CONCERT LIFE IN EIGHTEENTH-CENTURY BRITAIN

Concert Life in Eighteenth-Century Britain

Edited by
Susan Wollenberg and Simon McVeigh

LONDON AND NEW YORK

First published 2004 by Ashgate Publishing

Published 2016 by Routledge
2 Park Square, Milton Park, Abingdon, Oxfordshire OX14 4RN
711 Third Avenue, New York, NY 10017, USA

First issued in paperback 2016

Routledge is an imprint of the Taylor & Francis Group, an informa business

Copyright © Susan Wollenberg and Simon McVeigh 2004

Susan Wollenberg and Simon McVeigh have asserted their right under the Copyright, Designs and Patents Act, 1988, to be identified as Editors of this Work.

All rights reserved. No part of this book may be reprinted or reproduced or utilised in any form or by any electronic, mechanical, or other means, now known or hereafter invented, including photocopying and recording, or in any information storage or retrieval system, without permission in writing from the publishers.

Notice:
Product or corporate names may be trademarks or registered trademarks, and are used only for identification and explanation without intent to infringe.

British Library Cataloguing in Publication Data
Concert life in eighteenth-century Britain
   1. Concerts – Great Britain – History – 18th century 2.Music
   – Social aspects – Great Britain – History – 18th century
   3. Music – Great Britain – 18th century – History and
   criticism 4.Great Britain – Social life and customs – 18th
   century
   I.Wollenberg, Susan II.McVeigh, Simon
   780.7'841'09033

Library of Congress Cataloging-in-Publication Data
Concert life in eighteenth-century Britain / edited by Susan Wollenberg and Simon
  McVeigh.
     p. cm.
  Includes bibliographical references and index.
  ISBN 0-7546-3868-5 (alk. paper)
    1. Music–Great Britain–18th century–History and criticism. 2. Concerts–Great
  Britain–History–18th century. I. Wollenberg, Susan. II. McVeigh, Simon.

  ML285.3.C66 2003
  780'.78'41–dc22

2003057857

  ISBN 13: 978-1-138-24544-0 (pbk)
  ISBN 13: 978-0-7546-3868-1 (hbk)

Contents

List of Figures	*vii*
List of Tables	*ix*
List of Music Examples	*x*
Notes on Contributors	*xi*
Foreword	*xiv*
Acknowledgements	*xv*
Abbreviations	*xvi*

1   Introduction   1
Simon McVeigh

Part 1   Towns and Cities

2   Concert Topography and Provincial Towns in Eighteenth-Century
England   19
Peter Borsay

3   Clergy, Music Societies and the Development of a Musical Tradition:
A Study of Music Societies in Hereford, 1690–1760   35
Elizabeth Chevill

4   Competition and Collaboration: Concert Promotion in Newcastle
and Durham, 1752–1772   55
Roz Southey

5   Musical Culture and the Capital City: The Epoch of the *beau monde*
in London, 1700–1870   71
William Weber

Part 2   Sources and Genres

6   'The first talents of Europe': British Music Printers and Publishers
and Imported Instrumental Music in the Eighteenth Century   93
Jenny Burchell

7   Musicians and Music Copyists in Mid-Eighteenth-Century Oxford   115
Donald Burrows and Peter Ward Jones

8	The Catch and Glee in Eighteenth-Century Provincial England *Brian Robins*	141
9	The String Quartet in London Concert Life, 1769–1799 *Meredith McFarlane and Simon McVeigh*	161

Part 3   Contexts for Concerts

10	Music and Drama at the Oxford Act of 1713 *H. Diack Johnstone*	199
11	The Pleasures and Penalties of Networking: John Frederick Lampe in the Summer of 1750 *Roy Johnston*	219
12	'So much rational and elegant amusement, at an expence comparatively inconsiderable': The Holywell Concerts in the Eighteenth Century *Susan Wollenberg*	243
13	Gigs, Roadies and Promoters: Marketing Eighteenth-Century Concerts *Rosamond McGuinness*	261
14	Women Pianists in Late Eighteenth-Century London *Nicholas Salwey*	273

Index   *291*

List of Figures

7.1   Letter from John Snow to James Harris, 10 March 1737/38 (Hampshire Record Office, 9M73/G580/1). By courtesy of the Earl of Malmesbury and Hampshire Record Office   120

7.2   William and Philip Hayes: *David*. Hand of William Hayes, *c*.1774 (Bodleian Library, MS Mus. d.74, p. 98). By permission of the Bodleian Library, Oxford   122

7.3   William and Philip Hayes: *David*. Hand of Philip Hayes, 1781 (Bodleian Library, MS Mus. d.76, p. 46). By permission of the Bodleian Library, Oxford   123

7.4   William Croft: *O give thanks unto the Lord*. Hand of John Awbery, 1745 (Bodleian Library, MS Mus. d.27, p. 41). By permission of the Bodleian Library, Oxford   125

7.5   William Hayes: Concerto in D major. Autograph, *c*.1740 (Bodleian Library, MS Mus. b.6, p. 7). By permission of the Bodleian Library, Oxford   126

7.6   William Hayes: *Peleus and Thetis*. Autograph, *c*.1748 (Bodleian Library, MS Mus. d.79, p. 1). By permission of the Bodleian Library, Oxford   127

7.7   Emanuele d'Astorga: *Stabat Mater*. Hand of John Awbery, 1749 (Bodleian Library, MS Mus. d.19, fo. 71). By permission of the Bodleian Library, Oxford   128

7.8   G. F. Handel: *Messiah*. Hand of William Hayes?, 1750s? (Pierpont Morgan Library, New York, Cary MS 122, p. 127). By permission of the Pierpont Morgan Library, Mary Flagler Cary Music Collection   130

7.9   William Hayes: *Ode to the memory of Handel*, 1759. Anon. copyist (Bodleian Library, MS Mus. d.119, fo. 12^v). By permission of the Bodleian Library, Oxford   132

7.10   G. F. Handel: *Ode for St Cecilia's Day*. Hand of William Walond, *c*.1742 (Durham Cathedral Library, MS E23/9, p. 2). By permission of Durham Cathedral Library   134

7.11   G. F. Handel: *The Choice of Hercules*. Hand of William Walond, 1750s (Bodleian Library, Mus. 52 c.14, p. 47). By permission of the Bodleian Library, Oxford   136

LIST OF FIGURES

7.12	G. F. Handel: *L'Allegro, il Penseroso ed il Moderato*. Hand of John Lambourn?, 1750s (University of Birmingham Library, Shaw–Hellier Collection 177, p. 16). By courtesy of the JWP Loan Shaw–Hellier Collection, University of Birmingham	139
9.1	Newspaper advertisement for the first concert of the 1790 Professional Concert series (*The Public Advertiser*, 15 February 1790)	163
9.2	String quartet performances as a percentage of total number of known concerts	165
9.3	Subscription list from Dieudonné-Pascal Pieltain, *Six Quartettos for Two Violins, a Tenor and Violoncello* ..., op. 2 (London: Printed for the Author [1785])	172
10.1	William Croft, *Musicus Apparatus Academicus* [1720], title-page designed by John Devoto. By permission of the Bodleian Library, Oxford	206
10.2	William Croft, 'Laurus cruentas', first page of the first vocal movement as copied by James Kent in 1713. By courtesy of the Music Library, University of Washington Libraries, call-number M 782.8 C874t	213
11.1	Nixon's watercolour of High Street, Belfast. Photograph reproduced with the kind permission of the Trustees of the Museums and Galleries of Northern Ireland (Ulster Museum)	232
11.2	Agreement of Thomson and Davies with Lampe and Storer, 22 August 1750. Reproduced with the permission of Edinburgh University Library, Special Collections Department	234
12.1	Holywell Music Room, architectural sketch. By permission of the Bodleian Library, Oxford	250
12.2	Eighteenth-century map of Oxford city centre with the Holywell Music Room marked as 8. © Oxfordshire Photographic Archive, Centre for Oxfordshire Studies, Oxford	257

List of Tables

3.1	Performing subscribers at Hereford Music Society 1749–1750	44
3.2	Schedule of payments	45
3.3	Itinerary: Charles and son 1741–1755	50
3.4	Music Society's accounts	51
6.1	Analysis by genre of works published by subscription	95
6.2	Composers and their locations	97
6.3	Analysis of publication method for individual composers	99
6.4	Carl Friedrich Abel: distribution of publication methods	102
6.5	J. C. Bach: publications by end of 1763	102
6.6	F.-H. Barthélemon: publications	104
6.7	Samuel Arnold: instrumental publications	105
6.8	James Hook: publications	106
6.9	Selective list of publishers with European connections	113
9.1	Number of advertised concerts including string quartet performances, 1769–1799	164
9.2	Types of concert featuring string quartet performances, 1769–1799	166
9.3	Advertised string quartet performers	170
9.4	Advertised string quartet performances, 1769–1779	175
9.5	Advertised string quartet performances, 1780–1784	176
9.6	Advertised string quartet performances, 1785–1789	182
9.7	Advertised string quartet performances, 1790–1794	191
9.8	Advertised string quartet performances, 1795–1799	194
10.1	Structural breakdown of Croft's two Oxford odes showing number of movements, metre, scoring and key	204
11.1	Chronology of 1750	238

List of Music Examples

9.1   Felice Giardini, *Six Quartetto's*, op. 22 (London: J. Blundell, *c.*1779), no. 1 in F major, first movement   177

9.2   Felice Giardini, *Six Quartetto's*, op. 22 (London: J. Blundell, *c.*1779), no. 5 in E major, first movement   180

9.3   Dieudonné-Pascal Pieltain, *Six Quartettos*, op. 2 (London: Printed for the Author [1785]), no. 1 in A major, third movement   183

9.4   Dieudonné-Pascal Pieltain, *Six Quartettos*, op. 2 (London: Printed for the Author [1785]), no. 2 in D major, first movement   184

9.5   Ignaz Joseph Pleyel, *Three Quartettos … Dedicated to the King of Prussia*, op. 9, book 4 (London: W. Forster, 1787), no. 2 in C minor [B.341], first movement   187

Notes on Contributors

Peter Borsay is Professor of History at the University of Wales, Lampeter. His books include *The English Urban Renaissance: Culture and Society in the Provincial Town 1660–1770* (Clarendon Press, 1989), *The Image of Georgian Bath 1700–2000: Towns, Heritage, and History* (OUP, 2000) and, with L. Proudfoot (eds), *Provincial Towns in Early Modern England and Ireland* (British Academy and OUP, 2002). Recent essays include 'Sounding the Town', *Urban History*, 29 (2002), and 'Music, urban renaissance and space in eighteenth-century England', in H. E. Bodeker et al. (eds), *Le concert et son public* (2002). He is working at present on a history of leisure in Britain since 1500.

Jenny Burchell (née Pickering) was born in New Zealand and moved to England in 1987 where she completed a D.Phil., 'Polite or commercial concerts?', at the University of Oxford in 1993. Her main area of research is the organization of musical activity in Britain in the second half of the eighteenth century, and she has several publications in this field. She is now living in Dunedin, New Zealand, and is a freelance musicologist and guest lecturer at the University of Otago.

Donald Burrows is Professor of Music at the Open University (GB) and is the author of a major biography of Handel as well as *A Catalogue of Handel's Musical Autographs* (with Martha J. Ronish) and *Music and Theatre in Handel's World* (with Rosemary Dunhill). He has also edited many of Handel's works for publication, including *Messiah*, *Belshazzar*, *Imeneo* and the complete violin sonatas. He conducted the first modern performances of some of Handel's music for the Chapel Royal, and in 2000 was awarded the Handel Prize from Halle an der Saale, the city of Handel's birth.

Elizabeth Chevill completed her Ph.D., 'Music Societies and Musical Life in Old Foundation Cathedral Cities 1700–60', in 1993 at King's College, London. She has presented papers on various aspects of the history, repertoire and development of music societies in the first half of the eighteenth century and has done much work on musical references in archives and provincial newspapers of that period. Having taught for a number of years, she is currently undertaking further postgraduate study in theology at Oxford University.

Roy Johnston completed his doctoral thesis on Belfast concert life in the eighteenth and nineteenth centuries in 1996 at Queen's University, Belfast. He has published *Bunting's 'Messiah'* (Belfast, 2003), is a contributor to vol. 7 of *The New History of Ireland* (OUP, 2003) and the *Dictionary of Irish Biography* (CUP, forthcoming), and was a contributor to *Music and British Culture, 1785–1914: Essays in Honour of Cyril Ehrlich*, ed. Christina Bashford and Leanne Langley (OUP, 2000).

H. Diack Johnstone was formerly Reader in Music at the University of Oxford, and is now Emeritus Fellow in Music at St Anne's College, Oxford and General Editor of *Musica Britannica*. Co-editor (with Roger Fiske) of *The Eighteenth Century*, vol. 4 of The Blackwell History of Music in Britain (1990), he has published many articles, reviews and editions, mainly concerned with music in eighteenth-century England, Handel, and various aspects of performance practice of the period.

Meredith McFarlane graduated from the University of Queensland (Australia), and moved to England in 1994 to pursue further academic and performance studies in early music at the Royal College of Music. She went on to work as a violist with leading period-instrument ensembles and was recipient of numerous awards including (in 1998–99) the Grove Junior Research Fellowship (RCM) and an International Federation of University Women Fellowship. She successfully defended her D.Mus., 'The String Quartet in Late Eighteenth-Century England', at the RCM in December 2002 and her research continues to focus on musical life in that context.

Rosamond McGuinness has for decades, with her particular interest in an interdisciplinary approach to the study of London's music from *c*.1660 to *c*.1750, been engaged in studying the interaction between commerce, culture and communication in London during that time. To facilitate her study she has compiled the Royal Holloway Computer Register of Musical References in London Newspapers. An Emeritus Professor of Music at Royal Holloway, University of London, she has published mainly in a variety of non-musical publications. Her particular interests are in urban history, the book trade and the newspaper and periodical press, and aesthetics.

Simon McVeigh is Professor of Music at Goldsmiths College, University of London. He is the author of *Concert Life in London from Mozart to Haydn* (CUP, 1993) and of numerous articles on musical life in eighteenth- and nineteenth-century London. He has recently completed (with Jehoash Hirshberg) a study of the Italian concerto around Vivaldi; current projects include a book on London concert life from 1880 to 1914, and an edition of Arne's *Judith* for *Musica Britannica*.

Brian Robins is a freelance writer and lecturer who specializes in the music of eighteenth-century England. His edition of the *John Marsh Journals* was published in 1998 (Pendragon Press). He is a regular reviewer for *Fanfare* (USA)

NOTES ON CONTRIBUTORS

and the UK editor of *Goldberg Early Music Magazine* (Spain), in addition to which he is a contributor to the most recent edition of *The New Grove Dictionary of Music and Musicians*, and the *New Dictionary of National Biography*.

Nicholas Salwey graduated from Oxford University in 1990 with a first-class degree in music, and gained diplomas in piano performance from the Royal College of Music and the Guildhall School of Music in the same year. After taking a Master's degree in politics at the London School of Economics and a brief stint at the European Commission in Brussels he returned to music, teaching, performing, and working on a doctorate at Oxford entitled 'The Piano in London Concert Life: 1750–1800' which was completed in 2001. He is currently on the staff at Winchester College where he teaches piano and academic music.

Roz Southey completed a history degree at Hull University in 1973 before working as a freelance writer and researcher. In 1997 she graduated from Newcastle University with a first-class degree in music and went on to receive her doctorate from the same university in 2001. She currently lectures part-time at Newcastle. She is particularly interested in the historical and social contexts of eighteenth-century music making in the north-east of England and is the regular lecturer at the Newcastle Early Music Festival. She has also published a number of science-fiction short stories.

Peter Ward Jones has been Head of the Music Section of the Bodleian Library, Oxford since 1969. His eighteenth-century studies have included articles on British music publishers and composers for *New Grove*. He has also published extensively on Mendelssohn, including an edition of the Mendelssohns' honeymoon diary (1997), and is a member of the editorial board of the new Mendelssohn collected edition.

William Weber teaches history at California State University, Long Beach. He has published *Music and the Middle Class* (1975/2003), *Wagnerism in European Culture and Politics* (1985), and *The Rise of Musical Classics in Eighteenth-Century England* (1992). In 2002 he gave lectures on the history of concert programmes as Leverhulme Visiting Professor at the Royal College of Music, London.

Susan Wollenberg is Reader in Music at the University of Oxford, Faculty of Music. She has contributed on a variety of subjects to many scholarly publications and conferences. She is the author of *Music at Oxford in the Eighteenth and Nineteenth Centuries* (OUP, 2001). Her recent articles include 'Handel in Oxford: The tradition c.1750–1850', *Göttinger Händel-Beiträge*, 9 (2002), and 'The Oxford Commemorations and Nineteenth-Century British Festival Culture' in *Nineteenth-Century British Music Studies*, 3, ed. Peter Horton and Bennett Zon (Ashgate, 2003).

Foreword

The idea for the present volume originated in the symposium 'Concert Life in Eighteenth-Century Britain' held under the auspices of the University of Oxford, Faculty of Music at Wadham College, Oxford in July 1998 to celebrate the 250th anniversary of the Holywell Music Room. A number of the topics discussed on that occasion, and in this volume, link with eighteenth-century Oxford musical life in general and the Holywell Music Room in particular. Ranging over a wide area, the symposium as a whole highlighted the way in which research into concert life can contribute to the broader interest in the social perspective of eighteenth-century British cultural life which has developed in the last decade or so. This approach has attracted not only musicologists but also social and cultural historians, and the work that is gathered here brings together representatives of these various disciplines. Several of the essays included in the volume represent revised versions of papers given at the original conference, and to complement these, additional contributions have been commissioned from a range of scholars working in the field of concert history.

It is a pleasure to record our thanks to the Faculty of Music and to Wadham College, as well as to all the individuals who helped with the arrangements for the symposium.

Peter Franklin
H. Diack Johnstone
Reinhard Strohm
Susan Wollenberg
(symposium committee)

Acknowledgements

Thanks are due to the British Academy for research funding in connection with the preparation of this volume. The commissioning editors at Ashgate, especially Heidi May, offered invaluable support of the project at every stage; and Ian Taylor, of Lady Margaret Hall, Oxford, provided superb research assistance. Humaira Erfan Ahmed's sterling work enabled both the symposium and this book to take shape, while Will Goring's technical expertise helped to bring the volume to completion.

Susan Wollenberg
Simon McVeigh

Abbreviations

BL	London, British Library
DNB	*Dictionary of National Biography*
Hawkins, *History*	Sir John Hawkins, *A General History of the Science and Practice of Music*, 5 vols (London, 1776); facs. repr. of 2nd edn (1853), introd. Charles Cudworth, 2 vols (New York, 1963)
Highfill et al., *Biographical Dictionary*	Highfill, Philip J. jr, Burnim, Kalman A. and Langhans, Edward A., eds, *A Biographical Dictionary of Actors, Actresses, Musicians, Dancers, Managers & Other Stage Personnel in London, 1660–1800*, 16 vols (Carbondale: Southern Illinois University Press, 1973–93)
New Grove2	*New Grove Dictionary of Music and Musicians*, ed. Stanley Sadie and John Tyrrell, 2nd rev. edn, 29 vols (London: Macmillan, 2001)
OS	old style [dates]
PRMA	*Proceedings of the Royal Musical Association*
RMARC	*R.M.A. Research Chronicle*

CHAPTER ONE

Introduction

Simon McVeigh

As we struggle to imagine what a concert in the eighteenth century looked like, even perhaps what it felt like, we can hardly do better than start with Oxford's Holywell Music Room; and it is fitting that this book should have had its origins in a celebration of its history. This small symmetrical room – with its tiered seating around three sides and performers only marginally separated from the audience behind a low balustrade – reminds us how very close they were in terms of social as well as acoustical space.[1] Today the room is used as a recital hall, yet in the eighteenth century it witnessed orchestral and even choral concerts, the power and immediacy of a 'grand crash' that we can scarcely imagine.[2]

The very translation of the Oxford music society from tavern to specially built room is symptomatic of the increasing formality and gentility associated with the public concert (see Ch. 12). The Holywell room contrasts markedly with the 'bung hole' above Thomas Britton's coal warehouse in Clerkenwell, where those 'willing to take a hearty Sweat' heard some of the best music in London around 1700; or the Whitefriars tavern, 'rounded with seats and small tables alehouse fashion' (a shilling and 'call for what you please') where John Banister put on the first recorded public concerts in 1672.[3] The seventeenth-century concert was

---

1   The tiered arrangement was added in 1754 (Jenny Burchell, *Polite or Commercial Concerts? Concert Management and Orchestral Repertoire in Edinburgh, Bath, Oxford, Manchester, and Newcastle, 1730–1799* (New York: Garland, 1996), pp. 175–7). The platform or 'orchestra' was also tiered, rising gradually from the front to an organ at the top. On the Holywell Music Room and Oxford concerts, see John Henry Mee, *The Oldest Music Room in Europe: A Record of Eighteenth-Century Enterprise at Oxford* (London and New York: John Lane, 1911) and Susan Wollenberg, *Music at Oxford in the Eighteenth and Nineteenth Centuries* (Oxford: Oxford University Press, 2001); and Ch. 12 below.

2   On British musical life in this period, see Stanley Sadie, 'Concert Life in Eighteenth Century England', *PRMA*, 85 (1958–59), 17–30; E. D. Mackerness, *A Social History of English Music* (London: Routledge, 1964); H. Diack Johnstone and Roger Fiske, eds, *The Eighteenth Century*, Blackwell History of Music in Britain, 4 (Oxford: Blackwell, 1990); John Caldwell, *The Oxford History of English Music*, vol. 2 (Oxford: Oxford University Press, 1999); and David Wyn Jones, ed., *Music in Eighteenth-Century Britain* (Aldershot: Ashgate, 2000).

3   On early London concerts see Hugh A. Scott, 'London Concerts from 1700 to 1750', *Musical Quarterly*, 24 (1938), 194–209; Michael Tilmouth, 'Some Early London Concerts and Music Clubs, 1670–1720', *PRMA*, 84 (1957–58), 13–26; and Michael Tilmouth, 'A Calendar of References to Music in Newspapers Published in London and the Provinces (1660–1719)', *RMARC*, 1 (1961), 1–107. Rosamond McGuinness is compiling a database *Register of Music in London Newspapers 1660–1750* at Royal Holloway, University of London. On later London concerts, see Simon McVeigh, 'The

haphazard in its organization even at the fashionable York Buildings: 'Here was consorts, fuges, solos, lutes, Hautbois, trumpets, kettledrums, and what Not but all disjoynted and incoherent for while ye masters were shuffling out & in of places to take their parts there was a totall cessation, and None knew what would come next ...'.[4]

By the time the Holywell Music Room opened in 1748, the concert had crystallized into an event of its own, independent of the usual activities to which music formed an accompaniment, such as eating or drinking, dancing or conversing, praying or marching. The concept referred to all kinds of social models – tavern entertainment, gentlemen's society, assembly, private soirée, and so on – but it modelled itself on the play or opera in presenting a self-contained programme in two 'acts', a remarkably resilient structure as it has turned out. The miscellaneous Concert of Vocal and Instrumental Musick had also developed a logical inner organization of sorts, alternating some 10 to 12 instrumental and vocal items in formal symmetry.

Yet if at first sight all of this is at least recognizable to the modern observer, indeed comfortingly so, on closer acquaintance we find ourselves constantly surprised. Take the shape of programmes themselves. At London's subscription concerts in the later decades of the century it was fashionable not to arrive until well into the first half, while many wandered off before the end of the three-hour concert; so major items had to be placed somewhere around the interval, in clear distinction from the later preference for building programmes towards a climactic resolution, where the programme mirrored the aesthetic of nineteenth-century music itself. In the eighteenth century, the evening usually ended with an ill-defined 'full piece' as a light conclusion or play-out. The unquestioned alternation of vocal with instrumental items recognized both the centrality of vocal music (albeit usually borrowed from operas or oratorios) and the essentially instrumental *raison d'être* of a concert. Orchestral, solo and chamber items were carefully blended into the varied programme: no eighteenth-century organizer would have contemplated programming half a dozen Handel concertos in a row, a concept to which modern CD packaging and a 'collected works' mentality have somehow given a quite misplaced credibility.

At most London concerts there was a 'buzz of conversation' and members of the audience wandered around, visiting the refreshment room as they chose. Fanny Burney used her novel *Cecilia* to censure audiences at the Pantheon concerts:

> They entered the great room during the second act of the Concert, to which as no one of the party but herself had any desire to listen, no sort of attention was paid; the ladies entertaining themselves as if no Orchestra was in the room, and the gentlemen, with an equal disregard to it, struggling for a place by the fire.

Professional Concert and Rival Subscription Series in London, 1783–1793', *RMARC*, 22 (1989), 1–135; Simon McVeigh, *Concert Life in London from Mozart to Haydn* (Cambridge: Cambridge University Press, 1993); and Simon McVeigh, *Calendar of London Concerts 1750–1800, Advertised in the London Daily Press*, database, Goldsmiths College, University of London.

4   Roger North, quoted in Tilmouth, 'Some Early London Concerts', 17.

INTRODUCTION

Since London audiences regarded the concert hall as an extension of their own drawing room (the Hanover Square room even had sofas round the sides), they naturally behaved much as they did at private soirées. Yet their ready appreciation of solo virtuosity or striking new passages suggests a visceral engagement with the music that is familiar to us only from modern jazz concerts. Mrs Papendiek, writing in her customarily overblown style, recalled Salomon's debut in 1781:

> The "Tutti" of his favourite concerto, by Kreutzer, commenced rather mezzo-piano, and increased to a crescendo that drew down volumes of applause ... [The solo] was in the minor key, and the cadence he introduced was a long shake, with the melody played under – something new, which put Fischer almost into fits ... Such a *début* has scarcely ever been experienced. We were jumping from our seats.[5]

Salomon's performances of Haydn symphonies were similarly interrupted with spontaneous applause from listeners unable to contain their enthusiasm even 'in the midst of the finest passages in soft adagios'.[6]

Etiquette at musical societies, usually directed more towards bourgeois self-improvement and definitely more devoted to music itself, was stricter: but the need for the Castle Society to exhort members not to talk or wander around during concerts, on pain of substantial fines, suggests that the point still needed to be emphasized even there. At an early Oxford music club, meeting at the Mermaid Tavern around 1690, 'THE Steward is obliged to sconce any that makes a noise in time of performance, or to be sconced himself': downing a tankard of ale might not, one would have thought, be the most effective remedy.[7] Presumably quiet reigned at more august societies such as the Concert of Ancient Music, founded in 1776 to revere older music and often attended by George III: certainly by the mid-nineteenth century silent attention was demanded at classical chamber-music societies.[8]

Two surviving rooms intended for local musical societies seem extraordinarily small for their explicit purpose. The Holywell room at 65' × 32' was designed to accommodate 400 people; the still more elegant oval-shaped St Cecilia's Hall in Edinburgh was of similar size but intended for 500. London's Hanover Square room (where most of Haydn's 'London' symphonies were premiered) was only marginally bigger at 79' × 32', but it too was meant for 500. Of course not everyone attended at the same time, but it is not surprising that there were often complaints about crowded and over-heated public spaces.

---

5 Charlotte Papendiek, *Court and Private Life in the Time of Queen Charlotte*, ed. V. D. Broughton, 2 vols (London, 1887), vol. 1, pp. 185–7. This is a fanciful description, for Salomon would certainly not have played Kreutzer at this time.

6 *Journal des Luxus und der Moden* (1794), cited in H. C. Robbins Landon, *Haydn in England 1791–1795*, Haydn Chronicle and Works, vol. 3 (London: Thames & Hudson, 1976), p. 246.

7 Wollenberg, *Music at Oxford*, p. 46.

8 See William Weber, *The Rise of Musical Classics in Eighteenth-Century England: A Study in Canon, Ritual, and Ideology* (Oxford: Clarendon Press, 1992); and Christina Bashford, 'Learning to Listen: Audiences for Chamber Music in Early-Victorian London', *Journal of Victorian Culture*, 4 (1999), 25–51.

Another surprising feature is the interaction between professional and amateur musicians at most eighteenth-century venues. John Marsh, the attorney and land-owner who tirelessly organized concerts in Canterbury and Chichester, assumed that he could call on local professionals at will. He also took every opportunity to harangue the country's leading virtuosi into trying out his music, whether they were in Salisbury for the festival or assisting at Napier's amateur concert in London (see Ch. 9, p. 174 below). Failing to get a place in the audience at the Anacreontic Society, he simply took out his violin and joined the orchestra. Nevertheless, for all his desperate desire to be regarded as a musician of professional standing – a barrier as hard to cross as any social divide – Marsh made sure never to relinquish his amateur status: though an accomplished violinist, he chose only to play 'a ripieno bass' at the Salisbury Festival in 1776 and the timpani three years later.[9]

But perhaps the most striking feature of all is the constant expectation of novelty and thus new repertoire. A myth has grown up around British musical conservatism that would suggest concert repertoire was entirely dominated by Handel to the end of the eighteenth century. It is true that there were those who resisted the new *galant* style (as in Durham; Ch. 4), and Britain certainly continued to enjoy older music, to the extent that the music of Handel began to achieve classic status. But the vociferousness with which early music was advocated in the later eighteenth century only goes to emphasize the general thirst for the latest symphonies and operas: it was simply taken for granted that London subscription concerts would parade the most up-to-date music, often only just imported from the continent. And the value of new music as a commodity was unquestioned. After all the attempts to lure Haydn to England during the 1780s, generating a febrile anticipation right up to his eventual arrival in 1791, Salomon was not about to lose out by allowing anyone to get hold of the new symphonies, delaying publication (except for domestic arrangements) as long as he could.

Music simply permeated everyday life right across the country, a theme that leaps out of this book. Church, theatre and the military may have provided the bedrock of the nation's music, but concerts too were everywhere, from formal series and festivals, through musical societies to fashionable soirées and sociable glee clubs. Particularly inspiring are the enthusiasts who lived for music: the Yorkshire choral singers who walked from one festival to the next, before the establishment of the Halifax Harmonic Society and the like;[10] the untutored Lancashire handloom weavers (the 'Larks of Dean'), who made their own instruments and were so fond of 'singing and fiddling' that they worked day and

---

9   *The John Marsh Journals: The Life and Times of a Gentleman Composer (1752–1828)*, ed. Brian Robins (Stuyvesant, NY: Pendragon Press, 1998), pp. 251, 400, 147, 203–4. See also ch. 14, ' "The Harmony of Heaven": John Marsh and Provincial Music', in John Brewer, *The Pleasures of the Imagination: English Culture in the Eighteenth Century* (London: HarperCollins, 1997), pp. 531–72.

10   See Rachel Cowgill, ' "The most musical spot for its size in the kingdom": Music in Georgian Halifax', *Early Music*, 28 (2000), 557–75.

INTRODUCTION

night in order to indulge their hobby at weekends.[11] Scarcely any social event or entertainment, whether scientific demonstration or equestrian display, lacked music – and, at the risk of stating the obvious, live music.

Music provided enjoyment as well as erudition at every social level. By the late eighteenth century, the concert had largely shed its image as dangerous or immoral, and was in most quarters regarded as a worthwhile pastime, even an uplifting moral experience – without as yet carrying the burden of worthiness or educational and social mission. The concert had begun to be perceived as something of symbolic importance, even of lasting significance. Provincial festivals – usually three-day events in the autumn, with top performers from London – made an important civic statement, contributing to pride in local cultural institutions and providing a focus for local gentry, professionals and leaders of commerce.[12] Of course it was taken for granted that major national events would be celebrated by music: when in 1713 the 'Oxford Act' ceremony was revived to celebrate the Treaty of Utrecht, the two new Croft odes conveniently doubled as his submission for the degree of D.Mus. (see Ch. 10). More subtle, perhaps, in its message was the massive 1784 Handel Commemoration at Westminster Abbey, almost a state occasion, which vicariously reasserted national values and the established social order, unifying the country around the King and the new Pitt government after the shattering loss of the American colonies.[13]

This centrality of music has been increasingly recognized by social and urban historians. As Chapters 2 and 5 suggest, music was not just an idle fancy but an important shared experience. As a national form of entertainment and ritual, the concert or oratorio performance fitted most circumstances, offering a context for social status to be negotiated in an atmosphere of sociability, while at the same time providing a common ground that did not expose those conventions of conversation that differentiated social classes. If national identity was not yet strongly expressed in musical creation – there was not even a sense that this was lacking – by the late eighteenth century *Messiah* had undoubtedly assumed a national role.

Why then were concerts put on in eighteenth-century Britain, and why did the public concert develop so spectacularly here by comparison with the continent? Neither of these questions can be simply answered and it might be more helpful to address an apparently more straightforward question: who put on concerts? Two quite different modes of organization can readily be distinguished: the (often amateur) musical society, designed not for profit but for the enjoyment of the

---

11 See Roger Elbourne, *Music and Tradition in Early Industrial Lancashire 1780–1840* (Woodbridge: Brewer, 1980 for the Folklore Society), pp. 23–43.

12 See Brian Pritchard, 'The Music Festival and the Choral Society in England in the Eighteenth and Nineteenth Centuries: A Social History', Ph.D. diss. (University of Birmingham, 1968); and Douglas J. Reid, Brian Pritchard et al., 'Some Festival Programmes of the Eighteenth and Nineteenth Centuries', *RMARC*, 5 (1965) to 8 (1970).

13 William Weber, 'The 1784 Handel Commemoration as Political Ritual', *Journal of British Studies*, 28 (1989), 43–69.

6   SIMON McVEIGH

performers, and the professionally organized subscription or benefit concert, which was largely commercial in intent. Yet even this distinction proves much less rigid than might be imagined, as on the one hand musical societies became more professional in their performance and relationship with a paying audience; while on the other, commercial concert promoters endeavoured to hide their money-making intent. It is sometimes remarkably hard to discover into which category a particular concert series falls.[14]

Musical societies grew up in every town, formalizing the gathering of like-minded enthusiasts – perhaps cathedral singers and clergy, or amateur string-players – who met to sing sacred music or to play through concertos (this is why the concerti grossi of Corelli, Geminiani and Handel were so especially popular in Britain). Such societies reflected the propensity of eighteenth-century male society to organize itself in clubs and associations: often there were committees, drawn primarily from the performing members, and strict regulations about attendance and behaviour.[15] Catch clubs were no different in kind, for all their more convivial atmosphere (see Ch. 8): indeed they shared a tavern setting with many musical societies, unlikely to afford the grandeur of their own music rooms.

The patronage of local dignitaries was of significant influence in such societies. Some operated on a grand scale, most remarkably that at Edinburgh with its sizeable subscription from the cream of Edinburgh society and professional classes: some professional stiffening was hired from London (where Robert Bremner, the Scottish music publisher, acted as an agent) or even directly from Europe.[16] More typical were those based around a cathedral, such as the Hereford Society described in Ch. 3, formed by vicars choral bringing their experience of Oxbridge music societies to these cities.[17] Still others were dependent on the

---

14   The Durham concerts put on by the cathedral musicians provide an example, as there were apparently no amateur musicians (see Ch. 4, p. 57).

15   Peter Clark, *British Clubs and Societies 1580–1800: The Origins of an Associational World* (Oxford: Clarendon Press, 2000).

16   See Burchell, *Polite or Commercial Concerts?*, ch. 2; Sonia T. Baxter, 'Italian Music and Musicians in Edinburgh c.1720–1800: A Historical and Critical Study', Ph.D. diss. (University of Glasgow, 2000); and Jennifer Macleod, 'The Edinburgh Musical Society: Its Membership and Repertoire 1728–1797', Ph.D. diss. (University of Edinburgh, 2001). Edinburgh had particular pretensions in this regard, negotiating directly through contacts in Italy; yet it was a constant concern that they could not expect to attract artists of the very highest calibre, even as they aspired to international standards of performance.

17   On musical societies and music outside London in general, see Burchell, *Polite or Commercial Concerts?*, and Elizabeth Chevill, 'Music Societies and Musical Life in Old Foundation Cathedral Cities 1700–60', Ph.D. diss. (University of London, 1993). More specific studies include Wilfred Allis, 'The Gentlemen's Concerts, Manchester, 1772–1920', M.Phil. diss. (University of Manchester, 1995); Brian Boydell, *A Dublin Musical Calendar 1700–1760* (Blackrock: Irish Academic Press, 1988); Brian Boydell, *Rotunda Music in Eighteenth-Century Dublin* (Dublin: Irish Academic Press, 1992); Henry G. Farmer, *Music Making in the Olden Days: The Story of the Aberdeen Concerts 1748–1801* (London: Peters, 1950); Trevor Fawcett, *Music in Eighteenth-Century Norwich and Norfolk* (Norwich: University of East Anglia, 1979); David Griffiths, *'A Musical Place of the First Quality': A History of Institutional Music-Making in York, c.1550–1990* (York: York Settlement Trust, 1994); Peter Holman, ed., 'Music in Georgian Britain', *Early Music*, 28 (2000), including Brian Robins, 'The Catch Club in Eighteenth-Century England', pp. 517–29, Rachel Cowgill, '"The most musical spot for its size in

INTRODUCTION

vigour of a local genius for organization, such as John Marsh in Canterbury or Chichester, where the performing members were a hotchpotch of church musicians, militia, and more or less gifted amateurs. Marsh himself described the even more informal nature of a concert at Winchester, where

> we immediately went paid our halfcrowns & play'd a duplicate 2d fiddle part together of Abel's 3d. set of Overtures etc. which I then heard for the 1st. time & much liked. If Mr Day's friend on whom we had called, judg'd of the concert (as many ladies do) by the company attending it, he might have been right enough in his disparagement of it, there not being above 6. or 8. people besides the performers, but the band being pretty good (with 2 or 3 singers, which was not the case at Portsm'o) & considering it as opportunity of practice I co'd not now elsewhere get, I was very well pleas'd & should not have car'd if there had been no audience at all. As we had assisted in the orchestra & Mr Day was a professor, our half crowns were return'd to us by the doorkeeper (at the direction of Mr Fussell the manager) as we went out of the room.[18]

Unrestricted by the constraints of the London season, provincial societies often operated more or less all year round, with a regular meeting, perhaps weekly or monthly, taking care to avoid dates when there was no moon to travel by.

Often such societies attracted growing numbers of listeners, enrolled as 'auditor members', and put on special ladies' nights. This switch of emphasis caused tensions between the gentlemen players and audience members wanting to import more professionals, perhaps to replicate their experiences in London during the season. In its later years the Edinburgh musical society in effect became a subscription concert, with greater ladies' involvement; much the same happened to the Academy of Ancient Music in London, which had by the 1780s deserted its roots in older choral music in favour of a public series with a professional orchestra. The tension between the amateur performer and professional standards was exacerbated by the technical demands of the new symphonies, with Haydn defeating those violinists used to a Corelli ripieno part and requiring wind-players of a competence that the local militia could only sporadically supply.

At the other extreme from the amateur society was the purely commercial concert, undertaken by the professional with a readily identifiable product to sell: not only virtuoso and musical skills, but also access to the latest continental music (such marketing techniques are described in Ch. 13). At the forefront were London

---

the kingdom": Music in Georgian Halifax', pp. 557–75, and Peter Holman, 'The Colchester Partbooks', pp. 577–95; Kenneth James, 'Concert Life in Eighteenth-Century Bath', Ph.D. diss. (University of London, 1987); David Johnson, *Music and Society in Lowland Scotland in the Eighteenth Century* (London: Oxford University Press, 1972); Frida Knight, *Cambridge Music: From the Middle Ages to Modern Times* (Cambridge: Oleander Press, 1980); E. D. Mackerness, *Somewhere Further North: A History of Music in Sheffield* (Sheffield: Northend, 1974); Macleod, 'The Edinburgh Musical Society'; Rosemary Southey, 'Commercial Music-Making in Eighteenth-Century North-East England: A Pale Reflection of London?', Ph.D. diss. (University of Newcastle upon Tyne, 2001); R. P. Sturges, 'Harmony and Good Company: The Emergence of Musical Performance in Eighteenth-Century Derby', *Music Review*, 39 (1978), 178–95; Wollenberg, *Music at Oxford*.

18   *The John Marsh Journals*, pp. 65–6. Further on music in Salisbury, see Donald Burrows and Rosemary Dunhill, *Music and Theatre in Handel's World: The Family Papers of James Harris 1732–1780* (Oxford: Oxford University Press, 2002).

8   SIMON McVEIGH

promoters such as J. C. Bach and Abel (whose concerts ran from 1765 to 1781), and subsequently Salomon, with Rauzzini in Bath bringing a similar European perspective. The purpose of the subscription concert series, with audiences reaching as high as 800 at the Opera Concerts in the 1790s, was ostensibly to make money for the promoter. But although London and Bath subscription series were run on commercial lines – widely advertised, with tickets publicly on sale – the system was still to some extent modelled on others that provided an element of control. The weekly concert was borrowed from the gentlemen's society, and sometimes public concerts were even overseen by a committee who advised on artistic policy (and royal patrons such as the Prince of Wales were anyway hugely influential). The structure was also shared with the fashionable assembly, with a group of ladies sometimes exercising control over admission: indeed, the Bach–Abel concerts actually originated from a *beau monde* assembly at an opulent West End mansion. In this way commercial aspects were mitigated, even to the point of concealment: Bach and Abel, for example, advertised with such discretion that their concerts retained something of the aura of a private society.

For the subscriber, the public series was a way of sharing the expense of private concerts on a grand scale, since hardly any could contemplate maintaining a musical establishment of their own (James Brydges, Duke of Chandos, provides a very rare exception). By virtue of expensive tickets on the one hand and a restricted product on the other (Haydn's 'London' symphonies could hardly be heard outside Salomon's concerts), the subscription concert reinforced social exclusivity. In rewarding but not requiring close attention through a succession of discrete musical items, it provided a focus for social interaction: in effect the London concert sustained all the benefits of opera without the theatre, and it is not surprising that during the 1770s the subscription concert came to rival opera in the fashionable calendar.

Related to the subscription series was the benefit concert, a single one-off event organized by an individual musician as an annual reward for good service, whether to a musical society or to his patrons in general. The benefit concert was a kind of tip dressed up as a commercial undertaking, again modelled on practices at the theatre and opera. This pretence – which came to be seen as demeaning or merely deceptive – was already beginning to wane towards the end of the eighteenth century, and it was to be abandoned altogether in the nineteenth.[19]

On the face of it, such concerts provide a prime example of the commercialization of leisure.[20] Yet London's commercial concerts were in fact directed at the extended *beau monde* described in Ch. 5, rather than a bourgeois emulation of upper-class pleasures. London's concert halls were therefore all in the West End (indeed the City of London had no major concert hall until the

---

19   Simon McVeigh, 'The Benefit Concert in Nineteenth-Century London: From "tax on the nobility" to "monstrous nuisance"', in Bennett Zon, ed., *Nineteenth-Century British Music Studies*, 1, (Aldershot: Ashgate, 1999), pp. 242–66.

20   Cf. Neil McKendrick, John Brewer and J. H. Plumb, *The Birth of a Consumer Society: The Commercialization of Eighteenth-Century England* (London: Europa, 1982).

INTRODUCTION

Barbican opened in 1982). Concert promoters, usually musicians themselves, were ingenious entrepreneurs, but only in the most limited way. They were conspicuously reluctant to maximize the commercial potential by taking a whole orchestra to the wealthy bourgeoisie of the City or to the provinces – not even to such obvious markets as Bath or the newly fashionable resorts of Margate or Weymouth. Curiously, the unregulated commercial concert, far from opening up concerts to a wider public, was actually manipulated so as to have the opposite effect. Salomon's desire to maintain his own exclusive product (Haydn's latest symphonies) thus resulted in complaints that only those who could afford his high-priced subscription series could ever hear them.

Where a broader public could experience high-quality music in London was in two quite different contexts. Equally commercial were London's Lenten oratorios, arising out of Handel's various series from 1733 onwards. Not only was the genre itself essentially new, but so too was the notion of exploiting it in this populist way, especially when the subscription principle was abandoned in 1747, allowing a broad playhouse audience access through single tickets for the night. That there was real money to be earned here is evidenced by the blind organist John Stanley's assertion that the annual oratorio series was the basis of his whole livelihood, his profits (shared with J. C. Smith) reaching well into four figures. In the 1790s, profit was John Ashley's sole motive in promoting oratorio selections at Covent Garden: with potential audiences of over 2000 he could easily have pocketed £4000 each season.[21] A still wider section of London society would have been able to attend *al fresco* concerts at the summer pleasure gardens, where the one-shilling audience at the Vauxhall bandstand could hear everything from popular ballads to Haydn symphonies: the idea was imitated in many towns around the country.

London erected no barriers to anyone wishing to put on a public concert: it was an entirely free trade with no state or civic limitations, no guild restrictions, no quality control and no obstacles to foreigners. It was this freedom, as much as the readily available wealth, that encouraged public concert promotion in Britain. All of this contrasted markedly with the situation on the continent, with its centralized concert series (Paris Concert spirituel), orchestral societies (the Leipzig Gewandhaus) or semi-public concerts at aristocratic residences (Vienna) – leaving aside court music, which is a different story altogether. Yet for all the opportunities that the free market offered in Britain, there was nothing inevitable in this development of public concerts. We tend to take it for granted that regular public concerts are the norm, something to which all instrumentalists aspired; but this derives from an essentially nineteenth-century perspective. The evidence does not suggest that musicians regarded themselves as born to give public concerts: indeed, many avoided doing so if they could survive without. Geminiani promoted one major concert series in 1731–32 and a few concerts in Dublin and London, but according to Burney, he was 'seldom heard in public during his long residence in England. His compositions, scholars, and the presents he received from the great,

---

21   McVeigh, *Concert Life in London*, pp. 173–5.

10 SIMON McVEIGH

whenever he could be prevailed upon to play at their houses, were his chief support'.[22] The famous Parisian pianist Nicolas Hüllmandel lived in Britain for many years, but he appeared at only a handful of concerts in the early 1770s, and never promoted even a single benefit of his own. Even Clementi abandoned public piano performance after 1790, concentrating instead on teaching and his new business career as a piano-seller.

Outside London, commercial opportunities for concert promotion were still more limited. Bath, the resort of high society, naturally attempted to replicate the entertainments on offer in London: thus when Rauzzini took over the management of the Assembly Room concerts, many celebrated soloists were enticed away from the capital to appear there. Charles Avison in Newcastle also had the entrepreneurial spirit, his regular winter concerts (though initiated by a group of gentlemen) being essentially his own promotions, often supplemented by a summer series. Otherwise leading lights of local music societies might take the occasional benefit, and travelling musicians also put on concerts as they passed through: for the audience a one-off curiosity, for the musician the fare to the next town. Exceptionally, the French horn-players Mr Charles and his son seem to turn up everywhere in the years around 1750, marketing themselves like a travelling circus with performances on the oboe d'amore 'and two foreign instruments, the shallamo and clarinet': see Ch. 3, pp. 49–50. While it might sound like a concert tour, this would be overstating both intention and planning: usually musicians simply arrived and put on a concert with some local performers at a few days' notice. The idea that an international virtuoso might deliberately travel around the country in a planned succession of money-making concerts (as Hummel and Paganini were to do in the 1830s) was still in the future. At this point such naked commercialism would seriously have damaged both a musician's reputation and his standing with patrons.

If the divide between musical societies and commercial concerts was not nearly as rigid as it might at first appear, it is not surprising that concert types often extended or even crossed boundaries. Thus the societies that met in Gloucester, Hereford and Worcester led eventually to the first public music festival, the Three Choirs Festival, which added a strong link with charity. Amateur societies became more professionalized as they metamorphosed into concert societies with hired performers. In a similar way the private sphere crossed over into the public. The string quartet, essentially a private genre for the players, became a public virtuoso showpiece (see Ch. 9). The after-dinner glee also gained a much more public presence in formal glee clubs, eventually even becoming a concert item, sung by women and published under such titles as *The Ladies' Collection*. One might even regard in the same light the translation of women pianists into public performers with their own careers (explored in Ch. 14), essentially transferring a domestic pastime onto the concert stage.

---

22   *A General History of Music*, ed. Frank Mercer, 2 vols (London: Foulis, 1935), vol. 2, p. 992.

INTRODUCTION 11

All of this suggests that concerts were part of a fluid network of different types of music making and ways of making a living. By comparison with other artistic endeavours (even the theatre), eighteenth-century concert life was extremely fragile and largely unstructured. Even in London the number of public concerts was small, the season short, the economics risky: the targeted clientele was simply not a large enough market for any musician to be able to describe himself as a 'concert artist'.[23] All musicians were involved in numerous different activities – from performing at the Opera or playhouses, through composing, publishing and instrument-selling, to teaching and private concerts for wealthy patrons, which for many was the primary objective. It is striking that on the death of his patron the Duke of Cumberland, London's premier viola-player, Benjamin Blake, actually took piano lessons from Clementi so as to start a new career teaching piano to well-heeled young ladies. Thus while concerts could be lucrative – profitable oratorio seasons or a benefit making over a hundred pounds – their principal aim was to enhance the musician's reputation, and thus infiltrate the traditional orbit of aristocratic patronage.

Certainly for musicians outside London there was no question of being able to make a career purely from concert activities. Smaller towns could support only a handful of professionals at most, who made a living by teaching at the houses of the local gentry, selling music, dealing in music and instruments, and probably tuning and repairing them too. A Newcastle musician advertised in 1724 that he 'makes and sells all Sorts of Musical and Mathematical Instruments, Musick, Books, Tunes and Songs, Bows, Bridges and Strings, and any Sort of Turn'd Work, at reasonable rates: He also makes and sets Artificial Teeth so neatly, as not to be discovered from natural ones'.[24] Such musicians would play at the local musical society or at a major festival at the nearby cathedral; they might also form a small band to accompany a more famous soloist passing through. Not much over a hundred years later, Elgar's father, with his small music shop and piano-tuning business in Worcester, was still working in much the same way.

The concert was an essential part of a wider business network closely allied to the selling of piano music and songs for ladies' accomplishment, or symphonies and chamber music 'as performed at Mr. Salomon's concert' (see Ch. 6). Such epithets were not merely accidental, but a well-planned business transaction, as is exemplified by the negotiations of Kozeluch concerning performance and publication of his string quartets, as well as the achievement of Bland and Salomon in securing Haydn's op. 64 in 1791.[25] The intertwining of performance and publication was encouraged by London newspaper reviews, which were

---

23 See Simon McVeigh, 'The Musician as Concert-Promoter in London, 1780–1850', in Hans Erich Bödeker, Patrice Veit and Michael Werner, eds, *Le concert et son public: Mutations de la vie musicale en Europe de 1780 à 1914 (France, Allemagne, Angleterre)* (Paris: Editions de la Maison des sciences de l'homme, 2002), pp. 71–92.

24 Southey, 'Commercial Music-Making', p. 30, quoted from the *Newcastle Courant*, 1 Feb. 1724.

25 Ian Woodfield, 'John Bland: London Retailer of the Music of Haydn and Mozart', *Music & Letters*, 81 (2000), 210–44.

subsequently reported elsewhere, and in general publications such as the *European Magazine*. Through the national retail network, as music publishers increasingly emulated the highly developed book trade, printed music found its way across the country, vicariously disseminating the concert culture. Concerts were also involved in the promotion of pianos: though not as explicitly as in the next century (when piano-makers began to be named in programmes and on the side of concert instruments), nevertheless makers such as Broadwood and their latest technical advances were clearly flagged up in reviews.

It goes without saying that from the musician's point of view it was absolutely essential in this precarious profession to take every chance as it arose and to keep as many options open as possible. With few official organizations to call upon, the main task was to nurture networks among musicians and patrons – through family connections, through teachers, through freemasons' lodges, and through carefully pursued good fortune. Though Burney was undoubtedly exploited by Thomas Arne, he did gain a place on the viola in Handel's oratorios as a consequence of his apprenticeship; John Field, similarly exploited by Clementi to show off his instruments, received concerto opportunities as a result. J. C. Bach was regarded as the best teacher for professional musicians because of his connections: he first taught and then hired the Bath singer Ann Cantelo, who went on to a distinguished career as Mrs Harrison. In this regard the career of R. J. S. Stevens is particularly instructive: following frustrating early years as a choir-singer and organist, he used both professional and aristocratic connections to lever himself from one level to the next. Teaching at girls' schools brought him a lucky break: by teaching the daughter of the Lord Chancellor, he eventually got a place at the Concert of Ancient Music, becoming a leading composer and director of glees at private parties – a highly lucrative branch of the profession.[26]

It was also important to keep a variety of geographical connections alive. Outside the short London concert season (extending at the outside from late January to early June) there was little work in the public arena, except for those willing to take on the comparatively paltry rewards of the summer pleasure gardens. For the most fortunate this fallow period was filled with an invitation to a patron's country estate – Giardini at Blenheim, Madame Mara at Burleigh at the top of the chain – but there were many other ways to make money and forge new connections. Bach and Abel fostered their European contacts, visiting the continent in the summer months partly in order to engage new performers: many of their soloists came from Mannheim – Cramer, Wendling, Ramm, Carl Stamitz – a point insufficiently recognized. Others travelled the country, and musicians were much more mobile than we might suppose: even if the concert tour was yet to come, top singers and instrumentalists mapped out a path between Assize and

---

26   *Recollections of R. J. S. Stevens: An Organist in Georgian London*, ed. Mark Argent (London: Macmillan, 1992). See also Cyril Ehrlich, *The Music Profession in Britain since the Eighteenth Century: A Social History* (Oxford: Clarendon Press, 1985); and Deborah Rohr, *The Careers of British Musicians, 1750–1850: A Profession of Artisans* (Cambridge: Cambridge University Press, 2001).

INTRODUCTION

13

Race weeks, autumn festivals and perhaps theatre appearances. In 1758, for example, Giardini was in Ipswich in July, meeting Gainsborough for the first time; later that month he played at Avison's concerts in Newcastle, and in August at Garth's Race Week concerts in Durham; he went on to perform at the York Assembly rooms during Race Week there, no doubt at the instigation of his patron Mrs Fox Lane (Lady Bingley).

A more commercial agenda was pursued by John Ashley and his family, who toured whole festivals around the provinces in the years around 1790, capitalizing on the Handel vogue after the Commemoration. Ashley brought well-known London soloists to join local choirs and orchestras, astutely targeting developing towns without cathedrals, such as Portsmouth, Sheffield, Coventry or Leeds.[27] Such towns were unaccustomed to major festivals, and Ashley thus played upon local vanities as well as the deep-rooted love of Handel's music in the northern towns in particular.

As the century progressed, improving travel meant that London performers could easily make trips to Oxford even during the winter season, so that such celebrities as Fischer or Cramer, Tenducci or Mrs Billington, regularly appeared there. They were also engaged at Bath, Tunbridge Wells or the Newmarket Races, especially in the interstices around Easter. In 1794–95, for example, careful interlocking of engagements allowed Viotti to appear regularly in Bath, while still directing the Opera Concerts at London's King's Theatre.[28] By 1820, a week in the diary of the singer Mrs Salmon illustrates a remarkable mobility: Monday, rehearsal at the Concert of Ancient Music and performance at the Philharmonic Society; Tuesday in Oxford; Wednesday in London at the oratorio and Ancient Music; Thursday in Oxford; Friday in Bath; Saturday in Bristol.[29]

Conversely provincial musicians dipped into London culture before taking back new ideas about concert organization and new repertoires. The Newcastle musician Charles Avison, for example, was in London in 1734–35, and in 1751 he must have met Giardini, prime exponent of the new Italian *galant*: a frequent visitor to the north-east, Giardini was evidently a strong influence on both Avison and Garth in their espousal of the most up-to-date music. Perhaps Giardini also encouraged them in their surprising choice of music by Rameau; he had himself recently arrived from Paris, and directed at least one concert in London at which Rameau's music was performed.[30]

Some well-established London musicians, perhaps disappointed by competition, moved permanently to the provinces: leading violinists such as Dubourg went to Dublin, Janiewicz to Liverpool. Frustrated by failure in London, the

---

27   Brian Pritchard, 'The Provincial Festivals of the Ashley Family', *Galpin Society Journal*, 22 (1969), 58–77.

28   Burchell, *Polite or Commercial Concerts?*, p. 128.

29   *Quarterly Musical Magazine and Review*, 2 (1820), p. 382.

30   A 'harpsichord concerto' was performed by Ogle at the Dean Street series on 28 December 1751. If this was one of Avison's arrangements, it is of course possible that the influence worked the other way; at the next concert, on 4 January, Ogle performed a similar work by Avison.

14 SIMON McVEIGH

Passerinis promoted their own subscription series (mainly oratorios) in Edinburgh, Newcastle and Bath during the 1750s. The example set by the experienced theatre composer Lampe and his younger rival Pasquali in attempting new careers in Dublin is discussed in Ch. 11: both were to end up in Edinburgh. Most striking of all, Venanzio Rauzzini, the famous opera singer and composer, seized the opportunity to make his base in Bath. Yet sometimes such emigrants later hankered to return to the capital, and the committee of the Edinburgh Musical Society was caused endless grief by unauthorized absences and recriminations.[31]

Evidently there were networks that operated both nationally and at local levels. One nexus operated in north-east England, which was also on the musician's trade route between London, York and Edinburgh; there was another in the choral world of the northern counties, where the celebrated 'Lancashire witches' were in demand for every festival and choral performance. A third operated around the Three Choirs cathedrals, taking in both Bath and Bristol, but reaching as far as Shrewsbury – resulting in a hitherto unknown episode in Charles Burney's life (see Ch. 3, p. 46). Oxford stood at a crossroads, looking towards London and the Three Choirs, but also north-west to Lichfield and Birmingham, and south to Salisbury. Direct connections between Dublin, Belfast and Edinburgh presented an alternative periphery that was to develop further as transport improved in the nineteenth century.

Another kind of network operated at the level of patrons and amateurs, who themselves exerted a strong influence on taste in general: we should not forget the potent role of their private concerts in forming public taste, nor the effect on musical dissemination as they journeyed between London and their country seats. We know that George III was particularly influential on the Handel cult, his brothers and the Prince of Wales on the vogue for Pleyel and Haydn. More directly, patrons advanced musicians' careers, encouraging friends to buy tickets for benefits, obtaining positions at public concerts (the Duke of Cumberland got William Parke into the Professional Concert) or discovering 'unknowns', as when Sir Watkin Williams Wynn plucked Edward Meredith from a cooper's workshop into a successful concert career.

Some amateurs were more directly involved in concert promotion and thus with obtaining music. James Harris, the Salisbury MP and writer on aesthetics who organized the Salisbury concerts, worked directly with Handel; he was also in touch with Oxford copyists about Handel's unpublished music (see Ch. 7), in a network of collectors and copyists that stretched as far as Durham. Later his family concerts in London provided an opportunity for eminent musicians such as Sacchini to try out music in an informal setting, where Harris's daughter was accomplished enough to take part as a singer.

---

31 For example, Giuseppe Puppo was engaged to lead there in 1774, but in 1778 – complaining about the severity of the climate – he travelled without permission to Dublin, and went on to Bath as principal viola for Rauzzini: the Edinburgh directors had to write to Bremner in London to secure his return (Burchell, *Polite or Commercial Concerts?*, p. 44).

INTRODUCTION

Such intricately intertwined networks – of musicians across the country, of publishers and instrument-makers, patrons and concert organizers – might suggest a uniform cosmopolitanism that smoothed out any regional quirks. It is true that they resulted in broadly shared attitudes and an international repertoire (channelled through London), always allowing for the ideological division between ancient and modern music. Yet particular prejudices – for example, the aversion to opera in puritanical Edinburgh – resulted in distinct individual slants to the concert repertoire. Local societies took particular stances on the introduction of the new *galant* symphonies and Italian arias, and on the preservation of older concerto grosso and choral idioms. Usually this resulted in a more even mix than in London, but in Durham there was outright hostility between the two camps. Musical societies and concert series also offered scope for personal endeavours, such as those of Felton in Hereford or Avison and Garth in the north-east, where a truly local concert repertoire placed their own compositions alongside such novelties as the music of Rameau.

British composers negotiated the pressures of style change in their own fashion, adapting oratorio and instrumental idioms in a robust harmonic idiom and a direct tunefulness that defies conventional stylistic divisions into Baroque and Classical; and in the glee, admittedly a minor genre in the grander scheme, the British developed an indigenous achievement that was unique. Certainly Britain's concert life in the eighteenth century impresses by its individuality, its variety, its unselfconscious vitality – above all by those genuine and diverse musical enthusiasms that permeated British culture right across the social spectrum.

PART ONE

Towns and Cities

CHAPTER TWO

Concert Topography and Provincial Towns in Eighteenth-Century England

Peter Borsay[*]

Eighteenth-century Britain, particularly England, saw a remarkable growth in fashionable, high-status music making. What was novel about this was not only the unprecedented volume of activity, but also the public and commercial character of the performances – so much so, that it is possible to see in the long eighteenth century the origins of what we would recognize now as the modern concert system. Research by musicologists and historians has established the broad contours of this development, including the principal vehicles through which change was delivered: the subscription concert, the musical club and the festival.[1] By and large the phenomenon was an urban one. London, with its huge concentrated market – in 1700 the metropolis with half a million inhabitants was over 16 times larger than its nearest rival, Norwich with 30 000 souls – pioneered many of the key changes.[2] However, in some ways the most impressive feature of the process was the extent to which the regions and provinces of England picked up on and fostered the fashion for concerts. Town after town (many of them small)

---

[*] This chapter was originally given as a paper to the conference 'Concert, lieux et espaces musicaux en Europe, 1700–1920; approche architecturale, culturelle et sociale', Brussels, November 2001, as part of a project sponsored by the European Science Foundation, on 'Musical life in Europe 1600–1900; circulation, institutions, representation'. The paper in an earlier form will appear as part of the published conference proceedings. I am grateful to the organizers for their invitation to take part in the conference, and to those participating for their comments and suggestions during the conference.

1 E. D. Mackerness, *A Social History of English Music* (London: Routledge & Kegan Paul, 1964), ch. 3, pp. 87–126; John Harley, *Music in Purcell's London* (London: Dobson, 1968); J. H. Plumb, *The Commercialisation of Leisure in Eighteenth-Century England* (Reading: University of Reading, 1973), pp. 14–16; *New Grove2*, vol. 6, pp. 616–25; Cyril Ehrlich, *The Music Profession in Britain since the Eighteenth Century: A Social History* (Oxford: Clarendon Press, 1985), pp. 1–29; H. Diack Johnstone and Roger Fiske, eds, *The Eighteenth Century*, Blackwell History of Music in Britain, 4 (Oxford: Blackwell, 1990), pp. 31–95, 205–60; William Weber, *The Rise of Musical Classics in Eighteenth-Century England: A Study in Canon, Ritual, and Ideology* (Oxford: Clarendon Press, 1992); Simon McVeigh, *Concert Life in London from Mozart to Haydn* (Cambridge: Cambridge University Press, 1993); David Wyn Jones, ed., *Music in Eighteenth-Century Britain* (Aldershot: Ashgate, 2000); S. McVeigh, 'Concerts and music societies', in Iain McCalman, ed., *An Oxford Companion to the Romantic Age: British Culture 1776–1832* (Oxford: Oxford University Press, 2001), pp. 461–3.

2 For London as a centre of cultural innovation see Peter Borsay, 'London, 1660–1800: a distinctive culture?', in Peter Clark and Raymond Gillespie, eds, *Two Capitals: London and Dublin 1500–1840* (Oxford: Oxford University Press, 2001), pp. 167–84.

20 PETER BORSAY

established music clubs, subscription series and festivals. Some regions were stronger than others, but during the course of the century a measure of concert-going became, for the better off in society, a nationwide pastime.[3] Underpinning this was the powerful and pervasive presence of urbanization in eighteenth-century Britain, at this time the most dynamically urbanizing society in Europe and perhaps in the world. During the sixteenth and seventeenth centuries London's expansion had dominated the urban system, but regional industrial and commercial growth in the eighteenth century ensured that provincial towns were able to challenge the metropolis's supremacy.[4] Moreover, with quantitative demographic and economic growth came qualitative change, so that the efflorescence of provincial musical life was part of a broader urban cultural renaissance that affected high-status leisure as a whole.[5]

Most research undertaken on the rise of provincial concert life has focused on the personnel (entrepreneurs, enthusiastic amateurs, performers) behind the phenomenon, and the mechanisms through which it was delivered. Relatively little detailed attention has been paid to the physical surroundings of performances. The purpose of this study, therefore, is to examine *where* provincial concerts took place; to explore what may be called the topography of the concert. But before addressing this question it is necessary to define what is meant by a concert. The focus here will be on performances that possessed some measure of public and commercial character, and in which the musical element (as opposed to say the theatrical content) and function was predominant. On this basis one might seek to exclude private house parties, music theatre, and dance. However, in practice hard and fast lines of definition are difficult to sustain, particularly given that concert life at this point in time was still at a formative stage. For example,

---

3   Stanley Sadie, 'Concert Life in Eighteenth Century England', *PRMA*, 85 (1958–59), 17–30; David Johnson, *Music and Society in Lowland Scotland in the Eighteenth Century* (London: Oxford University Press, 1972); Trevor Fawcett, *Music in Eighteenth-Century Norwich and Norfolk* (Norwich: Centre of East Anglian Studies, University of East Anglia, 1979); Michael Tilmouth, 'The beginnings of provincial concert life in England', in Christopher Hogwood and Richard Luckett, eds, *Music in Eighteenth-Century England* (Cambridge: Cambridge University Press, 1983), pp. 1–17; M. Reed, 'The cultural role of small towns in England 1600–1800', in Peter Clark, ed., *Small Towns in Early Modern Europe* (Cambridge: Cambridge University Press, 1995), pp. 134–5; John Brewer, *The Pleasures of the Imagination: English Culture in the Eighteenth Century* (London: HarperCollins, 1997), pp. 531–72; Peter Clark, *British Clubs and Societies 1580–1800: The Origins of an Associational World* (Oxford: Clarendon Press, 2000), pp. 51, 80, 121–3, 441; J. Stobart, 'In search of a leisure hierarchy: English spa towns and their place in the eighteenth-century urban system', in Peter Borsay, Gunther Hirschfelder and Ruth-E. Mohrmann, eds, *New Directions in Urban History* (Münster: Waxman, 2000), pp. 27–8.

4   Penelope J. Corfield, *The Impact of English Towns 1700–1800* (Oxford: Oxford University Press, 1981); Peter Borsay, ed., *The Eighteenth Century Town: A Reader in English Urban History 1688–1820* (London: Longman, 1990); Rosemary Sweet, *The English Town 1680–1840: Government, Society and Culture* (Harlow: Longman, 1999); Peter Clark, ed., *The Cambridge Urban History of Britain*, vol. 2, *1540–1840* (Cambridge: Cambridge University Press, 2000); Christopher W. Chalklin, *The Rise of the English Town 1650–1850* (Cambridge: Cambridge University Press, 2001); Joyce M. Ellis, *The Georgian Town 1680–1840* (Basingstoke: Palgrave, 2001).

5   Peter Borsay, *The English Urban Renaissance: Culture and Society in the Provincial Town 1660–1770* (Oxford: Clarendon Press, 1989).

CONCERT TOPOGRAPHY AND PROVINCIAL TOWNS

much 'concert' music was delivered by clubs that were a mixture of public and private institutions, and that drew upon both amateur and professional resources. Instrumental interludes were frequently inserted into plays, and many of those who attended assemblies may not have danced but contented themselves with listening to the music. Further blurring the boundary between the concert and something which might more properly be called a domestic soirée was the later eighteenth-century fashion for private concerts, which though located in the home (often in a specially designated music room) of a gentleman or aristocrat, attracted such numbers as to suggest that the events were in some measure part of the public sphere.[6]

The single most striking feature about the topography of provincial concert life is the scarcity of either purpose-built accommodation, or premises exclusively (even predominantly) devoted to music making. Modern notions of concert halls or rooms specially constructed to meet the acoustical and aesthetic aspirations of discerning performers and audiences had little meaning in the provincial towns of eighteenth-century England. By and large these early concerts took place in multi-functional public spaces. The few seemingly attested eighteenth-century cases of purpose-built rooms are the Holywell Music Room in Oxford, built *c*.1742–48,[7] the Music Hall (Bold Street) Liverpool opened in 1786, and (outside England) the St Cecilia Hall built in Edinburgh in 1760–62. Another case might be the rebuilding, for an oratorio festival in 1788, of the disused Blackfriars' church in Norwich to form St Andrew's Hall (capable of accommodating an audience of 900), which subsequently became the home of a music society called the Hall Concert.[8] Though there are several instances of Georgian premises possessing or acquiring the nomenclature of 'music room', their status as sites devoted principally to public music making is often dubious. The so-called Music Room at Lancaster, built in the 1730s, was an ornate summer house, and appears to have acquired its name only in the nineteenth century, perhaps in reference to the depiction of the nine muses (including, in a prominent position, one holding a lyre) in the highly decorative plaster work in the upper room. The elegant Music Room of Number 51 Keldgate, Beverley (described as 'lately rebuilt' in 1753), appears to be an addition to a private residence rather than a public room.[9] During her travels

---

6 Michael I. Wilson, *The Chamber Organ in Britain, 1600–1800* (Aldershot: Ashgate, 2001), pp. 53–6; Johnstone and Fiske, *The Eighteenth Century*, pp. 319–20.

7 Further on the Holywell see Ch. 12 below.

8 John Henry Mee, *The Oldest Music Room in Europe: A Record of Eighteenth-Century Enterprise at Oxford* (London and New York: John Lane, 1911); George Chandler, *Liverpool* (London: B. T. Batsford, 1957), p. 435; A. J. Youngson, *The Making of Classical Edinburgh 1750–1840,* 1st pub. 1966 (Edinburgh: Edinburgh University Press, 1993), pp. 248–9; Weber, *The Rise of Musical Classics*, p. 136; Fawcett, *Music in Eighteenth-Century Norwich*, pp. 5, 9.

9 Andrew White, *The Buildings of Georgian Lancaster* (Lancaster: Centre for North-West Regional Studies, University of Lancaster, 1992), pp. 17, 49; Ivan and Elisabeth Hall, *Historic Beverley* (York, 1973; Beverley: Beverley Bookshop, 1981), pp. 56–9 (esp. p. 59). Subscription concerts were being held in the assembly rooms at Beverley from the 1750s: Victoria County History, *The County of York East Riding*, vol. 6: *The Borough and Liberties of Beverley* (Oxford: Oxford University Press, 1989), p. 132.

in the 1690s Celia Fiennes noted at Astrop 'a Roome for the Musick and a Roome for the Company', though the tiny size and remote location of the spa – it scarcely survived the eighteenth century – must leave some doubt as to how substantial these facilities were.[10] Bath was a spa on an altogether grander scale. In 1755 the local newspaper advertised a two-part programme for a concert room near the Parades. But given the availability of tickets for the pit, galleries and boxes, and the fact that wedged in between the two sections of the concert was a performance of a comedy called *The Suspicious Husband* (most probably the play of that name by Benjamin Hoadly, given at Covent Garden in 1747), it seems quite likely that the so-called concert room was in fact the theatre recently built (1750) in Orchard Street adjacent to the Parades.[11]

Given that in London during the course of the eighteenth century only two major halls appear to have been primarily designed and built with public concerts in mind,[12] it is not surprising that the vast majority of performances in provincial towns occurred in premises which served some non-musical function. Public buildings containing a large room or hall provided one obvious resource to call upon. Town halls were widely used. So, for example, in 1772 a concert was given by an orchestra of 14 players in Romsey town hall, which attracted an audience of nearly 100, and in 1789 the town hall at Bridgnorth accommodated a 'grand miscellaneous concert'. In mid-eighteenth-century Norfolk the town halls at King's Lynn and Thetford were used, and the splendid Guildhall at Worcester, built in 1721–23 with an impressive great room on its upper floor, was regularly employed by the Three Choirs Festival until a dispute in 1755.[13] Craft company (or guild) halls were also commandeered, such as that of the Merchant Taylors in Bristol (rebuilt in 1740–41) and the Drapers in Coventry.[14] At Oxford and Cambridge the rich physical heritage of university and college buildings, allied to the inherent performing resources of the institutions, provided ample opportunities for concerts. The three days of celebrations at Oxford in 1756 to honour Lady Pomfret, after a benefaction to the university, were accommodated in Wren's

---

10   *The Journeys of Celia Fiennes*, ed. Christopher Morris (London: Cresset Press, 1947), pp. 31–2; C. Tongue, 'Thomas Thornton at Astrop Spa', *Northamptonshire Past and Present*, 4 (1970–71), 281–5.

11   *The Bath Advertiser*, No. 1, 18 Oct. 1755; Sybil Rosenfeld, *Strolling Players and Drama in the Provinces 1660–1765* (Cambridge: Cambridge University Press, 1939), pp. 182–3. The concert hall in Vicar Lane, Leeds referred to in the *Leeds Gazetteer* in the 1760s also served as a theatre: Kevin Grady, *The Georgian Public Buildings of Leeds and the West Riding*, Publications of the Thoresby Society, vol. 62 for 1987 (Leeds: Thoresby Society, 1989), p. 162.

12   McVeigh, *Concert Life in London*, p. 56. For the wide variety of venues used in London during the first half of the eighteenth century see Johnstone and Fiske, *The Eighteenth Century*, pp. 38–43.

13   Brewer, *Pleasures of the Imagination*, p. 563; John Money, *Experience and Identity: Birmingham and the West Midlands 1760–1800* (Manchester: Manchester University Press, 1977), p. 81; Fawcett, *Music in Eighteenth-Century Norwich*, pp. 13, 37; Watkins Shaw, *The Three Choirs Festival: The Official History of the Meetings of the Three Choirs of Gloucester, Hereford and Worcester, c.1713–1953* (Worcester and London: E. Baylis & Son, 1954), p. 12.

14   Kathleen Barker, *Bristol at Play: Five Centuries of Live Entertainment* (Bradford-on-Avon: Moonraker Press, 1976), p. 8; Walter Ison, *The Georgian Buildings of Bristol*, 1st pub. London: Faber & Faber, 1952 (repr. Bath: Kingsmead Press, 1978), pp. 94–5; Money, *Experience and Identity*, p. 81.

CONCERT TOPOGRAPHY AND PROVINCIAL TOWNS 23

Sheldonian Theatre and included – in addition to the rich musical accompaniment to the formalities – a performance of Handel's *Judas Maccabaeus*, while in the following year a concert was mounted at Trinity College Cambridge by 'the Fiddling Gownsmen', before an audience of nearly 580, to raise money for the city's poor.[15]

Churches were, in a very real sense, part of the public fabric of a town. Usually constituting the largest covered space in the community, they were benefiting from the first major wave of investment in religious building since the Reformation.[16] Increasingly furnished with comfortable pews and galleries,[17] possessing their own teams of choral and instrumental performers (and with more and more town churches acquiring impressive organs and the services of professional organists), they were a natural home for concert performances. Though within the post-Reformation Anglican liturgical tradition there was some ambivalence about what, if any, sort of music should be performed in churches, a broad consensus seems to have emerged in the eighteenth century that as long as music of an appropriately sacred character was performed, churches were a suitable venue for concerts.[18] It was a process facilitated by the narrowing gap between provincial psalmody and art music in the period.[19] The boundary of propriety can be seen to have been drawn at the provincial festivals, often located in diocesan centres, where sacred pieces would be performed in the cathedral or a church and the remaining programme in secular premises. So for example at the Three Choirs Festival of 1756, based that year in Hereford, the two morning concerts in the cathedral accommodated Te Deum and Jubilate settings by Purcell and Handel, and anthems by Handel and Boyce, whereas the three evening concerts in the College Hall included Handel's *Samson* and *L'Allegro, il Penseroso ed il Moderato*, Boyce's *Solomon*, and various instrumental pieces.[20] At this stage the general practice appears to have been to perform oratorios, despite their religious subject matter, in secular premises, whereas by the later eighteenth century churches were also being used. This was a sign, as William Weber has argued, of 'how firmly the oratorios had become established as a bridge between the sacred and the secular', and more broadly of the extent to which the church had developed

---

15   *A Parson in the Vale of White Horse: George Woodward's Letters from East Hendred, 1753–1761*, ed. Donald Gibson (Gloucester: Alan Sutton, 1982), pp. 84–6; Suffolk Record Office, E2/20/1A (Cullum correspondence), John Hey to Rev. John Cullum, 31 March 1757; Sadie, 'Concert Life', 20.

16   Christopher Chalklin, 'The financing of church building in the provincial towns of eighteenth-century England', in Peter Clark, ed., *The Transformation of English Provincial Towns 1600–1800* (London: Hutchinson, 1985), pp. 284–310.

17   Marcus Whiffen, *Stuart and Georgian Churches: The Architecture of the Church of England outside London 1603–1837* (London: B. T. Batsford, 1947–48), p. 7 and *passim*; Basil F. L. Clarke, *The Building of the Eighteenth-Century Church* (London: SPCK, 1963), ch. 3, 'Accommodation', pp. 22–32.

18   Brewer, *Pleasures of the Imagination*, pp. 552–7; Wilson, *Chamber Organ*, pp. 17–18.

19   Sally Drage, 'A reappraisal of provincial church music', in Wyn Jones, *Music in Eighteenth-Century Britain*, pp. 183–8.

20   *The Gloucester Journal*, 7 Sept. 1756; see Ch. 3 below.

24   PETER BORSAY

as a site of concert performance.[21] One reason for such adaptability may well have been the church's need to respond to the competition from the proliferating body of secular entertainments. It is significant that church organists often played a vital role in developing all-round local musical life, brokering a rapprochement between the sacred and profane elements in this.[22]

Religious establishments contained rooms and halls other than those simply devoted to worship. The College Hall ('georgianized' during the eighteenth century) at Hereford was part of the medieval College of Vicars Choral, and it was the 'Close' (or Vicars') Hall at Wells where the music club, of which the physician Claver Morris was such an enthusiastic member, held its regular meetings and annual St Cecilia's Day concerts in the early eighteenth century.[23] The former chapel constructed in the fourteenth century over St Ann's Gate in the Close at Salisbury is reputed to be the location of Handel's first concert in England. Whatever the truth of this, the gate was situated next door to the fine town house of the literary theorist, politician and musical impresario James Harris, who used the room for rehearsals during the Salisbury Festival, and – as an account of 1770 makes clear – as a semi-private theatre:

> The Chapel makes a good theatre, the stage is near three feet high, there is room for between forty and fifty spectators, giving a good space for the orchestra, which consists in a proper band for the Pastorale of "Daphnis and Amaryllis" ... Dr Stevens leads the orchestra ... To fill up the choruses properly we are obliged to take two small choristers, and they make pretty shepherds.[24]

However great the value of public buildings as a home for the new world of concerts, the principal locations utilized were commercial premises devoted to sociability and entertainment; inns, assembly rooms, theatres, pleasure gardens and similar venues. As part of the wider urban renaissance, investment in the cultural sector of the urban fabric, as Christopher Chalklin has demonstrated, expanded rapidly in the eighteenth century, so that there developed a wide range of spaces, with the suitably fashionable ambience in which public, commercially

---

21   Weber, *The Rise of Musical Classics*, p. 137; J. Sutcliffe Smith, *The Story of Music in Birmingham* (Birmingham: Cornish Brothers, 1945), pp. 19, 26; K. James, 'Venanzio Rauzzini and the search for musical perfection', *Bath History*, 3 (1990), 111–12; Jack Simmons, *Leicester Past and Present*, vol. 1, *Ancient Borough to 1860* (London: Eyre Methuen, 1974), p. 120.

22   Clark, *British Clubs*, pp. 165, 186–7; Reed, 'Cultural role of small towns', p. 135; Adrian Henstock, ed., *A Georgian Country Town: Ashbourne 1725–1825*, vol. 1, *Fashionable Society* (Ashbourne: Ashbourne Local History Group, 1989), pp. 69–70; Borsay, *English Urban Renaissance*, p. 126.

23   Shaw, *Three Choirs Festival*, p. 12; Nikolaus Pevsner, *The Buildings of England: Herefordshire* (Harmondsworth: Penguin, 1977), pp. 170–71; *The Diary of a West Country Physician A.D. 1684–1726* [Claver Morris], ed. Edmund Hobhouse (London: Simpkin, Marshall, 1934), pp. 39–43, 58, 59, 65, 82, 113; cf. Ch. 3 below.

24   *The Diary of Thomas Naish*, ed. D. Slatter, Wiltshire Archaeological and Natural History Society, Records Branch, 20 (1964), p. 4; *Salisbury: The Houses of the Close*, Royal Commission on the Historical Monuments of England (London, 1993), p. 47; Elizabeth Harris quoted in Clive Probyn, *The Sociable Humanist: The Life and Works of James Harris 1709–1780* (Oxford: Clarendon Press, 1991), pp. 223–4, 233.

CONCERT TOPOGRAPHY AND PROVINCIAL TOWNS 25

based music could be performed.[25] In itself this reduced the pressure to construct specialized auditoriums. Traditionally hostelries constituted the premier leisure centre for the local community, and it was natural that concerts – especially as they first began to emerge, and before other suitable buildings were constructed – should find a home here. Indeed, it could be argued that in England the concert, just as the music hall was to do in the nineteenth century, grew out of a tavern-based culture of music making. The influence was certainly considerable in London.[26] What lay at the heart of the link between hostelries and music was their inherently convivial atmosphere (owing not a little to the presence of food, tobacco and alcohol), since this provided the essential sociable context for the clubs responsible for delivering much of the new concert music. The book of rules for the Musical and Amicable Society formed in Birmingham in 1762, which met at the Sea-Horse, contained on its front page a picture of four gentlemen singers with a decanter and wine glass, and a banner above inscribed with the words:

> To our Musical Club here's long life and prosperity;
> May it flourish with us, and go on to posterity.
> May concord and harmony always abound,
> And divisions here only in our music be found;
> May the Catch and the Glass go about and about,
> And another succeed to the Bottle that's out![27]

The musical society founded at Norwich in the 1720s flitted from one of the city's inns to another; about 1760 it was located at the Maid's Head, renting a room which it considered its own. In the 1780s substantial series of subscription concerts were being staged at the Rose and Crown Inn in Leeds and at the Royal Hotel (mounted by the Dilettanti Musical Society) in Birmingham, and it is significant that when in 1726 the Wells music club was forced out of the Close Hall after a quarrel between Claver Morris and the vicars, it reconstituted itself in the Mitre Inn.[28] Much of the appeal of hostelries was due to what Peter Clark has called 'the efflorescence of the urban inn' in the post-Restoration period, which involved heavy investment in additional space, decoration and furnishing – and in some cases the purchase of organs and later pianos – to enhance their role as upmarket social and recreational centres.[29]

---

25   C. W. Chalklin, 'Capital expenditure on building for cultural purposes in provincial England, 1730–1830', *Business History*, 22 (1980), 51–70; Borsay, *English Urban Renaissance*, pp. 144–72.

26   *Roger North on Music: Being a Selection of his Essays written during the Years c.1695–1728*, ed. John Wilson (London: Novello, 1959), pp. 351–3; Harley, *Music in Purcell's London*, pp. 135–51; Wilson, *Chamber Organ*, pp. 17–18.

27   Smith, *Music in Birmingham*, p. 13; for tavern-based musical culture see also Money, *Experience and Identity*, pp. 85–6; Clark, *British Clubs*, pp. 62–3, 121–3.

28   Fawcett, *Music in Eighteenth-Century Norwich*, pp. 5–6; J. Looney, 'Advertising and society in England, 1720–1820: a statistical analysis of Yorkshire newspaper advertisements', Ph.D. diss. (Princeton University, 1983), p. 171; *Diary of a West Country Physician*, ed. Hobhouse, pp. 42, 133–4.

29   Clark, *British Clubs*, p. 162; P. Clark, *The English Alehouse: A Social History 1200–1830* (London: Longman, 1983), pp. 195–9, 275–6; Fawcett, *Music in Eighteenth-Century Norwich*, p. 3; Alan Everitt, 'The English urban inn, 1560–1760', in A. Everitt, ed., *Perspectives in English Urban History* (London: Macmillan, 1973), pp. 100–104, 113–20.

26   PETER BORSAY

Inns also provided a welcome home for the new fashion of assemblies and the rapidly expanding theatre circuit that were such a feature of the cultural life of English towns after the Restoration.[30] However, from the early eighteenth century both these forms of entertainment began to benefit from the construction of purpose-built premises, which, together with dancing masters' rooms, became popular venues for concerts. Theatres staged not only opera and oratorio but also performances of songs and instrumental pieces; indeed, it was common practice to interpose instrumental works between the acts of oratorios. The relationship between theatres and music was strengthened by the potentially draconian terms of the Theatre Act of 1737; to circumvent this plays were often advertised as concerts, with the drama billed as taking place during the interludes in the music. In 1760, when anxieties had resurfaced about the strict implementation of the Act, a concert of music in six parts was advertised in Manchester, with *Theodosius: or the Force of Love* (presumably the play written by Nathaniel Lee for which Purcell composed incidental music) performed between the parts, and Norwich's first purpose-built theatre (erected in 1757) was described in publicity as 'the Grand Concert-Hall'.[31] Even more popular than theatres for the performance of concerts were assembly rooms. Once constructed these often became the premier site for performances, as appears the case at Bristol, Norwich, York and Bath.[32] The York music club, or 'music assembly' as it was known, had a particularly close association with the city's Blake Street Rooms, designed by Lord Burlington. The club was among the original subscribers who financed the construction of the Rooms in the early 1730s, purchasing a £25 share in the venture; in 1733 it agreed to pay the proprietors £20 annually for permission to use the premises for its regular Monday concerts during the winter season and morning concerts in August Race Week; and significantly – when the club was going through a rocky patch in the 1740s – the directors of the Rooms ordered enquiries to be made as to whether the club's representative would 'deliver up the instruments, and music books belonging to the Music Assembly, in order to be safely deposited for the use of any future concert'.[33] Of all English towns, Bath was the best equipped with purpose-built assembly rooms, acquiring its first establishment in 1708 and a second one, facing it across the Terrace Walk, in 1730. The latter closed down when the spectacular Upper Rooms, which still survive today, opened near the Circus in

---

30   Borsay, *Urban Renaissance*, pp. 117–21, 150–62, 329–31, 336–49; Mark Girouard, *The English Town* (New Haven and London: Yale University Press, 1990), pp. 127–44; A. Dain, 'Assemblies and politeness 1660–1840', Ph.D. diss. (University of East Anglia, 2001); Rosenfeld, *Strolling Players, passim*.

31   10 Geo. II, c. 28 (Theatre Act 1737); J. L. Hodgkinson and Rex Pogson, *The Early Manchester Theatre* (London: A. Blond for the Society for Theatre Research, 1960), pp. 25, 29; Fawcett, *Music in Eighteenth-Century Norwich*, pp. 21, 22, 23, 25.

32   J. Barry, 'The cultural life of Bristol 1640–1775', D.Phil. diss. (University of Oxford, 1985), p. 187; Fawcett, *Music in Eighteenth-Century Norwich*, pp. 5, 7–8, 39.

33   York Civic Archives, M.23/1, Assembly Rooms: Directors' Minute Book (1730–58), 24 March 1732/3, 23 April 1742; M.23/3, printed 'Proposals for Building, by Subscription, Assembly Rooms in the City of York'.

1771. Over time a lavish diet of concerts evolved around the various rooms. This reached its zenith under the leadership of the renowned Italian castrato Venanzio Rauzzini, who masterminded the programmes of 12 Wednesday concerts that were a feature of the winter season at the Upper Rooms, 'in three of which choral and ancient music is performed. A very reasonable subscription', as Richard Warner put it in 1801, 'admits to this rich feast of harmony'.[34]

Another major venue for music making in Bath, at least during the summer months, was the pleasure gardens. The model was set by the great London gardens, especially Vauxhall (originally Spring Gardens), Ranelagh and Marylebone.[35] Several of the leading provincial towns – such as Norwich, Bristol, Birmingham and Newcastle upon Tyne – opened gardens, often deploying the names of the metropolitan establishments and copying their practice of presenting various types of musical events, including concerts. The two principal gardens in late eighteenth-century Norwich adopted the titles Vauxhall and Ranelagh, and like their London counterparts built indoor auditoriums to protect their customers from the vagaries of the English weather.[36] As might be expected Bath also established a range of pleasure gardens during the course of the eighteenth century, mounting concerts on a regular or occasional basis. What differentiated these from the ones held in other venues was the exploitation of the gardens' open-air environment and cultivated rural ambience, and the manner in which the music was embedded in some wider entertainment experience. Pyrotechnic displays accompanied the regular concerts at the Spring Gardens (opened $c.1740$), as they did the spectacular gala concert nights at Sydney Gardens (opened 1795), when as Pierce Egan wrote in 1819, 'the music, singing, cascades, transparencies, fire-works, and superb illuminations, render these gardens very similar to Vauxhall'.[37]

In 1784 *The New Bath Guide*, describing the Monday and Thursday public breakfasts at the Spring Gardens, noted that 'music attends at breakfasts, and for dancing, with horns and clarionets'.[38] This inevitably raises the question: where does a concert end and a less defined musical experience begin?[39] It is a question which confronts any observer of the eighteenth-century town, with musical sound – of one form or another – seemingly an ever-present phenomenon. It was

---

34   Richard Warner, *The History of Bath* (Bath, 1801), p. 356; *The New Bath Guide* (Bath, 1809), pp. 20–21; Trevor Fawcett, *Bath Entertain'd: Amusements, Recreations and Gambling at the 18th-Century Spa* (Bath: Ruton, 1998), pp. 29–32.

35   Warwick W. Wroth, *The London Pleasure Gardens of the Eighteenth Century* (repr. London: Macmillan, 1979); Mollie Sands, *The Eighteenth-Century Pleasure Gardens of Marylebone* (London: Society for Theatre Research, 1987); J. Nicolson, *Vauxhall Gardens 1661–1859* (London: The Vauxhall Society and St Peter's Heritage Centre, 1991).

36   Fawcett, *Music in Eighteenth-Century Norwich*, pp. 29–32; Barry, 'Cultural life of Bristol', p. 192; Money, *Experience and Identity*, pp. 80, 83; Sadie, 'Concert Life', 19.

37   Fawcett, *Bath Entertain'd*, pp. 57–62; Brenda Snaddon, *The Last Promenade: Sydney Gardens Bath* (Widcombe: Millstream, 2000), pp. 16–18; Pierce Egan, *Walks Through Bath* (Bath, 1819), p. 182.

38   *The New Bath Guide* (Bath, 1784), p. 42.

39   On defining concerts, cf. Ch. 13 below.

28   PETER BORSAY

common practice in English spas – for example Bath, Epsom and Bristol Hot Wells – for a band of musicians to accompany the morning drinking and bathing routine of the company.[40] Quite what was performed is unclear, and it could be argued that this was mere mood music, which would be largely inaudible above the hubbub of conversation. Nonetheless, something was being played that amounted at the very least to a semi-concert. Nor can it be assumed that all the visitors took no interest in the sound that surrounded them, even if it was not always easy to discern exactly what was being played. In 1766 John Penrose reported from the Pump Room at Bath, 'We staid about an Hour, and heard the Tweedle-dum and Tweedle-dee of ten Musicians, seated in a Music Gallery at the West End of the Room. A great Number of Gentlemen and Ladies were there who kept such a Prating that the Pleasure of the music was lost.'[41] Open-air performances of music were by no means uncommon, and these were not confined to the pleasure gardens. Promenaders on the growing number of formal walks laid out in English towns might expect to take their perambulations to the sound of a small band. This was the case for those using the Gravel Walks (or Orange Grove) at Bath, while fashionable visitors to Tunbridge Wells were expected to contribute at least half a guinea towards 'the music … to pay them for their public play on the parade'.[42] There appears also to have been something of a fashion for aqua-concerts. The case of Handel's *Water Music* is well known, but the provinces shared this modish form of summer entertainment. Boats filled with musicians accompanied river parties at Norwich and Bristol Hot Wells; at the latter it was reported that the music – capitalizing on the acoustical properties of the Avon Gorge – 'when echoed and re-echoed by the rocks, has a most delightful effect, not only on those on the water but also to the auditors on land'.[43]

Concerts, of one sort or another, therefore took place in a wide variety of settings. Given the growth in demand, why were they so slow to acquire specialized premises? In answering this question, it is important to realize that the concert form was still at a very early stage of its development, and that there was no tradition of constructing specialized musical venues to accommodate it. Moreover, many of the provincial towns in which concerts were given were tiny places, and even if we take into account the population of the surrounding region,

---

40   J. Wood, *A Description of Bath*, 2nd edn 1749, repr. 1765 (Bath: Kingsmead Reprints, 1969), pp. 269, 437–8; Reginald Lennard, 'The watering places', in R. Lennard, ed., *Englishmen at Rest and Play: Some Phases of English Leisure 1558–1714* (Oxford: Clarendon Press, 1931), p. 63; Barry, 'Cultural life of Bristol', p. 192.

41   *Letters from Bath 1766–1767 by the Rev. John Penrose*, ed. Brigitte Mitchell and Hubert Penrose (Gloucester: Alan Sutton, 1983), p. 55.

42   John Collinson, *The History and Antiquities of the County of Somerset*, 3 vols (Bath, 1791, repr. Gloucester: Alan Sutton, 1983), vol. 1, p. 34; Thomas Benge Burr, *The History of Tunbridge Wells* (London, 1766), p. 115.

43   Fawcett, *Music in Eighteenth-Century Norwich*, pp. 32, 56; quoted in Vincent Waite, 'The Bristol Hotwell', in Patrick McGrath, ed., *Bristol in the Eighteenth Century* (Newton Abbot: David & Charles, 1972), p. 120; Barry, 'Cultural life of Bristol', p. 192; Richard Leppert, *Music and Image: Domesticity, Ideology and Socio-Cultural Formation in Eighteenth-Century England* (Cambridge: Cambridge University Press, 1988), pp. 205–8.

there was simply not a large enough market to support specialized auditoriums, or to guarantee those investing in such facilities an adequate return on their capital. However, all these arguments could apply equally well to theatres and assemblies, but these did acquire dedicated buildings from an early point in time. One reason may be that it was important for theatre company managers to have well-equipped auditoriums, with scenery and props, which offered the audience a good view of the stage. On the other hand music, particularly that of a purely instrumental nature, was highly portable and could in theory be performed in virtually any open space. Nor was it a complete disaster, as it would be with a play, if the audience had a poor or even no view of the performers. Dancing would also appear a highly flexible recreation, demanding little more than bodies and floor space. Yet dance – as it was practised at the new assemblies – was part of a complex social routine that required good catering facilities, high-quality furnishings and decoration, and, preferably, multiple spaces in which to take refreshments, play cards and gossip. Music was thus, in terms of defining its own particular space, a victim of its own adaptability.

However, it would be quite wrong to assume from this that concerts had no impact on, or took nothing from, the spaces which they occupied. Those who designed, remodelled and fitted out fashionable public arenas would have been well aware that these spaces might be called upon to accommodate musical performances. For assembly rooms and theatres it was a commercial priority that they were capable of housing as wide a variety of recreations (including music) as possible. Catering for concerts may even have affected the ecclesiastical fabric. The galleries frequently inserted into Georgian churches were no doubt primarily there to expand the capacity of the building to hold those attending divine service, an important requirement given the pace of urbanization, but they also provided excellent seating for concert-goers. It is difficult to imagine how the highly popular oratorios (in spring of 1791 a reputed 1500 attended one performance) mounted at Bath Abbey could have been accommodated comfortably without the double-tier aisle galleries erected – to judge from illustrative evidence – at some point in the second half of the eighteenth century, and stripped out during the 'restorations' of the nineteenth century.[44] Queen Square Chapel, Bath, built to service the residents of the fashionable new square of the 1730s, was opened with 'a concert of Vocal and Instrumental Musick, performed by ten of the best Hands at that time in the City', which included an anthem by the abbey organist Thomas Chilcot, 'O how pleasant is thy Dwelling'.[45] Comfort and exclusiveness were the hallmarks of the proprietary chapels, like that at Queen Square, that sprang up over Bath and other towns. Some appear to have been almost purpose-built as concert auditoriums. The Octagon Chapel, opened on Milsom Street (which became

---

44   James, 'Venanzio Rauzzini', pp. 111–12; James Lees-Milne and David Ford, *Images of Bath* (Richmond-upon-Thames: Saint Helena Press, 1982), gallery, nos. 95–100; John Britton, *The History and Antiquities of Bath Abbey Church*, continued to the present time by R[obert] E. M. Peach (Bath, 1887), pp. xvi, 58–9.
45   Wood, *Bath*, pp. 314–15.

Bath's premier shopping mall) in 1767, was constructed along the most elegant and commodious lines. In 1808 a character in one satirical account commented, 'I am acquainted with no place of worship which is so well calculated for *genteel* people ... here is every contrivance for warmth, ease, and repose'. The galleries and octagonal form of the building provided excellent views for those attending, particularly of the splendid Snetzler organ. The instrument was inaugurated in October 1767 with a performance of *Messiah* and an organ concerto, the latter played by the chapel's resident organist, the composer and Bath concert impresario William Herschel, who went on to compose many sacred pieces for the chapel.[46]

Elevated seating for the audience was paralleled in many public social spaces by special galleries and platforms for the performers. Music galleries were erected at Bath in the Pump Room (from at least 1734) and Cross Bath, and in the 'great rooms' constructed for the new mansion house built at York, as well as in the town halls at Bath and Warwick.[47] The York assembly rooms contained a music gallery (rebuilt in 1755), as well as a stage specially constructed for Race Week concerts, and the Upper Rooms at Bath possessed an interlinked complex of elegant musicians' galleries to service the various rooms.[48] Many walks and pleasure gardens probably contained galleries and stands from which music would be delivered to an open-air public, though it is difficult to ascertain the precise form of these ephemeral structures. A small gallery still survives on the Pantiles (or paved walks) at Tunbridge Wells, from which, according to a letter of 1767, the musicians played three times a day. The garden front of the tavern in the Sydney Gardens, Bath had a deep loggia, supporting, in its central segmental bay, an open orchestra; in John Nattes's drawing of 1805 this contains vacant music stands – no doubt the performers were taking a breather.[49]

Concerts, therefore, though they may not have acquired their own specialized auditoriums, shaped the spaces which they occupied. There is also a powerful sense in which those spaces themselves played a vital part in shaping the musical experience, and this may be a reason why purpose-built halls were slow to develop. Concerts did not take place in just *any* convenient location. Listening to 'classical' music was as much a social as an aesthetic experience, and it

---

46   [Richard Warner], *Bath Characters: Or Sketches from Life* (2nd edn, London, 1808), pp. 41–2; Anthony J. Turner, *Science and Music in Eighteenth Century Bath* (Bath: University of Bath, 1977), pp. 31–4; Walter Ison, *The Georgian Buildings of Bath from 1700 to 1830*, 1st pub. 1948 (Bath: Kingsmead Reprints, 1969), pp. 72–3, plate 23.

47   Bath Record Office, Bath Council Minutes, 24 May 1734; Wood, *Bath*, p. 269; Jean Manco, 'The Cross Bath', *Bath History*, 2 (1988), 61; Thomas Allen, *A New and Complete History of the County of York*, 3 vols (London, 1828–31), vol. 2, p. 287; Ison, *Buildings of Bath*, p. 88; Thomas Kemp, *A History of Warwick and its People* (Warwick: Henry T. Cooke, 1905), p. 177.

48   York Civic Archives, Assembly Rooms: Directors' Minute Book, 4 August 1732, 30 July 1733, 20 December 1733, 24 February 1735/6, 24 May and 6 September 1755; Ison, *Buildings of Bath*, p. 51.

49   John Newman, *The Buildings of England: West Kent and the Weald* (Harmondsworth: Penguin Books, 1969), p. 559; Margaret Barton, *Tunbridge Wells* (London: Faber & Faber, 1937), pp. 341–2; Ison, *Buildings of Bath*, p. 96; Snaddon, *The Last Promenade*, pp. 32–3.

CONCERT TOPOGRAPHY AND PROVINCIAL TOWNS 31

was essential that the place chosen conveyed the necessary mixture of prestige, fashionability and exclusivity if the performances were to meet the social expectations of those who attended them. Town and guild halls were popular not simply because they contained a large covered space, but more critically because they were centres of civic authority closely associated with the urban elite, and like assembly rooms could be carefully policed to keep out hoi polloi. High standards of decoration, furnishing and lighting, reflecting the most up-to-date taste, were important in concert locations to ensure that visual and aural stimuli combined to create a heightened sense of social kudos. The refined but exhilarating quality of the experience generated when sight and sound fused together is nicely captured in an account of a concert held in 1779 at the Bath Upper Assembly Rooms, eight years after their opening:

> The Elegance of the room, illuminated with 480 wax Candles, the prismatic colours of the Lustres, the blaze of Jewels, & the inconceivable Harmony of near 40 Musicians some of whom are the finest hands in Europe, added to the rich attire of About 800 Gentlemen & Ladies, was, altogether a scene of which no person who never saw it can form any adequate Idea ... Near 60 of the Nobility were present & several foreigners of Distinction.[50]

Such occasions reflect the fact that during the eighteenth century concert locations – theatres, assembly rooms, walks and pleasure gardens – were among the key sites for the acquisition and exchange of status, and that music lay at the heart of the processes by which social identities were created and the social order reproduced.

Churches, proprietary chapels apart, were open potentially to a wide cross-section of society. But the opportunities for segregating the audience provided by pews and galleries would have preserved a strong sense of status and the social hierarchy. Moreover, church buildings imbued the music performed in them with a special mixture of *gravitas* and spiritual intensity which appealed to the growing thirst for moral improvement, respectability and religiosity among the urban middling orders and social elite. This sense of an elevating experience was enhanced by the frequent association between church-based concerts and philanthropic projects, a link dating back to the annual service-cum-concert of the Corporation of the Sons of the Clergy (from 1697 held in the newly consecrated St Paul's), and continued in the provincial musical festivals, which were frequently underpinned by some charitable objective. The fact that churches became such crucial auditoriums for concerts benefited the profile of classical music as a whole, and helped protect it from the moral and commercial stigma that attached to the theatre. Much commentary on the church concert scene emphasized the relationship between musical and social harmony. In 1729 Thomas Bisse described the origins of the Three Choirs Festival as a 'fortuitous and friendly proposal between a few lovers of harmony ... to commence an anniversary visit ... which voluntary instance of friendship and fraternity was quickly strengthened by

---

50   Edmund Rack, quoted in Turner, *Science and Music*, p. 39.

32   PETER BORSAY

social compact'.[51] Music's perceived capacity to harmonize social relationships fitted closely with a central plank of the English Enlightenment, the notion of sociability.[52] The siting of concerts in what were seen as the secular temples of sociability – such as assembly rooms and pleasure gardens – can thus be seen as a way of drawing out of the music its harmonic potential and strengthening its broader cultural and social function. Significantly, it was a common practice to follow up a concert with an assembly. At the Three Choirs Festival in Hereford in 1756, the evening concert in the college hall was followed by a ball in the same room, to which 'no person will be admitted without a concert ticket'.[53] This linking together of pastimes not only ensured an efficient use of the spatial resources available, but also suggests that the two forms of leisure were conceived as intimately bound together, sharing a common sociable agenda.

This agenda, and music's role within it, was further facilitated by the way in which concert venues were often located in close proximity to each other, forming distinctive and tightly knit cultural quarters. In Birmingham the higher part of the town, elevated above the smoke and grime of the suburbs, was from the early eighteenth century the focal point for upmarket residential development. It was in this area that the various assembly rooms (in the Square, Bull Street and Colmore Row) and the Baroque St Philip's church (built 1709–15, the principal site of the Birmingham musical festival) were situated.[54] Norwich's pleasure gardens and walks were largely sited on the western side of the city, and the first purpose-built assembly rooms (1754) and theatre (1757–58) lay next to each other, close to the formally laid out walks on Chapel Field, and within easy striking distance of St Peter's Mancroft (the location of the morning concerts during the first Norwich festival in 1788).[55] The most sophisticated cultural quarter established in any English provincial town by the mid-eighteenth century was that sited in the south-east corner of Bath. In a remarkably small space this accommodated several paved walks lined with prestige lodgings and shops, two assembly rooms (Simpson's and Wiltshire's), two sets of tree-planted walks (Simpson's and the Orange Grove), a theatre (Orchard Street), pleasure gardens (the Spring Gardens, accessible by ferry across the Avon), together with the Abbey church, the Pump Room and the baths. During the latter part of the eighteenth century this highly concentrated pattern of cultural topography began to fragment, as the city expanded rapidly and

---

51   T. Bisse, *A Sermon Preached in the Cathedral Church of Hereford, at the Anniversary Meeting of the Three Choirs* (London, 1729), p. 20.

52   Roy Porter, *Enlightenment: Britain and the Creation of the Modern World* (London: Allen Lane, 2000), p. 22; Brewer, *Pleasures of the Imagination*, pp. 102–7; Anna Bryson, *From Courtesy to Civility: Changing Codes of Conduct in Early Modern England* (Oxford: Clarendon Press, 1998), pp. 68–71, 283; P. Borsay, 'Sounding the town', *Urban History*, 29 (2002), 101–2.

53   *Gloucester Journal*, 7 Sept. 1756.

54   Borsay, *Urban Renaissance*, p. 98; William Hutton, *An History of Birmingham to the End of the Year 1780* (Birmingham, 1781), p. 131; Joseph Hill and Robert K. Dent, *Memorials of the Old Square* (Birmingham: Achilles Taylor, 1897), pp. 84–5; Smith, *Music in Birmingham*, pp. 15, 24.

55   Dain, 'Assemblies and politeness', pp. 59–61; Borsay, *Urban Renaissance*, pp. 330, 344; *The Plan of the City of Norwich … Survey'd by Anthony Hockstetter* (1789); Fawcett, *Music in Eighteenth-Century Norwich*, p. 18.

fashionable Bath fanned out towards the north-west and north-east. However, this did not leave polite society cut off from cultural services. The construction of high-status residential accommodation (such as the Circus and Royal Crescent) on Lansdown Hill prompted the building of the Upper Assembly Rooms adjacent to the Circus to provide a prestigious base for leisure activities, including concerts, in the area.[56]

The eighteenth century saw the emergence and development of concert life in England. But generally this was not accompanied in provincial towns by the establishment of purpose-built or specialist musical auditoriums. By and large concerts had to make do with locations – such as town halls, inns, theatres and assembly rooms – constructed primarily to serve some other function. Such an apparently parasitic existence might be interpreted as a sign of the weakness and peripheral status of music among the arts and recreations of the social elite. However, the close and mutually beneficial association between concerts and other forms of cultural activity, a symbiotic rather than parasitic relationship, and the deployment of common spaces, might also be read as a sign of strength; of music's uniquely ubiquitous and pervasive presence, and its centrality to the eighteenth-century project. There is, indeed, a case for arguing that music was the substance that lubricated the whole machinery of fashionable culture, whose scale and complexity expanded so rapidly during the century.

---

56   P. Borsay, *The Image of Georgian Bath 1700–2000: Towns, Heritage, and History* (Oxford: Oxford University Press, 2000), pp. 11–13.

CHAPTER THREE

Clergy, Music Societies and the Development of a Musical Tradition: A Study of Music Societies in Hereford, 1690–1760

Elizabeth Chevill[*]

From his study of local newspapers, the late Michael Tilmouth concluded that concert-giving outside London did not really begin to develop until about 1720.[1] Since few provincial newspapers are extant before this date, this statement is hard to verify; however, it is certain that by the 1720s music societies existed in Gloucester, Hereford and Worcester (the Three Choirs cities),[2] and in other cities including Wells and York.[3] The societies at Hereford and Wells are likely to have been founded at the end of the seventeenth century: both appear to have existed before 1705. By the mid-1720s there are also advertisements in provincial newspapers for concerts in a number of towns and cities, including Canterbury, Exeter and Norwich.[4] From the 1730s, the names of music societies across Britain appear on subscription lists to works such as Festing's *Twelve Sonatas in Three Parts*, op. 2 (1731), Handel's *Alexander's Feast* (1738), Handel's *Twelve*

---

*   I wish to thank and acknowledge the help of Rosalind Caird, Archivist, Hereford Cathedral Library; York Minster [Library] Archives; Worcestershire Record Office.

1   Michael Tilmouth, 'Chamber Music in England, 1675–1720', Ph.D. diss. (University of Cambridge, 1960), p. 84.

2   Music societies in Gloucester, Hereford and Worcester pre-dated the founding of the Three Choirs, which according to Watkins Shaw had started by 1717. See Watkins Shaw, *The Three Choirs Festival: The Official History of the Meetings of the Three Choirs of Gloucester, Hereford and Worcester, c.1713–1953* (Worcester and London: E. Baylis & Son, 1954), p. 2.

3   From the beginning of the eighteenth century, a music club met every Tuesday in the vicar's hall in Wells. See *The Diary of a West Country Physician, A.D. 1684–1726* [Claver Morris], ed. Edmund Hobhouse (London: Simpkin, Marshall, 1934), pp. 39–43. From 1725 the accounts of Sir Darcy Dawes record subscriptions to various music societies in York. See York Minster Archives, Add. MS 65/1.

4   For example, *The Kentish Post*, 16–19 Nov. 1726 refers to plans for celebrations in Canterbury with a concert for St Cecilia's Day. The same advertisement also refers to changes to the week of the monthly meeting of the music society. *The Protestant Mercury* in Exeter carries a concert advertisement in the issue of 27 July 1722 (many more advertisements are to be found from 1727 in *Farley's Exeter Journal* and *Brice's Weekly Journal*). From 1714 the Norwich waits were obliged to give a concert on the first Monday of each month; see Trevor Fawcett, *Music in Eighteenth-Century Norwich and Norfolk* (Norwich: Centre of East Anglian Studies, University of East Anglia, 1979), p. 3.

36   ELIZABETH CHEVILL

Concertos, op. 6 (1740) and Boyce's *Solomon* (1743).[5] Detailed records of music societies in Hereford, Lichfield and Oxford give a fascinating insight into the organization and format of these societies, as do concert advertisements in the provincial press.[6] In examining the development of provincial music societies with particular reference to those at Hereford, I shall highlight the crucial role played by such societies in shaping the British musical heritage, and thereby contributing to the development of the oratorio tradition.

Music meetings in London date back to 1648. John Banister held public concerts from 1672 and one of London's earliest music societies is reputed to have been founded by Thomas Britton in 1678 at his house in Clerkenwell.[7] According to Hawkins, the 'small coal concerts' were 'the weekly resort of the old, the young the gay and the fair of all ranks, including the highest order of nobility'. Some of London's most eminent musicians also attended and performed free of charge. Precisely what was performed is not known: the catalogue of Thomas Britton's library, however, included seventeenth-century vocal and instrumental music, music by Corelli, Purcell and Handel, the 'overtures' of 'old English and Italian operas' and a variety of solos and sonatas from the continent. When Britton died in 1714, the society disbanded and former members started music societies in homes and taverns across London. The membership of these societies generally comprised amateurs, although professional musicians were sometimes employed to lead the band.

Musical societies in Oxford may have pre-dated Britton's gatherings: Hawkins states that in Oxford around the mid-seventeenth century, an association to 'promote the study and practice of vocal and instrumental harmony' was formed of 'many of the principal members of the university, heads of houses, fellows and others'.[8] This was one of several societies in which amateurs from the university formed the core of the membership. Hawkins may have been referring to the society at the Mermaid in Carfax which was owned by Anthony Hall until his death in 1691: this must have been one of the earliest music societies in Oxford.[9] Its rules and membership lists survive, and from these it appears that the club had

---

5   Subscriptions were made by provincial music societies to these publications as follows: Festing, *Twelve Sonatas in Three Parts*, op. 2: Edinburgh, Norwich, Oxford, Ripon, Catch Club at Oxford, York Musick Assembly; G. F. Handel, *Alexander's Feast*: Apollo Society at Windsor, Academy for Vocal Musick in Dublin, Oxford, Exeter; G. F. Handel, *Twelve Concertos*, op. 6: Canterbury, Oxford, Salisbury, Ladies Concert at Lincoln, Academy of Musick at Dublin; Boyce's *Solomon*: Canterbury, Chichester, Dublin Fishamble Street, Gloucester, Dublin Philharmonick Society.

6   Hereford Cathedral Library, HCA 6435 [Hereford Musical Society Accounts]; Stafford, William Salt Library, MS SMS 24 (iv). See Timothy Rishton, 'An Eighteenth-Century Lichfield Music Society', *Music Review*, 44 (1983), 83–6, and Margaret Crum, 'An Oxford Music Club, 1690–1719', *Bodleian Library Record*, 9/2 (Mar. 1974), 83–99: see also Oxford, Merton College Library, MS 4.33 [Records of an Oxford Music Society 1712–19].

7   Hawkins, *History*, vol. 2, p. 700. See also Edward Croft-Murray and Simon McVeigh, 'London (i), V: Musical Life, 1660–1800', in *New Grove2*, vol. 15, pp. 120–21.

8   Hawkins, *History*, vol. 2, p. 699.

9   Crum, 'Music Club', 83; Oxford, Bodleian Library, MS Top. Oxon. a. 76: 'Orders to be observ'd at the Musick Meeting' at Anthony Hall's Tavern.

MUSIC SOCIETIES IN HEREFORD, 1690–1760   37

40 members who met on the last Thursday of every month. The membership included James Brydges (later Duke of Chandos), and, significantly, a number of clergymen. One member, William Husbands, later became one of the vicars choral at Hereford; George Llewellyn, 'the Jacobitical musical mad Welsh parson', later became rector of Condover.[10] Similar societies existed in Cambridge: on a visit to Christ's College in 1710, the German traveller von Uffenbach commented that 'This music meeting is held generally every week. There are no professional musicians there, but simply bachelors, masters and doctors of music, who perform.'[11]

A large proportion of university graduates entered the clerical profession, which, as G. V. Bennett pointed out, was 'in large measure an extension of the universities' function into innumerable parishes spread throughout the country'.[12] Many graduates who had been involved in music clubs in Oxford and Cambridge became vicars in rural areas, and in what may have been an attempt to overcome problems of cultural isolation, formed themselves into musical societies. It appears therefore that some of the earliest provincial music societies were started by clergy in cathedral cities and modelled on societies in Oxford and Cambridge. The Hereford College Music Society was founded by members of the vicars choral before 1705, and we know from the diaries and accounts of Claver Morris, a physician, that at the beginning of the eighteenth century the music society at Wells met every Tuesday in the vicar's hall.[13] Another set of accounts shows that between 1739 and 1747 a music society met in the vicar's hall at Lichfield; we also know that from 1753, and for at least a decade beyond, a music society was meeting in the college hall at Exeter.[14] In the early years of the eighteenth century, sacred music seems to have had a prominent place in the repertoire: seventeenth-century motets by composers such as Borri, Carissimi, Fiocco and Steffani were performed in Oxford and almost certainly in York and Wells, together with secular music, including extracts from early Italianate operas such as *Thomyris* (1707) and *Camilla* (1706).[15]

---

10   William Cooke states that William Husbands graduated MA at Christ Church in 1687 before joining the vicars choral at Hereford in 1692. Hereford Cathedral Library, HCA 7003/4/3, 4 [William Cooke, 'Biographical Memoirs of the Custos and Vicars admitted to the College at Hereford from 1660–1823', no. 18]. Llewellyn became the rector at Condover in 1705: see Crum, 'Music Club', 88; Percy Scholes, *The Great Dr Burney: His Life, his Travels, his Works, his Family and his Friends*, 1 (Oxford: Oxford University Press, 1948), p. 6; and *Memoirs of Dr Charles Burney 1726–1769*, ed. Slava Klima, Garry Bowers and Kerry S. Grant (Lincoln, Nebr.: University of Nebraska Press, 1988), pp. 20–21.

11   *Herrn Zacharias Conrad von Uffenbach merkwürdige Reisen durch Niedersachsen Holland und Engelland*, ed. J. G. Schelhorn (Ulm, 1753–54), vol. 3, p. 12 quoted in J. E. B. Mayor, *Cambridge under Queen Anne* (Cambridge: Deighton Bell, 1911), p. 133.

12   G. V. Bennett, 'University, Society and Church, 1688–1714', in L. S. Sutherland and L. G. Mitchell, eds, *The History of the University of Oxford*, vol. 5: *The Eighteenth Century* (Oxford: Oxford University Press, 1986), pp. 360–61.

13   *Diary of a West Country Physician*, ed. Hobhouse.

14   Rishton, 'Lichfield'; for references to concerts in the college hall at Exeter see Elizabeth Chevill, 'Music Societies and Musical Life in Old Foundation Cathedral Cities 1700–60', Ph.D. diss. (University of London, 1993), p. 120.

15   Ibid., pp. 66–7; see also references in 'The account books of Claver Morris', *Notes and Queries for Somerset and Dorset*, 23 (1939), 100–101; 134–40; 164–6 and 345–7.

38   ELIZABETH CHEVILL

There are a number of signs of the clergy's involvement in concert life and music societies in the provinces in the early eighteenth century. Many of the special musical festivals and occasions were connected with the church in some way. In Salisbury as early as 1700 the Society of Lovers of Musick held concerts in the cathedral on or near to St Cecilia's Day. By 1717 the Three Choirs Festival had developed from the musical societies which were chiefly organized by the clergy of Gloucester, Hereford and Worcester cathedrals. By 1740 the Salisbury Festival had an evening concert at the assembly rooms, and by 1748 the festival had become a two-day event which took place at the end of September or at the beginning of October, just before the start of the London season.[16] The Salisbury Festival had a similar format to the Three Choirs Festival, with performances of church music at the cathedral in the morning and (from 1751) oratorios in the assembly room at night. Handel oratorios seem to have been a feature of evening festival concerts: as Winton Dean observed, 'Provincial performances of the oratorios [of Handel] were very numerous, especially after 1745'.[17]

The late seventeenth and early eighteenth centuries witnessed a remarkable development of English towns, which had a profound effect on the country's musical life. This development was prompted by economic expansion which in turn led to cultural growth. Sixty to seventy towns throughout England were established as regional centres, and places such as Bristol, Newcastle and York developed as provincial capitals.[18] In the early years of the eighteenth century assemblies, music societies, coffee houses and bookshops were established in towns throughout the country. Newspapers and printing presses were set up in many, and in some of the largest, such as Bath and York, newly built assembly rooms were acquired. Regional centres attracted increasing numbers of people to events such as assemblies, the Assizes and Race Week, and many gentry purchased town houses in order to participate in the cultural and social life.[19] Many of the gentry who had traditionally gone to London for the season became involved in assemblies and music societies in county towns;[20] members of the professional classes also became involved. Some of the artists who had poured into London from all over the continent were recruited to work in the provinces;[21] others

---

16   Information in this paragraph about the Salisbury Festival comes from Eileen Hornby, 'Some Aspects of the Musical Festivals in Salisbury in the 18th Century', *Hatcher Review*, II, 2/12 (Autumn 1981), 78–85. Also see the advertisement in the *Salisbury Journal*, 17 Oct. 1748.

17   Winton Dean, *Handel's Dramatic Oratorios and Masques* (Oxford: Oxford University Press, 1959), p. 84. For a list of performances of oratorios during this period, see appendices C and D, ibid., pp. 629–39, 640; see also Hans Joachim Marx, *Händels Oratorien, Oden und Serenaten. Ein Kompendium* (Göttingen: Vandenhoeck & Ruprecht, 1998), *passim*.

18   Peter Borsay, 'Urban Development in the Age of Defoe', in Clyve Jones, ed., *Britain in the First Age of Party, 1680–1750: Essays Presented to Geoffrey Holmes* (London: Hambledon, 1987), p. 199.

19   See Peter Borsay, 'The English urban renaissance: the development of provincial urban culture c.1680–c.1760', *Social History*, 5 (1977), 581–603.

20   See York Minster Archives, Add. MS 65/1 for references to payments for opera tickets and to Loeillet for music lessons, as well as tickets for plays.

21   See Chevill, 'Music Societies', esp. pp. 89–97, on paid musicians in Dublin, Edinburgh, Salisbury and York.

MUSIC SOCIETIES IN HEREFORD, 1690–1760

worked with the Royal Academy, which from 1720 was the first of several opera companies to provide Italian opera in London on a continuing basis. Reports of the Italian opera in London were read avidly in the provincial press; arrangements of tunes from it were performed across the country. The services of foreign musicians were in constant demand both as teachers and as performers. Instrumentalists and singers who were based in London during the season often toured the country appearing in concerts. Even musicians who remained in London were patronized by a musical establishment that received considerable support from gentlemen from the country.[22]

Music societies in Hereford

One of the earliest music societies in the English provinces began at the college of the vicars choral in Hereford. An important nineteenth-century source relating to the Hereford College Music Society is William Cooke's 'Biographical Memoirs of the Custos and Vicars'.[23] Cooke, who was himself a member of the vicars choral, died aged 70 in 1854. His memoirs, covering the period 1660–1829, are essentially biographies of the vicars choral. They include details of each individual's qualifications, the name of the college where he was educated and any details pertinent to his career. The biography of William Felton is particularly interesting since it includes a brief history of the college music society from 1723 to the mid-1750s. The information was probably at least partly based on a set of accounts which according to Daniel Lysons, the Three Choirs historian, covered the period from 12 February 1723 to November 1733.[24] According to Cooke, the source was based on 'various and distant resources' in which 'nothing has been inserted without substantial qualification'. Assuming it is reliable, it has much to say both about the early history of the Hereford College Music Society and about the Three Choirs Festival.

From Cooke it appears that by 1705 there was a music club meeting in the college of the vicars choral at Hereford. Cooke states that Peter Senhouse, a graduate of St John's College, Cambridge, was described in the records of this music club as 'a regular performer in the music club at that time existing in the college'. Unfortunately, records of the music society prior to 1749 are no longer extant; nevertheless Cooke clearly indicates that Peter Senhouse was a member of the music club while he was a vicar choral. Since Senhouse resigned from the college in 1705 in order to fulfil his duties as vicar in Leighton, the society appears to pre-date 1705.

---

22   See York, Add. MS 65/1.

23   Hereford Cathedral Library, HCA 7003/4/3, 4. Unless otherwise stated, the information in the ensuing paragraphs comes from this source.

24   Daniel Lysons, *History of the Origin and Progress of the Meeting of the Three Choirs of Gloucester, Worcester, and Hereford, and of the Charity Connected with it* (Gloucester: D. Walker, 1812), p. 160.

40 ELIZABETH CHEVILL

The second statement Cooke makes in connection with Senhouse is that the college music society formed the nucleus of what he refers to as 'the triennial music meetings'. This event soon commenced under the auspices of Bishop Bisse and 'other leading personages of the 3 Dioceses'. According to Lysons the Three Choirs Festival 'originated in a compact entered into by the members of certain musical clubs or societies in those cities, to make an annual visit to each other'.[25] The precise origin of the festival is hard to ascertain, but in his recent history of the Three Choirs, Anthony Boden suggests that the first embryonic meeting may have been in 1709 in Gloucester and the first meeting in Hereford, in 1711.[26] This chronology would accord with Lysons's comment that the musical clubs in each of the three cities had probably 'existed some time even before the Annual joint Meeting was established'.[27]

Around the end of the seventeenth century a number of distinguished musicians were to be found among the ranks of the Hereford vicars choral, and it is probable that they were founder members of the music society. As mentioned above, William Husbands, who joined the vicars choral in 1692, was formerly a senior member of the Mermaid Club, the prestigious Oxford musical society which met in Anthony Hall's tavern at Carfax. Husbands may also have participated in Henry Aldrich's weekly meetings at Christ Church in Oxford where he served as chaplain and organist. Husbands had been a boy chorister at Christ Church, entering in 1673;[28] however, his adult career in Hereford was cut short by his premature death in 1701. The then organist at Hereford Cathedral, Henry Hall ($c.1656$–1707), was also a distinguished musician, having trained at the Chapel Royal and served at Wells and Exeter before becoming assistant organist in Hereford, then vicar choral, and finally permanent organist in 1688. (Bruce Wood describes Hall as 'the most distinguished among the lesser composers of Purcell's generation'.[29]) Little is known about the musical interests of his successors, Henry Hall II and Edward Thompson, but Henry Swarbrick, who was elected organist on 10 November 1720, took a leading role in the Hereford College Music Society.

At the time when he wrote his memoirs, Cooke had access to dated records of the music society from 1723 to 1733. These are unfortunately no longer extant, although in his biography of William Felton, Cooke mentions that these records tell us that during the period 1723–33 the College Music Society met fortnightly in the hall belonging to the vicars choral. The room was 'comparatively small' and its flooring of brick and stone made it 'altogether ineligible as a receptacle for vocal and instrumental performances'. Lysons also consulted the society's account books for this period:

---

25   Lysons, *History*, p. 159.
26   Anthony Boden, *Three Choirs: A History of the Festival. Gloucester, Hereford, Worcester* (Stroud: Alan Sutton, 1992), p. 10.
27   Lysons, *History*, p. 161.
28   Crum, 'Music Club', 87.
29   Bruce Wood, 'Hall, Henry (i)', *New Grove2*, vol. 10, p. 699.

It appears by the Hereford book, that the club at that city comprised mostly of members of the *College*, who met weekly in the evening, in the hall belonging to the Vicars Choral. It was an establishment of little expence: the performances were all *gratis*, except that of Mr Woodcock, their leader, whose nightly pay was five shillings. The members were regaled with ale, cyder and tobacco. The names of the attending members, distinguished as performers and non-performers, (generally about fifteen or sixteen of the former and seven or eight of the latter.), were inserted each night of meeting in the book, with those of strangers introduced as visitors. The non-attendants paid a forfeiture of sixpence; these probably were applied to the purchase of music for the use of the club. In one year, I find an entry of the purchase of Geminiani's concertos, Shuttleworth's and Lully's solos, &c.[30]

It seems that at this stage the society was organized by 'non-paid' performers who were all college members; indeed Cooke suggests that it was only when the society relocated in the 1740s to the coffee house that performers were admitted from outside the college. It is probable, however, that even at the earlier stage, non-performing subscribers attended from outside. Since there were only 12 vicars choral, it is likely that most of these would have been involved as performing members. Some of those who were still at the college in 1749 are listed in the records of the music society extant from that period, and some acted as stewards at the Three Choirs.[31] For example, Thomas Dew is listed as a non-paid performer in the music society's records of 1749 and also served as steward in the Three Choirs in 1729 and 1735. He joined the college in 1711 and was probably involved in the music society from that time. Henry Swarbrick, the cathedral organist from 1720, is likewise listed in the records of the music society from 1749. Advertisements in the *Gloucester Journal* show that he engaged in a variety of musical activities. Every Wednesday and Friday he visited pupils within a 10-mile radius of Hereford to give harpsichord and spinet lessons. At least one concert at the college hall was held for his benefit, in 1737.[32] In 1726 Swarbrick is listed as a subscriber to Cluer and Creake's *Pocket Companion*, claimed to be a collection of 'the finest opera songs'.

The Woodcocks were one of the most important families in Hereford in the first half of the eighteenth century. The family may have been Italian: the International Genealogical Index records the christening in 1705 of a Francis or Franciscus Woodcock born to a 'Gulielmi' and 'Franciscae' Woodcock of the Parish of Winforton, Hereford. According to Hawkins, the branch of the family at Hereford was related to Robert Woodcock, whom he describes as 'a famous flautist'. Hawkins states that Robert Woodcock's brother, whom he names as Thomas, kept a coffee house in Hereford; he was 'an excellent performer on the violin ... [who]

---

30   Lysons, *History*, pp. 161–2.

31   See Lysons, *History*, pp. 141–57 for lists of stewards of the Three Choirs Festival.

32   See advertisements in the *Gloucester Journal*, 9 Aug. 1737 and 25 Oct. 1748; and Watkins Shaw, *The Organists and Organs of Hereford Cathedral* (Hereford: Friends of Hereford Cathedral Publications Committee, 1976), p. 17. In his memoirs, James Parry records having lessons from Swarbrick. See James Parry, *The True Anti-Pamela: or Memoirs of Mr. James Parry, Late Organist of Ross in Herefordshire* (London, 1742), p. 33.

played the solos of Corelli with exquisite neatness and elegance'.[33] Commenting on the popularity of Vivaldi's 'Cuckoo concerto', Charles Burney remarked that 'Woodcock, one of the Hereford waits, was sent far and near to perform it'.[34] Since there are no other references to Thomas Woodcock either in the society's records or in concert advertisements, nor is he mentioned in the International Genealogical Index, Hawkins was probably referring to Francis (also known as Frank), and not to Thomas Woodcock. An advertisement in the *Gloucester Journal* on 14 March 1727 reads:

> 𝔉𝔬𝔯 𝔱𝔥𝔢 𝔅𝔢𝔫𝔢𝔣𝔦𝔱 of Mr. Fra. Woodcock,
> ON MONDAY the 20th Instant, will be performed a Consort of Vocal and Instrumental Musick, in the College-Hall, in the City of Hereford. Beginning at Six a-clock.
> N.B. Tickets to be had at Mr. John Hunt's, Bookseller, and at Mr. Ford's at the Redstreak Tree.

This event was almost certainly held under the auspices of the Hereford College music society since, according to Lysons, Francis Woodcock was employed to lead the band. The concert, which coincided with the end of the season, may have been one of his privileges of office.

According to Cooke, the college concerts ceased in about 1733 and lay dormant for 17 years before being revived by William Felton.[35] No reasons are given to support this claim, but the evidence suggests that they continued for at least part of this period. William Felton joined the vicars choral in 1741 and it is unlikely that he would have waited for eight years before restarting the music society. Although Cooke states that Felton refounded the music society in 'a more favourable locality' at Woodcock's coffee house, the college hall remained in use. There are no records of repairs being made to the hall; it was used for the evening concerts of the Three Choirs Festival in 1741 and 1747, and again for a benefit concert for Swarbrick and Woodcock in 1747.[36] It is doubtful that the society folded for lack of interest, since many people from the city, including members of the vicars choral, continued to serve as stewards at the Three Choirs Festival. By March 1742 concerts were being held at the 'Great Room' at Francis Woodcock's coffee house in Milk Lane; in March 1749, a benefit for Dyer and Woodcock was also held there.[37] There is also an advertisement in the *Gloucester Journal* for a benefit for Francis Woodcock during Assize Week; the venue is not given. In any case the music society was fully operational from November 1749, as manuscript records survive covering the period from then until October 1753, and again from

---

33 Hawkins, *History*, vol. 2, p. 826.
34 Fragment dated Shrewsbury 1742–43, quoted in *Memoirs of Burney*, ed. Klima et al., p. 32 (see n. 10 above).
35 Unless otherwise stated, information on the music society at Hereford comes from Hereford, HCA 7003/4/3, 4, no. 49.
36 See advertisements in the *Gloucester Journal*, 9 Aug. 1737; 21 July 1741; and 7 July 1747.
37 *Gloucester Journal*, 9 Mar. 1742; 21 Mar. 1749.

MUSIC SOCIETIES IN HEREFORD, 1690–1760

September 1755 to March 1757.[38] These appear to be one of the most extensive sets of records for music societies in the eighteenth century. They include details of the society's rules, lists of members (both performing and non-performing) and the names of visitors and guests.

The accounts show that by 1749 the society, now simply known as 'The Music Society', was meeting at 'Frank Woodcock's Great Room' in Milk Lane on Tuesdays from October or November until March. Concerts started at 5.30 p.m. and ended at 10 p.m., after which time members were free to drink and smoke. Occasional advertisements in the *Gloucester Journal* show that benefit concerts, and concerts during Assize Week, were also put on at this venue. Balls invariably took place after such events.

According to the society's rules, there were two categories of membership: performing subscribers and non-performing subscribers. There were normally 12 performing subscribers who were responsible for the decision-making and general organization of the society. Cooke states that now for the first time these posts were open to non-college members. With the exception of the treasurer, the performing subscribers acted as stewards, taking one night each in turn. Performing subscribers were 'oblig'd to perform according to the scheme of Performers', although the rules decreed that 'the Steward shall oblige none but hired Performers to play Solos without their Consent'. Vocalists were expected to perform at least twice during the season and failure to do so resulted in a fine of 10 shillings over and above their subscription and any other fines. There were also fines for lateness and absence. Rule 13 stated that

> Performers who are not paid, if they attend before the first Act is begun shall pay one Shilling, if they are absent the first Act, & attend before the second Act is begun, shall pay two Shillings, & ev'ry Night they are absent & in Town shall pay three Shillings, but if out of Town, two Shillings only; & not coming before the second Act is begun, shall be deem'd an Absence.

To close all loopholes, rule 14 concluded: 'Every Performer paid or not paid absenting himself without Leave ... before either the first or second Act shall be deem'd as absent the whole Night'. Every year the rules included a list of the performing subscribers, and in the season 1749 to 1750 they also stated which instrument each played. Although six of the 13 were listed as vocalists, some may have doubled as instrumentalists. Five of the performing subscribers were vicars choral; at least some of the others were members of the gentry.[39] William Felton, a prolific composer and gifted performer, directed the band from the harpsichord (see Table 3.1).

---

38   Hereford Cathedral Library, HCA 6435.

39   Charles John Bodenham came from one of Hereford's most important families: he owned manors at Rotherwas, Dewchurch and Dinedor. Price Clutton may have been a member of the Clutton family who resided at Pensax, and John Ravenhill of the Ravenhills of Lower Eaton. Charles Robinson, *The Mansions of Hereford and their Memories* (London: Longmans & Co., 1873), pp. 30, 96, 164 and 113.

44 ELIZABETH CHEVILL

Table 3.1 Performing subscribers at Hereford Music Society 1749–1750

Name	Instrument	Date of admittance as vicar choral (if applicable)	University/college (if applicable)
John Woodcock	Vocal	1737	Catherine Hall, Cambridge
William Felton	Harpsichord	1741	Queen's College, Oxford
John Arnold	'Bass' and vocal	1748	New College, Oxford
Charles J. Bodenham	Violin		
[John] Ravenhill	Violin		
Thomas Clarke	Violin		
Richard Moore	Violoncello		
Egerton Leigh	German Flute		
Cornelius Rowlandse	Vocal		
Morgan Cove	Vocal	1744	New College, Oxford
Price Clutton	Flute		
Thomas Dew	Vocal	1711	Magdalen College, Oxford
Robert Dobbyns	Vocal		

The rules also set out the stewards' responsibilities: 'The Steward for the Night shall regulate the Concert, appoint the Musick, defray the Expenses & deliver the Balance of the Account to the Treasurer.' For the first two seasons, Thomas Porter acted as the steward's assistant. His duties included collecting tickets and money at the door, for which he was paid 2*s*. 6*d*. a night. On 29 March 1751 he was paid 10*s*. 6*d*. 'for Transcribing the Articles for the ensuing Season &c'. It was the steward's responsibility to ensure that the concert began at half past five and to lock up the gallery room and secure the coffee-house shutters at the end of the evening. The steward for the night did not play, but he was responsible for finding a replacement. Both the steward and the treasurer kept accounts for the evening; although the treasurer was a performer, he was exempt from taking a turn as steward. From November 1749 until November 1752, John Woodcock was

MUSIC SOCIETIES IN HEREFORD, 1690–1760

Table 3.2   Schedule of payments

	£	s	d
To Frank Woodcock	0	7	6
To Mr Dyer	0	7	6
To Mr Swarbrick for Tuning the Harpsichord	0	7	6
To Jemmy George	0	10	6
To Francisco Woodcock	0	2	6

treasurer; he was replaced by Robert Shenton who held the position until October 1755, when Henry Colebatch was elected in his place.

The society also engaged performers: the rules of 1749 stated that the treasurer should provide 'a Hautbois to perform each Night at as cheap a Rate as he can' and that the players should be paid for each evening as listed. The rules went on to say that no other performers were to be paid unless this was agreed by a majority of the performing subscribers. Rule 10 sanctioned payments as shown in Table 3.2. Payments of 15s. were also listed to 'Frank Woodcock for the use of his Room, Fires, Forms and Candles for the two Sconces, Desks and Harpsichord'; 2s. 6d. to 'Thomas Porter the Stewards Assistant' and a further 2s. to 'a person to be provided by the steward of the Night to go on Errands to carry Forms, Books and Instruments etc'.

Francis Woodcock and Dyer were the 'Principals' who were 'to play the acts alternately' as the steward directed. Mr Bodenham, Mr Ravenhill, Mr Clarke, Mr George and Francisco were the violinists; Mr Clutton and Egerton Leigh played the German flute, Mr Moore the violoncello and Mr Arnold the double bass. Since William Felton presided at the harpsichord, Mr Swarbrick's payment was presumably only for tuning. Mr Arnold Rowlands, Mr Dew, Mr Cove and [John] Woodcock were listed as vocalists, and had to perform at least twice during the season: Francisco Woodcock was almost certainly the son of Frank (known as Francis) Woodcock, the owner of the Great Room in Milk Lane. In the period prior to November 1752 regular payments 'To Mr Woodcock for himself & Son & c' were recorded along with payments for fires, forms and candles. In the season 1751–52, Francis Woodcock is listed as a paid performer for the last time; from November 1752 payments to him cease. For the season commencing in 1752, the society moved to 'the Great Room' of the Green Dragon; there are gaps in the records from 1753 to 1755, but by 1755 Francisco seems to have taken his father's place as one of the principal violinists. The identity of Dyer is not known but since his fee does not seem to have included an allowance for travel, he was probably local. Some of the paid performers travelled quite a distance: up to 1753 several payments are recorded to Mr Jemmy George from Abergavenny, which was a distance of about 20 miles. We know from newspaper advertisements

46   ELIZABETH CHEVILL

that Mr James George appeared in benefit concerts in Brecon, Cheltenham and Bath.[40]

Throughout the period covered by the accounts, payments are recorded to a Mr Charles Clarke, an oboist from Worcester. According to Worcester City Records, Charles Clarke was one of the city waits, and (from 1720) freeman of the city. Until February 1749, and on some occasions thereafter, he received £1. 6s. each evening for his services. At other times, regular payments were made of amounts ranging from £2. 2s. to £2. 15s. 6d. to 'Mr Charles Clarke from Worcester' and 'his partner', possibly a man named in the accounts on other occasions as 'Mr Jones from Worcester another Hautboy'. In 1756 and 1757, payments are recorded to 'Clarke's son', possibly William Clarke who was admitted to the Worcester waits in 1760.[41] Mr Jones and the Clarkes gave concerts in and around Worcester; their involvement in the society at Hereford is indicative of the links between musicians in the two cities. From time to time other musicians from Worcester also participated in concerts in Hereford. An advertisement in November 1758 for a performance of Boyce's *The Chaplet* at the college hall stated that 'Master Bond is expected from Worcester';[42] and on 23 March 1756, the accounts record payment of £1. 6s. to Mr Bond. Another eminent visitor to the music society was Charles Burney. In the last season covered by the accounts, from October 1756 to March 1757, he participated in nine out of ten concerts in the series, the exception being 7 January 1757. Burney may have come by invitation of Felton, with whom he seems to have been personally acquainted.[43]

According to Cooke, the admission of non-performing subscribers from outside the college may have been a new feature of the concert series from 1749. Although Lysons states that seven or eight non-performing subscribers were admitted in the period covered by the accounts (1723–33) they may have been college members.[44] In any case the re-establishment of the society at Woodcock's coffee house enabled a far larger number of non-performing subscribers to be admitted than was possible when the society was using the college hall. The accounts list the names of the subscribers: in 1749 there were 50; in 1750, 51; in 1751, 44; in 1752, 34; in 1755, 81; and in 1756, 76. Many were professional people (particularly clergymen), local tradesmen and members of the gentry. In October 1755 the list of non-performing subscribers included Mr Severine, an apothecary;

---

40   *Gloucester Journal*, 30 Aug. 1748; 26 July 1757.

41   Worcestershire Record Office [WRO], Worcester City Chamber Order Books, p. 153: 6 October 1720, 'Order'd that Mr Charles Clark is admitted freeman of this city'; Chamber Order Books, 1722–42: 25 November 1729: 'Ordered that Charles Clarke Junr shall have a share of the proffits as one of the waits of this city during such time as he shall officiate'. WRO, City Accounts, 1714–35: All Saints Day 1735, 'Paid Charles Clarke one of the City Waits' £2. 10s.; Chamber Order Books, 1742–72: 19 December 1760, 'Orderd that William Clarke is admitted one of the waites of this City & that he be allowed the same sallary as the other waits have and that the Chamberlain do provide him a cloak and a hat'.

42   *Gloucester Journal*, 14 Nov. 1758. The identity of Master Bond is not certain; he was probably related to Capel Bond, organist at Coventry at this time.

43   Further on Burney and Felton see p. 50 below.

44   Lysons, *History*, p. 161.

James Wylde [Wilde], a bookseller; Doctor Campbell, presumably a physician; the Mayor; Councillor Hoskins; George Phelps, the College Custos; and Sir John Morgan, MP;[45] from the gentry, Chandos Hoskyns of Harewood Hall; Harcourt Aubrey of Clehoger Hall, and Charles Fitzroy Scudmore from either Holme Lacy or Kentchurch.[46] The assistant steward delivered the tickets to the subscribers at least three days before the concert; they paid 2s., which enabled them 'to introduce one Lady'. Ladies were not permitted to subscribe, but 30 'new Tickets' were printed for their use which they could purchase from Mr Wilde, the bookseller, at 2s. each 'some time before every Night's Performance'. Subscribers may not always have been forthcoming with their money, since on 1 January 1751 Thomas Porter, the steward's assistant, was paid 10s. 6d. 'for his Extraordinary trouble in Collecting the Arrears &c'.

The society had a variety of rules. The fifth stipulated 'All Liquor to be paid for by those who call for it', and that there was to be 'no sitting to smoak or drink till the Concert is over'. According to rule 4, guests were permitted to attend concerts on payment of 2s. 6d. provided they were not residents of Hereford: 'Gentlemen, who are not Inhabitants of the City of Hereford may be introduc'd by a Subscriber, paying as a Subscriber; but no Inhabitant to be admitted unless he subscribe'. The weekly accounts list the names of visitors, and although the number of 'strange Gentlemen and Ladies' varied, in the 1749–50 season an average of nine was admitted each evening.

Instruments repaired out of the society's funds appear to have been owned by the college: indeed on 7 May 1751, an entry states 'it is Agreed that the Double bass belonging to the College of Hereford which has been damaged in the Service of the Society shall be repaired under the Direction of Mr Felton ... and furnish'd with brass pins, Screws &c ... and the Carriage of it to and from London for this purpose said'. Repairs were subsequently carried out locally: on 28 January 1752, the bill for £11. 9s. 6d. was paid to Mr Johnson for the repairs and a further 2s. to Mr Felton for packing the instrument.[47] Almost every time the society met, the accounts record payment of 2s. to 'Messengers for carrying instruments' and 1s. or 2s. to 'harpsichord messengers'. Although Woodcock's room was equipped with a harpsichord, on at least one occasion the society used one which belonged to Thomas Dew.[48] On several occasions payments are recorded for drums. On 21 November 1749 they may have been needed for the St Cecilia's Day celebrations a day later, and in January 1750 for a performance of 'Boyce's Overture' which the society had hired earlier in the month.[49]

---

45 October 1755 is taken as a random example. With the exception of James Wilde, who is referred to elsewhere in the records as a bookseller, the occupations noted are as recorded in the membership lists.

46 Robinson, *Mansions*, pp. 134 (Hoskyns), 65 (Aubrey), 142 (Scudmore) and 155 (on Kentchurch).

47 Mr Johnson was the cathedral odd-job man and carpenter.

48 Hereford Cathedral Library, HCA 6435, 29 March 1750.

49 Hereford Cathedral Library, HCA 6435, 2 January 1750, 2s. 6d. 'For the use of Mr. Boyce's Overture'.

Every year, 20 per cent of the cash in hand belonging to the society was put aside for music. The performing subscribers decided what should be bought, and it was acquired by Mr Wilde, the local bookseller. References in the accounts show that the society purchased two sets of instrumental music by Geminiani, Greene and Handel.[50] Greene's overtures, published by Walsh in 1745, were scored for a string body, 2 flutes, 2 oboes and a harpsichord. The two oboe parts of Handel's op. 3 concertos were presumably played by Clarke and Jones, the oboists from Worcester. Handel's op. 6 concertos and Geminiani's of op. 2 and op. 4 were scored for strings and continuo. The paid performers probably formed the concertino. It is difficult to ascertain how large the ripieno was, but if it included only the five performing subscribers listed as instrumentalists, the proportion of concertino to ripieno players would have been only 1: 2. It is possible that some of the performing subscribers listed as vocalists doubled as instrumentalists.

On 2 November 1752 it was decided to use £8 of the balance of £13. 10s. 3½d. to purchase music. An article of agreement was drawn up whereby the vicars of the college were made 'trustees and guardians' of the music books. This is particularly interesting since it shows that although the music society was no longer known as the 'College Music Society', the vicars still played a central role in its organization. Not all the music the society used was bought. Some was hired and some written out by hand. On 5 April 1753 Mr Cove was paid £1 for writing out the parts of *The Chaplet*. This was almost certainly Boyce's 'musical entertainment', published in 1750. The first known performance in Hereford took place in November 1758.[51]

With the exception of a production of Boyce's *Solomon* in April 1749 and *The Chaplet* in November 1758, the only records of the performance of large-scale dramatic or choral works were those given at the meetings of the Three Choirs Festival. Evening performances may well have been started to facilitate such performances. Songs from the opera and pleasure gardens probably had a fairly prominent place in the music society programmes: according to Cooke, Richard Shenton, who joined the vicars choral in 1752, 'introduced from Oxford, a variety of modern Songs & Duetts, which rendered him very acceptable to the Society'. His brother Robert Shenton, who had joined the vicars choral in 1750, sang duets with him which were 'so captivating' that the brothers became known as 'Richard & Robert, the two singing Birds'.[52]

In addition to the winter series of concerts, newspaper advertisements show that in the period from 1748 to 1758, benefit concerts for various members of the Woodcock family were held in summer, or during Race and Assize Week.[53] No

---

50   Hereford Cathedral Library, HCA 6435, April 1753.
51   *Gloucester Journal*, 14 Nov. 1758; its first public performance took place at Drury Lane in 1749.
52   Hereford Cathedral Library, HCA 7003/4/3, 4, I, nos. 52 and 53.
53   For advertisements see *Gloucester Journal*, 19 July 1748 and 30 July 1751, benefit Francis Woodcock; 13 May 1755, benefit Widow Woodcock; and 12 Sept. 1758, benefit Francisco Woodcock.

MUSIC SOCIETIES IN HEREFORD, 1690–1760

details of the programmes were given, but members of the music society would almost certainly have been involved. The society also held two fund-raising concerts in 1758 in aid of improvements to the Castle Green.[54] The second concert included a performance of Boyce's *The Chaplet* followed by the customary ball. In March 1750, the society gained permission from the College Custos to raise money in order to restore the college hall.[55] This was necessary so that it could be used for the evening meetings of the Three Choirs Festival.

Mention has already been made of the visits of Bond and Charles Burney to the music society, and there were almost certainly other visitors of whom we have no record. Newspaper advertisements show that a number of musicians toured the provinces;[56] the Charles brothers, who gave concerts in Hereford in 1749 and 1753, were among the most travelled. The first known appearance of Mr Charles in London was on 6 October 1733 when he was described as being 'lately arriv'd from Paris'.[57] Following his debut, he made occasional appearances in London and from 1740 began to tour the British Isles, giving concerts in different towns (see Table 3.3). Charles played a variety of instruments, including the French horn, clarinet, oboe and chalumeau. Most of his concerts included items featuring each of these instruments; advertisements claimed that many of them had never been heard before in England. Charles seems to have stayed in each place for only a couple of days, and, as can be seen from the schedule in Table 3.3, he may have planned his itinerary so that he visited most of the major regional musical centres during the course of a year. What appears to have been his first concert in Hereford took place 'By DESIRE of the MUSICAL SOCIETY' at five o'clock in Woodcock's 'Great Room', on Tuesday 3 January 1749.[58] The programme included a performance of 'a Variety of PIECES on the French-Horns, Shallamo, *and* Clarinett' and a concerto and a solo on the violin by Mr Charles junior. On 23 October 1753 a notice appeared in the *Gloucester Journal* announcing the arrival of Mr Charles and son from London:

> *On* Friday *Evening, the 26th Instant, will be performed,* at Hereford, *A* CONCERT *of* MUSIC, Vocal *and* Instrumental: Particularly several Select PIECES on the *French-Horns* by Mess. Charles, Sen. and Jun. from *London.*
> Tickets to be had at the *Swan* and *Falcon* in *Hereford,* at 2*s.* 6*d.* each.

The venue for the concert was not stated and no further details are known.

Musicians from Hereford also gave concerts in the surrounding districts. Few of these concerts seemed to have been advertised in newspapers, although on 30 August 1748 an advertisement in the *Gloucester Journal* announced a benefit concert in Brecon for Woodcock and George:

---

54   *Gloucester Journal*, 26 Sept. 1758; 14 Nov. 1758.
55   Hereford Cathedral Library, HCA 7003/1/4 [Vicars Choral Act Book], March 1750.
56   See Chevill, 'Music Societies', p. 159.
57   'Charles, Mons.', Highfill et al., *Biographical Dictionary*, vol. 3, p. 178.
58   *Gloucester Journal*, 3 Jan. 1749.

50 ELIZABETH CHEVILL

For the BENEFIT *of Mr.* FRANCIS WOODCOCK *and Mr.* JAMES GEORGE, *On Monday* the 5th of *September* next, being *Assize-Time*, At *Mr. Harper's* GREAT-ROOM at the *Golden-Lyon* in *Brecon*, Will be perform'd a CONCERT of *Vocal* and *Instrumental* MUSIC, By a Sett of *Good Hands*. To begin precisely at 7 o'Clock. *After the* CONCERT *there will be a* BALL, *to which no Person will be admitted without a Ticket for the Concert*. TICKETS to be had at the *Golden-Lyon*, and at Mrs. *Prosser's*, at the *Castle-Green*, in *Brecon*, at 2s. 6d. each.

Table 3.3   Itinerary: Charles and son 1741–1755

Source	Date	Venue
Stamford Mercury	10 Dec. 1741	Stamford: Great Assembly Room
York Courant	9 Feb. 1742	York: Assembly Room
Biographical Dictionary[*]	Mar. 1742	Dublin
Dublin Journal	17 May 1742	Dublin: Smock Alley
Biographical Dictionary[*]	24 Dec. 1743	Bristol: Assembly Rooms St Augustine's Back
Biographical Dictionary[*]	20 Feb. 1744	London: Haymarket (played a horn concerto after a production of *Othello*)
Worcester Postman	22 Dec. 1748	Worcester: Town Hall
Gloucester Journal	3 Jan. 1749	Hereford: Woodcock's coffee house
Gloucester Journal	17 Jan. 1749	Gloucester: Bell Great Room
York Courant	27 Mar. 1750	York: Assembly Room
Gloucester Journal	31 July 1750	Gloucester: Bell Great Room
Gloucester Journal	23 Oct. 1750	Hereford
Bath Journal	4 Feb. 1751	Bristol
Salisbury Journal	11 Feb. 1751	Salisbury: New Assembly Room
Bath Journal	6 May 1751	Bath
Bath Journal	12 June 1751	Bristol
Gloucester Journal	1 Oct. 1751	Ross
Bath Journal	18 May 1752	Bristol: opening concert at Hotwells
Newcastle Courant	9 Nov. 1754	Newcastle: concert for King's birthday
Biographical Dictionary[*]	1755	Edinburgh: Mr Charles appears as a clarinettist

[*]   Highfill et al., *Biographical Dictionary*.

In his memoirs, Charles Burney recorded hearing the 'Celebrated Felton, from Hereford & after him the 1st Dr Hayes, from Oxford' performing on the organ while on tour in Shrewsbury. Burney noted that their performances 'struck and stimulated me so forcibly … that I went to work with an ambition & fury that w[d] hardly allow me to eat or sleep'.[59]

---

59   *Memoirs of Burney*, ed. Klima et al., p. 33.

MUSIC SOCIETIES IN HEREFORD, 1690–1760   51

Table 3.4   Music Society's accounts

	£	s	d
To Raikes by Bill	0	10	6
Paid Carr: of tickets from Gloucester	0	0	6
Candles 2 Stone & 2lb	0	10	14
2 Sets of Handels 6 Overtures bound	7	0	0
A Box for the Musick	0	17	0
A Lock and Keys for the Box	0	3	6
paper to pack up the Worcester Books	0	0	1½
paid Carriage of them to Worcester	0	0	6
Paid Swarbrick for Jacks	0	0	6
To Holland Joiner by Bill	0	13	6
To Mr Wilde by Bill	2	3	0
Paid Swarbrick for tuning the harpsichord	0	5	0
A Bridge for the Tenor	0	0	4
To Lotters [sic]	0	0	11
Binding Shepherd's Lottery	0	1	6

The Hereford music society also took an active part in the Three Choirs Festival. Subscribers acted as stewards, and the band would almost certainly have included amateur players from the music societies of each of the three cities. The festival began on a Monday night with a rehearsal for all the performers. On Tuesday morning there was a meeting for subscribers, and that evening a dinner for the performers hosted by the steward. Music making began on Wednesday with a service with music in the cathedral at 11 a.m. and a concert in the evening; in the case of Hereford this was normally held in the college hall. The same timetable was adhered to on Thursday, and in 1753 the festival was extended to include a Friday evening concert.[60] Preparations for the festival began well in advance. In 1753 it was held at Hereford, and in April of that year several entries appeared in the music society's accounts in this connection (see Table 3.4).

Payments are shown to Mr Raikes, presumably the printer and owner of the *Gloucester Journal*, and payments for *The Shepherd's Lottery*, a work which was performed on the Friday evening concert of the festival in 1753.[61] The Handel Overtures mentioned may have been played between the acts of the performance of his oratorio *Samson* given on the Thursday evening, or at the Wednesday evening concert. The accounts suggest that the festival continued to be organized primarily by members of the music societies in each of the three cities.

---

60 See advertisements in the *Gloucester Journal*, 7 July 1747; 10 July 1750; and 7 Aug. 1753.
61 *Gloucester Journal*, 7 Aug. 1753.

52 ELIZABETH CHEVILL

Clearly conclusions based on the study of one particular society need to be drawn with caution. However, the music societies at Hereford do display national trends.[62] To sum up: the society in the market town of Hereford was founded by vicars choral in the late seventeenth or early eighteenth century. By 1723 membership was extended to non-college members, and, in common with many other music societies, by the mid-1740s the society moved from cathedral premises to an independent assembly room. Despite this move, the vicars choral continued to play a major part in the society. Instruments belonging to the college were used; and when, in 1753, the society purchased music, the vicars choral were appointed trustees. The popularization of the music society is evident from the account books of 1749 which show increasing support by the gentry and a potential attendance at meetings of over 170. As music societies became more fashionable, balls were introduced after at least some concerts; and in 1758, and again in 1759, concerts were held in order to raise money for laying out walks on the Castle Green where the company could stroll.[63] These developments were all fairly typical of societies in other cities.

The picture presented by records of music societies and emerging from a study of the provincial press is very much one of a network of music societies patronizing itinerant musicians and teachers. Details of subscriptions and concert advertisements suggest a diet of music from the London stage and instrumental music in the Italian style as standard fare. From the late 1740s, oratorios seem to have been a feature of special concerts and music festivals. Prior to that, marches, songs and tunes from both oratorio and opera featured in many concert programmes.[64]

An understanding of the history of provincial music societies in early eighteenth-century England is vital if we are to appreciate the musical tradition to which it gave rise. I have highlighted here the role played by Oxbridge-trained clergy in provincial music societies and drawn attention to how cathedral communities became the focal point for much of the country's musical activity. This influence shaped the course of music in England even after the 1720s when urban growth and the national obsession with the Italian opera had popularized music societies. Music festivals lasting several days became prevalent and many music societies, particularly those in major cultural centres such as Bath, Edinburgh and York, employed several foreign musicians, usually Italians, to lead the band.[65] The obsession with the Italian opera had made music a fashionable

---

62   For more details of other societies see Chevill, 'Music Societies'.

63   *Gloucester Journal*, 26 Sept. 1758 and 14 Nov. 1758.

64   For transcripts of concert advertisements in provincial newspapers, see appendices in Chevill, 'Music societies'.

65   For musicians employed in Edinburgh see David Johnson, *Music and Society in Lowland Scotland in the Eighteenth Century* (London: Oxford University Press, 1972), pp. 37–8 and 54–5; in Bath see Kenneth James, 'Concert Life in Eighteenth-Century Bath', Ph.D. diss. (University of London, 1987), pp. 53–63. Records of the Music Assembly at York show that from 1743 we can be reasonably certain that a number of musicians were employed to lead the band. These included one

commodity and it was against this background that instrumental music in the Italian style flourished and the tradition of Handelian oratorio emerged. At a time when the clergy's influence was so strong on the nation's musical life, the use of biblical subject matter in oratorios was ideal. The instrumental and vocal forces required were readily available, and for special occasions, top singers from London or Oxford could be engaged to take the solo vocal and sometimes instrumental parts. This brought something of the glamour of the London stage to the provinces. It has become almost a historical truism that Handel was adopted as the champion of music in England; his cultivation of the oratorio did much to secure his ascendancy over the musical scene in Britain for the remainder of the century. The ramifications of this situation are still being uncovered. The role played by clergy and cathedrals in early eighteenth-century provincial musical life, as discussed in this chapter, was a key factor in the development and success of the Handel oratorio tradition.

---

violinist, one woodwind-player, a cellist, and from 1749 (or possibly earlier) a keyboard-player. See Chevill, 'Music Societies', pp. 89–97 and 264.

CHAPTER FOUR

Competition and Collaboration: Concert Promotion in Newcastle and Durham, 1752–1772

Roz Southey

The earliest known concert in the north-east of England was held in Newcastle in 1712 when unknown performers offered 'Opera-Tunes, Italian Solio's, Sonata's, Overtures, &c. upon the following Instruments, viz. Spinett, Trumpet, Hautboy, Violins, Bass-Viols, Bassoons, &c'.[1] Over the next two decades, a few isolated concerts were advertised in local newspapers; most of these were given by visitors to the area – a 'famous Lute-Master', for instance (Newcastle, 1723) and Charles and Nathaniel Love (in Sunderland and Newcastle in November 1733)[2] – but local musicians were also plainly capable of promoting concerts. Two Newcastle concerts in 1733, for example, were given 'by a Sett of the finest and best Masters from York, Durham, &c.' and 'by the best Masters in these Parts'.[3] Clearly, cooperation already existed between local musicians in different centres, although the extent of such cooperation cannot be ascertained. In the 1750s, however, a dispute arose in Durham over the establishment of a new winter subscription series which led both to collaboration and to acrimonious competition, involving not only local musicians but also the Gentlemen Amateurs who were their patrons and supporters.

In Durham, musical life – both sacred and secular – revolved around the cathedral musicians, principally the organist and choir. This latter officially comprised 10 choristers and eight singing men (known as 'the Gentlemen of the Choir'); in practice the choir was supplemented by a varying number of supernumeraries and by the minor canons. The choir was not the isolated, insular body that might be expected of a foundation so far from London. Early eighteenth-century organists were recruited from outside the area – William Greggs from York and James Hesletine from London – and many of the adult singers in the choir were recruited from a similar distance.[4] Amongst those singing men who

---

1   *Newcastle Courant* [*NC*], 19–21 May 1712.
2   *NC*, 22 May 1725; 10 Nov. 1733.
3   *NC*, 29 Sept., 1 Dec. 1733.
4   Brian Crosby, *Durham Cathedral Choristers and their Masters* (Durham: Dean and Chapter of Durham, 1980), pp. 25 (Greggs), 26 (Hesletine). Hesletine had been a chorister in the Chapel Royal

came to the city from the south of England was the celebrated London concert-singer Thomas Mountier; Mountier had been associated with the choir of Chichester Cathedral before becoming known in London as a singer in Handel's operas.[5] His reasons for moving north are not clear, but within six weeks of his arrival he had held a concert in Newcastle and another in Durham – the first recorded concert in the latter place.[6]

The first regular series of concerts in the north-east was held in Newcastle, from 1735. The apparent catalyst for the series was the return to the city of a young local musician, Charles Avison. Avison – the son of a Newcastle wait – had been in London, where he had held a concert in March 1734;[7] by the end of 1735, however, he had returned to the north-east and obtained an appointment as organist of St John's church.[8] The setting up of a winter subscription series in Newcastle was advertised shortly before Avison's appointment; 12 concerts, each lasting three hours, were offered for a subscription of 10s. 6d. Although Avison is traditionally given the credit for the establishment of this series, he himself (in a letter written some years later to the local paper, the *Newcastle Courant*) stated that 'it was undertaken by twelve Gentlemen, who procured above One hundred and seventy Subscriptions for twelve Concerts'.[9] Nevertheless by the fourth season, beginning in the autumn of 1738, Avison was in control of the series; following a number of ambitious – and all too expensive – schemes, the Gentlemen Directors 'resigned the Management of it to Mr. Avison' promising that they would continue to play in the band and 'assist ... with their Performance'.[10] Having implemented changes designed to re-establish the concerts on a sound financial footing, Avison maintained full (and almost entirely unchallenged) control of the series until his death in 1770.[11] Avison's vocal soloist was Thomas Mountier from Durham Cathedral.[12]

In Durham, a subscription series is not known until the 1740–41 season; the wording of the advertisement for the series, however, suggests that the concerts

---

under John Blow. In the first decade of the century, the Dean and Chapter paid a Mr Budney of Cambridge 'for his Care in supplying the Quire with good voyces'. Chapter Archives, Durham Cathedral [CA]: Dean and Chapter's Act Books [DAB], 20 July 1704.

5 L. M. Middleton, 'Mountier, Thomas', *DNB*, ed. L. Stephen and S. Lee (Oxford, 1963–64 [repr.], vol. 13, p. 1110).

6 *NC*, 24 May 1735; *Newcastle Intelligencer*, 21 June 1733.

7 Arthur H. Scouten, ed., *The London Stage 1660–1800* (Carbondale, Ill.: Southern Illinois University Press, 1961), Part 3, 1729–1747, p. 378. Travelling to London for 'improvement' was not unusual; the Dean and Chapter's minute books record frequent leaves of absence for singing men to go to London, and other Newcastle musicians throughout the century travelled there on a regular basis.

8 Tyne and Wear Archives, Common Council Minutes of Newcastle [Co. Co.], 17 October 1734.

9 *Newcastle Journal [NJ]*, 4–11 Nov. 1758.

10 *NC*, 29 July 1738.

11 Avison also ran regular mid-year concerts in Assize Week and, for a number of years in the 1750s, ran a benefit for the new Infirmary in Newcastle – one of the rare occasions in the north-east when concerts were promoted for charitable purposes.

12 No choirs of a similar standard to that of Durham existed in Newcastle at this time; no professional singer is known to have been resident in the city.

may have been established for some time – there is no hint of novelty or newness, and no explanation of ticket conditions. As in Newcastle, the series began in early October and cost half a guinea; no indication at this early stage is given of the number of concerts, their frequency, or the repertoire performed.[13] Nor are the organizers named; but it is clear from other sources that the series was organized by the cathedral personnel. In a letter to his brother in September 1749 the new Dean of the cathedral, Spencer Cowper, referred to the winter series as 'our' concerts;[14] in addition, a performance of Handel's *Alexander's Feast* put on by cathedral personnel in November of the same year to mark St Cecilia's Day offered admittance free to subscribers to the winter concerts. This suggests that the two events were organized by the same people.[15]

With regard to the St Cecilia's Day concert, the Dean remarked to his brother (Earl Cowper) that 'Our News Paper's may have informed you of the noble manner our harmonious Band celebrated St. Cecilia'.[16] The remark was intended to be ironic; he was amused by the *Newcastle Courant*'s comment that the performance was 'allowed, by several of the best Judges, to equal, if not exceed, the … Performance of it in London'.[17] He wrote: 'It certainly was better than we cou'd expect. … Our … Canons were of great service in the Chorus's, but all, except old Gregory, much above singing single songs, so we failed in them.'[18]

Cowper's letters make it clear that the singers in these concerts were drawn from the cathedral choir, including both singing men and minor canons, and that in addition a number of the singing men undertook instrumental roles. In the early 1750s the leader of the band was a local singing man, Cornforth Gelson; Gelson had been a chorister in the choir for six years and had then spent a further four years as a wait in Newcastle before returning to the cathedral as a singing man in late 1751.[19] Cowper wrote of him with varying degrees of tepid praise, remarking that 'he plays very tolerably' and that 'one of poor Guelson's failings is, and I think his cheif, that he does not draw a good tone from his fiddle'.[20]

The extent of the involvement of Gentlemen Amateurs in the Durham concerts is not possible to establish; no record survives of any gentleman playing in the public concerts, although some prebendaries (including the Dean) held private concerts in which they or their families took part.[21] But Cowper took a proprietary

---

13   *NC*, 20 Sept. 1740.

14   Spencer Cowper, *Letters of Spencer Cowper, Dean of Durham, 1746–1774*, ed. Edward Hughes, Surtees Society 165 (London and Durham: Andrews & Co. and Bernard Quaritch, 1950), p. 109, 28 Sept. 1749.

15   Cf. Cowper, *Letters*, pp. 117–18, 7 Dec. 1749; *NC*, 13–25 Nov. 1749.

16   Cowper, *Letters*, p. 118, 7 Dec. 1749.

17   *NC*, 13–25 Nov. 1749.

18   Cowper, *Letters*, pp. 117–18, 7 Dec. 1749. Edward Gregory was vicar of St Margaret's church, Durham.

19   Treasurer's Accounts of Durham Cathedral [TA], 1738/9–1746, *passim*: Co. Co. 19 January 1747, 15 December 1751: TA, 1751–52.

20   Cowper, *Letters*, pp. 156–7, 3 Nov. 1752; p. 161, 10 Dec. 1752.

21   Donald Burrows and Rosemary Dunhill, *Music and Theatre in Handel's World: The Family Papers of James Harris 1732–1780* (Oxford: Oxford University Press, 2002), p. 279, 25 Oct. 1751.

58 ROZ SOUTHEY

interest in the band, going so far as to acquire from his brother in London a better violin for Cornforth Gelson.[22] The Earl himself occasionally played in the cathedral band when visiting the city.[23] Support also came from other prebendaries such as the Sharps (Archdeacons of Northumbria for most of the second half of the century) and Sir John Dolben, extensively involved in musical organizations in London and elsewhere, and evidently an admirer of James Hesletine.[24]

Collaboration

Initially, relations between the organizers of the subscription series in Newcastle and the cathedral personnel seem to have been good. No objections were raised to Thomas Mountier acting as Charles Avison's vocal soloist in the Newcastle series, and a letter is extant from Charles Avison to James Hesletine asking for the loan of one of the choristers for a concert:

> Newcastle, July 19th 1737.
> I am to have a benefit Concert in the Assize Week, and if I cou'd have the Boy Paxton over it would oblige a great many of my Friends. I shou'd have requested the Favour of the Dean because when I went to serve Mountier, he was so kind as to promise the Gentlemen of our Concert (when they din'd with him) to let us have the Boy once to hear him – but as I know you have the care of him, and can favour us at present, I thought it best to apply to you.[25]

Not only does the letter indicate the continued involvement of Gentlemen Amateurs in Newcastle concerts but it also indicates a degree of collaboration between the two sets of musicians (and supporting gentlemen) which was at least civil, if not cordial. By the early 1750s, however, relations had soured, at least between Avison and James Hesletine. The Rev. George Harris of Egglescliffe – a friend of Spencer Cowper – recorded in his diary an occasion in October 1751 in which he dined with one of the prebendaries of the cathedral: 'After dinner ... Marcello Avison. Garth on the violoncello – Hesletine refused to join with the Newcastle party in music.'[26]

Harris's mention of the 'Newcastle party' makes it clear that he was referring to the man rather than merely his music when he mentioned Avison. This is the first suggestion of animosity between Hesletine and Avison; in a letter to his brother a year later, however, Cowper referred to the quarrel, remarking that it 'has subsisted

---

22 Cowper, *Letters*, pp. 161–2, 10 Dec. 1752. Cowper asked for a cheap but good instrument; his brother, Earl Cowper, sent instead a Cremona violin, called the Cardinal.

23 Burrows and Dunhill, *Harris Papers*, pp. 252–3, 19 Nov. 1748.

24 DAB, 26 March, 2 April 1748.

25 Gloucester Record Office, D3549, 7/1/3. There were three Paxton brothers: this was probably Robert, the oldest, aged about 17 at this time. For details of the Paxton family see B. Crosby, 'Stephen and other Paxtons: An investigation into the identities and careers of a family of eighteenth-century musicians', *Music & Letters*, 81 (2000), 41–64. The letter from Avison is torn at the bottom, through the signature.

26 Burrows and Dunhill, *Harris Papers*, p. 279, diary of G. W. Harris, 31 Oct. 1751.

CONCERTS IN NEWCASTLE AND DURHAM, 1752–1772 59

for so many years that there is no hopes of its ever being brought to an end'.[27] He attributed it to Hesletine, 'who cannot bear a Competitor'.[28]

The third musician mentioned by Harris at the dinner party – John Garth – was one of the few musicians resident in Durham who was not associated with the cathedral; about 30 years old at this time, he was some 20 years younger than Avison. His first known concert activity dates from 1745 and 1746 when he held a number of Race Week concerts in Stockton-upon-Tees and Durham;[29] he was also probably organist of Sedgefield church, south of the city, although he remained resident in Durham city itself.[30] In addition he was probably from an early date a member of the concert band in Newcastle.[31]

From at least 1750, Garth was in competition with the cathedral musicians in a professional sense when the latter also began to hold Race Week concerts in the city. The two sets of concerts offered very different repertoire: the cathedral band generally performed songs and choruses from Handel; Garth, who almost certainly used Avison's concert band from Newcastle, usually put on a miscellaneous concert with an emphasis on instrumental music. This difference, based on the natural strengths of both groups of musicians, probably encouraged concert-goers to attend both concerts; but the limited size of the audience in such a small city (even augmented by visitors from the surrounding countryside) clearly made the viability of two concerts doubtful.[32] As a solution to this problem, Avison and Garth therefore, according to Cowper, suggested that the Newcastle and Durham bands should be amalgamated to form one large band that would play in concerts in both cities; subscription series in Newcastle and Durham would take place in alternate weeks and the profits, presumably, would be divided between the two.[33]

The idea, put forward by Garth and Avison on a number of occasions, apparently foundered on the rock of Hesletine's animosity towards Avison. There is no indication that Avison had done anything to provoke this enmity; Hesletine was a touchy man of uncertain temper – in 1727 he had come very close to dismissal after refusing to apologize for 'notoriously abuseing one of the prebendaries'.[34] The offers of cooperation were turned down in no uncertain terms, a rejection which was to have unforeseen and, to the cathedral personnel, unwelcome consequences.

---

27 Cowper, *Letters*, p. 159, 26 Nov. 1752.
28 Ibid.
29 *NC*, 27 July–3 Aug. 1745; 28 June–5 July 1746; 12–19 July 1746.
30 Stanley Sadie, 'Garth, John', *New Grove2*, vol. 9, p. 552: the living of this church was in the gift of the Bishop of Durham, who may also have influenced the choice of organist.
31 Cowper, *Letters*, pp. 159–60, 26 Nov. 1752.
32 Durham's population at the 1801 census was approximately 7000.
33 Cowper, *Letters*, p. 159, 26 Nov. 1752.
34 DAB, 12 August, 19 August 1727.

A rival series

Late in 1752, Spencer Cowper became aware that Garth was planning a winter subscription series in Durham. Garth's proposed series, like the first series in Newcastle, depended upon the patronage of Gentlemen Amateurs. His teaching activities had brought him influential friends; amongst others, he taught the children of Lord Barnard at Raby Castle near Staindrop.[35] In the summer of 1752, Lord Barnard and a number of other gentlemen (whose names do not survive) proposed a winter series of concerts to be supported financially by subscription and to be directed musically by Garth, for whose benefit the profits would be dedicated. Twelve concerts were to be held fortnightly; the price of subscription is not recorded.[36] Avison too was involved; Cowper stated that 'the organist at Newcastle joyns his forces with all his Myrmidons'.[37]

The decision, logical as it was, to hold the new series in Durham city where Garth lived, brought the organizers into direct competition with the cathedral personnel; Cowper remarked that 'our Concert is threaten'd with a Rival Concert being open'd in Opposition to it'.[38] Garth and Avison, however, may not have seen the two series as competitors. As they had no singer, they approached members of the cathedral choir; this move, if tactless, suggests that they saw no reason for the cathedral personnel to object to their concerts.[39] Spencer Cowper was of the opposite opinion and wrote to his brother in martial terms: 'Having no vocal, they have bid high for one of the Boys of our Choir, but I have forbid either vocal or Instrumental to give the foe any assistance if they march this way.'[40]

Cowper seems to have successfully prevented the new series acquiring a vocal soloist, but Garth went ahead nevertheless and the first concert of the series took place on 6 December 1752. Cowper claimed, with some satisfaction, that the series had only 14 subscribers, described by the *Newcastle Courant* as 'several gentlemen in and about the city'.[41] Each subscriber had two tickets whose conditions restricted their transferral to women only; as a large number of the gentlemen subscribers played in the band, such transferrals meant a preponderance of women in the audience – another cause of derision for Cowper.[42] Cowper's reference to Avison's 'Myrmidons' suggests that the Newcastle concert promoter brought his own concert band with him, supplementing it with Garth's aristocratic supporters; the Durham concerts and Avison's Newcastle series were held in

---

35   Henry Vane, Lord Barnard, became Earl of Darlington in 1754.

36   *NC*, 9 Dec. 1752.

37   Cowper, *Letters*, p. 159, 26 Nov. 1752.

38   Ibid.

39   Thomas Mountier, Avison's original soloist at the Newcastle subscription series in 1735, had left the cathedral choir around 1741–42 after a series of financial problems and absenteeism. His later movements are not known [DAB, 19 October 1742 *inter alia*].

40   Cowper, *Letters*, p. 159, 26 Nov. 1752.

41   *NC*, 9 Dec. 1752. Cowper's triumphalism on this point may indicate that the choir concerts were better subscribed.

42   Cowper, *Letters*, pp. 160–62, here p. 161, 10 Dec. 1752.

CONCERTS IN NEWCASTLE AND DURHAM, 1752–1772

alternate weeks, as proposed by the two men to Hesletine in their rejected suggestions for collaboration.

Cowper refused to attend but could not bear to miss what happened and sent his wife instead; Mrs Cowper attended both lunchtime rehearsal and the concert itself in the evening, and brought back a programme of the music played and an account of the evening's entertainment. The Dean reported to his brother in London in one of his frequent letters:

> The Musick was cheifly Instrumental performers at least equal to our own; but the choice of it wretched. It open'd with the Overture of Clotilda,[43] an Opera many ages older than Camilla,[44] and consisted of Concertos and solos, from <u>Rameau</u>, <u>Giardini</u> and <u>Avison</u>. Poor Corelli, and Handel were excluded almost Nem. Con. only one man amongst them pleaded hard that Corelli might conclude the affair, but he was only hooted at for his pains, and told that there was not one part of Corelli that the children in the streets cou'd not whistle from beginning to end, and their music was to be all <u>New</u>.[45]

Cowper's account is confused, and confusing, on a number of points. He runs together the rehearsal (at which the last recounted incident must have taken place) and the concert, and having chided the organizers for playing music that was old-fashioned and out of date, mocks them for insisting 'their music was to be all New'.[46] His scornful tone was echoed by the cathedral musicians, who convinced themselves that the new series was no threat after all; Cowper told his brother with evident glee 'I shall not fear that my Crowds will be injured in their Concert'.[47] So amicable did the Dean and James Hesletine now feel towards this new competition that they even contemplated lending Avison and Garth one of the singing men after all. This was not a generous gesture, however; the Dean described the man in question as 'squeaking thro' his nose like a penny trumpet'.[48]

Repertoire

The Dean's contempt for the repertoire performed at the first of Garth's series (shortly after to be known as the Gentlemen's Subscription Concert) indicates the heart of the conflict between the two Durham series which lasted for the best part of a decade. Little information survives about the repertoire played in Newcastle concerts at this period – Charles Avison usually advertised only the time, place and cost of his concerts, omitting both programme and notification of soloists; the Durham concert of December 1752, however, clearly reflected Avison's tastes which were probably shared by his friend, John Garth. Apart from Avison's own

---

43 By Francesco Conti, composed 1706.
44 Performed in London, April 1706. (The Dean's memory was at fault here.)
45 Cowper, *Letters*, p. 161, 10 Dec. 1752.
46 He also wistfully remarked that 'I wish I cou'd pick up some of these children for my Entertainment' – he was an admirer of Corelli. Ibid.
47 Ibid.
48 Ibid.

music, the concert offered that of a personal friend, Felice Giardini, with whom Avison was later to collaborate in the writing of an oratorio, *Ruth*, for the Lock Hospital.[49] Rameau, too, had been played in Newcastle concerts; about a year previously, Avison had been given by 'a generous Encourager of the Art ... at his own Expence, all the works of this Author'. He had arranged them for the use of the concert band in Newcastle and these arrangements were presumably the pieces played at the Durham concert. These works deserved Cowper's assessment as 'entirely New' – it is likely that they had not been heard in Durham before; in an advertisement for the Newcastle performances, Avison had talked of having 'the Pleasure of introducing to a Northern Audience, the compositions of this celebrated Master, which, as yet, are but little known in England'.[50]

Cowper's opinion of Rameau is not recorded but he made very clear his views on modern Italian composers such as Giardini; in a letter to his brother a few years earlier, he had referred to their productions as 'riff-raff Music'.[51] Cathedral concerts were based around a very different repertoire. Their reliance on the choir naturally meant a greater preponderance of vocal music in general, and the works of Handel in particular. Subscription series frequently began and ended with performances (possibly complete) of the shorter works such as *Alexander's Feast* and *Acis and Galatea*; *Messiah*, or choruses from it, was repeatedly performed in subscription concerts, Race Week concerts and benefits for singing men.[52] On one occasion the first three concerts of a subscription series were given over to a complete performance of *Samson*, part one in the first concert, and so on.[53]

Charles Avison's alleged dislike of Handel was much commented upon in his own time. It originated with his *Essay on Musical Expression*, published only a few months before the Durham series with Garth began; his faint praise was anathema to many of Handel's supporters. Avison wrote of:

> our illustrious HANDEL; in whose manly Style we often find the noblest Harmonies; and these enlivened with such a Variety of Modulation, as could hardly have been expected from one who hath supplyed the Town with musical Entertainments of every Kind, for thirty Years together.[54]

Avison's comments provoked a caustic response from William Hayes of Oxford, which Avison promptly published together with his own *Reply*, at the back of a second edition of the *Essay* in 1753. In this *Reply* he stated even more clearly his opinion of Handel.

> Mr. HANDEL is in Music what his own DRYDEN was in Poetry; nervous, exalted, and harmonious; but voluminous, and, consequently, not always correct. Their Abilities equal to every Thing; their Execution frequently inferior. Born with Genius

---

49   Simon McVeigh, 'Music and the Lock Hospital in the 18th Century', *Musical Times*, 129 (1988), 235–40.
50   *NC*, 14–21 Sept. 1751.
51   Cowper, *Letters*, p. 77, 21 Nov. 1746.
52   *NC*, 15 Feb. 1755; 12 Mar. 1757; 29 Sept. 1759.
53   *NC*, 1 Oct. 1763.
54   C. Avison, *An Essay on Musical Expression* (London, 1752), p. 53.

CONCERTS IN NEWCASTLE AND DURHAM, 1752–1772

capable of *soaring the boldest Flights*; they have sometimes, to suit the vitiated Taste of the Age they lived in, *descended to the lowest*. Yet, as both their Excellencies are infinitely more numerous than their Deficiencies, so both their Characters will devolve to latest Posterity, not as Models of Perfection, yet glorious Examples of those amazing Powers that actuate the human Soul.[55]

The small amount of surviving information about the repertoire performed in Avison's concerts indicates that he had no objection to Handel per se; in his London concert of 1734 he had presented (as the advertisement stated) 'Favourite Songs of Mr. Handel's',[56] and in 1739, at the beginning of the War of Jenkins' Ear, he had played several Handel works as a grand patriotic gesture – these included choruses from *Acis and Galatea* and *Saul* and were performed by the choir of Durham Cathedral.[57] Avison was also wholeheartedly in favour of the music of Corelli (who had been the teacher of Avison's own master, Geminiani), describing him in the *Essay* as 'faultless' and his works as 'immortal'.[58] The criticism of Corelli at the rehearsal for the concert in Durham is highly unlikely to have originated with Avison.

The decision of Garth and Avison to base their new Durham subscription concerts around 'new' music, and around instrumental rather than vocal music, may not, therefore, have stemmed merely from personal inclination and the taste of their aristocratic supporters, as Cowper's comments tend to suggest, but may have been occasioned by a deliberate commercial decision. A concert of 'new' instrumental music would offer repertoire of a very different kind from that played in the cathedral series; in this way, Garth and Avison might avoid the appearance of direct competition and encourage the inevitably limited audience in the city to attend both series.

Continuing rivalry: 1752–1756

The Choir Concert's supporters were extravagantly confident that the new series would not prosper. Cowper remarked that the cathedral band were 'all in good spirits and make very merry with their antagonists'.[59] But Garth's series completed its first season successfully and the rivalry extended itself into the summer months, with competing concerts in both the Race and Assize Weeks; the difference in repertoire was continued. Considerable effort was expended on both sides to make these summer concerts attractive. In Assize Week (June), the choir offered an open-air concert in the gardens at Old Durham, a large house just outside the city which was a fashionable resort for ladies and gentlemen in the manner of the

---

55   C. Avison, *Mr. Avison's Reply to the Author of Remarks On his Essay on Musical Expression, &c.* (London, 1753), pp. 50–51.
56   Scouten, *London Stage*, p. 378.
57   *NC*, 1 Dec. 1739.
58   Avison, *Essay* (1st edn), pp. 51–2, 79.
59   Cowper, *Letters*, p. 161, 10 Dec. 1752.

London pleasure gardens.[60] In Race Week (July), Garth brought in heavyweight soloists – Felice Giardini and his wife, the singer Signora Vestris.[61] It is not clear what part, if any, Charles Avison played in these concerts, but Giardini had played at Avison's own summer concert in Newcastle shortly before; it is likely that both men played for Garth.

In the autumn of 1753, Garth may have tried to pre-empt the cathedral series (which generally began in the first week of October) by opening his own series unusually early on 13 September;[62] if he was hoping to steal some of the choir's subscribers in this way, his own series may have stood in need of support. Avison's continued involvement is attested by Harris who attended the second concert of the series and commented in his diary: 'Avison, Garth, &c. played. Only one Song. Began about ½ hour past 6 & ended quarter past 8 o'clock.'[63] The emphasis was clearly still on instrumental music.

The following summer, only Race Week concerts in the middle of July were advertised in local newspapers; the cathedral's offering was in the form of a benefit for two of the singing men – Cornforth Gelson and one of the Paxton brothers.[64] Less than two months later, Cowper was reporting to his brother a new development that threatened to undermine fatally the cathedral band. Avison and Garth had apparently not given up hopes of securing a singer from the choir and had at last succeeded:

> [Paxton] at [present] is in open Rebellion against me, and what is worse his Rebellion has brought our Concert to be on its last Legs, as he has gone over to our Enemies' quarters. I have not yet heard that he or Guelson, (the other Reprobate who I borrow'd your Fiddle for, and is also a Deserter) are as yet received by them, but their Desertion has made them incapable of being admitted into our own.[65]

The details of this 'rebellion' are difficult to ascertain. The Paxton in question was almost certainly the youngest brother, Stephen; as he was probably the cathedral band's principal cellist, his defection would indeed have had serious implications, as would Gelson's as leader. It is not clear whether Gelson and Paxton did perform in Garth's subscription series, but the incident had severe consequences for both men. Paxton left the choir – the last recorded payment of salary to him was in the middle of 1754 – and headed for London.[66] He may have gone of his own accord; Cowper's enmity almost certainly chased the other defector from the city. In December 1754, three months after Cowper's irate letter, Cornforth Gelson was suspended from the choir for fathering an illegitimate child;

---

60   *NC*, 9 June 1753.

61   *NC*, 21 July 1753. When the Italians moved on to perform at a Race Week Concert in York the following month, Garth went with them and returned the favour by playing in Vestris's benefit. [*York Courant* (*YC*), 21 Aug. 1753.]

62   *NC*, 8 Sept. 1753.

63   Burrows and Dunhill, *Harris Papers*, p. 293, 27 Sept. 1753.

64   *NJ*, 22–9 June 1754.

65   Cowper, *Letters*, pp. 174–5, 20 Sept. 1754.

66   TA, 1753–54.

CONCERTS IN NEWCASTLE AND DURHAM, 1752–1772   65

in January 1755, he was dismissed.[67] As the child was nearly a year and a half old at this time and Gelson had been openly supporting it financially, it is difficult to believe that the Dean had not heard of the matter before or that he was not using it as an excuse to be rid of Gelson.[68]

The defections did not have the effect Cowper feared; the Choir Concert replaced the 'defectors', and between 1755 and 1757 the situation continued much as before, with competing winter and summer concerts, to which the Gentlemen's Subscription series added the first of a regular series of concerts to celebrate the King's birthday in November.[69] Garth continued to offer miscellaneous concerts, chiefly of instrumental music; the cathedral-backed concerts were still based on Handel's works. In May 1756, the cathedral personnel mounted an ambitious mini-festival of four concerts: two held outdoors on the river banks and the river itself, the others – unusually – in the cathedral. The *Newcastle Courant* reported:

> We hear from Durham, that last Thursday se'nnight the Sons of Dr. Sharp, in company with most of the musical Gentlemen and Quire of that Place, gave a concert of vocal and instrumental Musick upon the Banks and upon the River ... consisting of several Overtures, Songs and Choruses. The Instruments were two French Horns, two Hautboys, two Bassoons, Flutes, Flageolets, Violins, and Basses. – On Saturday, the same was repeated in the Church, in that Part of the Steeple called the Lanthorn.[70] The Solemnity of the Pieces inspired the Hearers with an awful Kind of Satisfaction, infinitely superior to the Pleasure experienced by lighter Pieces. Tuesday was a second in the Church; and Wednesday Evening, there was another on the Water and the Banks.[71]

The reference to 'lighter Pieces' was clearly a jibe aimed at Garth's concerts and suggests that the review was written by a partisan supporter of the choir.

Decline

In mid-1757, Garth went ahead with his Race Week concert as usual.[72] But doubts were surfacing about the continued financial viability of his series. In September, Cowper wrote to his brother:

> When the Mich[aelma]s Geese are put to the Spit, our Concerts begin ... I believe one more Winter leaves us Masters of the field, for the Gentlemen-subscribers are

---

67   DAB, 4 January 1755.
68   Baptismal registers of St Margaret's church, Durham, 12 August 1753. The singing man was forced out of Durham altogether; he stayed briefly at Morpeth and in the following April found himself employment as 'Master and Teacher of Church Musick' in Edinburgh, where he seems to have remained for the rest of his life. His fellow singing men remained supportive, holding a benefit for his family a fortnight after his dismissal. [*NJ*, 4–11 Oct. 1755; *NC*, 11 Jan. 1756; 17 Apr. 1756.]
69   *NC*, 6 Nov. 1756; 8 Nov. 1755; 5 Nov. 1757.
70   i.e. under the tower.
71   *NC*, 5 June 1756.
72   *NC*, 23 July 1757.

heartily sick of the Expence of theirs, and the chief Manager has left this Town and Country for good and all.[73]

These financial difficulties may not have been confined to Garth's concert; a general decline in interest in concert-going may have been taking place, for in October, Cowper told his brother that 'we open'd our Concert last Tuesday se'night to a very thin Audience'.[74] However, financial problems may not have been Garth's sole concern; events in Newcastle may have occasioned Charles Avison's increasing withdrawal from the series.

Avison's part in the later seasons of the Gentlemen's Subscription series in Durham is unclear. His friendship with Garth was certainly as strong as ever; Garth still played in Avison's Newcastle concerts, and the Durham series could not have continued without the participation of the Newcastle concert band. It was Avison who also recommended to Garth the project of producing an English version of the Psalms of Benedetto Marcello, a project which Avison had originally planned to carry out himself.[75] Garth's preoccupation with this – eight volumes were published yearly between 1757 and 1765 – may have affected the energies he could devote to the Durham subscription series, as may his extensive teaching practice.

In Newcastle, Avison's attention was also increasingly directed to his own affairs. In 1757, after a number of apparently uneventful years, Avison made several changes to his regular musical routine. In May he started a new series of concerts, a summer subscription of four held at monthly intervals.[76] This may have been in response to the establishment of a pleasure garden in the city; the gardens – and concerts in them – were established by 1760 and advertisements suggest that they may have also been open in previous years.[77] Known at this time merely as Mr. Callendar's Gardens, but later christened Spring Gardens, these were in fact nursery gardens owned by a family of seed merchants and situated on the edge of the city beyond St Andrew's church. Avison's contempt for the quality of music performed in such locations had been forcibly expressed in the *Essay*;[78] his own series may have been intended to present the summer concert-goer with what he considered to be better-quality music. Unfortunately, and as usual, no indication of repertoire is given in Avison's advertisements.

In October of the same year (1757) Avison, like Garth, faced financial difficulties. For the new season of the winter subscription series Avison announced a substantial rise in the price of subscription tickets, increasing the cost by around a quarter.[79] His stated reason was a rise in expenses, although he disguised it as an

---

73 Cowper, *Letters*, p. 190, 11 Sept. 1757.
74 Ibid., p. 201, 15 Oct. 1758.
75 Avison, *Essay*, 2nd edn (London, 1753). [At back of volume: 'Proposals for publishing by subscription, specimens of the various stiles in musical expression. Selected from the Psalms of Benedetto Marcello'.]
76 *NC*, 30 Apr. 1757; *NJ*, 21–8 May, 25 June–2 July, 23–30 July 1757.
77 *NC*, 7 June 1760.
78 Avison, *Essay*, 1st edn, pp. 71–2.
79 *NC*, 24 Sept. 1757.

CONCERTS IN NEWCASTLE AND DURHAM, 1752–1772 67

improvement to the concerts, claiming it allowed him to light the concert room with wax candles 'to give more elegance to the Concert'.[80] He had at this time (he later estimated) 140 subscribers, a number to which Garth's concert probably never came close.[81] The following year, 1758, the price for admission to the summer concerts was astonishingly high: half a guinea for three concerts (compared to the same price for 12 winter concerts), or a near-prohibitive 5s. for individual tickets (2s. 6d. was the usual price).[82]

Further protests against ticket conditions in the winter of 1758 provoked Avison into a column-long letter to the *Newcastle Journal*, defending his position.[83] He detailed the history of the winter series and how he came to have financial and administrative direction of it as well as musical control.[84] According to one supporter, he had seriously considered giving up all but the musical direction. He had, the anonymous supporter wrote:

> been called to account for assuming the sole direction of both the performance and subscription, so thereby giving an offence where he intended a service. For that reason, he was desirous to give up the management of the concerts to any gentlemen who would undertake it; and at the same time to submit his best service to their commands, rather chusing to assist, than preside, where it was so precarious to please.[85]

Avison must have felt particularly under threat at this period as, in the summer of 1758, he faced – apparently for the first time – a major challenge from another musician on his own ground. Charles Claget, a young Irishman, arrived in Newcastle early in 1758; he divided his attention between giving dancing lessons (on Monday, Tuesdays and Wednesday mornings) and teaching various instruments – the 'Violin, Violoncello, Guitar, Citra, &c'.[86] Avison, despite having been in command of Newcastle's musical life for over 20 years, does not seem to have received the newcomer well (although it is fair to say that the evidence of the matter comes only from Claget). Claget's promotion of a number of benefits seems to have persuaded Avison that the Irishman intended to set up a rival subscription series, and in the light of what had happened, and was continuing to happen in Durham, that could only be a sensitive issue. The two men quarrelled – an event described by Claget as an 'unlucky Difference':[87]

> As some Persons misjudging Mr. Claget's Intention have taken Publication of a Concert as an Opposition; he desires they wouldn't look on it in that Light for the future, but consider Music is his Profession; that his is not a Subscription Concert,

---

80   Ibid.
81   *NJ*, 4–11 Nov. 1758.
82   *NC*, 25 Mar. 1757.
83   *NJ*, 4–11 Nov. 1758.
84   Ibid.
85   *NJ*, 10–17 Mar. 1759.
86   *NJ*, 29 July–5 Aug. 1758. For Claget's early career, see Brian Boydell, *Rotunda Music in Eighteenth-Century Dublin* (Dublin: Irish Academic Press, 1992), p. 77.
87   *NJ*, 9–16 Dec. 1758.

68 ROZ SOUTHEY

but one benefit night, what is commonly granted to any Performers, tho' they stay not a Week on the Spot.[88]

Claget's extensive use of the choir of Durham Cathedral in these concerts may also have caused offence, given the rivalry between the two Durham series.[89]

In the event, Claget did not prove a substantial threat; he stayed only two years, apparently giving up his concert activities in favour of appearances with the local theatre company.[90] His presence, however, together with the controversy over the Newcastle subscription series and the competition from the Spring Gardens (which continued into the late 1760s), may have directed Avison's energies away from the Durham series organized with Garth.

Despite Cowper's certainty that Garth's subscription series could not continue for want of funding, the 1757–58 season of concerts went ahead, as did the summer concerts of 1758, for which Garth again obtained the services of Felice Giardini.[91] In September 1758 the subscribers met to elect a treasurer for the coming year, and the finances were apparently sufficiently healthy for the series to go ahead from 12 October.[92] By the following year, however, Cowper's prediction of failure was plainly coming true, albeit later than he had anticipated; the 1759–60 season was the last for the Gentlemen's Subscription Concert. It may be that Garth's series, being less established than either the cathedral series or Avison's concerts in Newcastle, was less able to weather the increasingly difficult financial situation that clearly developed from 1757 and (as Cowper's remarks at the time suggest) may have been caused, or complicated, by a decrease in the number of concert-goers.

Personal and professional relations

Cowper's letters convey the impression that the people involved in the two series were not only professional but personal rivals. During the 1750s, however, Garth and many of the cathedral personnel seem to have been on good terms and performed together on a number of occasions. A concert in November 1754, for instance, put on by the Mayor of Durham to celebrate the King's birthday, included amongst the performers the visiting French-horn virtuoso, Mr Charles, 'several Gentlemen of the Town', John Garth, and 'the Gentlemen of the Choir who performed the Vocal Parts with great Applause'.[93] The Vestry Minutes of Stockton Parish Church detail payments (for the opening of the new organ) both to Garth and to 'players and singers' from Durham.[94] The annual dinner and pre-series

---

88   *NJ*, 9–16 Dec. 1758.
89   *NJ*, 16–23 June, 22 Sept., 21 Apr. 1759.
90   *NC*, 3 Nov., 10 Nov. 1759.
91   *NC*, 22 July 1758.
92   *NC*, 16 Sept., 30 Sept. 1758.
93   *NC*, 9 Nov. 1754.
94   Durham Record Office, EP/Sto/30: Vestry Book, Stockton Parish Church, 1762–1926.

CONCERTS IN NEWCASTLE AND DURHAM, 1752–1772

meeting of subscribers to the Gentlemen's Subscription Concert was held in an inn – the Star and Rummer – run by the singing man, Peter Blenkinsop,[95] and no fewer than nine people connected with the cathedral subscribed to the eight volumes of Garth's *Marcello's Psalms*. These subscribers included the Bishop of Durham, four prebendaries, the Dean and Chapter (who ordered two sets, presumably for the use of the choir), James Hesletine and – most surprising of all – Spencer Cowper himself.[96]

It may be that animosity had died with the passing of years, although Cowper's glee at the prospective demise of the series in 1757 hardly suggests so. A certain amount of the rivalry between the two series was due to the hostility between Hesletine and Avison; but much of Cowper's reaction may be attributed to his ever-volatile relations with 'Harry Vane' – Lord Barnard (later Lord Darlington), Garth's chief supporter. Cowper's dislike of Lord Barnard, whom he described in 1749 as 'wallowing in his own filth and nastiness',[97] was based on personal and political disagreements, and on what Cowper suspected were Barnard's attempts to undermine his (Cowper's) position in the local community. Cowper may have considered Garth's subscription series as one more of Barnard's schemes.[98]

Collaboration and withdrawal

After the disappearance of the Gentlemen's Subscription Concert in 1760, the last traces of rivalry lingered within the Race Week concerts. In 1760 and 1761, Garth's concerts of vocal and instrumental music were in competition with benefits for William Paxton;[99] in 1762 and in succeeding years, the cathedral-backed concerts were given by the entire choir and consisted of large-scale vocal works, chiefly by Handel – *Alexander's Feast, Acis and Galatea* – but also including Boyce's *Solomon*.[100] Garth continued to bring in well-known soloists from London; from 1768 he hired as first violin Giovanni Battista Noferi, leader of the Opera House ballet in London.[101] Noferi played in summer concerts in Durham until the mid-1770s and may have been recommended by his predecessor and friend, Felice Giardini.

In June 1763, James Hesletine died 'about six of the clock in the evening ... of a fit of the palsy'.[102] He had been organist of the cathedral for 52 years; his

---

95   *NC*, 23 Oct. 1756; 16 Sept. 1758. Blenkinsop was the singing man who hooted through his nose like a penny trumpet.

96   John Garth, *The first fifty Psalms set to Music by Benedetto Marcello – and adapted to the English Version by John Garth* (London, 1757–65), subscribers' list.

97   Cowper, *Letters*, p. 109, 28 Sept. 1749.

98   Ibid., p. 183, 2 Oct. 1756.

99   *NC*, 19 July 1760; 1 Aug. 1761. William was the middle brother.

100   See e.g. *NC*, 17 June 1762; 17 July 1762; 16 July 1763; 15 July 1764; 13 July 1765; 12 July 1766; 16 July 1768.

101   *NC*, 16 July 1768.

102   Thomas Ghyll (Recorder of the City of Durham), Diary, 1748–78, Surtees Society 118 (Durham and London, 1910), 213.

successor, appointed after some considerable wrangling between the Chapter and the Dean, was Thomas Ebdon, one of the singing men and a local man.[103] Ebdon also took over the direction of the concerts, and before long was mending relations with John Garth. In 1769 the customary two concerts of Race Week were reduced to one; the advertisement named Ebdon and Garth as joint promoters.[104] A fortnight later, in Assize Week, they collaborated again; although two concerts were put on, these were an obvious compromise between the parties. The concert on 3 August was of vocal and instrumental music with Noferi as first violin – a type of concert previously characteristic of Garth – and the second, on 4 August, was a Handelian concert of the cathedral type, a performance of *Acis and Galatea*.[105]

The collaboration continued over the next three years, although the winter subscription series was apparently organized by Ebdon alone. Garth's influence was steadily weakening throughout this period. In the mid-year concerts, vocal music began to predominate rather than miscellaneous concerts; of the eight concerts organized jointly by Garth and Ebdon between 1769 and 1772, only three were of vocal and instrumental music, the other five consisting of oratorio performances.[106] Ebdon was clearly the dominant partner in the collaboration and the logical result was that he should take over the entire organization of the concerts, an event which occurred in 1773.[107] Garth's withdrawal may have been accelerated by the death of Charles Avison in 1770; Avison's involvement in concerts in Durham during the last decade of his life is uncertain but it is probable that he continued to perform in Garth's concerts. Garth performed in Newcastle concerts throughout Avison's life.[108]

From the 1770s Garth appears to have dedicated himself principally to teaching, although he is known to have acted as the Bishop of Durham's organist at Auckland Castle in the 1790s.[109] About the same time he moved from Durham to family property in the parish of Wolsingham and in 1794 was married – apparently for the first time – to an heiress 30 years his junior, spending the remaining years of his life administering her property; he died in 1810 an extremely wealthy man.[110] His one-time collaborator in Durham, Thomas Ebdon, died in the same year. The cathedral winter subscription series, under Ebdon's direction, had lasted until 1793, was briefly revived in 1796 under a 'Committee of Gentlemen', then succumbed, apparently for lack of support.[111] The repertoire, based on Handel's works, seems to have remained unaltered to the end.

---

103   DAB, 1 October 1763; 17 November 1754.
104   *Newcastle Chronicle [NCh]*, 29 July 1769.
105   Ibid.
106   *NC*, 8 July, 29 June 1769; 14 July, 11 Aug. 1770; 13 July, 20 July 1771; 25 July, 8 Aug. 1772.
107   *NCh*, 17 July, 31 July 1773.
108   His withdrawal from Newcastle concerts after Avison's death evidently caused much resentment and resulted in a hostile anonymous letter to the *Newcastle Courant*. [*NC*, 25 Aug.–1 Sept. 1770.]
109   CA, Auckland Receiver General's accounts, Financial and audit, 1659–1856, Box 36.
110   He was buried in the north aisle of St Cuthbert's church in Darlington in March 1810.
111   *NC*, 12 Nov. 1796.

CHAPTER FIVE

Musical Culture and the Capital City: The Epoch of the *beau monde* in London, 1700–1870

William Weber[*]

During the period from about 1700 to 1870 London, and to various extents the capital cities of Europe generally, possessed a particular kind of elite social life. The capitals brought together increasing numbers of wealthy and influential people, generally more than courts were accustomed to do, and indeed robbed the courts of their former central role in politics and culture. These people knew one other individually less than was the case among courtiers, but much more than was to be the case by the end of the nineteenth century as a result of population growth and the rise of mass political movements. They most commonly referred to themselves as part of the *beau monde*, or simply as 'the World'. Political and cultural issues – *querelles*, as the French termed them – were debated in common within a tightly knit network of institutions and personal relationships. Letters of the period move back and forth between personal gossip, party politics and opera news with a naturalness that seems unusual, indeed quaint, in our day. The *beau monde* defined the sociability of elite life in London and Paris for this span of time for reasons essentially of demography and political culture.

Historians and literary scholars have taken the particular nature of the cosmopolitan elites during this period too much for granted. We all are well acquainted with this aspect of capital-city elites, but we have not looked closely enough into the process by which the concentration of elite groups reshaped the nature of sociability in the cities.[1] Though only some families or individuals lived

---

[*] I would like to thank Margaret Jacob and Larry Stewart for helping bring this chapter about. For a related piece, see William Weber, 'La culture musicale d'une capitale: l'époque du beau monde à Londres, 1700–1800', *Revue d'histoire moderne et contemporaine*, 49 (2002), 119–39.

[1] Among pioneers in this study, see E. H. Wrigley, 'A Simple Model of London's Importance in changing English Society and Economy, 1650–1750', *Past and Present*, 37 (1967), 44–70; Lawrence Stone, 'The Residential Development of the West End of London in the Seventeenth Century', in Barbara C. Malament, ed., *After the Reformation: Essays in Honor of J. H. Hexter* (Philadelphia: University of Pennsylvania Press, 1980), pp. 167–212; James Dyos and Michael Wolff, *The Victorian City: Images and Reality* (London: Routledge & Kegan Paul, 1973), 2 vols, esp. Lynn Lees, 'Metropolitan Types: London and Paris compared', pp. 413–28; and Bernard Lepetit and Peter Clark, eds, *Capital Cities and their Hinterlands in Early Modern Europe* (Aldershot: Scolar Press, 1996),

72   WILLIAM WEBER

year-round in the capitals, the fact that so many of them came together at key times of the year affected European society and culture profoundly.

The movement of elite families into capital cities seems to have begun first in London, where much was accomplished by 1600, followed to a significant extent by 1650 in Paris.[2] The nature of the *beau monde* awaited, however, the weakening of absolutist authority and the self-assertion of elites as a public. That began to occur in London upon the Restoration of the House of Stuart, a regime that is now seen as fragile and essentially impermanent.[3] By 1700 the life of the elite had shifted out of the court to public life in London.[4] Cultural life was central to the process by which this new group was formed; in some respects it evolved more in the theatres than in Parliament. By the same token, one can argue that in Paris as much as in London during the eighteenth century the broad population of wealthy and powerful people learned the dynamics of public partisanship originally in *querelles* within literary and musical life.

One can speak thus of an epoch of the *beau monde* existing between around 1700 and 1870 as a means of characterizing the life of the cosmopolitan elite. Some aspects of this world – the structure of public opera and concerts, for example – became established permanently in the capital cities during the eighteenth century, and for that reason can be seen as the start of the modern era. But in other respects the manners and mores of the elite world changed fundamentally after the middle of the nineteenth century. Around 1850 the tight little social world of nobility, gentry and professions, whose life was focused upon public places, receded increasingly into private spheres. Not only were there now so many people potentially part of the *beau monde*, but also the leadership of the middle classes in politics and culture disrupted its oligarchic rule. Cultural occasions increasingly became segmented into specialized and independent worlds of taste; among them there no longer existed a common sphere of acquaintance.[5] The year 1870 is necessarily only an approximation for the time when the *beau monde* ceased to exist.

Musical life, especially opera and concert life, is a particularly good place within which to study this problem. Here I will sketch out broadly certain main characteristics of this culture with musical life as a focus. As the most social of all the arts, music can tell us a lot about this subject. Musical life encompassed both

---

including David R. Ringrose, 'Capital Cities and their Hinterlands: Europe and the Colonial Dimension', pp. 217–40.

2   See Stone, 'The Residential Development of the West End of London'.

3   Tim Harris, *Politics under the Later Stuarts: Party Conflict in a Divided Society, 1660–1715* (London: Longman, 1993).

4   R. O. Bucholz, *The Augustan Court: Queen Anne and the Decline of Court Culture* (Stanford, Calif.: Stanford University Press, 1993).

5   I am indebted to the ideas of Lawrence Levine, in *Highbrow/Lowbrow: The Emergence of Cultural Hierarchy in America* (Cambridge, Mass.: Harvard University Press, 1988); Christophe Charle, *Naissance des 'intellectuels': 1880–1900* (Paris: Editions du Minuit, 1990); and Robert Ritchie, 'Cultural Riots: Nineteenth-Century Theater in England and America', Founders Lecture, Huntington Library (San Marino, Calif.: 1994).

THE *BEAU MONDE* IN LONDON, 1700–1870

public and private activities and figured prominently within both religious and civil ceremony, and as a result its culture spans major areas of society in unusually comprehensive ways. While the musical world has idiosyncratic traditions, its links with political and social structures make it a useful vehicle by which to see what the middle and upper classes were doing culturally in public places and how they related to one another.

We must confront the problem of modernity in this discussion. There is a fundamental difference between modernity and modernization: the former means a new epoch seen in the context of the society; the latter, by contrast, involves the notion that a universal, macrocosmic set of changes has transformed world society, a theory often put in linear and teleological terms. Since the widespread critique of modernization theory, the terms 'modern' and its cognate 'modernity' have become more common, used to maintain a certain flexibility in historical meaning.[6] One can define different levels of modernity in a society, not all of which became permanent, and thereby not exaggerate the unity of historical conditions.

The concepts of public opinion, public life and the public sphere have in the last 10 years or so become accepted widely by historians as fundamental to modernity within political culture. The early ideas of Jürgen Habermas in *The Structural Transformation of the Public Sphere* have provided the focus for thinking about English leadership in the development of ideologies and the rise of open-ended political discourse.[7] That kind of open-ended, indeed uncensored, political behaviour is now seen by many scholars as quintessentially modern, when one defines the term on a broad historical and conceptual plan. Much of what Habermas wrote is now a 'given'; in the cultural area his framework is the starting-point for more detailed research and rethinking of new and more specific areas.[8]

Essential to the idea of the public sphere in the early modern period is the recognition that politics, culture, religion and ideas mixed freely and can be difficult to separate. On a certain plane, public life was unitary in structure because

---

6 The best-known such conception is the idea of 'paradigm' advanced by Thomas Kuhn in *The Structure of Scientific Revolution* (Chicago: University of Chicago Press, 3rd edn 1970); on the discussion of the book, see Steve Fuller, 'Being There with Thomas Kuhn: A Parable for Postmodern Times', *History and Theory*, 31 (1992), 241–75. For discussion of modernization theory, see Joyce Appleby, Lynn Hunt and Margaret Jacob, *Telling the Truth about History* (New York: Norton, 1994), pp. 78–89, 217, 220, 229. In the conclusion of my book on the middle-class concert public of the 1830s and 1840s in London, Paris and Vienna, originally published some 30 years ago, I ventured to portray concert life of the period as bringing a kind of modernization in stricter, in some ways more rationalized, professional roles played by musicians within musical institutions differentiated from other areas of entertainment; see *Music and the Middle Class: The Social Structure of Concert Life in London, Paris and Vienna, 1830–48* (London: Croom Helm, 1975; Aldershot: Ashgate, 2003).

7 *The Structural Transformation of the Public Sphere: An Inquiry into a Category of Bourgeois Society* (Cambridge, Mass.: MIT Press, 1989), tr. Thomas Burger with the assistance of Frederick Lawrence. See also Terry Eagleton, *The Function of Criticism from The Spectator to Post-Structuralism* (London: Verso, 1984).

8 See the remarks by Orest Ranum, review of Hélène Merlin, *Public et littérature en France au XVIIe siècle*, *Modern Language Notes*, 111 (1996), 806–12.

74 WILLIAM WEBER

the elites and their company found in English society were small in number and relatively unsegmented in their activities. To be sure, each area – music, for example – had its own internal structure and in a sense its own politics. It is for that very reason that when we find strong networks among areas of society we need to take them very seriously. Margaret Jacob demonstrated a critically important set of links between science, religion, the universities and high politics; I have found a related grouping among Anglican church music, Tory ideology, university chapels, and the growth of canonic thinking on music.[9] Basic to the modernity of English life in this period was the dynamism with which ideas and influences moved back and forth between closely adjoining areas of culture and society, uninhibited by boundaries imposed by intellectual and corporate traditions. That took place because, on the one hand, England was the most homogeneous of the major European countries in language and culture and, on the other, the state held back from imposing controls upon the press and business that were standard in most other places.[10] Early eighteenth-century England offered an unusual wealth of possibilities for cultural change.

Year-round residence did not develop as extensively among elite groups in London as in Paris during the eighteenth century. Nevertheless, the post-revolutionary political context in Britain produced an open-ended elite 'world' over half a century earlier than in France. The number of noble, bourgeois and professional families living at least part of the year in London increased in the course of the seventeenth century, bringing about the construction of the West End, their principal place of residence at the turn of the next century.[11] As Bucholz has shown so effectively, the shift of elite social and political life out of the court to London took place quickly and decisively under the reign of Queen Anne as clubs, coffee-shops and public houses burgeoned in the wake of the 1689 constitutional settlement.[12] Similar changes in elite habits occurred in Paris under the Regency, though with less immediate or fundamental political consequences, and with residence patterns more widely dispersed, from the Boulevard Saint-Germain across the river to the rue de Rivoli and down to the Marais.[13] But in both cities a

---

9 Margaret C. Jacob, *The Newtonians and the English Revolution, 1689–1720* (New York: Gordon & Breach, 1976) and *The Cultural Meaning of the Scientific Revolution* (Philadelphia: Temple University Press, 1988); William Weber, *The Rise of Musical Classics in Eighteenth-Century England: A Study in Canon, Ritual, and Ideology* (Oxford: Clarendon Press, 1992). The evolution of musical thought was powerfully influenced by empiricism; musical life indeed had more intellectually to do with science than with the fine arts or the early field of formal aesthetics. See William Weber, 'The Intellectual Origins of Musical Canon in Eighteenth-Century England', *Journal of the American Musicological Society*, 47 (1994), 488–520; and Larry Stewart, *The Rise of Public Science: Rhetoric, Technology and Natural Philosophy in Newtonian Britain* (Cambridge: Cambridge University Press, 1992).

10 Keith Wrightson, *English Society, 1580–1680* (London: Hutchinson, 1982), Introduction, pp. 11–14.

11 Stone, 'The Residential Development of the West End of London'.

12 Bucholz, *The Augustan Court*.

13 Orest Ranum, *Paris in the Age of Absolutism* (New York: John Wiley, 1968); Bernard Lepetit, *Les Villes dans la France moderne (1740–1840)* (Paris: A. Michel, 1988).

large part of the elite began spending more of the year in the capitals; some in effect became Londoners and Parisians. What grew up among them was a distinct milieu, usually dubbed the World or the *beau monde*, such as could not be found numerously in any other cities.

Essential to the elite sociability within the two capital cities was the culture of consumption that developed from the extreme concentration of elites and the competitive tendencies this produced. While Amsterdam rivalled the two cities in its style of living, it was too small, too far from the court in The Hague and lacking in centralized political authority for it to develop a comparable new elite world.[14] Some historians in fact see a redistribution of wealth going on from the country to the capital cities, facilitated by the state and consumed by the cosmopolitan elites.[15] The centrality of these cities within their societies made consumption a much more visible, public phenomenon than it had been before, and from that came the economic power that made the dynamism of eighteenth-century musical life possible.

The rise of London's modern musical world

The musical world that arose in London around the turn of the eighteenth century established public musical institutions and social practices some of whose basic characteristics still exist today as foundations of musical culture. During the sixteenth and seventeenth centuries musical activities were quite limited in their number and scale; they took place chiefly in churches and court or municipal celebrations and thus had purposes larger than music itself. The inauguration of public opera presentations in Venice in the 1630s and dramatic productions with music in London in the 1670s, and of concerts for paying audiences in London in the same decade, marked major milestones in the social history of music. As Habermas puts it, 'For the first time an audience gathered to listen to music as such – a public of music lovers to which anyone who was propertied and educated was admitted.'[16] Roger North said that very thing in *The Musical Grammarian* (*c*.1728) in declaring: 'But how and by what stepps Musick shot up in to such request, as to croud out from the stage even comedy itself, and to sit down in her place and become of such mighty value and price as we now know it to be, is worth inquiring after.'[17] On a certain plane, in the concerts held in York Buildings just off the Strand in 1680 and in the Royal Festival Hall in the South Bank arts complex built in 1951 we see public spaces central to a capital city and the cultural activities

---

14 John Brewer and Roy Porter, eds, *Consumption and the World of Goods* (London: Routledge, 1993).

15 See Ringrose, 'Capital Cities and their Hinterlands'.

16 Habermas, *Structural Transformation of the Public Sphere*, p. 39.

17 *Roger North on Music*, ed. John Wilson (London: Novello, 1959), p. 302.

essential to its life.[18] The growing concentration of the elites, together with the professionals and artisans who worked for them, reshaped both the institutions and the discourse in musical life in profound ways. In that sense by 1780 London's musical life had become modern, or, one might say, entered into a new era of modernity.

London was either the first or the foremost in establishing public musical activities during the eighteenth century. Its opera, established at the King's Theatre in 1708, was the only example in a monarchical system where opera was founded on a commercial basis, legally independent of the court. The high fees given singers there came to set the standard throughout Europe. Public concerts not only began in London but also became far more numerous and specialized there than anywhere else in Europe, based on the petty capitalism of selling subscriptions to several concerts. Essentially, the modern concert world of entrepreneurial presentations originated in early eighteenth-century London.[19] Professional musicians became unusually independent in their dealings with wealthy families, establishing fee-for-service relationships much more consistently than was done elsewhere. And the first canon of works from the past, revered as great music, was established in England by the end of the century.[20]

The King's Theatre epitomized the ways by which cultural and political institutions were integrated in this society. It emerged as a solution to what the crisis of the 1690s did to the London theatre. The Manners Campaign had a devastating impact upon the theatre world, for the vicious moral attack Jeremy Collier made upon it in 1698 essentially made plays no longer a proper focus for the life of the upper classes.[21] Both sexual and political innuendo had become too strong for a community that feared a new civil war; the eventual outcome was the Licensing Act of 1737, which ended the theatre as a forum for political commentary. The King's Theatre was established as a replacement for what the theatre had been in the early decades of the Restoration, but one in which the peerage and indeed the entire British elite became concentrated. The theatre in effect became the main resort of Parliament at play. Though opera librettos made only muted political implications, the theatre made a powerful statement about the unity and the consolidation of the Hanoverian Succession.[22]

The world of public concerts had a less overtly political character than that of opera, since they did not intersect with the peerage as directly. But they became far

---

18 'London', *New Grove2*, vol. 15, p. 151; Robert Hewison, *Culture and Consensus: English Art and Politics since 1940* (London, 1995).

19 Simon McVeigh, *Concert Life in London from Mozart to Haydn* (Cambridge: Cambridge University Press, 1993).

20 Weber, *The Rise of Musical Classics*.

21 Jeremy Collier, *A Short View of the Immorality, and Profaneness of the English Stage, together with the Sense of Antiquity upon this Argument* (3rd edn, London: S. Keble, 1698).

22 See Elizabeth Gibson, *The Royal Academy of Music (1719–1728): The Institution and its Directors* (New York: Garland, 1989); William Weber, 'L'Institution et son public: l'opéra à Paris et à Londres au XVIIIe siècle', *Annales: Economies, sociétés, civilisations*, 48/6 (1993), 1519–39. I am indebted to Maximilian Novak for discussion of this point.

THE *BEAU MONDE* IN LONDON, 1700–1870

more numerous in London than anywhere else in Europe during the eighteenth century partly for a political reason – the weakness of cultural controls in the metropolis. Concerts began in the public houses and benefited from the liberties accorded these institutions under the Commonwealth and after the Restoration. The licences granted to the public houses were taken as sufficient for the musical activities put on within them, and while a few special kinds of concerts were asked to seek permits, the great majority had no regulation.[23] This situation was virtually unique in Europe, since the norm was monopolistic controls by either the court or the municipal theatre; in Leipzig, for example, the Gewandhaus gave permits for most concerts until after the middle of the nineteenth century. The Licensing Act of 1737 ignored concerts as it clamped down on entrepreneurial theatres and imposed censorship of scripts. No other city had as much musical entrepreneurism as London even in the nineteenth century, since elsewhere concerts tended to be more institutional and centralized.

The epoch of the *beau monde*

The *beau monde* was a social grouping basic to elite life during the intermediate epoch of modernity we are discussing here. It constituted a milieu significantly larger, more diversified, and less intimate than that of a court but at the same time one much smaller and more distinct than the upper classes of the metropolis such as developed in London and Paris in the second half of the nineteenth century. This was a public most of whose members knew most of one another by engaging in a closely linked set of social, cultural and political contexts. They at least knew *of* each other: thus different from a court, where one did know everyone, and from the amorphous, highly segmented elite worlds that emerged with the growth of the capital cities and the rise of mass politics and mass culture. During the early eighteenth century the terms *beau monde* and 'the World' emerged in both London and Paris, serving as handy ways to refer to an elite, cosmopolitan public that could be fairly easily identified in terms of individuals and families.

Public theatres, especially opera, stood at the centre of the elite public world. Going 'to be seen' should not be construed necessarily as an opportunistic act of attempted upward mobility; since being in public was so basic to elite life, attendance was presumed as a normal social act for anyone reckoned part of the *beau monde*. Opera became considerably more of an obligation than the spoken theatre, since it was linked to international elites and in London was run directly by members of the aristocracy. The *Weekly Journal* declared in 1725:

> Musick is so generally approv'd of in *England*, that it is look'd upon as a want of Breeding not to be affected by it, insomuch that every Member of the *Beau-Monde* at this Time either do, or, at least, think it necessary to appear as if they understand it; and, in order to carry on this Deceit it is requisite every one, who has the Pleasure of

---

23 McVeigh, *Concert Life in London*.

thinking himself a fine Gentleman, should, being first laden with a Competency of Powder and Essence, make his personal Appearance every Opera Night at the Haymarket ...[24]

Membership in the World was thought to be known to all of that station; it also provided upper-class society with a social reference point and a source of moral authority. The letters – in effect, the exceptionally detailed diary – that Lady Mary Coke, a divorced daughter of the Duke of Argyle, wrote to her sister between 1767 and 1791 portray vividly how she conceived of the *beau monde* and related with its members. Lady Mary invoked the authority of the World repeatedly. After a night at the King's Theatre in 1779 she remarked that 'Mr Fawkener & Sir Harry Featherstone at first sat in the Pitt over against the Box & then went in to it[;] each has his particular reasons as the World says.'[25] Members of the milieu deferred to its moral dictates. In 1778 Lady Mary said of Lady Carmarthen, who at the time was separated from her husband and was entertaining her lover at home: 'I don't hear she desires to see Company or that she intends to brave the World; however bad she may be at least there is some appearance of shame.'[26] One can see how tightly drawn the World tended to be from the fact that three-quarters of the more than 350 subscribers to box seats at the opera in the season of 1783 alone were cited in Lady Mary's journal at some point in time.[27]

The *beau monde* was by no means coextensive with the nobility. It included not only the baronetcy and relations of both titled groups, but also both men and women whose professional roles led them into the World – doctors, financial agents, high-level artists and musicians, cultural entrepreneurs, high-tone prostitutes, and so on. This is not to minimize the centrality and the ultimate authority of the nobility in eighteenth-century England in musical life as much as in society at large, as I have suggested elsewhere.[28] What it does mean is that despite the resurgence of aristocratic authority towards the end of the century, the social life of this elite avoided overtly caste-like conventions and favoured a fairly loose sense of social levels. Thus there was no strict separation between nobles and commoners in the seating at the King's Theatre (or indeed at the Opéra in Paris); only in the top level of boxes did one find no titled people. By comparison, in Vienna the seats at the Burgtheater placed a wooden barrier between the two

---

24 *Weekly Journal; or, Saturday's Post*, 18 Dec. 1725, quoted in Gibson, *Royal Academy of Music*, p. 388.

25 I am indebted to the Honourable Caroline Douglas-Home for access to the original of the letters and diaries of Lady Mary Coke, Coldstream, Berwickshire, 2 Jan. 1779. The first 15 years of the diary (1759–74) are found in *The Letters and Journals of Lady Mary Coke*, ed. J. A. Home, 4 vols (Edinburgh: D. Douglas, 1889–96).

26 20 Dec. 1778.

27 See the list of subscribers in the *Morning Herald*, 5 Feb. 1783, p. 5, and *A Descriptive Plan of the New Opera House with the Names of the Subscribers in each Box*, London, 1783 (BL). Research in this area is aided enormously by the card file of personal information on all individuals cited in the unpublished portion of her journal that was made by Wilmarth Sheldon Lewis and his staff and is held in the Lewis Walpole Library of Yale University, Farmington, Ct.

28 *The Rise of Musical Classics*, ch. 9, 'Conclusion'.

THE *BEAU MONDE* IN LONDON, 1700–1870 79

classes throughout the eighteenth century.[29] In London and Paris modernity meant fluid relations between elites such as did not evolve in Vienna until the 1830s and 1840s.[30]

We need to keep in perspective that while the *beau monde* was a diversified elite group, the nobility nonetheless played a central role in the evolution of the public sphere. One objection a historian might now make to Habermas's analysis is his insistence upon the centrality of the bourgeoisie in the rise of the public sphere. He is not as rigid on this score in discussing men of letters as he is on political discourse generally: 'The public sphere of the world of letters (*literarische Öffentlichkeit*) was not, of course, authochthonously bourgeois', he remarks (p. 28). But one must go well beyond that to recognize the leadership that noblemen – from Shaftesbury to Walpole to Lord Middlesex, impresario in the King's Theatre in the early 1730s – performed in the intellectual and political innovations Habermas is talking about. Leadership of different groups shifted decade by decade; as Terry Eagleton puts it, in the *Tatler* and the *Spectator* 'English criticism is able to glimpse its own glorious origins, seize the fragile moment at which the bourgeoisie enter into respectability before passing out of it again'.[31] By the same token, few concerts of any stature were presented in the City of London – virtually all major musical events were in the West End. While high business families went to the King's Theatre, to concerts at Hickford's Rooms or at the Pantheon on Oxford Street, musical entrepreneurs fashioning concert locales did not choose to do business in the traditional bourgeois part of London.[32]

Many of the manners and mores of the *beau monde* seem quite foreign, if not indeed offensive to us today. Attendance at a theatre was presumed to be a social act; to go was by definition to mingle with the assembled company as much as to see a production, and as a result a quite literate diarist saw no need to mention what he or she saw on a given night. An individual would often attend several theatres in an evening, arranging to see favourite scenes, players or singers or meeting with people in different halls and boxes.[33] The idea that musical pieces

---

29   Otto G. Schindler, *Das Burgtheater und sein Publikum*, 2 vols (Vienna: Österreichische Akademie der Wissenschaften, 1976).

30   Weber, *Music and the Middle Class*.

31   Eagleton, *The Function of Criticism*, p. 25.

32   McVeigh, *Concert Life in London*. For different perspectives on the issue of bourgeois or aristocratic dominance of eighteenth-century England, see Roy Porter, *English Society in the Eighteenth Century* (London: Allen Lane, 1982); Linda Colley, *Britons: Forging the Nation, 1707–1837* (New Haven: Yale University Press, 1992); J. C. D. Clark, *English Society, 1688–1832: Religion, Ideology and Politics during the Ancien Regime* (Cambridge: Cambridge University Press, 1985; 2nd edn, 2000); Donna Andrew, 'Aldermen and the Big Bourgeoisie Reconsidered', *Social History*, 6 (1981), 359–64.

33   In 1715, for example, Sir Dudley Ryder wrote in his journal, 'Went to the play into the side-box. Stayed the first Act. Then to the new Playhouse, into the side-box, where stayed the first Act. Supped at the Gill House ... [went home and] read part of Molière's comedy l'Escole des Femmes. To bed at 10, being sleepy.' Still, in March 1716 he reported going to see Addison's *The Drummer, or the Haunted House*. See *The Diary of Dudley Ryder, 1715–1716*, ed. William Matthews (London: Methuen, 1939), pp. 128, 195. Joseph Addison made a critique of such etiquette, but one doubts how deep his conviction went in this regard. See Henrik Knif, *Gentlemen and Spectators: Studies in*

80   WILLIAM WEBER

might comprise integral, permanent works of art was weak as yet; most operas were patchworks – *pasticci* – of arias from different works by various composers. But that should not impugn the seriousness of the public. Since many people saw an opera production often within a season, it was not thought obligatory to sit through it all. Although social behaviours – talking, moving about, some sources say playing cards – were tolerated such as is not normally done today, that does not mean that no one cared about what was happening onstage. Writers liked to say that nobody listened to an opera, or that nobody knew much about it, but that statement was a trope, an irony, essentially ambiguous in meaning. Least of all does it mean that there were no serious listeners; Handel, Rameau and Gluck was each admired deeply by the aficionados of his time.[34]

The etiquette of the *beau monde* in theatres was rather more multi-faceted and tolerant than ours today because before the late eighteenth century the opera world recognized little stratification among its listeners by levels of taste. Opera was assumed to be accessible, indeed attractive, to all members of the elites and the people from other social levels who formed part of their world; both aficionados and less serious listeners went to the same productions in the same halls. While Monteverdi composed his early works in Mantua for a quite intellectual public and a private context, from the founding of the Venetian halls in the 1630s onwards opera was what one might call 'general taste'.[35] All of this displays major respects in which eighteenth-century theatre life, with its variety of genres, cultural idioms and social behaviours, was foreign from the modern cultural world.

Thus did opera possess what we might call a mixed social etiquette. People took for granted that they would socialize during the performance; they had often made appointments to meet and would move between boxes or parts of the hall. But it is also clear that some people did watch and listen, and that at points the entire audience did so. The discovery that not everyone was absorbed in listening at every moment all the time seems offensive to us, given the highly idealistic aesthetic that defines our whole approach to musical experience. But the toleration in the earlier period of behaviours that might impede listening flowed from social necessity, as we shall see, not from a limited commitment to music as a serious pursuit on the part of the society as a whole.

Public display of sexual licence was another trait basic to the *beau monde* and the theatre world in both London and Paris. While freedom from moral codes had long been something of a privilege of the uppermost social orders, this right became far more open and more conventional within this milieu than it had been

---

Journals, Opera and the Social Scene in Late Georgian London (Helsinki: Finnish Historical Society, 1995), pp. 70–73. James H. Johnson is more critical of the old order of musical manners; see *Listening in Paris: A Cultural History* (Berkeley: University of California Press, 1995). Also see my contribution to this debate in 'Did People Listen in the 18th Century?', *Early Music*, 25 (1997), 678–91 (special issue, 'Listening Practice').

34   See Lydia Goehr, *The Imaginary Museum of Musical Works: An Essay in the Philosophy of Music* (Oxford: Clarendon Press, 1992).

35   See William Weber, 'Learned and General Musical Taste in Eighteenth-Century France', *Past and Present*, 89 (1980), 58–85.

THE *BEAU MONDE* IN LONDON, 1700–1870

before. The opera was the focal point for sexual gossip; Lady Mary always kept her sister well informed on such matters. One speculates whether the concentration of so many wealthy and influential people might have excited them and led them into extravagant sexual behaviours.[36] The pattern seems to have begun about the same time in both Paris and London in the 1720s, and became particularly prominent in public life during the 1770s and 1780s; we know most about what went on in Paris thanks to the detailed police reports on public immorality, which list well over half of *abonné(e)s* to the Opéra, or their spouses.[37] The publishing industry played an important role as well, since in both cities there were scandal sheets about upper-class individuals, including princes of the blood, in some cases with political overtones.[38]

The politics of cultural quarrels

Essential to public life during the extended eighteenth century of which we speak was the persistence of intimate, one might say incestuous relations between political and cultural worlds. Theatres provided a central forum for discourse after the Restoration; the rhetoric of party served as a key vocabulary of dramatic allusion and gesture.[39] The King's Theatre and then its first strong company, the Royal Academy of Music (1720–28), were born in a political context, essentially of Whig and Hanoverian parentage. Librettists and composers played upon people's

---

36   One does not, however, hear such gossip in the extensive autobiography of John Marsh (1752–1828), a gentleman of both landed and urban bourgeois stock in Sussex and Kent; see W. Weber, 'The Fabric of Daily Life and the Autobiography of John Marsh', *Huntington Library Quarterly*, 59 (1997), 145–69.

37   The documents are in the Archives de la Bastille in the Bibliothèque de l'Arsenal, and excerpts have been published in M. L. Larchey, *Documents inédits sur le règne de Louis XV* (Paris, 1863); Camille Piton, *Paris sous Louis XV: Rapports des inspecteurs de police au roi*, 5 vols (Paris: Société du Mercure de France, 1908–14).

38   In 1769 the *Town and Country Magazine* was launched; the focus of its monthly issues was on one to three articles called *Tête-à-Tête*, the history of some affair with enough specificity that many people knowledgeable about *le beau monde* would understand who was being discussed. By the 1780s pamphlets had begun to appear as well, the best known, by Charles Pigott, done from a radical Whig point of view (*The Jockey Club* and *The Female Jockey Club*). For Paris, see Thevéneau de Morande, *La Gazette cuirassée: ou anecdotes scandaleuses de la cour de France, Le Philosophe cynique, pour servir de suite aux anecdotes scandaleuses de la cour de France*, and *Mélanges confus sur des matières fort claires*, published in London in 1771. A slicker version of such reports was published by Imbert de Boudreaux in *La chronique scandaleuse*, 4 vols (Paris, 1782–92). See Jeffrey Merrick, 'Sexual Politics and Public Order in Eighteenth-Century France: The *Mémoires secrètes* and the *Correspondance secrète*', *Journal of the History of Sexuality*, 1/1 (1990), 64–84; Margaret C. Jacob, 'The Materialist World of Pornography', in Lynn Hunt, ed., *Eroticism and the Body Politic* (Baltimore: Johns Hopkins University Press, 1991), pp. 157–202; and Dror Wahrman, '*Percy*'s Prologue: From Gender Play to Gender Panic in Eighteenth-Century England', *Past and Present*, 159 (1998), 113–60.

39   W. L. MacDonald, *Pope and his Critics: A Study in Eighteenth Century Personalities* (London: Dent, 1951); John Loftis, *The Politics of Drama in Augustan England* (Oxford: Clarendon Press, 1963); Philip J. Finkelpearl, *Court and Country Politics in the Plays of Beaumont and Fletcher* (Princeton: Princeton University Press, 1990).

partisan sensibilities with a highly entertaining ambiguity.[40] Musical activities, of course, had long had close links with politics; what was new, indeed modern, was the shift from court celebration to public discourse in a highly unstable political community. The opera and the concert hall emerged along with the club and the coffee house as Shaftesburian social spaces where the elites who were then building the public sphere could be entertained. Musical events indeed provided an apolitical ritual context where many of these key groups could meet, activities of the sort that neither the Parliament nor the coffee-shop could provide. Shaftesbury wrote just as English musical life was shifting from the highly private contexts of seventeenth-century domestic and religious music making – Pepys's world – to the public arenas of the Georgian period, but just a few years too early for him to experience.[41]

The linkages between musical, literary and political discourse brought about periodic episodes where events in the three worlds intersected to ignite what was sometimes called a *querelle*. The pamphlets and essays written for these disputes were the epitome of one of the key growing-points in the eighteenth-century press: satires or polemics filled with highly nuanced allusions to contemporary affairs in different fields, but written for a broader reading public than had generally been the case in the seventeenth century. Essential to such episodes was the extent to which many readers knew or knew of the participants and the writers personally, since the social world of the upper classes was relatively small and concentrated in the capital city. People who did not involve themselves in high politics experienced factional dispute more directly within episodes such as these than within matters of state; indeed in many cases cultural disputes bore closely upon politics as such. It was through the commingling of political, literary and musical affairs that the public sphere was extended beyond those who held offices and exerted influence on an ongoing basis.

The best-known such disputes in music occurred in Paris – a brief and limited one over an essay promoting Italian opera by the Abbé Raguenet in 1706 (translated soon after into English), another over Rameau and Gluck in 1737, and then the two primary episodes, the Querelle des Bouffons of 1752–53 and the rivalry between Gluck and Piccinni in 1774–78. The last two episodes interacted closely with the political happenings around them – the *philosophes* fighting for Italian opera and the *Encyclopédie* jointly in the first, and *littérateurs* squaring off over the ambitious new Queen in the second.[42]

---

40 Curtis Price, 'English Traditions in Handel's *Rinaldo*', in Stanley Sadie and Anthony Hicks, eds, *Handel Tercentary Collection* (Basingstoke: Macmillan, 1985), pp. 120–37; and 'Political Allegory in Late-Seventeenth-Century English Opera', in Nigel Fortune, ed., *Music and Theatre: Essays in Honour of Winton Dean* (Cambridge: Cambridge University Press, 1987), pp. 1–29.

41 Lawrence Klein, *Shaftesbury and the Culture of Politeness: Moral Discourse and Cultural Politics in Early Eighteenth-Century England* (Cambridge: Cambridge University Press, 1994); and 'The Third Earl of Shaftesbury and the Progress of Politeness', *Eighteenth-Century Studies*, 18 (1984–85), 186–214.

42 William Weber, '*La musique ancienne* in the Waning of the Ancien Régime', *Journal of Modern History*, 56 (1984), 58–88; Robert M. Isherwood, 'The Third War of the Musical Enlightenment', *Studies in Eighteenth-Century Culture*, 4 (1975), 223–45.

THE *BEAU MONDE* IN LONDON, 1700–1870   83

Similar, and equally significant, disputes took place before then in London. Between 1706 and around 1740, literary men challenged the rise to prominence of Italian opera within elite cultural life in a rich literature of pamphlets and essays that raised a wide array of moral, political and aesthetic issues.[43] Soon after the first production of opera in the Italian idiom in 1705, John Dennis opened the controversy with *An Essay on the Opera's after the Italian Manner* and in *An Essay upon the Publick Spirit* (1711). A new round of pamphleteering opened up in the early 1720s and was intensified by the premiere of *The Beggar's Opera* in 1728. Party politics played a part in this literature, since court officers predominated among the Directors of the Royal Academy of Music, but a great variety of moral issues and personal digs were raised in the pamphlets that usually made them cut across party lines.

We can see how opera and politics mingled in this literature in a comment made in 1727 about the rivalries between the singers Faustina and Cuzzoni and between the composers Handel and Bononcini:

> Which of the two is the Aggressor, I dare not determine, lest I lose the Friendship of my Great Noble Personages, who espouse some the one, some the other Party, with such Warmth, that it is not now, (as formerly) *i.e.*, are you High Church or Low, Whig or Tory; are you for Court or Country, King *George*, or the Pretender: but are you for *Faustina* or *Cuzzoni*, *Handel* or *Bononcini*. This engages all the Polite World in warm Disputes; and but for the soft Strains of the Opera, which have in some Measure qualified and allay'd the native city of the *English*, Blood and Slaughter would consequently ensue.[44]

Here we see the King's Theatre depicted in Shaftesburian terms as a place where polite discourse would supplant faction and disorder, a place more aristocratic than the coffee house but still sharing in its civilizing virtues. Thus did writers amuse their readers, moving from fickle patrons to the deadly serious subject of the Pretender. Opera played an important role within the public sphere by providing a forum where members of the conflicting parties could meet, and the public could engage in a variety of factional disputes, the seeming result being a lessening of overall tensions. The Paris *querelle* of the 1750s interacted in similar fashion with the constitutional crisis between the royal house and the Parlement of Paris: dispute over the Italian company of *bouffons* provided the supporters of the *Encyclopédie* with a vehicle by which to irritate the King, and gave the public a vital debate over the direction that the state-managed Opéra should take.

This is not to say, however, that musical discourse was identical with civic discourse, or indeed that public life fitted exactly with what is known as the public sphere. The musical world should be seen not as a constituent member of the

---

43   Lowell Lindgren, 'Early Pamphlets on Italian Opera, 1706–14'; Gibson, *Royal Academy of Music*, pp. 383–438; Thomas McGeary, 'Shaftesbury, Handel and Italian Opera', *Händel Jahrbuch*, 32 (1986), 99–104; and 'English Opera Criticism and Aesthetics, 1685–1747', Ph.D. diss. (University of Illinois, 1985).

44   *Monthly Catalogue*, no. 50, June 1727, quoted in Gibson, *Royal Academy of Music*, p. 428. See for this kind of satire also *The Miscellaneous Works of the Late Dr. Arbuthnot*, 2 vols (Glasgow: James Carlile, 1750), vol. 1, pp. 213–23 (the attribution to Arbuthnot has been disproved).

84   WILLIAM WEBER

public sphere, the forum surrounding authority of state, but rather as a public world that interacted with that emerging domain. The sense grew up by the 1720s that musical life was a separately constituted sphere in society and as such had its own civic discourse. The small size and relative lack of differentiation within the upper-class musical world in this epoch gave it a unity and a self-consciousness as a distinct, though obviously not self-contained community. Again we need to recall the broad demographic parameters of the periods we are discussing. It was only after about 1700 that the idea of a republic of musical activities arose. But by 1870 much of that was largely to disappear with the expansion and specialization of cultural institutions and publics.

During the eighteenth century it was common to speak either of the musical world, or perhaps of the opera, in political similes. In England musical life took on an especially clear sensibility of this kind because the King's Theatre, for all intents and purposes the centre of that world, was funded and governed by noblemen and gentlemen, most of whom either were Members of Parliament or had offices in the Royal Bedchamber. People of Quality necessarily viewed the Directors of the King's Theatre rather as officers in government, since what was done to manage the theatre affected the daily life of their social World.[45] Thus in 1720 a satire on opera employed the term 'republic' in reporting the crisis that the failure of a diva to arrive in England had given the opera's directors: 'It gives me some concern, when I reflect how prodigiously the *demise* of this unfortunate Lady must disconcert the measures of the *Musical Republick*! What councils, and what matter for debate, it must occasion to provide against a disappointment of such importance to their schemes!'[46] Note that such an idea of a cultural 'republic' had a national rather than a cosmopolitan meaning; while in the early use of the term it meant learned men of all nations, it was now used within the context of an essentially national musical culture related to the public sphere.

Thus does the King's Theatre exemplify the extent to which England had moved into a new political era. In France the retreat of Louis XIV from public life in the 1680s and 1690s shifted authority over taste from the royal house to the public and to the musicians who ran the opera, but without nearly as clear a discontinuity as that made by the Glorious Revolution and the political turmoil that ensued for three decades in England. The satire just cited rightly spoke of a Republic rather than an oligarchy, since authority was public and broadly distributed rather than couched in the estates of a few noble families. Leadership passed into the hands not only of the noblemen, but also of theatrical entrepreneurs, musicians, publicists, and men of letters. The fact that writers such as John Dennis,

---

45   Weber, 'L'Institution et son public: l'opéra à Paris et à Londres au XVIIIe siècle'.
46   *The Anti-Theatre*, 29 Mar. 1720. Though musical discourse had its idiosyncrasies, and contained much less political theory than was found in commentary on the fine arts, such uses of the term 'republic' can be related to civic humanism, as discussed by John Pocock in *The Machiavellian Moment: Florentine Political Thought and the Atlantic Republican Tradition* (Princeton: Princeton University Press, 1975); and John Barrell, in *The Political Theory of Painting from Reynolds to Hazlitt: 'The Body of the Public'* (New Haven: Yale University Press, 1986; repr. 1995).

THE *BEAU MONDE* IN LONDON, 1700–1870   85

Joseph Addison and Richard Steele felt compelled to do so much to curb the Italian opera shows how powerful it became – and without a monarch to lead it.[47]

From one modernity towards another

We have argued that the public musical world which began in England at the start of the eighteenth century can be defined as an aspect of modernity, but one that can be seen differently when examined from contrasting time perspectives. On the broadest plane, the public culture of the new capital city became a constant in English society that has lasted to the present. London was the first capital where this kind of capital-city culture developed to a major extent; it has remained among the focal points of Western musical life ever since. Yet we can also see a different framework of cultural modernity from about 1700 to 1870, a musical world based upon closely knit elite groups natural to the urban demographics and the nature of politics in that epoch. The two aspects of modernity were complementary to one another; one could define the change in the nineteenth century as the reshaping of social and cultural modalities within continuing institutional structures.

From this viewpoint, the end of the eighteenth century was a secondary, but not insignificant, point of change. The new order of public cultural life that began at the turn of the eighteenth century moved to a higher level of intensity in the second half of that century, as the publishing industry boomed, theatres expanded and concerts proliferated; and sexual licence became ever more flagrant, especially by the royal princes. During the late 1780s in both London and Paris a movement of serious moral concern arose over the course that public life had taken. Even before the French Revolution one can see members of the World beginning to rethink their life and trying to establish stricter standards of behaviour, embracing a kind of early Victorianism.[48] The main consequence in musical life was a tapering off of public concerts and a shift to more private institutions.[49] Nevertheless, the tight little world of aristocratic musical culture, and all the social appurtenances of its life, continued right up to the middle of the nineteenth century.

England led European musical life much less vigorously in the middle of the nineteenth than in the eighteenth century. Despite London's precocity in its development of public musical life, it took such a role in part because it had long stood on the periphery of the Western musical world. The chief leadership in musical life since the early sixteenth century had come out of Italy, providing the

---

47   On the critique of Italian opera by Addison and Steele, see Knif, *Gentlemen and Spectators*, chs 1 and 2. We do know, however, that George I went to virtually all opera performances when he was in London, and that he gave gifts to major singers that amounted to an indirect subsidy of the company. See Donald Burrows and Robert D. Hume, 'George I, the Haymarket Opera Company and Handel's Water Music', *Early Music*, 19 (1991), 323–41.

48   Wahrman, '*Percy*'s Prologue: From Gender Play to Gender Panic in Eighteenth-Century England'.

49   McVeigh, *Concert Life in London*.

86 WILLIAM WEBER

most fundamental principles of craft, learning and patronage that defined music and its social contexts all over Europe.[50] England, by contrast, stood on the borders of the fast-moving traffic of music and musicians between Rome, Venice, Vienna, Dresden, Munich, Hamburg and Paris; the court went so far as to allow no foreigners, particularly Italians, into its royal chapel.

While the country was pulled much more closely into the vortex of continental musical life after 1700, its musical sensibilities never entirely engaged with it. English musicians held apart from the Italians when they arrived, focusing their careers in directions quite different from their guests. That happened in part because the 'Musical Republick' that constituted the King's Theatre maintained a rigidly Italian repertoire throughout the eighteenth century, presenting no music by English composers on its stage. In the process English composers were discouraged firmly from attempting to distinguish themselves within the more ambitious or publicly prominent genres of music – rather as was true of women composers as a general rule throughout Europe.[51] The modernity of eighteenth-century musical life brought English musicians much business as performers and entrepreneurs; this in turn put London on the international musical map but limited seriously their opportunities for musical creativity.

A wide variety of forces began to bring the elite culture of the long eighteenth century to a close around 1850. These changes did not happen as quickly as those that have been discovered in parliamentary party behaviour,[52] but they were in many respects related to what was going on in politics. First, the gradual growth in the London metropolis in terms of both demography and space distended the social framework that Lady Mary Coke called the World. There simply became too many people one ought to know and gossip about. Simon McVeigh has argued cogently that prior to the 1830s few musicians were at all active in attracting publics to concerts; their main concern was to extend their contacts within the *beau monde* to obtain lucrative opportunities for teaching at home and performing at salons. After 1850 concert life was dominated by a new order of entrepreneurs who became skilled in developing anonymous middle-class audiences.[53] Musicians became less dependent on individual patronage than their predecessors. Now being schooled in conservatories, they had less to do with the old elite social world that had dominated musical life formerly.

---

50   On Italian musical leadership, see especially Hellmut Koenigsberger, 'Republics and Courts in Italian and European Culture in the Sixteenth and Seventeenth Centuries', *Past and Present*, 83 (1979), 32–56; and Iain Fenlon, Introduction, *The Renaissance, Man & Music*, vol. 2 (London: Macmillan, 1989), pp. 1–62 ('Music and Society').

51   Marcia J. Citron, *Gender and the Musical Canon* (Cambridge: Cambridge University Press, 1993). See also Ch. 14 below.

52   See John A. Phillips and Charles Wetherell, 'The Great Reform Act of 1832 and the Political Modernization of England', *American Historical Review*, 100 (1995), 411–36.

53   Simon McVeigh, 'The Musician as Concert-Promoter in London, 1780–1850', in Hans Erich Bödeker, Patrice Veit and Michael Werner, eds, *Le concert et son public: Mutations de la vie musicale en Europe de 1780 à 1914 (France, Allemagne, Angleterre)* (Paris: Editions de la Maison des sciences de l'homme, 2002), pp. 71–92.

Secondly, the opening of politics to new groups that began in the 1830s undermined one of the principal underpinnings of this social world, since from the start it had been linked closely to aristocratic control of the political order. The Concert of Antient Music, the mainstay of the early musical canon run as an aristocratic patriarchy, ended in 1848. The aristocratic opera public, responding to political and cultural challenge, refashioned its etiquette around notions of high art. The public life of the World now became less focused on the opera and much more upon private visits than before.[54]

Thirdly, politico-musical disputes of the sort that had been the highlight of public life all but disappeared. The last major such affair in England was the attempt to found a competing theatre at Covent Garden in 1847, based on lesser nobles and bourgeois. The parallel final *querelle* in France was the visit of Richard Wagner for a production of *Tannhäuser* in 1859.[55] From this time on cadres of professionals, both musicians and critics, took control of the discourse in musical life increasingly away from the circles that had mixed professional and amateur. Christophe Charle's interesting book applies to Britain as much as to France.[56]

Changes in both musical and theatrical life formed an integral part of these shifts. After the middle of the nineteenth century the London theatres, now released from the long-standing monopolistic regulation, began branching out into separate locales for different kinds of entertainment. A similar process took place in the shift from the diversified programmes of the benefit concert to the specific taste of the individual recital; different kinds of concerts served different kinds of tastes. Moreover, repertoires of older works, now called 'classical' music, moved into the focus of musical life, as symphony orchestras and string quartets came to rival the opera, and levels of artistic worth established a new aesthetic and ideological frame of reference. It was from these assumptions that concert programmes began sorting themselves by musical taste.

In 1893 a variety of Society ladies wrote in the *Pall Mall Magazine* on the changes that had come about in their world during the previous 50 years. One said that she had seen evolving 'an entirely new condition of Society in that time' and went on: 'I don't suppose any one will deny that Society in England is as much altered as is possible to conceive in that period.'[57] Another writer declared that 'When – many years ago, alas! – I made my *début* in Society, I found it a collection of people all of the same social position, many of them bound together by ties of

---

54 Jennifer Hall, 'The Refashioning of Fashionable Society: Opera-going and Sociability in England, 1821–61', Ph.D. diss. (Yale University, 1996; Ann Arbor: UMI, 1997).

55 Gerald D. Turbow, 'Art and Politics: Wagnerism in France', in David C. Large and William Weber, eds, *Wagnerism in European Culture and Politics* (Ithaca, NY: Cornell University Press, 1984), pp. 134–66; Marc Baer, *Theatre and Disorder in Late Georgian London* (Oxford: Clarendon Press, 1992); Hall, 'Refashioning of Fashionable Society'.

56 Levine, *Highbrow/Lowbrow: The Emergence of Cultural Hierarchy in America*; Charle, *Naissance des 'intellectuels'*; and Ritchie, 'Cultural Riots: Nineteenth-Century Theater in England and America'.

57 Mary Jeune, 'More about Society', *Pall Mall Magazine*, 1/3 (1893), 422–3.

88   WILLIAM WEBER

relationship, knowing each other more or less intimately, and also tolerably well acquainted with each other's financial position. All belonging to the same *monde*, poverty was not looked upon as a crime.'[58] The new diversity of elite worlds bothered people; the Countess of Cork, another contributor, wondered if 'a series of different sets devoid of the elements of fusion cannot accurately be defined as Society'.[59]

The fragmentation of musical life into diverse worlds, indeed the split between popular and classical, formed part of this reordering of elites. Lady Frances Evelyn Brooke declared that 'it happens that in place of half a hundred grandees, the world of fashion has swollen to the enormous and unwieldy dimensions with which we are now familiar'. That did have good consequences, in large part in musical life, she suggested. She pointed to a 'satisfactory symptom' in 'the modern enthusiasm for music, which for the first time in our generation has made really good opera in London both possible and profitable; it may be that the intellectual gratification which comes from music is more valuable than all others ... bringing to-day the extreme relief of beauty, in the form of sound, to great numbers'.[60] By that she meant the relatively new principle of fidelity to the composer's score and intentions, found most vividly in the Wagnerian movement and in the early music movement.[61]

Does all this confirm the argument, made most directly by J. C. D. Clark, that eighteenth-century England should be seen as an *ancien régime*? On the one hand, too much of the most basic framework of musical culture throughout the modern period arose in England at this time for the term to be valid across the board. At the turn of the eighteenth century there were established structures of petty capitalism by musicians and the location of public concerts at the centre of elite social life, all of which became a permanent condition, a framework of modernity, within musical life. The leadership that high church Tories exerted in establishing the idea of 'ancient music' was quintessentially modern in its canonic ideology.

Yet on the other hand, the term does ring true in a significant respect. Many commentators of the 1830s and 1840s certainly thought that England needed to emerge from a 'Gothic' age in which the elites exercised their authority in oligarchic fashion. Musical commentators called for the transformation of operatic taste into what they thought would be a more serious mode and identified the manners and mores of traditional opera-goers as part of a kind of *ancien régime*.[62] These ideologists challenged the tight circles of nobles who had dominated the opera and used it as the cultural manifestation of the broad oligarchy of the Hanoverian regime; they were stunningly successful in redefining the most basic

---

58 'Society: A Retrospect', by 'A Woman of the World', *Pall Mall Magazine*, 1/4 (1893), 577.

59 Countess of Cork, 'Society Again', *Pall Mall Magazine*, 1/1 (1893), 39.

60 Lady Frances Evelyn Brooke, 'What is Society?', *Pall Mall Magazine*, 1/2 (1893), 236.

61 Harry Haskell, *The Early Music Revival: A History* (London: Thames & Hudson, 1988; New York, Dover Publications, 1996).

62 Hall, 'Refashioning of Fashionable Society'; Weber, *Music and the Middle Class*. J. C. D. Clark first used the term *ancien régime* for England of this period in *English Society, 1688–1832*.

terms in which opera was discussed. Both the rake at the opera and the catch-singing director of the Concert of Antient Music epitomized this Old Order. The new connoisseur of 'classical' music prided himself upon the lofty philosophical role that was now invested in his authority; he saw his predecessors – Horace Walpole and his friends – engaging in trivial enterprises in hunting for operatic talent.[63]

The argument that a broadly defined condition of modernity came into existence at the turn of the eighteenth century is not a Whiggish interpretation of this history. If anything, it goes in a quite different direction, since it suggests that the most basic aspects of modernity – open-ended politics and the public cultural life natural to the new capital city – came into place quickly at the start of the century. Change came less from linear development of a progressive order – liberalism or any rise of the bourgeoisie – than from shifts caused by the adaptation of upper-class life to social change and political crisis. What happened around 1700, 1750, 1790 and 1830 came from efforts by members of the ruling classes to come to grips with the big problems they faced. The closely knit interpersonal fabric of elite culture and politics during this period proved quite malleable to new and different needs.

Jacques Revel offers an elegant model for considering the problem of modernity.[64] He sees between 1650 and 1800 a set of shifts, as intellectuals and their society moved in contrasting directions in defining the authority by which popular culture was understood and controlled. While a professionally based field of anthropology was the product of this thinking in the late eighteenth century, Revel does not see it as a modernizing force and indeed argues that the shifts were non-linear in nature. One might locate such a point of view philosophically in the attempt to find a middle ground between system and relativism, a position recently termed 'pragmatic realism'.[65] Though by his analysis anthropology was established in a cultural context that should be considered modern, Revel does not interpret it as an all-encompassing modernizing process; the contrasts between these shifts are more important than any ongoing historical process. Social and intellectual structures did not necessarily grow from small to large, but rather society moved in different directions in succeeding periods to find solutions to new social needs and political conflicts. Thus while early modern English musical culture laid down structures we should consider modern, it was not undergoing a process of modernization.

---

63 See Jeffrey Hay, 'The Colloquial Musical Metaphysics of Francis Hueffer and George Bernard Shaw', Ph.D. diss. (University of California, San Diego, 1994).

64 Jacques Revel, 'Forms of Expertise: Intellectuals and "Popular" Culture in France, 1650–1800', in Steven L. Kaplan, ed., *Understanding Popular Culture: Europe from the Middle Ages to the Nineteenth Century* (Berlin, New York: Mouton, 1984), pp. 255–73.

65 Appleby et al., *Telling the Truth about History*, pp. 241–70.

PART TWO

Sources and Genres

CHAPTER SIX

'The first talents of Europe': British Music Printers and Publishers and Imported Instrumental Music in the Eighteenth Century

Jenny Burchell

The cataloguing of repertoire performed in miscellaneous concerts in Britain throughout the eighteenth century reveals an astonishing diversity in all genres and in all parts of the country. Although local repertoire was influenced by local taste and circumstances, a common core repertoire can be distinguished; the majority of it was published in London. A small amount of music was published in most of the larger centres, but only the population of London was large enough to support this activity to any great degree. London was not necessarily the entrance port for visiting musicians from Europe, but it was certainly the main entrance to Britain for their music.

A comparative investigation of printed music available in Britain in the period 1750–99, its sources and consumers, though highly desirable, is far beyond the scope of the present chapter. This study is a preliminary examination, intended for expansion into such an investigation, of two facets of the journey of instrumental music through the printed medium from composer to performer: the routes to publication, and the role of the publishers in defining repertoire.

Although music publishers covered all genres, styles and tastes, from circus tunes and the latest songs of the less salubrious theatrical entertainments and pleasure gardens, via a wide range of theatre music, dances, instruction books and church music, to the most demanding symphonic repertoire and Italian opera, this study is concerned only with instrumental music. Dances and marches are not included as these tended to be of primarily local interest and were rarely imported from or exported to other countries. Arrangements of works are also generally excluded from consideration because they were usually published after the original versions, and were therefore not significant in the introduction of those works in their primary form to the public.

If identifying concert repertoire is a tortuous process, constructing a reasonably accurate account of any given publisher's lists is all the more so. Although many publications from the second half of the eighteenth century include either a page

94   JENNY BURCHELL

or two listing works from the same publisher, or the titles of a handful of similar works at the foot of the title page, complete surviving catalogues for individual publishers are relatively few and their locations scattered, so that finding them involves a strong element of luck. In order to access as much material as possible this study is based largely on information extracted from the *British Union-Catalogue of Early Music*.[1] Short titles are used in the text. Two caveats must be observed: first, that conclusions are based on extant material, and there is no way of knowing what is lost; second, many dates of publication are approximate, so that extreme caution is required when classifying the sources of a given work. Despite these problems, and the preliminary nature of this study, nevertheless it is possible to reach some conclusions.

From composer to performer

Examination of title-pages of eighteenth-century publications reveals three basic routes to publication: publication by subscription; private printing; and publication by a third party.

Publication by subscription was a means of covering costs in advance. The intention to publish would be advertised, usually in London papers and often much further afield, by the composer or sponsoring organization, and publication would not proceed until sufficient subscriptions had been received. The British Library's card catalogue of music within their holdings which was published by subscription, though not comprehensive, provides a substantial list of music published in this way during the eighteenth century.[2] Some 345 items, of which 334 were published in Britain, are listed for this period; these are categorized by genre in Table 6.1. The majority of these works were composed or edited by native composers, and publication by subscription was the only one of the three basic routes into print which was used more by native than by foreign composers, perhaps because they were more likely to be able to raise a group of personal subscribers.

The earliest large-scale works to be published by subscription in Britain appear to have been the work of the publisher John Cluer, who, following the success of his two volumes of *A pocket companion for gentlemen and ladies* (1724 and 1726), used the same method to finance the printing of several of Handel's operas in score, including *Alexander* (*Alessandro*: 1726), *Scipio* (*Scipione*: 1726), and

---

1 *The British Union-Catalogue of Early Music printed before the year 1801: A record of the holdings of over one hundred libraries throughout the British Isles*, ed. Edith B. Schnapper, 2 vols (London: Butterworths Scientific Publications, 1957). See also Charles Smith and William C. Humphries, *Music Publishing in the British Isles from the beginning until the middle of the nineteenth century* (Oxford: Basil Blackwell, 1970).

2 This resource is discussed in Jenny Burchell, 'Musical societies in subscription lists: an overlooked resource', in Michael Burden and Irena Cholij, eds, *A Handbook for Studies in 18th-Century English Music IX* (Oxford: Burden & Cholij, 1998).

Table 6.1 Analysis by genre of works published by subscription

Small-scale vocal music, including songs, canzonets, cantatas, glees, etc.	88
Miscellaneous collections	10
National collections of songs and other music (mostly Scottish)	15
Dance collections, including Scottish dances	15
Church music	
Collections and services	25
Psalm collections	15
Anthems	14
Hymns	6
Total	60
Tutors	
Vocal	1
Instrumental (cello)	1
Composition	1
Total	3
Oratorio, opera and theatre music	35
Circus tunes	1
Instrumental music	
Overtures/symphonies	3
Concertos	23
Divertimenti	1
Marches	2
Quartets	1
Trios	4
Sonatas	41
Solos	11
Lessons	13
Suites	2
Variations	1
Voluntaries	4
Miscellaneous keyboard	1
Total	107

Admetus (*Admeto*: 1727). He had already published Handel's operas *Giulio Cesare* and *Tamerlane* (*Tamerlano*: both 1724) as commercial prospects. After Cluer's death in 1728 John Walsh became Handel's principal publisher. Walsh's successor William Randall published complete scores of *Messiah* (?1767), *Judas Maccabaeus* (1769), *Jephtha* (1770), *Israel in Egypt* (1771), *Saul* (1773) and *Joshua* (1774) by subscription, with a further series consisting of *Esther* (1783), *Belshazzar* (1784), *The Occasional Oratorio* (1784), *Susanna* (1784), *Joseph* (?1785), *Solomon* (?1787) and *Theodora* (?1787) by H. Wright, who also billed himself as Walsh's successor, but actually took over the business from Randall's widow. The editions of Randall and Wright are exceptional in that they published by subscription works which were already in circulation.

Subscription was the usual means of publication of large new collections of church music (or posthumous new editions) such as the collections entitled *Cathedral Music* of William Boyce (1760), Maurice Greene (*c*.1770), William Croft (*c*.1775), Samuel Arnold (1790), Matthew Camidge (1790), William Hayes (1795; and its earlier incarnation as *Forty select anthems in score*, 1743) and Thomas Sanders Dupuis (1797), as well as Thomas Ebdon's *Sacred Music* (?1790). All of these are extensive works, not only expensive to produce, but limited in their probable consumers. The same is true of the psalm and anthem collections, and indeed for several of the collections of Scottish music listed in the catalogue.

Publication of such monumental works by subscription usually appears to have been a matter of collaboration between composer and publisher, or even the responsibility of the publisher alone. The publisher William Napier found this process the most convenient (and certain) method of funding the publication of several collections of Scottish music including *A complete collection of the pastoral music of Scotland* (1789) and *A selection of original Scots songs* (1790–95); certainly the majority of the title-pages carry the imprint only of the publisher. But two exceptions to this are found with Handel, with the publication of *Alexander's Feast* (1738) and the *Twelve grand concertos in seven parts* (1740). Both were published by John Walsh by subscription, but both title-pages carry the words 'Publish'd for the Author. London. Printed for & Sold by I. Walsh'. Apart from these Walsh appears to have published only *Justin* (*Giustino*: 1737) by subscription, and there is no reference on its title-page to Handel as the publisher.

The remainder of the works listed in the catalogue are smaller in scale. The inclusion of 15 collections of glees is surprising at first sight, given the popularity of the genre and the number of these to be found on most publishers' lists, and that the composers include Samuel Webbe (the elder) and John Danby (three publications). Several of the other composers such as Pieter Hellendaal, James Brooks and Thomas Ebdon were not based in London, however, and although Ebdon's *Six glees, for three voices*, op. 3 (*c*.1785) was printed by 'Longman and Broderip, for the Author', Brooks's *Second set of twelve glees* (1798?) were published in Bath, and Hellendaal's by his own music shop in Cambridge.

The reasons for publication by subscription of the instrumental works, and indeed the majority of the remaining vocal works, are not always obvious at first sight. If we consider the categories listed in Table 6.1 there seems no reason for the large number of concertos, for example. Apart from the cost of engraving a large work for publication, the reputation of the composer would have been an important factor in the decision to publish by subscription. In all the instrumental categories examined here, a significant proportion are the work of composers usually resident outside London, and therefore perhaps perceived by publishers as not commanding a wide audience. All three of the overtures or symphonies, and more than half of the concertos, were composed outside London, as well as a number of small-scale works. The composers and their locations are listed in Table 6.2. Almost all of these works were printed in London. Avison's concertos provide the only examples of concertos by a native musician actually published elsewhere. Although his concertos were sold through London shops, with the exception of the *Twelve concertos*, op. 9 (1766) they were engraved and printed by Joseph Barber in Newcastle.

Table 6.2   Composers and their locations

Jane Guest	Bath
Capel Bond	Coventry
Thomas Ebdon	Durham
John Garth	Durham
Francesco Barsanti	Edinburgh
Giovanni Giornovichi	Edinburgh
Girolamo Stabilini	Edinburgh
William Jackson	Exeter
William Felton	Hereford
John Valentine	Leicester
Robert Wainwright	Manchester
Charles Avison	Newcastle
Robert Barber	Newcastle
Thomas Wright	Newcastle
Henry Hargrave	Nottingham
Samuel Wise	Nottingham
Philip Hayes	Oxford
Thomas Norris	Oxford

In the case of the works for small ensemble the proportion originating outside London is considerably smaller. Many of the remaining works are slight, the composers obscure even in the eighteenth century, and the list of subscribers correspondingly short, suggesting that these works were unlikely to appeal to a wide audience. It is notable that many of those publishing keyboard works by subscription (often optimistically labelled 'Op. 1') are known only by these works; there is no surviving evidence of any other compositional activity.

It is tempting to assume that publication by subscription can be used as qualitative assessment, or at least as a guide to popular taste, but although this is clearly an unsuitable indicator in the case of the church music, neither does examination of the complete publication history of instrumental works published first by subscription justify this assumption to any reliable degree. While it is certainly the case that a set of works published by subscription late in a composer's publishing career tends to suggest that earlier sales may not have been entirely satisfactory, as for example John Lewis Hoeberechts's *Three sonatas*, op. 11 (1799) or William Jackson of Exeter's *Eight sonatas*, op. 10 (1773), Charles Avison's *Twelve concertos*, op. 9 are an example of a work in which the reverse is true. Avison's first sets of concertos were published in Newcastle (op. 2 by subscription), but also sold in London. His op. 4 set was published only in London – by John Johnson, without subscription – and reprinted several times. Op. 9 was published by subscription by R. Johnson in London, then reissued for Avison and sold by Robert Bremner, who went on to publish his op. 10 set. It should be further noted that publishers often subscribed to multiple copies of a work, which would then be sold in their own shops.

Of those composers listed in the British Library's subscription card index with more than one piece of instrumental music published by any means, the majority had pieces published directly by a publisher, even if they also had works published privately. Table 6.3 outlines the proportion of the works by these composers according to method of publication. From examination of the works listed – and their lists of subscribers – it is clear that publication by subscription was chosen for one of two principal reasons: either the work in question was so large that its preparation for publication would be prohibitively expensive, or it was such that publishers would regard it as unlikely to sell in sufficient quantity, either because it was of limited use, the composer was not well known or because it came into the category of what could crudely be described as vanity press.

Even where a composer had an established reputation, residence in London did not guarantee unassisted publication. If no subscription was taken it was far from uncommon for relatively unknown composers to be obliged to accept at least partial responsibility for publication themselves. The words 'Printed for the Author' appear on many title-pages, and carry the implication that the work has been published at the instigation – and therefore almost certainly the expense – of the composer or occasionally the editor. This is borne out by the imprint of Tartini's *XII Sonatas for two violins and a bass* (1750), which were 'Printed at the Author's Expence'.

The arrangements for selling these works varied, but two methods were most common. In the first, the printer's name is not given, and the words 'Printed for the Author' are followed by 'and may be had of him at his House', followed by the

Table 6.3 Analysis of publication method for individual composers

Composer	Method of publication			
	Subscription	Author	Direct	No imprint
Barbandt	1	2	2	—
R. Barber	1	1	—	—
Barsanti	1	1	1	1?
C. Barthélemon	1	1	1	1
W. Bates	1	—	3	—
J. C. Beckwith	1	—	2	—
George Berg	1	3	2	—
H. Burgess (younger)	1	1	—	—
Cattanei	1	1	—	—
Cervetto (elder)	1	1	4	1
Defesch	2	—	4	1
Felton	1	—	7	—
Festing	5	—	4	—
John Garth	1	2	3	—
Joseph Gibbs	1	1	—	—
Henry Hargrave	1	1	—	—
John Hebden	1	1	—	—
Henry Heron	1	—	1	—
John Lewis Hoeberechts	1	5	10	—
Charles Frederick Horn	1	2	1	—
William Jackson (Exeter)	1	—	2	—
Samuel Jarvis	1	—	1	—
Peter Anton Kreusser	1	1	—	—
James Lyndon	1	—	1	—
J. C. Mantel	1	2	—	—
Maria Hester Park	1	2	—	—
Pasquale Ricci	1	—	6	—
P. Sazoi	1	—	—	?
Robert Wainwright	1	—	2	—

100   JENNY BURCHELL

address, rendering them a useful resource for biographical research. It was also common practice for composers to sign such publications in an attempt to prevent fraud. In the second – probably more common – version of this arrangement the printer's name was given. When this was the case the printer generally also acted as distributor and seller, which would have provided additional income for the publisher without major outlay.

Private publication was common among newcomers to Britain, and among musicians who were perhaps known more as performers; as with the large collections of church music which were published by subscription, it is probable that publishers were wary of publishing works for which they could not readily identify a reasonable market. Independent private publication and the consequent personal advertising could work in the composer's favour, however, notwithstanding the costs of engraving and advertising the work. When Carl Stamitz arrived in Britain in 1777, for example, almost his first action was to publish two sets of works – *Six trios*, op. 14 and a set of symphonies, op. 13, which he advertised in the *Gazetteer and New Daily Advertiser* on 10 and 17 May. As he was primarily a performer it was obviously to his advantage to have his address broadcast as widely as possible in the hope that more work would follow, and the title-page of the symphonies described him as 'Compositeur du musique de Monsieur le Marechal et Duc de Noailles', which by that point was certainly no longer the case. As Stamitz established his reputation as composer and performer in London he was able to sell the plates, and the symphonies were reprinted first by John Welcker in 1780, then by John Preston (1781), Preston & Son (1790) and T. Preston (1800).[3]

So far we have considered two possible routes to dissemination in printed form – publication by subscription, and private publication, whether independent or under the aegis of an established publisher. But the publication of the majority of printed music in Britain seems to have been the sole responsibility of the publisher. From the composer's perspective this third route – publication financed by a publishing house – was almost certainly the simplest, since it involved no financial outlay in preparation, nor the considerable attendant complications of storing engraved plates once printing was complete. Subsequent reissue by the publisher without the author's direct participation must have been seen as a desirable outcome, and it is scarcely surprising to find that a relatively high proportion of works printed privately were indeed later reissued, or published in new editions – once their marketworthiness was proved. In practice most composers used a combination of private and direct publication as outlined by the examples which follow.

The diversity of routes to publication was particularly helpful to the many foreign composers who either visited Britain or settled there. Carl Friedrich Abel,

---

3 See Jenny Burchell, 'Printing, publishing and the migration of sources: the case of Carl Stamitz', *Brio*, 27 (Nov. 1990), 59–66; reprinted with minor revision in *Fontes Artis Musicae*, 38 (1991), 130–38.

BRITISH MUSIC PRINTERS AND PUBLISHERS 101

who arrived in London in the 1757–58 season and remained there as impresario, gamba-player and composer until his death in 1785, published 25 pieces or sets of instrumental music (and no vocal works) in London. His first publication to which a definite date can be assigned is the set of *Six sonatas*, op. 2, published in London by Robert Bremner in 1760, and followed in 1761 by the publication of his *Six overtures*, op. 1 by John Johnson. With the exception of one contribution to Bremner's series *The Periodical Overture in 8 parts* (1766), and two sets of trios published by Longman, Lukey & Co. (*c*.1775 and *c*.1777), they were the only compositions which Abel either chose or was able to sell directly to a publisher until 1783 when Bremner published *Six trios*, op. 16. The three publications which followed the opp. 1 and 2 sets – *Six overtures*, op. 4 (1762), *Six sonatas*, op. 5 (1764) and *Sei sonate*, op. 6 (1765) – were produced privately.

The chronological list of earliest editions of each work (Table 6.4) summarizes the distribution of publication methods. Over half of the works published by Abel in London appeared first at his own instigation, and the obvious implication is that neither Bremner nor Johnson regarded either the op. 1 or op. 2 publications as a success. But both works were reprinted, as indeed were many of the others – the op. 2 sonatas by Bremner (*c*.1765), and the *Six overtures*, op. 1 by Thompson & Son (*c*.1763), then by C. & S. Thompson (*c*.1765), and finally by Robert Bremner (*c*.1770). Bremner also published Abel's keyboard adaptation of the overtures (*c*.1765). It is notable, however, that after Abel's death the original versions of his works were not reprinted, though a number of arrangements were.

J. C. Bach, on the other hand, seems to have had little difficulty in getting his work into print. Having settled in London in 1762, he had published five sets or individual works by the end of 1763 (see Table 6.5). Of Bach's entire list of published music only two sets of instrumental works were printed privately – *Six sonatas*, op. 2 and *Six simphonies*, op. 3 (1765), possibly because of the success of the Bach–Abel concerts and the opportunity which they presented for his instrumental works to reach a wide audience, though this does not seem to have assisted Abel. The *Six concertos*, op. 1 proved particularly popular and new editions by both [Peter] Welcker and R. Bremner appeared *c*.1765; Welcker reprinted them again *c*.1770. Welcker also acquired the *Six simphonies*, op. 3, with a new edition *c*.1768 and reissue *c*.1770. Bremner then published a new edition of the same symphonies *c*.1775.

Although Bremner published two more of Bach's symphonies in *The Periodical Overture in 8 parts* as No. 15 (1766) and No. 44 (*c*.1775), the rest of Bach's instrumental works – and the vast majority of his vocal ones – were published first by [Peter] Welcker, then from 1777 to 1781 by John Welcker. The *Four sonatas and two duets*, op. 18 were the only pieces published by John Welcker after his insolvency in 1780, although after a break of a mere two months he resumed business as a publisher until about 1785. The last new work to be published while Bach was still alive, *Six grand overtures*, op. 18 (?1781), was published by W. Forster.

JENNY BURCHELL

Table 6.4 Carl Friedrich Abel: distribution of publication methods

1760	*Six sonatas*, op. 2	Author (Bremner)
1761	*Six overtures*, op. 1	John Johnson
1762	*Six overtures in eight parts*, op. 4	Author
1764	*Six sonatas*, op. 5	Author
1765	*Sei sonate a solo*, op. 6	Author
*c.*1765	*Six sonatas for two violins*, op. 3	Author
*c.*1765	*Six overtures*, op. 1 (adapted for the harpsichord or piano forte by the author)	Robert Bremner
1766	*Periodical Overture in 8 parts* no. 16 [in D]	Robert Bremner
1767	*Six simphonies*, op. 7	Author (Bremner)
1769	*Six quartettos*, op. 8	Author (Bremner)
*c.*1770	*Six sonatas*, op. 9	Author (Bremner)
1773	*Six simphonies*, op. 10	Author (Bremner)
1774	*Six concerts pour le clavecin*, op. 11	Author (Bremner)
1775	*A second set of quartettes*, op. 12	Author (Bremner)
*c.*1775	*Three trios for a violin, violoncello and bass*	Longman, Lukey & Co.
1777	*Six sonates pour le clavecin*, op. 13	Author (Bremner)
*c.*1777	*Les suites des trois premieres trios*	Longman, Lukey & Co.
1778	*Six overtures*, op. 14	Author (Bremner)
*c.*1780	*Six quatuors*, dediés à Monseigneur le Prince de Prusse	Author
	Six quartettos, op. 15	William Napier
1783	*Six trios*, op. 16	Robert Bremner
*c.*1785	*Six overtures*, op. 17	Robert Bremner
	Duetto for two violoncellos	Birchall & Andrews
	Six sonatas for the piano forte with an accompaniment for a violin, dedicated to the Queen	Harrison & Co.
	Four trios, op. 16	John Preston

Table 6.5 J. C. Bach: publications by end of 1763

The Favourite Songs in the Opera call'd Orione	John Walsh
Six favourite overtures [*Orione, La Calamità, Artaserse, Il Tutore e la Pupilla, Cascina* and *Astarto*]	John Walsh
Periodical Overture in 8 parts no. 1 [in D]	Robert Bremner
Six concertos for keyboard, op. 1	No imprint
Six sonatas, op. 2	Printed for the Author

These were by no means the only works to appear under Bach's name during his lifetime or indeed after it. Other works were published by A. Hummel, Longman, Lukey & Co., Longman & Broderip, and James & John Simpson before Bach's death, and by John Preston, James Cooper, W. Campbell, and Longman & Broderip after it. But with the exception of the *Favourite overture in the opera of Carattaco*, published by Longman & Broderip (*c*.1780), and *A favourite concerto for the harpsichord, or piano-forte, etc.* [Op. XIII, no. 4] also published by Longman, Lukey & Co. in 1777, the remaining works published in Bach's name are not actually by Bach. The majority of his authentic works were reprinted at least twice, and reprinting – as well as the publication of spurious works in his name – continued until at least the end of the eighteenth century. Many of the new editions or reissues were carried out by whichever Welcker happened to be the current publisher.

Despite the differences in level of compositional activity and consequently in volume and means of publication, both Bach and Abel, after an initial trial of several publishers, maintained a working relationship with a single publisher. Other composers were not so consistent. Muzio Clementi arrived in England in 1766–67 at the age of about 14, and settled in London in 1774. Both the *Six sonatas*, op. 1 and a *Duett*, op. 6 were published *c*.1775, by Welcker and S. Babb respectively. By 1786, when Longman & Broderip published *La Chasse*, op. 16, Clementi had published some 12 sets of works in England, under no fewer than 10 imprints (including reprints): Welcker, S. Babb, J. Welcker, S. A. & P. Thompson, J. Blundell, Preston & Son, J. Dale, Longman & Broderip, John Kerpen, and J. Preston – as well as several which were privately printed. After this chaotic beginning, however, Clementi settled with Longman & Broderip – later Longman, Clementi & Co. – with a return to both J. Dale and Preston & Son whom he had favoured slightly before 1786, from 1791 to about 1795.

The inconsistency of publishing method, not only between private and commercial publication, but in variety of imprint, considered with the sheer volume of material produced, suggests less a prolific composer – though Clementi undoubtedly was one – than one desperate to get every note into print with the utmost dispatch in order to reach the widest possible audience, although with increasing age and reputation Clementi was able to reduce the number of imprints.

The list of works published by the violinist François-Hippolyte Barthélemon, who settled in London (from France) in 1764, falls somewhere between Clementi and Bach in its coherence, although the list is one of the most diverse found (Table 6.6). Barthélemon apparently had no difficulty in persuading publishers to buy his music, since none of the early works was published privately. Again the familiar names of Welcker, John Welcker, and Longman & Broderip appear more or less in succession, though here they are interspersed with the imprints of publishers who are either minor or more inclined to deal with the cheap end of the market.

It seems that the common pattern for foreign musicians visiting or resident in Britain was to publish a group of works rather quickly, often distributed between

Table 6.6 F.-H. Barthélemon: publications

1765	*Six sonatas*, op. 1	Welcker
*c.*1765	*Six sonatas*, op. 2	Welcker
*c.*1770	*A favourite Irish air made a rondeau* [vln, hpd]	S. Lee: Dublin
	Six duetts for two violins, op. 4	C. & S. Thompson
1775	*Two favourite solo concertos*	Longman, Lukey & Broderip
*c.*1775	*Six concertos*, op. 3	Welcker
	Six petites sonates pour le piano forte	Welcker
	A quartetto [op. 12 no. 1]	R. Wornum
*c.*1776	*Six overtures*, op. 6	Author
1776	*Six overtures*, op. 6	J. Welcker [later edn]
*c.*1780	*Six duettos*, op. 8	John Welcker
1784	*Six duets*	J. Fentum
*c.*1785	*Six quartettos*, op. 9	Wm Napier
	Six solos, op. 10	Longman and Broderip
	Six voluntaries, op. 11	Longman and Broderip
*c.*1790	*A new tutor for the violin*	Author
	Preludes for the violin	Author
	Six quartetts, op. 12	R. Wornum
	A new tutor for the harpsichord or piano forte	Author
*c.*1795	*Tutor for the harp*	Longman and Broderip
1796	*Three favourite duets*	Culliford, Rolfe & Barrow

several publishers, with as few as possible published privately. Even within the works of the composers detailed above, a common group of publishers emerges: the Welckers and J. Blundell, Robert Bremner, Longman & Broderip, and the Prestons – with an outer group on the periphery consisting of the Thompsons, William Napier, R. Wornum, J. Fentum, and W. Forster (and others). The same group can be identified in publications by native composers, though native composers who were prolific publishers produced more printed vocal music than instrumental – William Boyce, for example, published only four instrumental works.

With Samuel Arnold's works we see the familiar pattern of clusters of publications from a single house, at a particular period. Although the list in Table 6.7 gives only the instrumental music, the pattern is generally replicated by his vocal music. Arnold's earliest instrumental works were published by Welcker; J. Blundell, as Welcker's business successor, seems to have been a logical progression. Longman & Broderip published an edition of the *Second set*

BRITISH MUSIC PRINTERS AND PUBLISHERS

Table 6.7   Samuel Arnold: instrumental publications

1768	*A favourite lesson*	Welcker
*c.*1770	*Eight lessons*, op. 7	Welcker
1775	*A second sett of eight lessons*, op. 10	Welcker
*c.*1775	*Twelve minuets*	Welcker
	Six overtures for the harpsichord, op. 8	Welcker
*c.*1777–79	*A set of progressive lessons*, op. 12, bk. 1	Author (John Welcker)
*c.*1779	*Eight lessons*, op. 7	J. Blundell
*c.*1780	*A third sett of eight sonatas*, op. 11	J. Blundell
*c.*1780	*Six overtures in eight parts*, op. 8	Longman and Broderip
1780–85	*A set of progressive lessons*, op. 12, bk. 1	Author (Longman & Broderip)
1782	*Three concerto's*, op. 15	Author
1783	*Three grand sonatas*, op. 23	Author
*c.*1785	*Eight lessons*, op. 7	Longman and Broderip [later edn]
*c.*1785	*A second sett of eight lessons*, op. 10	Longman and Broderip [later edn]
*c.*1785	*A third sett of eight sonatas*, op. 11	Longman and Broderip [later edn]
1787	*Dr Arnold's New Instructions for the German-flute*	Harrison

of lessons, op. 10 (published by Welcker in 1775) during this period, however, and the *Progressive lessons*, op. 12 (*c.*1777–79) were privately printed, though they were sold for Arnold by [John] Welcker, then by Longman & Broderip (1780–85). In spite of Longman & Broderip's apparent interest in publishing Arnold's works – they published more of his vocal works than any other publisher – they produced only one publication which was not already in print; two other publications from this period were privately printed, and the *New Instructions for the German-flute* (1787) were published by Harrison.

James Hook's publications, contemporaneous with those of Arnold, were also issued predominantly by Welcker for the first few years. Until the 1790s, however, Hook seems to have been less inclined to settle with any one publisher, and C. & S. Thompson, later S. A. & P. Thompson, recur throughout the list (Table 6.8). Instrumental works represent only a small fraction of Hook's compositions; his œuvre includes many stage works and some 2000 songs, many of them composed for performance at pleasure gardens. His list of instrumental works is not short, however, and it is notable that not one item on it was published either privately or by subscription.

JENNY BURCHELL

Table 6.8   James Hook: publications

1767	*Five lessons and a favourite overture*	John Johnson
1769	*Favourite concerto with variations on Lovely Nancy* [op. 5]	Welcker
*c.*1770	*Chiling o Guiery, with variations*	J. Preston
1774	*Six concertos for harpsichord*	Welcker
	Six solos for a German flute	C. and S. Thompson
*c.*1774	*Concerto* [*Six concertos*, no. 1]	Welcker
*c.*1775	*For Sally I sigh, with variations*	Welcker
	Lovely Nymph, with variations	Welcker
	Rural Felicity, with variations	Welcker
	Saw you my father, with variations	Welcker
	To thee oh gentle sleep, with variations	Welcker
	Tweed side, with variations	Welcker
	When I followed a lass, with variations	Welcker
	Six sonatas, op. 16	Welcker
	Martin's minuet, with variations	C. and S. Thompson
	Six sonatas for two German flutes	C. and S. Thompson
1776	*Twelve sonatinos* [op. 12?]	C. & S. Thompson
*c.*1776	*The Jolly Young Waterman, with variations*	Welcker
1778	*Favourite concerto* [op. 5]	S. & A. Thompson [later edn]
	Lady Priscilla Bertie's minuet, with variations	S. & A. Thompson
	Six sonatas, op. 17	Wm Randall
1779	*A second sett of twelve sonatinos*	S. A. & P. Thompson
*c.*1780	*Six sonatas*, op. 16	Longman and Broderip [later edn]
	When war's alarms, with variations	S. A. & P. Thompson
1781	*Duetto*, op. 44	J. Preston
1782	*Third set of twelve divertimentinos*, op. 25	T. Skillern
	Six solos, op. 24	S. A. & P. Thompson
*c.*1783	*Chanson de Malbrouk, with variations*	J. Preston
1784	*Twelve divertimentinos*, op. 33	T. Skillern
	Six grand lessons, op. 30	J. Preston
*c.*1785	*Six conversation pieces*, op. 40	S. A. & P. Thompson
	Guida di Musica, op. 37	J. Preston
	Lesson of the harpsichord	T. Skillern
1788	*Six sonatas*, op. 54	Preston
1790	*Six grand concertos*, op. 55	Preston & Son
*c.*1790	*The Royal Chace, a favourite sonata*	Preston & Son
1793	*Three sonatas*, op. 72	A. Bland & Weller
1794	*Guida di Musica*, pt 2, op. 75	Preston & Son
1795	*Three grand sonatas*, op. 78	Preston & Son

Table 6.8 *continued*

c.1795	*Six sonatas*, op. 77	A. Bland & Weller
1796	*New Guida di Musica*, op. 81	A. Bland & Weller
1797	*Three favourite duetts*, op. 82	A. Bland & Weller
	Three grand sonatas, op. 84	A. Bland & Weller
1798	*Six trios*, op. 83	Bland & Weller

The publishing pattern of the Durham composer John Garth (*c*.1722–*c*.1810) is similar to that of J. C. Bach though the scale is quite different. Garth was the organist at Durham and organizer of the subscription concerts there in the 1750s (see Ch. 4 above). His printed compositional output is relatively small (a total of six items) and consists entirely of instrumental music, but whereas Avison – his near-neighbour and fellow impresario in Newcastle – had his works printed locally, Garth's were produced entirely in London. His cello concertos – his first publication – were printed privately by John Johnson in 1760, but there was a gap of some eight years before he published his *Six sonatas*, op. 2 by subscription with Bremner. The sonatas evidently proved popular; subsequent editions were produced by Welcker (*c*.1770), J. Blundell, Welcker's son-in-law (*c*.1780), and 'J. Bland for the Proprietor' (*c*.1786). John Welcker also produced a new edition of the cello concertos *c*.1780. *A second sett of six sonata's*, op. 4 was published directly by [Peter] Welcker in 1772, following a set of *Six Voluntaries*, op. 3 in 1771, but it was not reprinted in London. *A fourth sett of six sonatas*, op. 6 was also directly published by John Welcker (*c*.1778), but the fifth and final set, op. 7, was 'Printed for the Author & sold by Robson' in 1782. No record is found of a third set, though both set and opus numberings suppose its existence.

While the vast majority of music composed in Britain was published in London, it has already been observed that a small amount was published in other centres by composers such as Pieter Hellendaal (Cambridge), Charles Avison (Newcastle) and Philip Hayes and Paul Alday (Oxford). Many composers also sought publication in Europe.

Although composers of European origin who were resident in Britain unquestionably had the tastes of their immediate audiences in mind, and had no particular intention of leaving the country, many of them clearly remained essentially cosmopolitan in outlook. J. C. Bach, whose reputation as a composer was well established before his arrival in England, is a particularly good example. The *Six simphonies*, op. 3 were privately printed in London in 1765, and were also published by J. J. Hummel in Amsterdam at about the same time; and the *Six sonatas*, op. 16 were published by J. J. Hummel in Berlin *c*.1785, after publication by Welcker *c*.1776. Other European editions which appeared subsequent to London publication include *Six sonatas*, op. 2 (A. Hummel, London, *c*.1770; S. Markordt, Amsterdam, *c*.1780), *Six quartettos*, op. 8 (Welcker, London, *c*.1770;

108 JENNY BURCHELL

Stechway, The Hague, *c.*1780), and *Four sonatas and two duets*, op. 15 (John Welcker, 1778; J. Schmitt, Amsterdam, *c.*1785).

Even though Bach was resident in London new publications did not necessarily appear there first – publication of *Six concertos*, op. 7 by Welcker in 1770 may have been preceded by that of J. J. Hummel (*c.*1768), and J. J. Hummel's edition of *Six sonatas*, op. 17 (1779) preceded that of Welcker by a year. The *Four sonatas and two duets*, op. 18 printed by Welcker in 1781 were published by Chevardière and also by de Roullede, in Paris, possibly in the previous year, while of the *Six grand overtures*, op. 18 (W. Forster, ?1782), nos 1 and 2 had already been published in Amsterdam by J. Schmitt as early as *c.*1775, with an additional printing of no. 2 by the same publisher possibly a year earlier.

Several sets of symphonies do not appear to have been published in London at all; *Six simphonies*, op. 6 was published by Hummel in Amsterdam (1770), *Six simphonie périodique*, op. 8 was published by S. Markordt, also in Amsterdam (*c.*1775), and *Trois simphonies*, op. 9 was published at The Hague by B. Hummel in 1773.

The pattern of European publications often mirrors that of London activity. It is not surprising to find that Clementi achieved a collection of European imprints as diverse as his British collection, beginning with Bailleux (Paris) in 1782 whose edition of *Three sonatas*, op. 5 (1782) may well have pre-dated J. Dale's edition. The rest of the European publications were either virtually simultaneous or obviously later. Publishers include Artaria (Vienna): *Three sonatas*, op. 7 (1783), *Six sonatas*, op. 25 (1790), *Two sonatas* (*c.*1790) and *Four sonatas*, op. 12 (1794); Sieber (Paris): also *Four sonatas*, op. 12 (*c.*1787); Bossler (Speyer): *Six sonatas*, op. 13 (1788); J. J. Hummel (Amsterdam): *La Chasse*, op. 16 (*c.*1790); and Boyer (Paris): *Three sonatas*, op. 10 (*c.*1790) and *Sonata*, op. 20 (*c.*1791), as well as two publications with John Lee in Dublin.

Abel's European publications numbered only three: *Six quartettos*, op. 8 (Robert Bremner, 1769; S. Markordt, Amsterdam, *c.*1780); *Six sonatas*, op. 2 (Author, by Bremner, 1760; 'Aux Addresses Ordinaires', Paris, *c.*1765); and *Four trios*, op.16 (John Preston, *c.*1785; J. J. Hummel, Amsterdam, *c.*1775). As well as Abel, other composers who were perhaps better known as performers such as Luigi Borghi, Wilhelm and Johann Baptist Cramer, and Venanzio Rauzzini had compositions published by European houses while living in Britain, though a very large number – including Barthélemon – did not.

Utilization of the extended market was not confined to foreign composers in Britain. John Garth's *Seconde sett of six sonatas*, op. 4 (Welcker, 1772) was published by S. Markordt (Amsterdam) *c.*1790; Joseph Tacet's *Six solos for a German-flute* [op. 1], for example, were privately published in 1767, but although they were not reprinted in Britain, they also appeared 'Chez le Sieur le Marchand' in Paris in 1771. More surprising are the publications of Robert Valentine in the early eighteenth century. The majority of his quite numerous works were published by Walsh & Hare, or Walsh alone, with a few published by Daniel Wright, but two – *XII Sonatas or solos for a flute*, op. 2 and *XII Sonatas or solos*, op. 3 – had already been published in Europe some years before their appearance under Walsh & Hare's imprint. His *XII Sonatas or solos for a flute*, op. 2 was published 'Per il Mascardi' in Rome (1708; Walsh & Hare, 1713), and the *XII Sonatas or solos*, op. 3 'Chez Estienne Roger', Amsterdam in *c*.1712. The German composer Theodore Smith, mainly active in England, published no fewer than four collections in Europe: *Six concertos*, op. 4 (J. Hummel in Amsterdam *c*.1783), *Trois trios en duos*, op. 1 (J. J. Hummel, Berlin, *c*.1775) and *Trois sonates en duo*, op. 4 (J. J. Hummel, Berlin, *c*.1775) and while op. 1 was published by Longman & Broderip in 1779 as *Three favourite duets, for two performers on one harpsichord or piano forte. Dedicated to Lady Ann and Lady Sarah Windsor*, there is no documented surviving evidence that they were published in their original form in Britain at all.

It is evident from the lists discussed here and from the catalogues of other composers that a number of conclusions can be drawn. First is the matter of qualitative judgement and its relationship to publishing method. Publication by subscription of instrumental music does not automatically imply lack of compositional stature; this is shown by the number of composers who published other works directly. Similarly, private publication was at times more an indication of caution on the part of the publisher, and was often followed by a reprint or new edition in the publisher's name alone. Second, although composers were certainly anxious to get as much material into print as possible, sometimes apparently to the point of using any publisher who would accept the work, they tended to be loyal to the current house, and to stick with them unless obliged by circumstance to change. Finally, while it is not surprising to find foreign composers duplicating publication in Europe, the practice was not confined to these.

The role of the publisher

The second part of this study is concerned with the other side of the process – the selection and acquisition of music by the publishers themselves. In Britain there was to be found a ready market for printed instrumental music in the many musical societies and subscription organizations, as well as private groups too nebulous to be described as formal societies, and an increasing domestic market as the divide between professional and amateur competence grew towards the end of the century. But in order to survive, publishers had not only to supply their customers with music, but to provide them with the sort of music they wanted to play or hear, not just the sort of music that composers thought they should publish. The problematic nature of this endeavour may be one of the reasons for the bankruptcy of so many eighteenth-century music publishers, including John Welcker; Longman & Broderip; Corri, Dussek & Co., and William Napier – though few of them seem to have been out of business for long.

The most prolific publishing house was Longman & Broderip (et al.), who clearly sought financial security by maintaining a wide-ranging catalogue of

110 JENNY BURCHELL

works of all genres. As well as introducing previously unpublished instrumental music, they were enthusiastic reprinters and producers of previous editions (often acquiring plates from other publishers), which number roughly a quarter as many as the original works. The list is further augmented by works they published 'For the Author'. The Longman & Broderip list embraces all levels of endeavour. They printed works by both native and foreign composers resident in Britain, and they imported music from Europe both printed and for their own publication.[4] It should be noted, however, that they were not always scrupulous in authenticating the authorship of their publications, even when the putative composer was resident in London. Their edition of *Thirty six preludes in different keys for the German flute, hoboy or violin* (1771) appeared under the name of the flautist Joseph Tacet, but an advertisement by Tacet states that these were not his works; in addition, as has already been observed, several compositions purported by them to be by J. C. Bach are spurious or at least doubtful. Less prolific but none the less clearly significant were Robert Bremner, John Johnson, the Welckers, the Prestons and the Thompsons, followed by J. Bland, Robert Birchall, Joseph Dale, William Forster and William Napier, all of whom published music from the same variety of sources as Longman.

The flow of new music to publishers from within Britain has already been discussed. But analysis of concert programmes, catalogues of music owned by musical societies, concert advertisements and publishers' lists shows a strong interest in works imported from Europe, and indeed a relatively large proportion of such works. All of the publishers identified above printed imported music.

Publication of imported music was established practice long before the middle of the eighteenth century. Walsh's publications of works already published elsewhere include – among many others – music by Corelli, Tibaldi, Giuseppe Valentini, Veracini, Ricciotti, F. X. Richter and Vivaldi, from as early as *c*.1710. Walsh was certainly the first publisher to print C. P. E. Bach's works in Britain, with *Sig.^{r} Bach (of Berlin) concertos for the harpsichord, or organ. Op.3^{2a}* [H. 414, 429, 417] (*c*.1750), *Sei sonate per cembalo* [H. 136–9, 126, 140] (1763), and *A 2^d set. Sei sonate per cembalo … Opera seconda* [H. 150–51, 127–8, 141, 62] (1763). Longman, Lukey & Co. published *A favourite concerto for the harpsichord, or piano forte* (*c*.1770), following it with *Six sonatas* [H. 162, 180–82, 163, 183] (*c*.1775) and *A second sett of three concertos for the organ or harpsicord* [H. 421, 444, 428] (*c*.1775) – presumably preceded by a first set. Robert Bremner published *Six sonatas for harpsichord or piano forte* [H. 525–30] in 1776, and William Forster caused to be printed *Six progressive lessons* (1783). *A favourite concerto* [A major] *for the harpsicord or piano forte*, printed for C. & S. Thompson *c*.1775 in C. P. E. Bach's name is not actually by him, suggesting

---

4 See David Wyn Jones, 'From Artaria to Longman & Broderip: Mozart's music on sale in London', in Otto Biba and David Wyn Jones, eds, *Studies in Music History presented to H. C. Robbins Landon on his Seventieth Birthday* (London: Thames & Hudson, 1996), pp. 105–14.

BRITISH MUSIC PRINTERS AND PUBLISHERS 111

that Longman & Broderip were not the only company to be careless with their attributions.

If we may attribute the establishment of music importation to Walsh, even the brief list of C. P. E. Bach's works serves to show that it was embraced with enthusiasm by later publishers. Of the above-named publishers Longman, Lukey & Co. (later Longman & Broderip) were responsible for the introduction of unquestionably the largest volume of European-sourced music into Britain. David Wyn Jones states that by 1781 Longman & Broderip advertised 'a Correspondence with all the Publishers of Music in Europe', and had set up a connection with Artaria, in Vienna, by which means they became 'in effect ... Artaria's agent in London',[5] though they were not the only publishers to import music directly from Artaria.[6] This enabled them to import works selected from Artaria's lists, including no fewer than 34 works by Mozart.[7] Labels pasted on extant copies show that Longman & Broderip sources also included Boyer (Paris) and Bailleux (Paris), and it is clear that much of the music they imported came in printed form directly from publishers. There is no reason to suppose that other importing publishers did not follow the same practice.

Some publishers also undertook travel in order to locate works. An entry dated 15 February 1773 in the Sederunt Books of the Edinburgh Musical Society notes that

The Treasurer further informed the Meeting that Mr Bremner had while in France & Holland made a collection of Overtures which he had imagined would be proper for the Society to have in their Library & which were now lying at London[8]

and earlier correspondence between the Society and Bremner suggests that he chose and bought music for the Society.[9] Bremner's choice of destinations is certainly significant, since many of the works already identified here as published elsewhere besides Britain were published in France; most of the rest were published by J. J. Hummel in Amsterdam. Although we may reasonably assume that Bremner visited publishers on his travels it is also very likely that he solicited works directly from composers.

Bremner's role in the importation of new music was an important one. In 1763, a year after his expansion from Edinburgh to London, Bremner began what turned out to be a 60-part series, *The Periodical Overture in 8 parts*, with the express intention of introducing music which had not been printed elsewhere – an intention

---

5   Ibid., p. 108.

6   'Torre & Co' labels are to be found on a number of works including Haydn and Sterkel, *6 sonatas*, op. 17 (Artaria, 1785), 'Imported from Vienn. Publish'd & Sold by Torre & Co. ... London, July 1785', and John Kerpen published a number of works also published by Artaria.

7   Wyn Jones, 'From Artaria to Longman & Broderip', p. 110.

8   Edinburgh Central Library, Edinburgh Musical Society Sederunt Books, vol. 3, p. 9 (15 February 1773).

9   Jenny Burchell, *Polite or Commercial Concerts? Concert Management and Orchestral Repertoire in Edinburgh, Bath, Oxford, Manchester, and Newcastle, 1730–1799* (New York: Garland, 1996), p. 73.

112   JENNY BURCHELL

that with one exception appears to have been upheld.[10] He began with a symphony by J. C. Bach – one of the earliest of his works to be printed in London – and by the appearance of the last overture in 1783 on surviving evidence he seems not only to have published 59 previously unpublished symphonies, but also to have been the first to publish in Britain the works of some 17 composers, including Pasquale Ricci, Anton Filtz, Pietro Crispi, Christian Cannabich, the Earl of Kelly, Niccolò Piccinni, Joseph Herschel, Ignaz Holzbauer, Gossec, Franzl, Dittersdorf, Michael Haydn, Vanhal, Sacchini, Schmitt, Boccherini and Schobert – some of whose other works he had previously published. For the remaining composers he was one of the earliest publishers, although not the first. Outside the series he also introduced Eichner, Alessandri and Traetta.

Bremner's influence on the orchestral repertoire of Britain is demonstrated by the prominence of those composers whose works he included in *The Periodical Overture* in concert programmes during the last quarter of the eighteenth century in all parts of Britain.[11] His list was more selective than Longman & Broderip's, and it should be noted that works by many of the composers he published first soon appeared on Longman & Broderip's list. His plates passed to Preston, who regarded it as one of the most valuable collections in Europe. It is surely no coincidence that J. J. Hummel in Amsterdam published a series of 20 'sinfonies periodiques' beginning in November 1769, nor that Sieber (Paris), Markordt (Amsterdam) and Joseph Schmitt (Amsterdam) followed suit in the 1770s.

But although Bremner's influence is obvious, he was not the sole importing publisher at that period. William Forster managed to import Haydn's symphonies before Longman, and John Johnson was a small-scale importer in the 1750s and 1760s. Of particular interest, however, are the activities of William Napier, who set up in business as a publisher in 1772 in London. Napier had been a violinist for the Edinburgh Musical Society from about 1758, and would certainly have known Robert Bremner from that time. Napier's list of publications is notable for the predominance of small-scale chamber music, and in particular for the number of quartets, which significantly outnumber every other instrumental genre; many of these works also exist in earlier European prints. In its emphasis on small ensembles Napier's list seems to balance Bremner's, which though by no means devoid of chamber music contains a relatively high proportion of larger works. In view of the number of shared imported composers it does not seem unreasonable to suggest that the two worked together in some way. A selection of these and other publishers whose lists include works previously published in Europe is given in Table 6.9.

A full assessment of the significance of these publishers requires considerably more space than is available within the limits of a single chapter, but several points can be stated with some certainty. Although the practice of importing music was

---

10   See also D. Wyn Jones, 'Robert Bremner and *The Periodical Overture*', *Soundings*, 7 (1978), 63.

11   Burchell, *Polite or Commercial Concerts?*

BRITISH MUSIC PRINTERS AND PUBLISHERS

Table 6.9   Selective list of publishers with European connections

Birchall & Andrews; Birchall & Co.; Robert Birchall
S. Babb
J. Bland
J. Blundell
Robert Bremner
Corri & Sutherland; Corri, Dussek & Co.; Corri & Co.
J. Dale
J. Fentum
William Forster
G. Goulding
Harrison
John Johnson; Mrs Johnson; R. Johnson (plates sold to Bremner, 1777)
J. Longman & Co.; Longman, Lukey & Co.; Longman, Lukey & Broderip;
     Longman & Broderip
William Napier
J. Oswald
John Preston; Preston & Son; T. Preston; Preston
William Randall
Thompson & Son; Thompson & Sons; C. & S. Thompson; S. A. & P.
     Thompson
Henry Thorowgood
J. Walsh
Peter Welcker; Welcker; John Welcker
R. Wornum

established early in the eighteenth century, and in spite of the enthusiasm for foreign musicians in the 1750s, it was only with the 1760s that this became accepted practice for any publisher with pretensions to a wide audience. It is also clear that a large list of imported music was no substitute for sound business practice, as is shown by the financial difficulties of Longman, Napier and John Welcker. But success or failure of individual houses aside, it is plain that by the last part of the eighteenth century the importation of foreign instrumental works was the primary distinguishing feature of the more sophisticated publishing establishments, and that these houses went to considerable lengths to be able to uphold the claim that on their lists was indeed to be found music 'by the first talents of Europe'.

CHAPTER SEVEN

Musicians and Music Copyists in Mid-Eighteenth-Century Oxford

Donald Burrows and Peter Ward Jones[*]

Surviving manuscript scores and part-books provide us with evidence of musical activity in Oxford, not only filling out our knowledge of musical repertoire, but also offering insights into practical aspects of the performances. A basic need for these was the provision of performing material, and in Oxford this task was sometimes shared among many people. Some contributed more substantially than others, and some were undoubtedly also themselves performers. This essay is devoted principally to the Oxford music copyists and their role in the city's music making.

The serious documentary record of Oxford's concert life may be said to have begun in 1753, five years after the opening of the Holywell Music Room, with the first publication of *Jackson's Oxford Journal*. In 1753 itself the *Journal* had only one item relating to a musical event, a brief report of a performance of Handel's *Alexander's Feast* during the Commemoration celebrations in July, but from the next year onwards the paper carried frequent notices and reports of concerts, and indeed became the regular organ for advance concert notices.[1] For the preceding half-century documentary information about Oxford performances comes principally from very sporadic reports in the London newspapers, mainly concerning performances in Act Week: in 1713 when Croft and Pepusch received their doctorates, in 1733 when Handel did not receive his, and in 1738 when 'Mr Church and Mr Hayes' gave a benefit performance of *Alexander's Feast*.[2] An intriguing performance of Handel's *Samson* for Hayes's benefit on St Cecilia's Day 1743 is known from an advertisement in the London newspapers,[3] and this may have been part of a series of regular annual celebrations for music's patron saint in Oxford: in 1736 a London newspaper reported that Handel's *Acis and*

---

[*] The authors have prepared a full study of Oxford hands of the period, published as 'An Inventory of Mid-Eighteenth-Century Oxford Musical Hands', *RMARC*, 35 (2002), 61–144. It includes a fuller range of reproductions of the various copyists' hands than has been possible here.

[1] See further Ch. 12, below.

[2] On the 'Acts' generally, see H. Diack Johnstone, 'Handel at Oxford in 1733', *Early Music*, 31 (2003), 248–60, and 'Music and Drama at the Oxford Act' (Ch. 10), below; on other aspects of Oxford's music making in the period, see Susan Wollenberg, *Music at Oxford in the Eighteenth and Nineteenth Centuries* (Oxford: Oxford University Press, 2001), and Donald Burrows, 'Sources for Oxford Handel Performances in the First Half of the Eighteenth Century', *Music & Letters*, 61 (1980), 177–85.

[3] *Daily Advertiser*, 10 Nov. 1743.

115

Galatea was to be given in Magdalen College hall, also for Hayes's benefit, and James Harris's correspondence with Oxford musicians reveals a comparable performance in 1738 for the benefit of the violinist Philip Phillips, and a further concert in 1739.[4] In April 1749 the award of Hayes's doctorate and the celebrations for the opening of the Radcliffe Camera were accompanied by a three-day Handel festival at the Sheldonian Theatre conducted by Hayes.[5] This seems to have initiated an annual sequence of similar musical performances at the Commemoration of Benefactors: according to one correspondent in April 1750, 'about the beginning of July, the first commemoration will be celebrated, & there is to be forever hereafter an annual Festival, with entertainments of Musick and Oratory, in praise of our Benefactors'.[6] There were also other university occasions (such as the ceremony for the Installation of a Chancellor) in which special musical performances featured, and more regular – though more modest – concerts were given by a succession of musical clubs and societies, culminating in the Oxford Musical Society by the 1740s. But there is no continuous record before 1753, and even information on Handel's famous visit in 1733 relies on some very strange sources – such as the diary of Thomas Hearne, who stayed away from the performances, and the published journal of a Frenchman who was best known as a writer of fiction.[7] The evidence for William Hayes's attendance at Handel's performances comes from a preface to a collection of his church music published more than 60 years later:[8] in 1733 Hayes was still organist of Worcester Cathedral, but he moved to Oxford the next year as organist of Magdalen College, and was appointed as Professor of Music following the death of Richard Goodson junior in 1741.

Although, as Watkins Shaw has noted,[9] William Hayes was the first Professor to have had any known role in the examination of exercises for music degrees, his various posts in Oxford were primarily concerned with practical music making, and he has been assumed to have been a leader in Oxford's musical activities in the mid-century period. Something of his musical character is known through his compositions and through his regular promotion of performances of Handel's music. However, he did not work alone. Although direct documentary sources for the first two decades of his residence in Oxford are sparse, there are other sources

---

4   *Daily Advertiser*, 13 Nov. 1736; Donald Burrows and Rosemary Dunhill, *Music and Theatre in Handel's World: The Family Papers of James Harris 1732–1780* (Oxford: Oxford University Press, 2002), pp. 62, 64, 77–8.

5   See Otto Erich Deutsch, *Handel: A Documentary Biography* (London: A. & C. Black, 1955), p. 664.

6   Letter from Theophilus Leigh to Lydia, Dowager Duchess of Chandos, 30 April 1750, Balliol College, Oxford, MS 403, fo. 127[r].

7   Concerning the 1733 'Act' see also Thomas McGeary, 'New accounts of Handel and the Oxford Act', *Handel Institute Newsletter*, 13/1 (Spring 2002), pp. [6–7], and Johnstone, 'Handel at Oxford'.

8   William Hayes, *Cathedral Music in Score* (London, 1795).

9   H. Watkins Shaw, 'The Oxford University Chair of Music, 1627–1947, with some account of Oxford degrees in music from 1856', *Bodleian Library Record*, 16/3 (Apr. 1998), 247.

which tell us about Oxford musicians and music making, the repertoire performed and the varied activities of key musicians.

Of prime importance for this early period is some surviving musical material: a set of part-books in Christ Church library, complemented by other sources now in the Bodleian Library and at Durham Cathedral library.[10] This material originated from the later years of Richard Goodson junior (1688–1741), and the Christ Church part-books seem to have become separated from the rest because they comprised the material copied by Goodson and therefore presumably regarded as his own property. The sharing of such work between copyists seems to have been a frequent occurrence in Oxford. Goodson's annotations on the inside covers of the part-books provide hints about how the music was used, and lead us to the names of other people involved in Oxford's musical activity. On Christ Church MS 69 one intriguing annotation reads: 'Score and parts lent to Mr Dobson to carry to the clubb. Mon July 9'. That date fell on a Monday in 1733 and 1739: if the annotation was made in 1733, it would have been in the middle of Handel's visit to Oxford, and on the very day that, according to Hearne, Goodson had performed a 'sham concert' at the Theatre as his contribution to the Act. The 'club' referred to was presumably that which met at the King's Head, the regular meeting-place of the Oxford musical society until the opening of the Holywell Music Room. Several of the society's surviving copies of printed music now in the Bodleian Library carry annotations referring to the King's Head Club, the latest ones being editions of Handel's *Saul* and *Deidamia* from 1739 and 1741. It is uncertain how far Goodson himself was active with the society at that time.

Another of Goodson's annotations, in Christ Church MS 72 and this time including secure year-dates, leads us to the name of Richard Fawcett (1714–82) of Corpus Christi College, who in 1735 had borrowed (and returned) music from Goodson's library, and also presented an older set of part-books to Goodson, presumably for secure preservation. Fawcett turns out to be an important person for this period of Oxford's music, but we must pause for a moment to consider what that might mean. The annotation by Goodson refers to Fawcett borrowing scores of music by Lully and Clérambault, but we cannot be sure that he used the music for performances. It is quite clear from music copied by Fawcett, and from his annotations on music that had been copied by other people, that he was involved with the copying and adaptation of music for Oxford performances. But he was also a semi-professional music copyist (or perhaps rather copyist-master) who produced material for other purposes.

By a lucky accident, a vivid picture of his activities emerges from his letters to James Harris of Salisbury. From these it seems that he also managed the copying of scores for private libraries (including his own) and of performing material for other organizations, such as the Salisbury musical society that Harris directed. In a letter written from London on 6 April 1736, Fawcett refers to music that he has

---

10   See Burrows, 'Sources for Oxford Handel Performances', 179.

promised to copy for Harris, and asks in return for a loan of Harris's manuscript copies of Handel's Coronation Anthems:[11]

> Tis some time since I sent orders that a copy of the anthem O Sing &c should be prepared and sent to you at Salisbury, by this time I hope you have received it. My stay in this place has been longer than I imagined it would have been when I had the pleasure of seeing you last, but if nothing extraordinary happens I shall be in Oxon by Friday next when I shall hasten the transcribing The Lord is my light &c[,] & take care that you may have it as soon as possible. If you send the two anthems you promised me by the next weeks carrier they will certainly find me at home, and if you would be so good as to send the other two Coronation Anthems at the same time (if you can conveniently spare 'em) I shall take it as a favour, and after having taken copies of them with expedition will take care that they shall be safely return'd to you. I shall be mighty glad to communicate any thing in my possession, and hope you are sufficiently convinced that it would be infinite pleasure to me to do it.

The trade in manuscript material was important here because the Handel anthems involved (*O sing unto the Lord*, *The Lord is my light* and the two Coronation Anthems) were not publicly available in published editions. In another letter written from Oxford about three months later, Fawcett revealed the problems that he had encountered in trying to fulfil his plans:[12]

> At last I have been able to send you part of the musick I promis'd you. I am sorry I could not send it sooner but as the delays were quite unavoidable, I am only to beg pardon for not acquainting you with them. Both the peices I intended to send you belonged to Goodson. Soon after I came from London he was taken dangerously ill, in the beginning of his sickness he called in all his books & took the Mass from me before I had time to transcribe 4 pages. The man during his illness was in so ill a humour that notwithstanding his having received favours from me I could not prevail upon him to part with the book before last Sunday. It happen'd then that the person who generally writes for me was taken ill, so that as I thought myself obliged to fullfill my promise to you I have been at the trouble of transcribing the whole thing since that time. By this accident you have not so fair a copy of this as you had of the anthem I sent you[,] but I hope you will be able to read it & that it is pretty correct. I dare say the composition will please you[;] to me it is a very fine one.
>
> As to the other anthem[,] as Goodson is employed in taking a score of it you may be sure his illness has put a stop to that, so that I am afraid you must be obliged to wait a little longer for it. It was but last Tuesday that he lett me know he was able to go on with it. As fast as he does it a copy shall be taken for you. My writer's illness obliges me to desire leave to keep your Coronation Musick a little while longer[;] as soon as I have done with it I shall take care to return it by a safe hand.

As well as providing us with a vivid picture of Goodson in his later years, this is interesting for the give-away phrase 'the person who generally writes for me'. It is apparent that Fawcett was running something of an industrial unit in music copying, comprising at least this person, Goodson and Fawcett himself. Furthermore, while some of the Oxford copyists were undoubtedly professional musicians – practising as organists or lay clerks, for example – Fawcett was not

---

11   Burrows and Dunhill, *Harris Papers*, p. 14.
12   Letter of 24 June 1736, ibid., pp. 18–19.

MUSICIANS AND MUSIC COPYISTS IN OXFORD

one of those: his formal biography is of an academic and clerical career, from which we would not even guess that he had an interest in music. Later on, indeed, his letters to Harris range over more conventional topics for classically trained eighteenth-century intellectuals. On the subject of music copying, Fawcett's subsequent letters name John Snow, who apparently failed to secure the post of organist of Winchester Cathedral in 1737 but served in that post at St John's College, Oxford, from the 1730s until his death in 1766. Snow himself enters Harris's correspondence in 1738, when he was copying orchestral parts for the concertos to accompany *Alexander's Feast* for a Salisbury performance:[13]

> I am sorry I have not finish'd the concerto's yet but I have been so much employ'd with schoolars & scoreing some anthem's & services which I am obliged to do that I have not had time[;] another oportunity I will send the instrumental parts of the organ concerto's & the organ concerto in the Ode with all the parts[,] and I am promised the violin concerto in the Ode[;] when I have it I will send that[.] I will not fail to send the rest as soon as posibly I can.

Clearly Snow was a significant music copyist, but we have not yet managed to identify any musical manuscript that matches his handwriting (Fig. 7.1).

Such was the rather predatory nature of the copyists' activities that Fawcett wrote in 1741 as soon as he heard that Harris had received the sumptuous and authoritative collection of manuscript scores that we now know as the Malmesbury Collection:[14]

> I take the liberty of writing to you by one of our Oxford musicians, and as I have heard of a valuable collection of Mr Handel's musick which you have had given you lately I beg leave to acquaint you [that] if you have any duplicates of entire pieces operas or scores &c which you care to part with[,] I should take it as a particular favour if you would give me leave to treat with you about them.

One final letter, from Snow in January 1742, is of particular interest not only for its reference to copying activities but for news of the first Oxford music room project:[15]

> I have these anthems of Mr Fawcett and he of Sir John Dolbin[,] where by Mr Fawcett at a proper oportunity I could get any of Handels musick or any other Sir John has[,] but I am so much engag'd in writing musick at present I cannot make use of the oportunity as much as I wish I could[.] I must beg that you take no notice how you come by this anthem or any other that I may hereafter send[,] tho I am not any way engaged to keep them to my self[,] but perhaps a private spirit of emulation in some people to get a larger collection scarcer or better then others may deprive me of an oportunity of geting things if known I part with them.
>
> We are raising a subscription to build one of the rackett courts into a musick room but cannot yet be able to judge what success we shall have in it.

---

13 Letter of 10 Mar. 1738, ibid., p. 43.
14 Letter of 24 Nov. 1741, ibid., pp. 126–7.
15 Letter of 1 Jan. 1742, ibid., p. 132. In this letter, and in one of 24 Nov. 1741 (ibid., p. 127), Snow refers to making copies for Harris of English anthems by Handel that were unpublished.

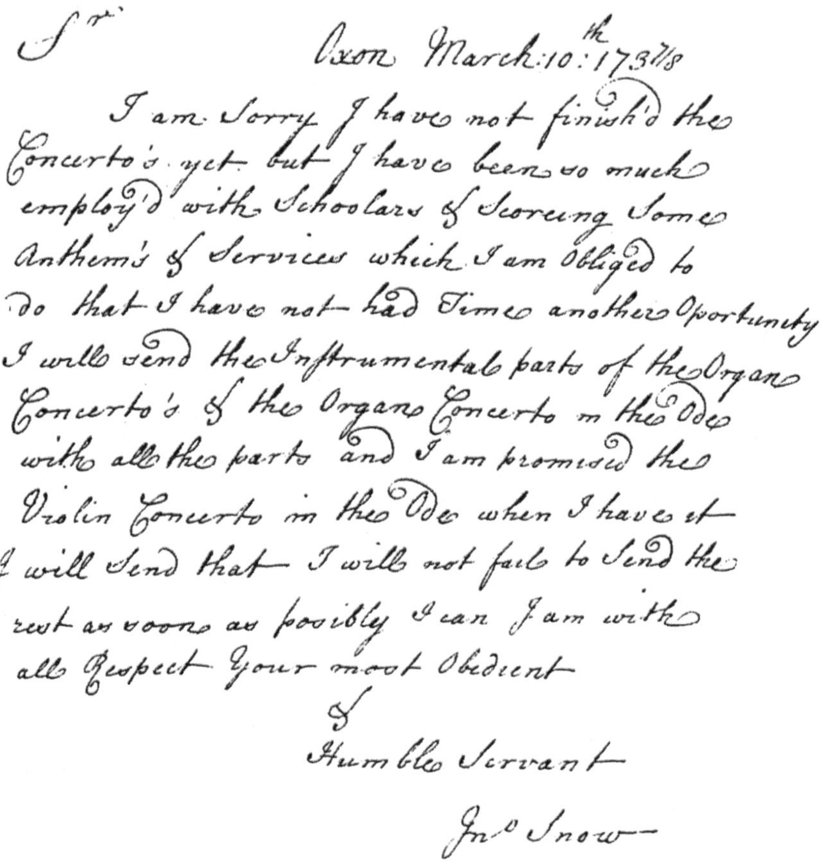

Sr

Oxon March:10:th 1737/8

I am Sorry I have not finish'd the
Concerto's yet but I have been so much
employ'd with Schoolars & Scoreing Some
Anthem's & Services which I am Obliged to
Do that I have not had Time another Oportunity
I will send the Instrumentall parts of the Organ
Concerto's & the Organ Concerto in the Ode
with all the parts and I am promised the
Violin Concerto in the Ode when I have it
I will Send that — I will not fail to Send the
rest as soons as possibly I can I am with
all Respect Your most Obedient
&
Humble Servant

Jno Snow —

Fig. 7.1   Letter from John Snow to James Harris, 10 March 1737/38 (Hampshire Record Office, 9M73/G580/1)

Sir John Dolben was at that time based alternately at his family home in Finedon, Northamptonshire, and at Durham Cathedral where he was a prebendary, though he was also Visitor of Balliol College from 1728 until 1755: the tentacles of copying connections obviously spread wide from Oxford.[16] Music collectors, copyists and performers were not isolated categories, and the various interconnections provided routes for the transmission and commissioning of copies. It is clear from various references in James Harris's correspondence that the leading Oxford musicians went to perform in the Salisbury concerts from time to time, and there was frequent traffic in the other direction as well: in particular, the Salisbury trumpeter William Biddlecomb was a regular performer at Oxford concerts

---

16   Concerning Dolben, see Donald Burrows, 'Sir John Dolben, Musical Patron' and 'Sir John Dolben's Music Collection', *Musical Times*, 120 (1979), 65–7; 149–51.

from the mid-1750s onwards. One hitherto undocumented event in Oxford is revealed by accident through letters to Harris in autumn 1739 from two Oxford musicians – the violinist Philip Phillips and the alto singer Walter Powell – who wrote to apologize that they could not perform at the Salisbury Festival that year because Phillips had a benefit concert in Oxford on St Cecilia's Day.[17] Although the evidence is sporadic, it seems possible that concerts on (or near to) St Cecilia's Day were a regular and significant feature of the Oxford musical calendar during the 1730s and 1740s.

Snow was definitely a performer: Fawcett may have been, but in any case there is no doubt that he was actively involved with Oxford performances. In the surviving music from the period around 1740, in fact, there is more evidence of Fawcett's activity in Oxford's concert life than there is for Hayes's. Fawcett moved on from Oxford in 1754, and it is not certain that he had been so active in the Musical Society during his last decade there. It seems reasonable to assume that William Hayes was in practice the manager and policy-maker for the mid-century period, as he must surely have been for the concerts accompanying university celebrations such as the Commemoration of Benefactors, but again James Harris's correspondence gives us pause on this matter. In 1763 Harris's son was a student at Merton College and he was asked to act as an intermediary for the loan of performing material for two of his father's pieces, in the following terms:[18]

> Now let me tell you that I have acquainted Dr Bever with your father's kindness in indulging us with the Hymn & Pastoral – He is much oblig'd to Mr Harris & if convenient would be glad of it immediately – Now the noble Mr Kemp's coach sets out next Monday from the Blue Bell Holborn (I think), so if it could be sent by that conveyance directed for the Doctor at All Souls, he would have it that evening – Why we would be glad to have it so soon is, that Norris will be here at that time when (as he is acquainted with the thing) he can adjust the parts &c – Dr Bever will be responsible for all: care of all the parts &c – Our first fiddle is Melchier [Malchair] a most excellent stick – Lates second & many other good [players] – Vocal performers will be Norris[,] Corfe & Millard[,] a boy we have here who sings very prettily – We can have it perform'd either Monday senight the 13th instant or either [of] the two following, the 20th or 27th – But either of the two first will be most convenient as not interfering with the Encænia as that will draw nigh – I wish Mr Harris could settle & you let me know, if he could contrive to be here with you either of the above days, for the accompanyment on the harpsichord is no small addition to the delicacy of some of the songs – Indeed an air is destroy'd entirely by being ill-accompanied.

It is clear from this that the management of the Oxford concerts in the 1760s was in the hands of Thomas Bever (1725–91) of All Souls. We know Bever as a music collector from his frequently encountered book-plate, though his musical hand is known only from a single volume in which he copied works of Phocian Henley.[19]

---

17 Burrows and Dunhill, *Harris Papers*, pp. 77–8; the letter was written from London.
18 Letter of W. Benson Earle to James Harris jun., 3 June 1763, ibid., pp. 406–7.
19 Bodleian Library, MS Tenbury 537. Concerning Bever's collection, see Richard Charteris, 'Thomas Bever and Rediscovered Sources at the Staats- und Universitätsbibliothek, Hamburg', *Music & Letters*, 81 (2000), 177–209.

Fig. 7.2   William and Philip Hayes: *David*. Hand of William Hayes, *c*.1774 (Bodleian Library, MS Mus. d.74, p. 98)

During Fawcett's later years in Oxford we find another prolific copyist, and one who was also to follow a clerical rather than musical career. This was John Awbery (1720–75), who matriculated at St John's College in 1739 and was a Fellow of New College from 1740 to 1762. He seems to have been primarily involved with copying full scores, probably for his own library.[20] However, we can establish that he was well known to the Hayes family. His link to William Hayes may have gone back to his schooldays, for amongst the subscribers to Hayes's *Twelve Arietts or Ballads* of 1735 is a 'Mr Aubry jun. of Winton Coll.' (i.e. Winchester College). Awbery would have been 14 at the time, having been there since 1731.[21] In the 1740s he was already copying music in score for his own interest, including Morley canzonets, Bassani motets, Croft anthems and Handel's *St Cecilia Day Ode*. What survives probably represents only a fraction of his activity in this direction, and William Hayes, in a letter of 12 October 1775 to John Alcock, attributes Awbery's poor health at the end of his life to his over-preoccupation with

---

20   Some scores bear Awbery's annotations for copying dates, between 1745 and 1772.

21   A note of caution should be sounded in this identification, since there was a John William Aubrey at Winchester from 1729, born near Oxford (son of the rector of Stanton St John), who also became a Fellow of New College 1738–40, although with no known musical interests – his subsequent career was as army officer and brewer.

Fig. 7.3　William and Philip Hayes: *David*. Hand of Philip Hayes, 1781 (Bodleian Library, MS Mus. d.76, p. 46)

copying.[22] He was a Fellow of Winchester College from 1762, and also rector of Stratfield Saye, Hampshire.

Awbery may have been more closely involved in the practical side of Oxford's concert life than his surviving scores suggest: there is one hint of this in a source which is quite remarkable for other reasons. In the collection at Durham there survive two performing parts of Oxford provenance for the original Part One of Handel's *Israel in Egypt* as performed by the composer in 1739–40, which consisted of an adaptation from Handel's Funeral Anthem for Queen Caroline from 1737, with altered words.[23] One of the parts, for 2nd soprano (Canto 2), is in the hand of a music copyist from Handel's own circle;[24] but apparently it had lost

---

22　The letter is transcribed in Percy M. Young, *Lichfield Cathedral Library: A Catalogue of Music*, vol. 1 (Birmingham: University Library, 1993), p. 2.

23　Durham Cathedral Library MS E35(i): see Brian Crosby, *A Catalogue of Durham Cathedral Music Manuscripts* (Oxford: Oxford University Press for the Dean and Chapter of Durham, 1986), p. 76; and G. F. Handel, *Israel in Egypt*, ed. Annette Landgraf, *Hallische Händel-Ausgabe*, Serie I, Band 14/1 (Kassel, 1999), p. 579.

24　Copyist S1 in the classification by Jens Peter Larsen, in *Handel's Messiah: Origins, Composition, Sources* (London: A. & C. Black, 1957), ch. 4.

124 DONALD BURROWS AND PETER WARD JONES

its outer bifolium, which was made up by Awbery, presumably from a duplicate copy. The parts seem to reflect some performance of *Israel in Egypt* in Oxford for which we have no other record; it probably took place *c*.1746–48 judging by the style of Awbery's hand. It may be that the Oxford musicians did not then have the resources for a complete performance of *Israel in Egypt*[25] and performed Part One alone. This would have been remarkable enough, for Handel himself gave only four performances with this version of Part One, and no other provincial performances are known so early. It seems very likely that the Oxford musicians borrowed Handel's own performing material – as the Salisbury musicians are also known to have done for other works – and that these two part-books were never returned. The returned set was probably not checked very carefully, since Handel had no immediate use for the music. Another equally interesting similar remnant of the Oxford musicians' activity is an orchestral bass part for the Italian cantata *Cecilia volgi un sguardo* (HWV 89), again in the hand of the same copyist from Handel's circle and probably from a set of parts borrowed from the composer.[26] Like Handel, the Oxford musicians may have performed the cantata along with *Alexander's Feast*, a few years after Handel himself had abandoned the cantata. The part includes rests lightening the scoring of the bass line which are not explicit in Handel's score or any other extant sources for the work.[27]

When Awbery arrived in Oxford as an 18-year-old student in 1739, William Hayes would have been 31, his sons Thomas and Philip six years and one year old respectively. (Philip would much later succeed his father as Professor of Music.) One of the most curious forms of evidence of a connection between William Hayes and Awbery concerns a change in the latter's musical handwriting, but to approach this subject requires a small excursion on the subject of the handwriting of the Hayes family themselves. The two major musical scribes of the family, William and Philip, have very similar writing styles: we see the two together in the score of the oratorio *David* from the 1770s, which William began but left unfinished at his death, and which Philip completed.[28] (Fig. 7.2 and Fig. 7.3.)

Here the difference in the hands is quite clear: even in his later years William has a firm and solid hand, while Philip was tending towards a thinner, narrower style. However, at earlier periods, and given momentary changes of mood and circumstance, it is not always so easy to tell the two apart. But are the similar hands confined to William and Philip? We have to take into account not only the possibilities of similarities between the musical handwritings of different scribes, but of changes of style on the part of individual scribes.

---

25   The oratorio required a double SATB chorus and an orchestra including trumpets and trombones.

26   Durham Cathedral Library, MS E20 (iv)/6.

27   See the commentary to HWV 89 in G. F. Handel, *Cantaten mit Instrumenten* III, ed. Hans Joachim Marx, *Hallische Händel-Ausgabe*, Serie V, Band 5 (Kassel, 1999), p. 143.

28   Oxford, Bodleian Library, MSS Mus. d.74–76.

Fig. 7.4   William Croft: *O give thanks unto the Lord*. Hand of John Awbery, 1745 (Bodleian Library, MS Mus. d.27, p. 41)

In the course of investigations into the surviving musical sources from the Hayes circle in Oxford, it has become apparent that such changes of style were indeed a factor for many of the music copyists. Where changes in a copyist's handwriting style can be chronologically documented they are of course a useful tool in assigning dates to manuscripts. It can, however, often be hard in the first place to decide whether similar manuscripts, showing for example various styles of clef, are really the work of different hands, or of one copyist changing his style. Such a problem occurs in distinguishing the work of John Awbery from that of William Hayes. Fig. 7.4 is an example of Awbery's hand from 1745, with his characteristic forms of C clef and bass clef. For comparison Fig. 7.5 shows an example from William Hayes, probably written around 1740: a very different C clef (one of four early types he used) and a different bass clef. By the later 1740s, however, Hayes had changed style and Fig. 7.6 shows a new C clef, as well as a new and very characteristic shape of the naturals.[29] Awbery too begins to use this

---

29   The form of the natural we have referred to informally as the 'Powergen', from its similarity to the logo of that company during the 1990s.

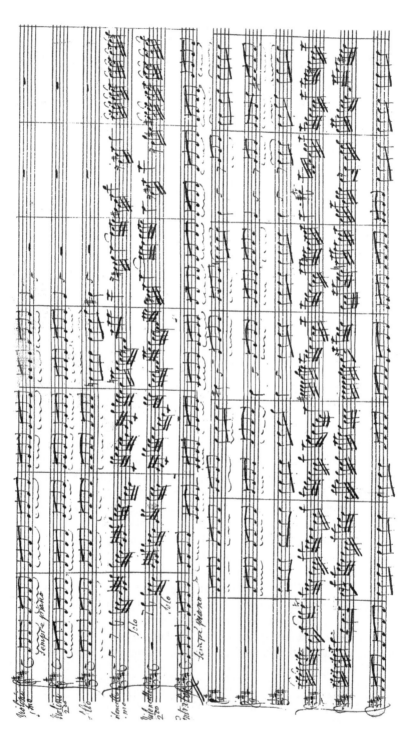

Fig. 7.5 William Hayes: Concerto in D major. Autograph, c.1740 (Bodleian Library, MS Mus. b.6, p. 7)

Fig. 7.6   William Hayes: *Peleus and Thetis*. Autograph, c.1748 (Bodleian Library, MS Mus. d.79, p. 1)

form of natural, and by 1747 his bass clef has mutated into the same type as Hayes's.[30] Then in January 1749, on consecutive pages in the middle of copying Astorga's *Stabat Mater*, Awbery suddenly switches his C clefs to the latest Hayes style (Fig. 7.7).

From now on the two have almost identical hands, and this has led to much confusion and misattribution. The problem is seen at its clearest in two scores of Hayes's *Peleus and Thetis*, composed around 1748.[31] One (Bodleian Library, MS Mus. d.79) is Hayes's autograph score; the other (MS Mus. d.80), owned by Awbery in 1749, has been described as another copy in Hayes's hand,[32] but in fact it was written by Awbery. Although the styles are so close, Awbery, fortunately for us, retains one very particular characteristic from his earlier days: when he comes

---

30   Oxford, Bodleian Library, MS Mus. d.56.
31   It may have been performed as part of the opening celebrations of the Music Room: see Simon Heighes, *The Lives and Works of William and Philip Hayes* (New York: Garland Publishing, 1995), p. 233.
32   Heighes, *Hayes*, p. 339.

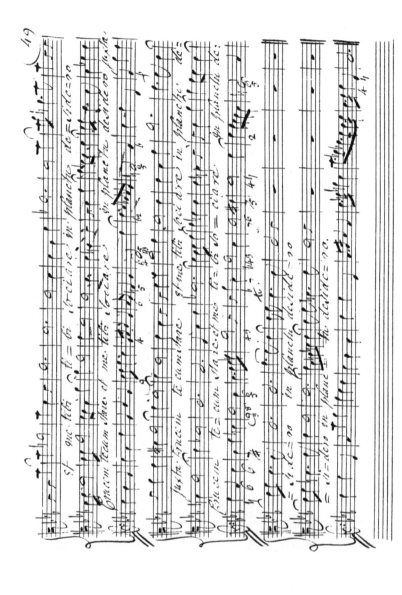

Fig. 7.7   Emanuele d'Astorga: *Stabat Mater*. Hand of John Awbery, 1749 (Bodleian Library, MS Mus. d.19, fo. 71)

to write semibreve rests, he almost invariably hangs them from the middle line of the stave (see Fig. 7.7), rather than from the fourth line up, as Hayes and almost everybody else does. It is a habit that he clung to throughout his life, during the course of which he copied various other works of William and Philip Hayes, as well as indulging in the occasional composition of his own. From this time onwards neither Awbery nor William Hayes made any significant changes to their musical hands.

Philip Hayes, born in 1738, naturally enough learnt his musical hand from his father in the 1750s, and by the end of that decade had developed his own style, still closely resembling William's but usually sufficiently distinct to be identifiable. In general his notes are more rounded in style, and he did not follow his father's form of naturals, but used the conventional rectangular shape. As he grew older his musical hand became smaller and even more rounded: it may not be altogether frivolous to suggest that, given Philip's legendary corpulence which grew with age, it is not improbable that the smaller size of his script reflects constrictions placed on his hand movement by the rest of his body.

The real problem period for disentangling the hands of William and Philip lies mainly in the 1750s, and it seems impossible to be 100 per cent sure of attributing certain manuscripts of this period. The problem can be found, for instance, in a score of Handel's *Messiah* which William owned. This score, famous in literature about *Messiah* sources as the 'Goldschmidt' copy, originated in the 1740s, probably before 1745, and was copied by two of Handel's circle of scribes, S1 and S5.[33] The musical contents have a tantalizingly oblique relationship to the form of the oratorio that Hayes conducted at Oxford in 1749, and it is possible that he did not acquire the score until after that date. The Hayes family made two insertions in the score in Part One. The original scribe had accidentally omitted the recitative 'There were shepherds abiding in the field', but had thoughtfully left enough space at the end of the page for it to be added. There is no doubt that this addition is in William Hayes's hand – the 'classic' firm hand with slightly square shoulders to the C clefs. The score's original musical contents had reflected Handel's 1743 performances in this section of the oratorio, including the arioso version of 'But, lo, the angel of the Lord', but Hayes inserted the (now more familiar) version of 'And lo, the angel of the Lord' (Fig. 7.8). The question is 'Which Hayes'? At first sight this might appear to be a later contribution by Philip – the more spindly style and the thinner clefs look like his style – but it includes the form of the natural sign which was more characteristic of William, and the balance of probability would seem to indicate attribution to him, even though Philip himself also seems to have employed his father's style of natural in his youth (*c*.1755).

The confusion between the hands of the two Hayeses occurs particularly in the sets of performing parts of William and Philip's works. These parts survive for

---

33　See Donald Burrows and Watkins Shaw, 'Handel's "Messiah": Supplementary Notes on Sources', *Music & Letters*, 76 (1995), 359.

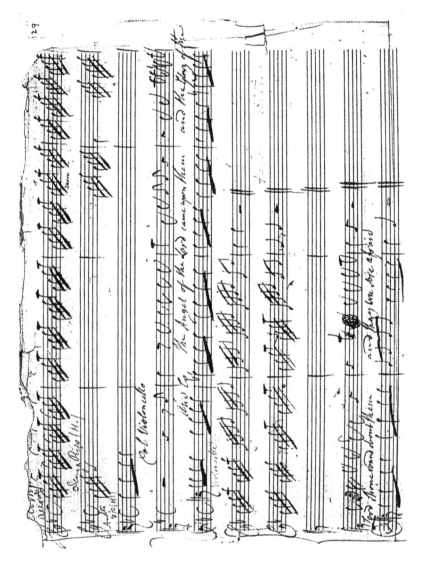

Fig. 7.8   G. F. Handel: *Messiah*. Hand of William Hayes?, 1750s? (Pierpont Morgan Library, New York, Cary MS 122, p. 127)

MUSICIANS AND MUSIC COPYISTS IN OXFORD 131

quite a number of their compositions, especially the odes, masques and similar works written for university and other festivities from the late 1740s onwards. Documentary evidence, and the sets of parts themselves, indicate that substantial forces were often involved: a body of two dozen strings, appropriate wind (sometimes with doubled parts) and brass, and perhaps a chorus of 25–30. The parts for the three major William Hayes works from around 1750 – *Peleus and Thetis*, *Ode on the Passions* and the 1751 Commemoration Ode, *Where shall the muse* (to a text by Thomas Warton), are comparatively straightforward as regards copying and will be considered further in a moment. But for later works like the 1759 Ode, *Hark! hark from ev'ry tongue*, written for the Installation of the new Chancellor (Lord Westmorland), the *Ode to the memory of Handel* from the same year and Philip Hayes's *Telemachus* (1763–65), we come across situations where a multiplicity of copyists is involved.[34]

In fact we have identified over 80 Oxford scribal hands from the period 1740 to 1780, most of them as yet anonymous. The Installation Ode, for example, has seven such hands (plus William and Philip Hayes), of which four reappear in the Handel Ode, which has no fewer than 11 anonymous hands (again plus William and Philip). The really odd thing about these sources, and several later sets of parts, is the apparent lack of a logical pattern in the copying process. In a multiple-copyist situation it might be imagined, for example, that one copy of each string part would be written out by the composer or a principal copyist, with other people being employed to produce the duplicates – and such a pattern can sometimes be found within the Hayes corpus of parts. But in the Handel Ode, for example, even a single violin part may be the work of up to three copyists, with duplicate parts also the work of multiple hands, but not necessarily the same in number or identity. One or two reasons suggest themselves to account at least in part for this situation. It may be that the works were hastily composed to a deadline, and that parts were prepared 'en courant' as various sections were finished, rather than waiting until the completion of the whole. The presence of some of the hands may suggest that revisions or additional parts were needed for later revivals, since at least the Handel Ode received repeat performances, and Philip's *Telemachus* had a complex performance history.[35] Be that as it may, the general impression left by these works is often of an 'all hands on deck' approach when it came to the preparation of performing parts. Many of the copyists contributed only a couple of pages or so, but others played more substantial roles.

Although few definite names can be put forward, there is among these pages a hand which is very close to that of William Hayes, yet distinct from it and from Philip's (Fig. 7.9).It is important to remember at this point that William had other children besides Philip, and of these we know that at least two were musical: Thomas (b. 1733) and William junior (b. 1741). Thomas, after a choristership at

---

34 For source references, see the Catalogue of Works in Heighes, *Hayes*, and Ward Jones and Burrows, 'Inventory'.
35 See Heighes, *Hayes*, pp. 236–8.

Fig. 7.9 William Hayes: *Ode to the memory of Handel*, 1759. Anon. copyist (Bodleian Library, MS Mus. d.119, fo. 12^v)

MUSICIANS AND MUSIC COPYISTS IN OXFORD

Christ Church, was active as a bass singer in Oxford up to 1759, when he went to Durham as precentor at the cathedral and vicar of St Oswald's. Since the hand does not appear after these 1759 works, it is tempting to attribute this pseudo-William hand to him, though we cannot at present provide firm proof. Of course William had pupils, whose hand may have imitated their master, and other Hayes offspring may have been drafted in, though it should be observed that the musical hands in these parts, almost without exception, appear to be fluent ones and do not indicate inexperience. It should be added that later on we also encounter two pseudo-Philip hands, one of which turns out to be that of John Beckwith (1759–1809), who was in Oxford from 1775 to 1784 as a pupil-assistant, first to William and subsequently to Philip Hayes. The other contemporaneous hand is equally likely to have been another of the pupils; several of these are known by name.

It would not be surprising to find many of Oxford's known professional musicians, especially organists and lay clerks, working as music copyists. While it seems inevitable that most of these copyists are destined to remain anonymous, our investigations have enabled us to identify at least one major Oxford copyist of the time. An early manifestation of this musical hand is found in association with Richard Fawcett in a basso continuo part for movements from Handel's *Ode for St Cecilia's Day*, where Fawcett's work is directly continued by the other copyist (Fig. 7.10). The set of part-books from which this is taken[36] is of particular interest in several ways. It can be dated fairly precisely because a page of a London newspaper from January 1742 was used for the cover of one of the violin parts. The present material consists of a score and eight part-books, but Fawcett helpfully wrote an inventory of the original set on the cover of the score and this consisted of:

> 2 Violin I, 2 Violin II, Viola, Oboe I, Oboe II, obbligato Cello, obbligato Bassoon, Double Bass, Cello Repieno [*sic*], 1 Canto, 1 Alto, 2 Tenor, 1 Basso and 1 Basso Continuo part

Thus we know that some time early in 1742 the Oxford musicians performed extracts from the ode, composed three years previously, and we can make a fair guess at the size of the performing forces. The music consisted of the opening and closing solos and choruses of the work: the orchestral forces apparently did not run to the inclusion of trumpets in the last chorus.

We also encountered this copyist's hand in two manuscript full scores of Handel's *Athalia* from the 1750s and 1760s, which belonged to the Oxford Musical Club.[37] The scores pose interesting questions – not least in that one is not a copy of the other – and we thought initially that we were dealing with two different copyists, albeit with very similar hands. It soon became apparent that the same hands occurred frequently, not only in the vocal and orchestral parts for the

---

36 Durham Cathedral Library, MS E23.
37 Now the property of the Oxford University Musical Society, and deposited in the Bodleian Library.

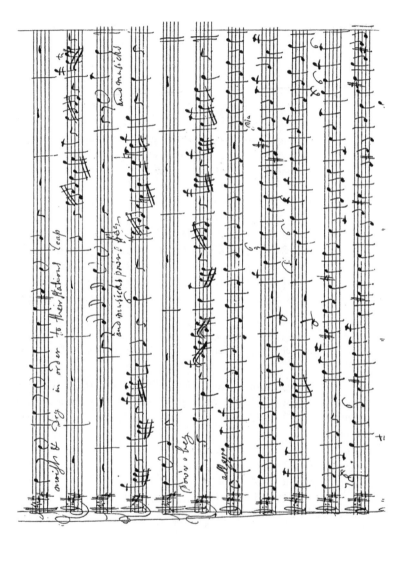

Fig. 7.10 G. F. Handel: *Ode for St Cecilia's Day*. Hand of William Walond, c.1742 (Durham Cathedral Library, MS E23/9, p. 2)

MUSICIANS AND MUSIC COPYISTS IN OXFORD 135

Hayeses' works but also in the New College Choir Books (which have been in the Bodleian Library since 1919),[38] and it also emerged that they were in fact two manifestations of the same hand. Examination of the New College account books (the 'Long Books')[39] revealed that between 1745 and 1767 the sole music copyist to whom payments were made was William Walond; even more helpful were a number of Walond's surviving receipted bills,[40] the best of which give exact particulars of which anthems and services he copied and when. Apart from confirming the identity of Walond's hand, these links provide a most useful tool for dating the various layers of the New College part-books, and also the contemporary organ books which came to light a few years ago and are still at the college.

Walond has hitherto remained a very obscure figure biographically. Even the 1980 edition of *New Grove* offered only a date of death (incorrect as it turns out) and little seemed to be known of his life apart from the fact that he described himself as 'Organist in Oxford', obtained a B.Mus. in 1757 and had musical sons.[41] His publications consisted of two sets of organ voluntaries and a setting of Pope's *Ode on St Cecilia's Day*. A little research into local Oxford archives has, however, enabled us to fill out the biography somewhat. He was born in Oxford in 1719, the son of William and Mary Walond. He himself married a Mary about 1749, and over the next 18 years they produced 14 children, including William junior (b. 1751), the future organist of Chichester Cathedral. He died in August 1768. His role as 'Organist in Oxford' was in fact that of deputy to Richard Church, as we gather from Woodforde's diary.[42] Church, in addition to his New College and Christ Church posts, was also organist of the parish church of St Peter in the East. Walond was thus the essential cog that enabled Church to hold his posts in plurality – a common state of affairs in eighteenth-century Oxford. But in addition to whatever payments he received from Church (for such a deputy's post was purely unofficial), it is clear that music copying was a major source of income for Walond with his growing family. He made extensive contributions not only to the New College books but also at Christ Church (where only the organ books survive).[43]

On the concert front, it is Walond who turns out to be the principal copyist in all the sets of parts of William Hayes's early odes and masques around 1750, and he was still at work in Philip's *Telemachus* in 1763 (though oddly absent from William Hayes's 1759 works). Besides the *Athalia* scores belonging to the Musical

---

38   Bodleian Library, MSS Mus. c.46–51, d.149–169, e.22–25 and f.32.

39   New College Archives, Oxford.

40   e.g. New College Archives, 11388.

41   'Walond, William', *New Grove* (1980). In the 2nd edn (2001), an updated biography appears.

42   W. H. Hargreaves-Mawdsley, *Woodforde at Oxford 1759–1776* (Oxford, 1969), e.g. entry for 20 Dec. 1762, 'William Walond our dep. Organist tuned my Harpsichord this Morning'.

43   Walond's hand was tentatively identified as that of Richard Church by Donald Burrows in the article cited at n. 2. We have not been able firmly to identify Church's authentic hand in the copies of music from Oxford, but see Ward Jones and Burrows, 'Inventory', p. 64.

Fig. 7.11 G. F. Handel: *The Choice of Hercules*. Hand of William Walond, 1750s (Bodleian Library, Mus. 52 c.14, p. 47)

Society (the earlier of which can now almost certainly be linked to a 1755 performance), manuscript additions to three volumes of printed editions of Handel's works, formerly owned by the Society, are all in his hand.[44] These few manuscript remains of the Society's library would thus seem to indicate that Walond was its main copyist in the middle of the century. He was also a viola-player, as indicated on a part-book from William Hayes's *The Passions*,[45] and he may well have been a regular member of the Music Room band. He was granted benefit concerts by the Society at the Music Room in 1758 and 1763. Beyond Oxford, Walond's hand is also found in the manuscripts of Samuel Hellier's collection, formerly at the Wombourne Wodehouse near Wolverhampton.[46] Hellier, who was at Exeter College in the 1750s, clearly commissioned Oxford copyists in the 1750s and 1760s to prepare performing material, including works like *Alexander's Feast*, for his library and for performance by the Wombourne ensemble. As with Awbery and William Hayes, however, certain features of Walond's hand changed considerably over his career, and his various forms of the C clef in particular offer a useful chronological tool. Fig. 7.11 shows his style in the 1750s, which was also his most prolific period.[47]

No autographs survive for Walond's published compositions, and the only other works known by him are an anthem in the New College books and the organ part of an evening service at Christ Church – both naturally enough in his hand, and dating from the 1750s. Two manuscripts now in the British Library, both at one time owned by Thomas Bever, have old attestations that they are in Walond's hand, and show that hand in various stages of evolution.[48] One of them, a volume of anthems by Croft, Purcell and others in score (purchased by Bever in 1777), formerly belonged to William Scroggs, another Oxford collector, for whom Walond may have copied the music.[49] It should also be noted that Walond's eldest son, William junior (1751–1836), who went off to Chichester in 1775, appears to have taken on his father's mantle after his death in 1768, both as deputy to Church and as a copyist at New College and Christ Church – although (atypically) his hand does not imitate that of his father.

Walond, however, is not the predominant Oxford hand in Samuel Hellier's manuscripts, which are for the most part the work of a different copyist employing a style very similar to Walond's apart from the bass clef (Fig. 7.12). This hand,

---

44   Bodleian Library, Mus. 21.c.10 (*L'Allegro, il Penseroso ed il Moderato*), Mus. 52.c.5(1) and Mus. 52.c.14 (*The Choice of Hercules*).

45   Bodleian Library, MS Mus. d.121, fo. 107.

46   See Percy Young, 'The Shaw–Hellier Collection', in Terence Best, ed., *Handel Collections and their History* (Oxford: Oxford University Press, 1993), pp. 158–70; Ian Ledsham, *A Catalogue of the Shaw–Hellier Collection in the Music Library, Barber Institute of Fine Arts, the University of Birmingham* (Aldershot: Ashgate, 1999). The collection has subsequently been transferred to the Birmingham University Library Special Collections department.

47   See the illustrations in Ward Jones and Burrows, 'Inventory' for further examples.

48   Additional MSS 17842, 31402.

49   Scroggs was one of the subscribers to Walond's first set of voluntaries in 1752, and had earlier subscribed to Hayes's *Twelve Arietts*.

like Walond's, changes character between the 1750s and 1760s, and the two men were clearly associated. A letter of 1769 from Hellier to his agent John Rogers at Wombourne, which mentions a 'Mr Lamborn' copying Handel's Coronation Anthems for him, suggests that this prolific copyist may have been John Lambourn. We know little about Lambourn, but he evidently headed the 'University Musicians' for a time in the 1750s,[50] and subscribed to Walond's *Ode on St Cecilia's Day*. Surprisingly perhaps, comparatively little of this hand is found amongst other Oxford manuscripts, but it must be remembered that what has survived is but a fraction of what once existed – very little of the Musical Society's performing material, for example, is now extant. Among other college choir copyists, brief mention should be made of William Mathews (d. 1791), the well-known Oxford bass soloist, who was a lay clerk at Magdalen College from 1759 and owned a music shop in the High Street. Regular payments to him for copying at Magdalen are found in the college accounts from 1763 to 1771. Unfortunately no early choir material survives at Magdalen, but his hand is identified from an inscription by Thomas Bever in Fitzwilliam Museum Mus. MS 169 – a copy by Mathews of a Pergolesi mass[51] – and can be found in one or two other surviving manuscripts.

In order to form as good a picture of music making in mid-eighteenth-century Oxford as the surviving evidence permits, we need to draw upon both documentary and musical sources, and to interpret them in a complementary manner. In many respects the remaining musical material, scores and part-books, provides an unusually rich resource: we have music that we can relate to periods, or even specific dates, of performance, and in some cases to the names of many of the performers. The provision of the music was an essential prerequisite for the performances; thus the copyists played a vital role in the management of musical activity. We may reasonably assume that most of the copyists were also players or singers who participated in the performances. In addition to the music that was copied for immediate practical use, there are scores from the Oxford scribes that seem to have been copied for personal libraries, and hint at the repertoire that Oxford's musical connoisseurs considered to be valuable. A few figures – Fawcett, William and Philip Hayes, John Awbery, William Walond senior, John Beckwith and a couple of the anonymous hands – seem to have dominated the scribal activity, but they were surrounded by circles of other labourers whose work and significance is only now becoming recognized.

---

50 He signed for payment to the musicians in the Christ Church Disbursement Books for 1753 and 1756 (Christ Church Archives).

51 See Charteris, 'Thomas Bever'.

Fig. 7.12   G. F. Handel: *L'Allegro, il Penseroso ed il Moderato*. Hand of John Lambourn?, 1750s (University of Birmingham Library, Shaw–Hellier Collection 177, p. 16)

CHAPTER EIGHT

The Catch and Glee in Eighteenth-Century Provincial England

Brian Robins

The striking increase in the urbanization of England during the course of the eighteenth century represents one of the most important defining characteristics of the period. Just how dramatic was the acceleration in the process that took place may be illustrated by a single statistic. In 1700 it is estimated that around 7½ per cent of the population lived in provincial urban centres, a proportion that had risen to some 20 per cent a hundred years later.[1] Along with the growth in both the number and size of towns, the period also witnessed a significant parallel expansion in the establishment of a social structure that bound such communities together. Assemblies, clubs, lending libraries, theatres and public concerts may be counted among the numerous activities that contributed to the creation of modern civic unity. For the greater part such institutionalization followed a predominantly middle-class course, many educational and leisure pursuits falling beyond the financial means of the less well off. The present essay examines the unique role played by two indigenous musical forms, the glee and the catch, within the social fabric of music making during the latter half of the eighteenth century. While initially both were principally the province of gentlemen's clubs formed for the express purpose of combining conviviality with their performance, the glee's phenomenal rise in popularity ensured that it would also enter the concert hall and play a part in domestic music making.

The catch and glee are rare examples of genres created by native composers that owe little or nothing to outside influences. Both have origins earlier than the period under discussion, especially the catch, but reached the height of their popularity during the course of the eighteenth century in a process largely articulated by clubs formed specifically for their performance. During the Restoration it had become fashionable for music clubs to be formed. Roger North's description of one such club, meeting 'in a lane behind St. Paul's', establishes a framework that would become the basis for many eighteenth-century catch clubs. Here, North tells us, 'some shopkeepers and foremen came weekly to sing in consort; and to hear, and injoy ale and tobacco; and after some time the audience grew strong ... and their

---

1 Peter Borsay, ed., *The Eighteenth Century Town: A Reader in English Urban History 1688–1820* (London: Longman, 1990), p. 5.

142   BRIAN ROBINS

musick was cheifly out of Playford's Catch Book'.[2] The plebeian membership of
the club described by North is reflected in that of the Madrigal Society, one of the
most significant vocal music clubs formed during the first half of the eighteenth
century,[3] and also in some of the provincial catch clubs that sprang up during the
latter part of the century. The foundation of the Madrigal Society marked an
important milestone in the revival of old music, a movement that is one of the
defining features of musical activity in eighteenth-century England.[4] The preface
to the first extant publication devoted specifically to both catches and glees,
Catches, Glees, and Canons, published by the Oxford Professor of Music William
Hayes in 1757, explicitly acknowledges the debt owed to the composer's heritage:

> In the following Compositions, I have endeavoured to imitate that simplicity of Style
> which distinguishes the Works of those Masters who are allowed to have excelled in
> this Species of Music; particularly those of our Countrymen HILTON, LAWES,
> BREWER, FORD and others of the last Century; But above all, the famous
> PURCELL; whose incomparable Humour can never be outdone if equalled.[5]

According to John Wall Callcott, one of the most prolific composers of catches
and glees, devotion to the past was also at least in part responsible for the
establishment of what is generally known as the Noblemen and Gentlemen's
Catch Club (henceforth the [London] Catch Club) in 1761.[6] But it was also, in
Callcott's words, the objective of the Catch Club 'to encourage the efforts of rising
composers', an ambition that would gain fulfilment in a unique repertoire of native
music. As the full name suggests, the members of the Catch Club occupied a
position in society at the opposite end of the social spectrum to the shopkeepers,
mechanics and weavers of North's club and the Madrigal Society. Its principal
instigator appears to have been John Montagu, fourth Earl of Sandwich, while the
subsequent membership included not only royalty and peers of the realm, but also
prominent leading figures from the armed services and business. Membership was
firmly controlled and the club developed a strict set of rules that included fines and
expulsion for non-attendance. An important early innovation that quickly led to a
rapid expansion of new repertoire and an apparent lessening of interest in 'old'
music was the introduction of annually presented prize medals for the best catches,
glees and canons.[7]

---

    2   *Roger North on Music*, ed. John Wilson (London: Novello, 1959), p. 351. For a fuller
examination of the seventeenth-century background see Brian Robins, *A Thoroughly English Music:
Catch and Glee Culture in Eighteenth Century England* (forthcoming).
    3   See Hawkins, *History*, book XX, pp. 886 ff. for a well-known description of the Madrigal
Society.
    4   See William Weber, *The Rise of Musical Classics in Eighteenth-Century England: A Study in
Canon, Ritual, and Ideology* (Oxford: Clarendon Press, 1992) for a seminal survey of this topic.
    5   William Hayes, Preface to *Catches, Glees, and Canons* (Oxford, 1757).
    6   John Wall Callcott, 'Essays on musical subjects: Essay iii – On the Catch Club' (31 August
1801), BL, Add. MS 27646.
    7   Analysis of the 32 volumes published by Edmund Warren, the secretary of the Catch Club,
under its auspices between 1762 and 1793 reveals that while 'old' music took up approximately
5% of the contents during the 1760s, 1770s and 1780s, the proportion dropped to 3% in the 1790s.
Significantly, it was during this last decade that the glee became less contrapuntal in character,

THE CATCH AND GLEE IN PROVINCIAL ENGLAND 143

Roy Porter has drawn attention to the manner in which London fashions and institutions were taken as a model by provincial towns,[8] so it is hardly surprising to find that following the establishment of the aristocratic and politically dominated Catch Club the following decades witnessed the emergence of catch clubs in many cities and towns throughout Britain. Indeed, although little documentary evidence has as yet come to light, it appears probable that the earliest catch clubs in the provinces pre-date the Catch Club. The most likely candidate is Oxford, which had a long tradition of convivial music making in its colleges and inns. Elizabeth Chevill has drawn attention to the existence in the provinces of more generalized music societies during the first half of the century, including one that met at the Mermaid, Carfax (Oxford) as far back as the last decades of the seventeenth century.[9] Chevill's exhaustive research on musical clubs in Exeter, Hereford, Lichfield, Salisbury and York revealed no organization that could specifically be identified as a catch club, although she notes that the singing of catches not infrequently brought an evening's entertainment to a convivial close. A significant feature of these music clubs was the large number of clergymen and lay clerks who were members, thus establishing a precedence found in many provincial catch clubs, especially those located in cathedral cities. Little positive evidence of a commensurate involvement in catch and glee singing by choristers of parish churches has emerged, although William Gardiner's testimony suggests that it may have been more widespread than seems apparent. Recounting his youthful days in Leicestershire during the 1770s, Gardiner recalled that 'in addition to the church performances, these musicians of the forest were in the habit of singing the best of our English glees, with a taste and expression rarely equalled in a country village'.[10]

For evidence of the early existence of a catch club in Oxford we can return to William Hayes, who was also a professional (or privileged) member of the Catch Club from 1765. Hayes's 1757 Preface makes clear that he composed many of the works included here for a club he had been accustomed to attending for some time:

> Many of the former [compositions] were born under the happy Auspices of a most agreeable and well regulated Society that met weekly, and subsisted several Years, in very high Perfection, in this Place, and which I found to be productive of the desirable Effects: viz. *Chearfulness* and *Good-humour, Friendship* and a *Love of Harmony*; not to mention how much it contributed to the *Improvement* of the younger Practitioners, enabling them to sing readily at Sight, by being accustomed to a Variety of Cliffs and Movements, and this, not by Compulsion or Drudgery, but,

---

suggesting that there may have been an influence of earlier music on the pioneers of the glee repertoire that was not maintained by their successors.

8   'Science, Provincial Culture and Public Opinion in Enlightenment England', in Borsay, *The Eighteenth Century Town*, p. 252.

9   Elizabeth Chevill, 'Music Societies and Musical Life in Old Foundation Cathedral Cities 1700–1760', Ph.D. diss. (University of London, 1993). See also Ch. 3 above.

10   William Gardiner, *Music and Friends, or Pleasant Recollections of a Dilettante*, 3 vols (London and Leicester, 1828–53), vol. 1, p. 46 f.

144   BRIAN ROBINS

by Allurement, and the Gratification of a Pleasure they found in it themselves. Moreover: These good Effects having operated very greatly to my advantage, as well as to the Entertainment of the Public, it is with the utmost Pleasure and Sense of Gratitude, that I acknowledge the Obligation I am under to my assistant Friends upon that Account. Thus much may suffice as to the Utility and laudable Practice of frequently singing Catches, and other little detached Pieces of *Vocal Harmony*; and I cannot help wishing it may prove an inducement to others, my Brethren of Cathedrals especially, to encourage and promote such Societies as the above; well knowing it will contribute greatly to their own Satisfaction, the Improvement of those who may stand in need of their Assistance, and thereby, not a little, to the just Execution of *Church-Music*, or the Support of any *Choral Performance*.

Eight years later Hayes published a supplement in which the dedication specifically refers to an Oxford 'Catch-Club'; this may also help locate 'this Place' as the King's Head Tavern (the possibility exists that the venue may have changed during the intervening years).[11] Substantiation of the early existence of a catch club in Oxford comes from Edward Fawconer, a Fellow of Merton College, who in 1752 recorded that he visited a catch club in Oxford, 'of which Dr [William] Hayes & his son [Philip], with other good performers, were members, & was there very agreeably entertained'.[12] Hayes's Preface is important for defining not only once again the essentially convivial nature of catch club culture, but also his belief that the singing of catches and glees served a useful didactic purpose, particularly to the clergy, who as noted maintained a strong presence in musical clubs. While detailed discussion of performance practice lies beyond the scope of the present chapter, Hayes's following paragraph provides such valuable insight that it is worth quoting *in extenso*:

> Few I should imagine, need be informed, that the Manner of performing Catches, is, by one Person's leading off and singing so much as one of the Number of Parts whereof the Catch consisteth, before the Second begins; he then sings the same Quantity, and the Third begins; and so on, till as many are employed as it requires: But I must beg leave to suggest, that, so often as it is repeated, an Alternacy of *Forte* and *Piano* or *Loud* and *Soft*, in imitation of the *Chiaro Oscuro*, or *Light* and *Shade* in painting, has an agreeable effect; except in such, where the humour of the Subject requires a certain Jollity to be kept up throughout the whole, which the Performer will very easily distinguish. And if, amongst the following, any should be found worthy of being *pathetic*, or to have any thing *delicate* in their *Taste* or *Construction*, I would recommend *Mezzo Piano* (at least sometimes under the full Tone of Voice) as being more expressive of Tenderness.
>
> I shall hope for a Pardon from the *judicious Reader*, for having given these few Hints concerning the Manner of performing Catches, when I assure him, they were intended chiefly for the Information of *Novices* in the Art; and not to insult the better *Taste* and *Skill* of the Adept, by intruding Conceits of my own where they are not wanted. For this Reason, I have been very sparing in arbitrarily prescribing Graces,

---

11   William Hayes, *A Supplement to the Catches, Glees, and Canons lately published by Dr. Hayes* (Oxford, 1765).

12   Donald Burrows and Rosemary Dunhill, *Music and Theatre in Handel's World: The Family Papers of James Harris 1732–1780* (Oxford: Oxford University Press, 2002), p. 285: Letter from Edward Fawconer to James Harris, 10 November 1752.

THE CATCH AND GLEE IN PROVINCIAL ENGLAND 145

and in putting Marks for Expression; being persuaded that a Redundancy of such Marks not only perplex the Performer, but if his *Taste* in the Executive Part be better than the Composer's (a very possible Case) will certainly give him disgust, tho' calculated with the utmost Care and Precision. To such a One, the best Guide will be a true Perception of the Sense and Drift of the Design; and that Expression the most proper, resulting from his own instantaneous Feeling.

Here we find clear evidence that the performance of catches (and glees, since the two terms were frequently interchangeable during the 1760s) was ideally expected at this time to be far from rough and ready, but rather sophisticated musical interpretations that took account of such matters as dynamics, colour and expression. How often such ideals were achieved is another matter, especially in the provinces, but they obviously remained an issue. In January 1800 the amateur composer and diarist John Marsh attended a meeting of one of the most famous provincial catch clubs, the Harmonic Society of Bath. There he encountered his friend, the noted glee and catch composer Dr Henry Harington, who was apparently in agreement with Marsh that a selection of glees and catches was 'very accurately done, tho' in not quite so good a style as I had expected, as they sung rather too loud & in too boisterous a manner'.[13]

Further frustratingly brief evidence of the early existence of provincial catch clubs may be found in the preface to *The Essex Harmony*, another pioneering collection first issued in 1769. After referring to the Catch Club, its compiler John Arnold goes on to inform his readers that the great esteem in which part-songs, catches, canons and glees are held at present 'is evident by the great Number of Catch-Clubs, &c. which are now established both in Town and Country'. Regrettably, Arnold identifies only the London Catch Club, although significantly he also names Oxford as a place where a club or clubs exist. In addition Arnold takes up Hayes's didactic theme, indeed extending it to the view that the cultivation of singing in country areas would serve a social purpose since 'it would not only prevent the many Accidents, Mischiefs, and other bad consequences, generally attending those Diversions of Heroism, Cudgeling, Football Playing &c. but would be a means of encouraging the practice of one of the greatest of Sciences' .[14] Arnold's promotion of music in country areas was to find an echo in the singing contests held at local Oxfordshire inns (and doubtless elsewhere) during the 1770s. One such contest held at the Crown Inn, Farringdon in April 1777 informed 'Lovers of Vocal Harmony' that sides would compete for a prize of three guineas, each to sing 'two Songs, of two or three Parts, and two Catches or Glees'.[15]

Both Hayes and Arnold clearly imply the precedence of Oxford, and despite Arnold's teasing '&c.' no evidence of other provincial catch clubs being formed during the 1760s has to date come to light. The next three decades would, however,

---

13   *The John Marsh Journals: The Life and Times of a Gentleman Composer (1752–1828)*, ed. Brian Robins (Stuyvesant, NY: Pendragon Press, 1998), p. 707.

14   John Arnold, ed., *The Essex Harmony* (London, 1769).

15   *Jackson's Oxford Journal*, 5 Apr. 1777.

witness a vast expansion of the catch club culture both in London and in the provinces, where the existence has been established of clubs in historic urban centres such as Canterbury, Salisbury, Chichester, York, Lincoln, Norwich, Lichfield and Bristol, spa cities like Bath, and the newer, fast-growing industrial conurbations of Nottingham, Liverpool and Manchester. Doubtless others await discovery. One of the particular difficulties of uncovering detailed information on the organization and activities of clubs is the lack of newspaper advertising and reporting. Unlike concert promoters, who obviously needed to make the public aware of their activities, the organizers of private clubs rarely needed to promote their regular activities in the press. We are therefore largely reliant on a few extant records and personal observations. The most comprehensive records known today are those of the Canterbury Catch Club and the Bath Harmonic Society, while there is a useful account of the Bristol Catch Club.[16] In addition a set of Rules exists for the Lichfield Cecilian Society (founded in 1772), although the document on which they are preserved is damaged and partly illegible.[17] For personal accounts of the activities of provincial catch clubs we are hugely indebted to the indefatigable John Marsh, who not only was a member of clubs in Salisbury, Canterbury and Chichester (which he founded in 1787), but also recorded in his diaries anecdotal comments on catch clubs in Bath and Nottingham. It is therefore the clubs in Bath, Canterbury (established in 1779), Salisbury (before 1776), Chichester and Bristol (by 1774) that form the principal source of this study.

The inspiration for the formation of provincial catch clubs was, as already noted, almost certainly the exemplar of the London Catch Club and the part it played in elevating the glee to a popular indigenous art form. However, the provincial clubs could not (and did not) seek to emulate their grand London progenitor in certain major respects, most notably in terms of membership and structure. The London Catch Club was a highly selective organization dominated by parliamentarians from both Houses that could afford, with the professional assistance of some of the best London singers, to adopt the purist stance of admitting only the performance of unaccompanied catches, glees and (especially in its earlier days) canons. Provincial clubs necessarily took a more pragmatic line, invariably diversifying to include instrumental music and solo songs during the course of their evening's entertainment. Details of instrumentalists exist for both the Canterbury and Bath clubs. Around 1785 the Canterbury club employed an orchestra of around 14 players (3 violins, 1 viola, 5 'basses', 3 oboes and 2 horns).[18] The catalogue of the Canterbury Catch Club collection includes a

---

16   Graham Hooper, 'A Survey of Music in Bristol with special reference to the eighteenth century', unpublished MS, Bristol Record Office.

17   Lichfield Record Office [LRO], Add. MS D127.

18   Pencilled on the inside of vol. 3 of the Canterbury Catch Club collection, c.1785. The full collection consists of nine original manuscript volumes of catches, glees, duets and songs. Vols 5, 6 and 9 are missing. Apparently commenced around 1785 (the year appended to vols 1 and 3), entries in the same hand extend well into the nineteenth century. They are thereafter supplemented by later additions. The collection is now housed in the Library of Canterbury Cathedral.

THE CATCH AND GLEE IN PROVINCIAL ENGLAND

substantial number of instrumental works, among them the 'complete' orchestral works of Handel and an extensive list of modern symphonies by such composers as Abel, J. C. Bach and Haydn. John Marsh left a detailed account of the Canterbury Club that includes a description of the kind of programme he encountered when he first attended in November 1783:

> The plan of this club was as follows. About half past 6. an overture was played by the band (in a small orchestra railed off at one end of the room) after which follow'd a glee; then a quartetto, trio or concerto; after which follow'd another glee & then a catch, which constituted the first Act; the second of w'ch after a short cessation began with another overture, next to w'ch Mrs Goodban generally made her appearance & sung a song, after which another glee & a catch or chorus concluded the concert. The generality of the audience & performers however comonly remained 'till 11 or 12 o'clock, smoking their pipes (which they did all the time of the concert, except during Mrs Goodbans song, imediately preceding w'ch the company were always desired by the president to lay down their pipes) during which time single songs were sung, as called for by the president.[19]

Marsh's mention of the extremely unusual presence of a female singer at a catch club calls for a brief digression on the subject of the place of women in clubs. As Peter Clark makes clear in his recent study,[20] such institutions were almost exclusively a male preserve. One exception was more general music societies, frequently difficult to distinguish from concert series and which were often prepared to admit mixed audiences. Chevill, for instance, notes that women were somewhat controversially admitted to the New Musick Club in York as early as 1728, their presence causing one local observer to note that 'Filthy smoking, muddy Ale and Wine are all forbid during Musick Time'.[21] The greater openness of musical societies defines a paradigmatic difference between these and the entire catch club culture, which was dependent upon the basic tenets of male conviviality – drinking, smoking and male companionship. In addition the risqué nature of many catches made them unsuitable for performance in front of 'polite', or mixed, society. This is not to say that women had no role within the broader parameters of catch club culture. While they were not permitted to attend regular club evenings, the Catch Club had introduced an annual Ladies Night by the early 1770s, an initiative emulated in Canterbury, where Marsh informs us that he attended 'the annual Catch Club for *ladies* at Goodban's (of which there was always one as soon as the regular season was over)' in May 1785.[22] Rule XXVII of the Lichfield Cecilian Society states 'That the Lady-Patroness have a Ticket to the Concert on the Festival-Night [the celebration of St Cecilia's Day on or near 22 November] conveyed to her, with particular Compliments from the Stewards'.[23] Nevertheless, Marsh's use of italics implies that such events were sufficiently

---

19   *The John Marsh Journals*, ed. Robins, p. 302.
20   Peter Clark, *British Clubs and Societies 1580–1800: The Origins of an Associational World* (Oxford: Clarendon Press, 2000), p. 3.
21   Chevill, 'Music Societies', p. 78.
22   *The John Marsh Journals*, ed. Robins, p. 344.
23   LRO, reference as n. 17.

148 BRIAN ROBINS

unusual to require special emphasis, and there is no record of their being hosted in Salisbury, Chichester, Bath or, until 1810, in Bristol. Mrs Goodban's participation at the Canterbury club can almost certainly be attributed to the fact that she was the wife of the landlord of the Prince of Orange, the venue for its meetings.

The fashionable status of Bath must have been responsible for its Harmonic Society's following the lead of the Catch Club in appointing honorary professional members, both vocalists and instrumentalists. Four instrumentalists are appended to a list of club members dating from 1799, among them the cellist Alexander Herschel (brother of the famous astronomer) and one of the Mahon brothers (probably John), both eminent clarinettists. Apropos of this group, which was significantly smaller than the number of instrumentalists employed in Canterbury, Article XI of the Rules of the society implies that they were used only for the purpose of accompanying vocal music at meetings; for these occasions, members were expected to be in the room 'before the Abbey clock strikes seven':

> The President shall be absolute during the Meeting, *consistent with the Rules and Orders of the Society*. On his taking the Chair the MUSICAL PERFORMANCE shall commence, which shall consist of *Catches, Glees, Chorusses, Songs &c.* which shall continue until *nine* o'clock ... a cold supper, at *Four Shillings* each, (Port Wine and Sherry included) shall then be placed upon the table; before which the grace of *"Sodales Caenantes"* shall be sung, the whole Society standing up; and in like manner the Canon of *"Non nobis, Domine!"* shall be sung. Three Toasts only shall be given ... after which, such Catches, Glees, or Songs, shall be sung as may be called for by the PRESIDENT, or VICE-PRESIDENT. At *Eleven* o'clock the bill shall be brought in, when the PRESIDENT shall quit the chair.[24]

The singing of grace and toasting were common features in more formally constituted clubs, both musical and otherwise, though most would have found the Bath society's three toasts distinctly on the parsimonious side.

Although detailed records are lacking, a collection of 'Duets, Rotas [rounds], Canons and Glees' issued by the Bristol organist and composer Robert Broderip in 1795 and 'respectively inscribed To the Members of the Bristol Catch Club, and Cecilian Society' suggests that Bristol followed its West Country neighbour in restricting its repertoire to vocal music. The impression is supported by a surviving Ladies Night programme dating from March 1810, when only glees, catches and songs were performed.[25] Bath and Bristol thus differ in this from Salisbury, Canterbury, Chichester and Lichfield, where members were able to hear both vocal and instrumental music. As we have seen, in Canterbury the two were interspersed, while in Salisbury and Chichester the instrumental music preceded the singing of catches and glees, a format closer to that of another London club, the Anacreontic Society.[26]

---

24 *A Selection of Favourite Catches, Glees, &c. as Sung at the Bath Harmonic Society with the Rules of the Society, and a List of Members. Second edition with considerable additions* (Bath, 1799).
25 Hooper, 'Survey', p. 205.
26 *The John Marsh Journals*, ed. Robins, p. 149 (Salisbury), p. 419 (Chichester).

THE CATCH AND GLEE IN PROVINCIAL ENGLAND 149

Whatever degree of incursion instrumental music did or did not make into club meetings, its role naturally remained secondary to the main objective of the entertainment – the singing of catches and glees supplemented by drinking and (in most instances) some form of supper. The singers who took part in these performances ranged from the eight professionals retained by the Bath club (three of whom also appeared in Bristol) to the near total dominance of vicars choral in clubs based in cathedral cities. In Salisbury all four principal singers, Joseph Corfe, John Goss, a Mr Barrett and Francis Wellman were prominent members of the cathedral choir. Corfe, also a Gentleman of the Chapel Royal, played an active role in Salisbury's musical life over a long period, being appointed leader of the subscription concerts on the death of James Harris in 1780; he was succeeded 12 years later by his bitter rival Robert Parry as cathedral organist. During the period Marsh was there (1783–87), the Canterbury Catch Club could boast among its principal singers Israel Gore, a vicar choral who subsequently became a member of the St Paul's Cathedral choir and, like Corfe, a Gentleman of the Chapel Royal. In Chichester Marsh could also draw upon the services of four cathedral vicars choral, Moses Toghill, John Moore, Bartholemew (*sic*) Middleton, and a Mr Webber. Toghill was the possessor of what Marsh considered one of the finest counter-tenor voices he ever heard, while the diarist Sylas Neville heard Toghill on a visit to Chichester in 1781 and was much impressed by his 'most powerful & at the same time melodious Bass voice'[27] (it was not unusual to sing both counter-tenor and bass). Another distinguished founding member of the Chichester Catch Club was Theodore Aylward, a founder member of the Glee Club (in 1787), professor at Gresham College and subsequently appointed master of the choristers and organist of St George's Chapel, Windsor.

The presence of such names as those mentioned above tempts the suggestion that performance standards in the provinces, if hardly likely to have been on a level with those of the Catch Club, were often high. Such a notion must, however, be balanced against the fact that this was a period during which (as has been widely recognized) the standard of singing in cathedrals was generally poor. Contemporary clues to the levels attained are scarce. With the exception of the comments quoted above on the Bath society, even that acute observer John Marsh rarely passed judgement on the quality of performance he heard other than to castigate the hapless Mrs Goodban of Canterbury for 'screaming' the top notes of Stephen Paxton's popular glee 'How sweet, how fresh', an observation that supports a strong impression that the best performances of catches and glees were achieved by adult male ensembles. While assessment of general performance standards must therefore remain conjectural, it does seem entirely reasonable to propose that the expectation that both glees and catches should be performed with a degree of attention and refinement similar to that outlined by William Hayes in the 1760s remained unchanged.

---

27 *The Diary of Sylas Neville 1767–1788*, ed. Basil Cozens-Hardy (London: Oxford University Press, 1950), p. 288.

150   BRIAN ROBINS

The known repertoire of provincial clubs was to some extent predictably modelled on that of their grand London progenitor, and in at least two instances, those of Bristol and Chichester, clubs owned the volumes produced annually by Edmund Warren under the auspices of the Catch Club.[28] The Bristol Catch Club was additionally the co-dedicatee (with the city's Cecilian Society) of a more general collection including 20 catches and 19 glees compiled by the local composer and publisher Robert Broderip. Canterbury and Bath both produced their own collections, the former being the largest and most important manuscript collection in existence. Up to around 1820 over 1300 entries were made by the same hand, 62 per cent of them glees and 32 per cent catches, the remainder consisting of either solo songs or duets. In the instance of the Bath Harmonic Society, the proportion of catches and glees is even more heavily weighted in favour of the latter, no less than 77 per cent of the contents of its *Selection* consisting of glees. Such an imbalance runs directly counter to the contents of the Warren Collection, where near-equality of content is granted to the two forms. This is almost certainly partially due to the later date of the provincial collections, since for both musical and external reasons the glee progressively ousted its older companion. As the form better suited to lyrical expansion and sentimental expressive qualities reflecting the increasing gentility of society, it was better placed than its humorous masculine companion to survive entry into polite society. Indeed, the often risqué nature of the catch was a constant issue. Publishers frequently sought to distance themselves from the more questionable examples of the genre by assuring their readers that the contents of their collections entirely excluded 'obscenity and ribaldry ... as being foreign to the true nature of innocent mirth and good humour',[29] while as early as 1771 the critic of *The Monthly Review* was able to reassure his readers that a collection under consideration included 'none of those indecent, ribaldry pieces inserted, by which other collections have been disgraced'.[30]

The London Catch Club itself was attacked for singing crude catches on a number of occasions by critics such as the Exeter composer and essayist William Jackson,[31] but no uniform picture emerges of the attitude of provincial clubs to the more ribald catches. The Canterbury Collection certainly includes a number of such pieces, while as late as 1790 John Marsh records one Colonel Jones singing for his entry audition to the Chichester club a song 'the words of which were not more chaste than his manner of singing them'. Hooper suggests (without providing evidence) that the 'purposeful rearrangement of words to achieve a bawdy result

---

28   In Bristol a copy was owned by a prominent member, the surgeon Richard Smith: Hooper, 'Survey', p. 201. The Chichester Catch Club owned a copy shared with the subscription concerts, the gift of Thomas Steele, one of the city's MPs and himself a member of the Catch Club; cf. *The John Marsh Journals*, ed. Robins, p. 526.

29   Joseph Vernon, *The New London and Country Songster* (London, 1781).

30   *Monthly Review*, 44 (Jan. 1771).

31   In the tenth of his *Thirty Letters on various subjects* (3rd edn, London, 1795) Jackson makes a thinly veiled attack on the Catch Club and its espousal of a form 'not judged perfect, if the result be not the rankest indecency'.

THE CATCH AND GLEE IN PROVINCIAL ENGLAND   151

was characteristic of the catches performed by the Bristol club'.[32] In contrast the genteel Bath club seems to have eschewed such rough manners, at least by the end of the century, Rule 1 of its constitution sternly stating that 'This Society is established for the PROMOTION OF HARMONY, in its general signification; in order to preserve which, no POLITICAL DISCUSSION shall be suffered to take place, nor shall any INDECENT SONG or SENTIMENT be permitted to be sung or spoken on any account'.[33] As we shall later discover, harmony 'in its general signification' was more easily set in a rulebook than maintained in practice. The refinement of the Bath Harmonic Society may also have been responsible for the impressions of the irascible Charles Dibdin, who visited a catch club in Bath (in all likelihood the Harmonic Society) in 1787, finding 'the fashionable gravity' of the proceedings 'beyond credibility'. 'That a meeting', Dibdin fulminated, 'professedly convivial should apparently be held without mirth, is a kind of existence without a soul – a mental death – but it may be reconciled by saying that it is a refinement on politeness.'[34]

Such politeness is doubtless responsible for the unusually low proportion of catches found in the Bath Collection, a mere 29 in a collection consisting of a total of 253 works. We also find Bath to be out on something of a limb when it comes to an analysis of composers contributing to the overall repertoire. This is partly because of the number of locals featured in its collection, men like Henry Harington (also a glee and catch composer of national significance), and James Brooks, who were responsible for nearly a fifth of the contents.[35] Nonetheless it is surprising to find Samuel Webbe senior, not only the finest but also the most popular of all glee composers, relegated from his customary first place to third, behind Harington and John Wall Callcott, in the Bath Collection. Callcott, an immensely prolific composer who had to be curbed by the Catch Club after submitting too many prize entries, was comfortably the leading runner-up to Webbe in the popularity stakes, while other figures to feature prominently across the spectrum include John Danby, Benjamin Cooke and Luffman Atterbury. Yet perhaps the most striking aspect of the repertoire of the provincial clubs is its sheer diversity. Only 48 glees are found to be contiguous in the three sources covering the four clubs for which sufficient detail is available (Warren, as previously noted, was used in Chichester and Bristol). Further indication of the most popular glees sung in the provinces can be culled from those mentioned by John Marsh, although these include public concert performances in addition to catch club airings. Both listings include works whose popularity endured throughout much

---

32   Hooper, 'Survey', p. 204.
33   Bath *Selection*, reference as n. 24.
34   Charles Dibdin, *The Musical Tour of Mr. Dibdin* (Sheffield, 1788). Letter VII to T.S. Esq., pp. 24–5.
35   The Harmonic Society of Cambridge went one step further, issuing two collections of 'Glees and Rounds for three, four and five voices' (1796 and 1800) entirely composed by members who include Charles Hague, Richard Wheeler and William Dixon. The extensive list of subscribers on the title-page of the earlier book includes such names as Samuel Arnold, Thomas Attwood and R. J. S. Stevens, providing evidence that although local the publications achieved widespread circulation.

152   BRIAN ROBINS

of the nineteenth century: R. J. S. Stevens's Shakespearean settings 'Sigh no more, ladies' and 'Ye spotted snakes', and Samuel Webbe's 'You gave me your heart', 'Swiftly from the mountain's brow' and 'When winds breath soft'. While it is risky to derive categorical assertions from the restricted corpus of evidence available, the conclusion that the repertoire performed in the provincial clubs was drawn from a small number of canonic works supplemented by a huge and locally varied stock appears inescapable.

For an understanding of the proceedings and membership of provincial catch clubs, we are yet again much indebted to Marsh. Part of his vivid picture of the Canterbury Catch Club has already been quoted above and it can be supplemented by his accounts of the clubs in Salisbury and Chichester. By the time Marsh arrived in Salisbury in October 1776, he found the club well established:

> The winter Catch Club at the Spread Eagle now beginning, I on the 15th. went there & played with Mr Woodyear the leader ... At this meeting there was always a concert from about ½ past 6 'till after 8. at w'ch time a large table was set out ... [after w'ch] the company form'd a circle round the fire & catches & glees were perform'd by Mess'rs Corfe Goss Barrett & Wellman with now & then a song from some other member 'till 11. or 12 o'clock. – The subscription was 7/6s. per qu'tr w'ch paid for the room, fire, candles, bread, cheese & beer at supper pipes & tobacco (w'ch were never used 'till after supper) whatever else was drank being separately paid for by those that called for it. Besides subscribers however there were several professional performers who were admitted gratis & intitled to the same fare as the subscribers.[36]

When Marsh moved from Salisbury to an inherited estate in Kent in 1783 he again found a successful and well-patronized club in Canterbury, at which he made his first appearance in November of that year:

> The price of admission to this club was only 6d. for w'ch besides the music an unlimitted quantity of pipes & tobacco & beer was allow'd, in consequence of which many of the members, amongst the lower kinds of tradesmen etc. used by way of having a full pennyworth for their penny, to go at 6. and smoke away till 11. or 12. On account of this fumigation from 40. or 50. Pipes ... there were 3. ventilators in the ceiling in order, in some degree to get rid of the smoke but the room was so low pitched & bad that notwithstanding this, it appear'd as if we were all in a fog there. – The terms of admission being so low it will naturally be wonder'd how the landlord co'd possibly help losing instead of profiting by it, but the fact was that every member of the Club (of whom there were 50. or 60) paid his 6d. whether he came or not & a great many were always absent (the club being on every Wednesday throughout the winter) besides which many that were present instead of drinking beer had spirits & water & particularly *gin punch* (w'ch Goodban was famous for making particularly palatable) w'ch were paid for extraordinarily.[37]

Not surprisingly, comparison between the formats of the two clubs reveals common features. Both were held at inns, the traditional venue for male clubs during the eighteenth century. This ensured the essential ingredients of drink and social conviviality provided at a modest cost. The choice of inn in Canterbury and

---

36   *The John Marsh Journals*, ed. Robins, p. 149.
37   Ibid., pp. 302–3.

THE CATCH AND GLEE IN PROVINCIAL ENGLAND   153

Salisbury was in part obviously dictated by the accommodation available, but also in both instances by a landlord who actively participated, both Goodban of the Prince of Orange and Gibbons of the Spread Eagle in Salisbury being violinists. As Peter Clark notes, such close relationships between club and innkeeper benefited both and played an important part in the expansion of club life.[38] Lichfield, where the society met at the King's Head until 1790 when it moved to the Swan Inn, was almost certainly unusual in expressly forbidding the landlord membership of the society.[39] In Bath and Bristol the clubs also met at an inn, in the instance of the former at the White Hart.[40] The Bristol Catch Club met at the Bush Tavern in Corn Street, where the landlord Jack Weeks was apparently a well-known local character, although it is not clear whether or not he was actively involved. The club founded by John Marsh in Chichester in November 1787 broke with this tradition in meeting at what had become known as the Old Concert Room in East Pallant, a venue that involved food and drink having to be brought in from outside:

> Having now fully establish'd the plan of the Concerts & set them going, the next thing I wish'd to do was to settle a plan for the winter Catch Club at the old Concert Room, in which the vicars & Mess'rs Aylward Webber Humphry etc. all coinciding, we met on Tuesday the 23d. in the even'g at the Room, where we had some oysters etc. & settled the plan as follows – to meet together for 12 nights on every other Friday at the old Concert Room (but so as not to interfere with Subscript'n Concert nights) & amuse ourselves with instrumental music from half past 6. 'till half past 8 at w'ch time we were to sit down to a supper consisting only of oysters & Welch rabbits (to be provided for us at 10d. per head ... & afterwards sing catches, glees etc. around the fire, whetting our whistles with punch, wine etc. as agreed by the members present. These members were however to be confin'd to such gent'n as were capable of either assisting in the instrumental part, or of joining in at least one catch or glee etc. who were to subscribe 7s/6d per quarter to defray the expence of the supper, fire candles & attendance, & forfeit 6d per time for nonattendance or being too late. – To assist in the instrumental part we engaged Mr Payne (at ½ a crown a time) & invited Mr Mitchell the schoolmaster, who played the tenor at the Concerts, Mr Bailey a flute player & his son who played the flute & violin (also amateur players at the Concert) to join us, who except when particularly invited to stay used to go away as soon as the concert before supper was over. – The plan being thus settled, Mr Walker was appointed steward for the 1st. night (Friday Nov'r 2d.) w'ch office was to be taken by each member in rotation ...[41]

As is clear from the foregoing, Marsh, himself a gentleman, had ideas that differed from those he had encountered in Salisbury and Canterbury. The strict rules formulated are closer to London models than the more open atmosphere prevailing in Salisbury and, especially, Canterbury. Professional instrumentalists

---

38   Clark, *British Clubs*, p. 165.
39   LRO, reference as n. 17, Rule XVIII.
40   A second catch club may have existed in Bath. In 1804 *A Selection of Catches, Glees etc.* was published with a dedication to the 'Members of the Bath York-House Catch-Club'. There is of course also the possibility that the Harmonic Society had changed its name. York House was the principal inn in Bath, rated as 'one of the largest and best inns in the kingdom out of London' by Pierce Egan in his *Walks through Bath* (London, 1819), p. 34.
41   *The John Marsh Journals*, ed. Robins, pp. 419–20.

154 BRIAN ROBINS

were still hired, but were expected to leave after being given supper, itself a more ambitious affair than the bread, cheese and porter served at the Salisbury club. Additionally, Marsh's new club departed from provincial tradition in admitting only those capable of taking part in the singing, thus adding a qualification barrier that provided greater exclusivity than that pertaining to the other clubs under discussion. The use of fines to act as a deterrent against non-attendance or lateness was a common rule among eighteenth-century clubs, although no such mechanism is recorded as having been in place in Salisbury or Canterbury. Surprisingly, the more socially pretentious Bath Harmonic Society seems not to have levied such fines, although Rule X imposes a heavy punitive fine of half a guinea on a president for not being in his chair at the correct hour. The position of president, another standard feature of club life, was generally served by rotation among club members. While Bath and Canterbury had a president at their meetings, Salisbury, Chichester and Lichfield preferred a steward (or stewards), whose function was to manage rather than chair club nights.

The formality of the clubs under discussion thus varies considerably and was largely dictated by the social status of the membership. Canterbury unquestionably comes closest to what we might term today a working men's club, with a large membership including 'the lower kind of tradesmen' paying a low nightly admission charge (instead of a quarterly membership subscription) in order to drink cheap beer and smoke their pipes, the fumigation from which apparently caused one member to own what he called his 'catch club coat', a smoke-stenched garment he reserved especially for his visits to the Prince of Orange. At the opposite end of the scale Bath attempted to maintain something of the exclusivity of the original London Catch Club, considering as candidates for membership only 'NOBLEMEN, GENTLEMEN, and PROFESSIONAL MEN, who reside in Bath or its Vicinity, or who may occasionally visit it'.[42] As at the Catch Club, those who sought membership were balloted, at least nine members being necessary for an election conducted on the blackballing system. In Bath a ratio of one black ball to two white resulted in rejection.[43] Non-performing applicants in Lichfield also had to face a ballot.[44]

Membership numbers and the demand for membership apparently maintained a healthy level. In Bath the list of members in 1799 runs to no fewer than 276 names,[45] while the large attendance noted by Marsh in Canterbury was obviously replicated in Salisbury, as he makes clear in an entry dated only a month later than his first appearance at the established club:

> Mr Corfe having had some disagreement with some of the members of the Catch Club at the opening of that meeting this year, now suggested to me an idea of having (with my assistance as leader & Mr Burgatt's etc.) another club once a fortnight (on

---

42   Bath *Selection*, reference as n. 24, Rule II.
43   Ibid., Rule IV.
44   LRO, reference as n. 17, Rule II.
45   Given Bath's status as a fashionable spa with a fluctuating population, it is unlikely that attendance figures for any one meeting approached this figure.

THE CATCH AND GLEE IN PROVINCIAL ENGLAND

155

the intervening Tuesdays) upon a smaller scale than the other, where there were now so many members that it frequently became disagreable. This, as may be supposed, I readily acceded to, & on Tuesday Nov'r 5th. we had our first meeting at w'ch Mr Burgat & I played the 1st. fiddle, Mr Gibbons (the landlord) the 2d. Mr Corfe the pianoforte; Mr Still & Mr Beaumont (a musical amateur then at Sarum) the violoncellos Mr Chubb flute with tenors etc. making altogether a very good band. – Having amused ourselves for about 2 hours with instrumental music (in the course of w'ch we played one of Boccherini's quintettos for 2 violins, tenor & 2 obligato violoncellos, of w'ch Mr Beaumont was very fond) we about half past 8. had our bread & cheese etc. after w'ch Mess'rs Corfe Goss Wellman & Barratt sung some glees etc. with now & then a single song till between 11 & 12 o'clock.[46]

The passage is of significance not only for underlining the popularity of the catch clubs – henceforward Salisbury, like Canterbury, would for some years support a weekly meeting throughout the winter – but also providing further insight into the organization, activities and membership of the clubs. Here we find a social mix that encompasses cathedral choristers, the landlord of the Spread Eagle Inn, a dancing master (Burgat), an apothecary and middle-class professional men such as Chubb, an attorney. In Chichester, as already noted, the membership was much smaller (within a few months of its establishment Marsh records 30 people, including a number of visiting musical amateurs, attending a meeting in January 1788) and in general came from a rather higher social stratum. In addition to Theodore Aylward and the cathedral vicars, the membership named by Marsh at various times includes a clergyman, a surgeon, the sociably boisterous Colonel Jones, whose ribald qualification song has already been mentioned above, and two gentlemen. The local bookseller Humphry is the only name belonging to a humbler level of society, while Marsh significantly notes that two amateurs admitted as instrumentalists remained members only a short while, 'being not in the habits of intimacy with the other gent'n'.[47]

The Chichester club therefore sought to retain the intimacy of a gathering of friends meeting together to make music and enjoy convivial company, at least after the hired professionals had departed. Such an ethos is obviously quite different from that of the Bath Harmonic Society, where although the membership joined in a cold supper the large potential audience must have precluded any real atmosphere of intimacy. As Marsh's reportage of a breakaway catch club in Salisbury reveals, size was a common problem and many clubs sought to avoid becoming too large by placing a restriction on the number of members admitted. The London Catch Club passed an early resolution in April 1762 to restrict the number of members to 21 (the rule seems not to have been followed: by November 1764 there were 31 members),[48] while the Lichfield Cecilian Society restricted its membership to 60, excluding performers.[49]

---

46 *The John Marsh Journals*, ed. Robins, p. 151.
47 Ibid., p. 421.
48 Minutes of the Catch Club, BL Add. MS H.2788.rr.
49 LRO, reference as n. 17, Rule I.

156   BRIAN ROBINS

The relatively high cost of supper at the Bath Harmonic Society came in addition to an annual subscription of one guinea for a season that lasted from the last Friday in November until the last Friday in April, a total of some 22 meetings. Members who had not settled their dues one month after the commencement of their residency during the season were barred pending a new ballot, although not penalized for missing an entire season.[50] The 1799 Bath Harmonic membership list reveals a number of distinguished names led by George III's second son, Frederick, Duke of York, the exiled Stadtholder, William V of Orange and his son Prince Frederick of Orange. They are followed by the Marquises of Bath and Lansdown, and nine peers of the realm. The name of Sir Richard Pepper Arden, Master of the Rolls since 1788 and a friend of Prime Minister William Pitt also graces the list, as do a number of eminent military men and knights. Perhaps surprisingly, from this list only three names out of 42, those of Lord Hawarden (elected 1806), Sir Charles Talbot (1799) and Sir Walter James (1806), ever shared membership of the London Catch Club. The last named is also one of only two to be found among subscribers' lists of catch and glee publications, a striking comparison with members of the London Catch Club, many of whose members regularly supported such publications. Among the gentlemen and professional men whose occupations can be determined, it is hardly surprising to find a large body of service men (73, predominantly officers of the Royal Navy) and clerics (49), while medical men also feature strongly.

Thanks to Richard Smith junior, a member of the Bristol Catch Club from 1796, we also have some details of its membership.[51] In the fly-leaf of his copy of the Warren Collection, Smith recorded that when his father Richard Smith, a surgeon at the Bristol Infirmary, joined the club in 1785 notable members included four clerics, two attorneys, a silk mercer, a merchant, a Colonel Andrewes of the Somerset Militia, the composer and publisher Robert Broderip, whose publication dedicated to the club has already been mentioned, and the cathedral organist Rice Wasborough. Several were still members when the younger Smith joined, now supplemented by several members of the Wasborough family, a customs officer, James Hillhouse, a shipbuilder, a doctor, an attorney, 'a private gentleman' and, interestingly, one Applewaite, who is described by Smith as 'a West Indian'. Like the clubs in Salisbury and Canterbury, the Bristol club therefore appears to have admitted a diversity of membership that cut across class.

Although all clubs sought to maintain 'harmony, in its general signification', societies, as Clark notes, 'often experienced internal conflict'.[52] Provincial catch clubs were no exception. We have already seen how a breakaway club was formed in Salisbury because Joseph Corfe disagreed with some of the members, while John Marsh also records a new club being set up in opposition to the Canterbury Catch Club, ostensibly on account 'of the badness of the room at Goodban's', but

---

50   Bath *Selection*, reference as n. 24, Rules V and VII.
51   Quoted in Hooper, 'Survey', pp. 202 and 205.
52   Clark, *British Clubs*, p. 234.

THE CATCH AND GLEE IN PROVINCIAL ENGLAND 157

in reality a reflection of the rivalry between local musicians.[53] In Chichester the gradual erosion of the rules relating to visitors actually led to the demise of the club founded by Marsh. In November 1792 he records that 'by swerving from our original rules in the admission of unqualified members ... we had much injur'd the society'.[54] Marsh's remarks were specifically occasioned by a bad-tempered meeting at which a drunken local visitor (a 'gentleman') insulted one of the founder members, but there is an impression that this upset was only the culmination of a sequence of events. Subsequently many leading members of the club, including Marsh, resigned and the club was disbanded. The rowdiness that led to the demise of the Chichester club was by no means exceptional. Years earlier the breakaway Salisbury club was the scene of an episode that inspired a caricature entitled *Scene at a Catch Club*, now sadly lost:

> At our last Catch Club for this season (on the 10th.) a most extraordinary thing happen'd ... It may be recollected that on Capt Mitchell's kicking Burgat down the stairs at the Assembly in Dec'r 1779. the latter sent him a challenge w'ch the other declin'd noticing Burgat determin'd to insult him the 1st. time he met him afterw'ds w'ch ... did not happen 'till this even'g when during a performance of a violin concerto by Burgat, he came into the room with his friend Mr Richards who was a member of the club ... As soon as the concerto was finish'd, Burgat looking very significantly tow'ds that quarter of the room, gave a pretty strong *hiss* w'ch after a little pause being repeated, Mr Chafy got up & ask'd Burgat whether it was him & his friend that he did the honor to hiss. "No (replied he) it was *Mitchell*". This imediately brought up him & his introductor Richards who seizing little Burgat by the collar & proceeding to serve him as he had been serv'd at the Assembly, Mr De Hearle the French master (a great friend of Burgat's) imediately came up & threaten'd to be a witness of the assault of his friend, on which Mr Richards (without quitting his hold on Burgat) threaten'd to throw him behind the fire, & a fine hubbub was created ... Mr Richards perceiving that the little man wo'd hardly retire without force being used, very goodnaturedly, by way of putting an end to the business desired him that if he did not chuse to quit the room to resume his fiddle & take his place in the orchestra. But this was too great a condescension for Burgat to submit to who said he sho'd either play or not just as he pleased. Seeing however now a fair opportunity of closing this matter I imediately look'd out a full piece w'ch we all played (except Burgat who kept aloof with his fiddle in his hand) & w'ch concluded the concert after w'ch we according to custom on the last night adjourn'd to a foreroom to supper w'ch afforded Burgat & his friend De Hearle an opportunity of remaining behind & taking themselves off unnotic'd ... [55]

In 1790 the Lichfield Cecilian Society was riven with dissension of a different kind. A schism had apparently arisen between performing and non-performing members over the question of the powers to enforce the rules, a privilege granted only to performing members in the original statutes. In a magnanimous gesture the performers agreed to waive this ruling in the interest of 'preserving the Harmony

---

53　*The John Marsh Journals*, ed. Robins, p. 308.
54　Ibid., p. 526.
55　Ibid., pp. 233–4.

158   BRIAN ROBINS

of the Society', while at the same time adding a stern rider that the rules should in future be clearly understood by all new members.[56]

Following the break-up of the Chichester Catch Club attempts to form a new club meeting at the homes of members were apparently short-lived. The names listed by Marsh as attending the first meeting suggest that the new club was in fact little different from the ubiquitous domestic musical evenings that feature throughout Marsh's narrative, those mentioned including such genteel society as Lady Louisa Lennox, the sister-in-law of the Duke of Richmond. While it was the catch clubs in London and the provinces that provided the dynamic for establishing the enormous popularity of catches and glees, they had in fact entered the drawing room at an early stage. Marsh records innumerable instances when they were performed domestically, while it appears that Lord Sandwich, the driving force behind the Catch Club, propagated their performance at every opportunity. William Gardiner recalls a dinner party attended by his father at Gumley Hall in Leicestershire in September 1774. Sandwich and 'the London party' were present:

> On the cloth being drawn, his Lordship, addressing himself to Mr. Warren, secretary to the Nobleman's Catch Club, said, "Tom, have you got the catch-books here?" "Yes, my Lord," said Warren. "Then hand them to me." On their being placed at the head of the table, his Lordship said, "I shall choose first, and then each one in his turn".[57]

A number of catches and glees then followed, the ladies remaining until 'probably driven away by the unrestrained conversation of my Lord'. Gardiner concludes his account with a revealing observation: 'Chorus music, at that time was not understood, and not more than four singers could be found in Leicester to assist in the performance just described.' While the intended one-to-a-part performance of catches and glees was largely an unchallenged norm in London and more sophisticated provincial cities, it was by no means universally adopted. When Marsh first started reorganizing musical life in Canterbury he discovered that the boys

> were so badly taught by Porter, their master [Samuel Porter, the cathedral organist], that out of so many it was always difficult to find one or 2 fit to sing a single song & even the upper part of a glee without another to support him, on w'ch account when we came to try over the glee of Dr Harington's for a treble, tenor & bass ("Gentle Airs") at the rehearsal, Mr Porter brought 3 boys to sing the upper part, saying that if they were not enough I might have *more*, to w'ch I replied that as it was for a glee not a chorus that I wanted them, one or at most 2. wo'd be sufficient.[58]

Marsh's sarcastic dismissal of Porter's offer reveals a man accustomed to hearing glees and catches performed in more refined style, as does his observation on hearing the choir of the Dock Chapel in Portsmouth perform 'glees, elegies etc. in

---

56   LRO, reference as n. 17.
57   Gardiner, *Music and Friends*, vol. 1 (1828), p. 6.
58   *The John Marsh Journals*, ed. Robins, p. 300.

a very solemn style'. 'They might indeed', he continues, 'with as much propriety have been termed *chorusses* [Marsh's italics] there being about 9 or 10 singers & of course 2 or 3 to a part'.[59]

Marsh's request to Porter for boy trebles was made not on behalf of the Canterbury Catch Club, but for concert performance. The admission of the glee into concert programmes was an early development in its history for which Thomas Arne can be credited. As early as 1767 Arne had performed glees (with orchestral accompaniment) at London's Marylebone Gardens, a precedent that found few imitators until the early 1770s. Intriguingly, the earliest evidence yet discovered of glees and catches being given in a provincial concert comes from the Three Choirs Festival held in Gloucester in 1772. Included among the meeting's advertised events is a 'CONCERT, consisting of Full Pieces, & some of the most admired Catches and Glees, Solos and Concertos'.[60] Among the vocal performers listed are Elizabeth and Mary Linley, and Thomas Norris, who had become a privileged (professional) member of the Catch Club two years earlier. Whether or not the Linley sisters took part in the glees and catches is uncertain, but it is probable they did, there being of course no bar to female singers in the concert performance of such pieces. Three years later, in 1775, John Marsh attended a Race Concert at Winchester at which catches and glees were performed. They were, he notes, 'beginning now to be introduc'd in concerts', a comment that suggests that the Three Choirs concert must indeed have been something of a precedent. Marsh's references to this concert are also of interest for neatly encapsulating the difference between the two forms and providing an explanation for the glee's being more acceptable in the concert room than the catch, pointing out that although he was 'much pleas'd' with the performance of the glee, the catch 'requir'd humour' and was more suited to 'a convivial party then a public concert'.[61] Thomas Norris was also involved in the first concert to be devoted to catches and glees at a Salisbury Festival meeting (in 1776), leading to the suspicion that he may have been a prime mover behind the integration of the two forms into concert life. Once again John Marsh was on hand to report the event, having apparently revised his opinion regarding the concert performance of catches:

> in the evening [we went] to a performance of catches and glees at the Rooms which being something new they were very fully attended & were admirably sung by Norris Corfe Goss & Parry who all enter'd with great spirit into the humorous ones & made me laugh very much at the catch of "Mr Speaker", "Beviami tutti" etc.

By the 1780s the glee had firmly established itself in the concert programmes of provincial subscription concerts and festivals. Surviving programmes from the period suggest that it was rare for one or two glees not to be included.

---

59   Ibid., pp. 367–8.
60   *Jackson's Oxford Journal*, 25 July 1772 (and subsequent issues). The meeting took place between 9 and 11 September.
61   *The John Marsh Journals*, ed. Robins, pp. 132–3.

BRIAN ROBINS

Paradoxically it was the popularity of the genre, in particular within the context of domestic music making, that led to its gradual evolution from a skilfully wrought contrapuntal composition to more chordally based works scarcely distinguishable from a part-song. The demand for domestic glees also resulted in musicians turning popular ballads into glees, a procedure that drew the scorn of William Gardiner, who observed that after singers such as the noted James Bartleman, a privileged member of the Catch Club and a professional member of the Glee Club from the time of its establishment in 1787, had 'sung the classical glees threadbare, they introduced, as a novelty, a mawkish sort of composition – ballads harmonised for four voices – to which they improperly gave the name of glees. These ... being pretty well known as songs, were much applauded.'[62] The increasing and controversial employment of keyboard accompaniments also undoubtedly weakened the compositional structure of the 'pure' glee. John Marsh found himself embroiled in just such a controversy during a domestic evening's music making in January 1793:

> On Monday the 21st. we all went to a musical party at Mr Middletons to whom I lent my piano forte for the occasion on w'ch amongst other things I accomp'd a new glee sung by Mrs S.Heming, Mess'rs Moore & Toghill, the latter of whom imediately afterw'ds observ'd that it wo'd have a better effect another time *without* accompaniment ... tho' ... saying he did not mean to criticise on *my* accompaniment in particular, but on accomp'ts in general.[63]

The rise and decline of the catch and glee in Georgian England represents a unique and largely unexplored part of the nation's musical and cultural history. Taking their impetus from a small group of noblemen and gentlemen who met on a November evening in 1761 to form the London Catch Club, the two forms were disseminated throughout the length and breadth of Britain by the musicians and enthusiasts who founded their own clubs – supported by a broad cross-section of male society meeting for the pleasure and entertainment they gained from listening, singing, drinking and eating in a convivial environment. Despite all the schisms, unruly behaviour and occasional intemperance, many of the provincial clubs survived well into the nineteenth century. As late as 1819, long after the city had abandoned a regular concert series, a new catch club was founded in Chichester. Significantly its meetings were held not at a concert room or private houses, but at the Swan Inn.

---

62 Gardiner, *Music and Friends*, vol. 3 (1853), p. 108. The author is here referring to a concert given by a group of singers including Bartleman and Thomas Greatorex during Assize Week in Leicester, probably during the 1790s.

63 *The John Marsh Journals*, ed. Robins, p. 533.

CHAPTER NINE

The String Quartet in London Concert Life, 1769–1799

Meredith McFarlane and Simon McVeigh

Introduction

The string quartet's evolution as a musical genre coincided with an unprecedented profusion and diversification of London's public concert life. This intense concert activity, culminating in the so-called 'rage for music', affected all those involved in British musical life and, in turn, provided the impetus for new styles of chamber music. In charting string quartet performances over a period of 30 years, this chapter highlights the contribution of London's many foreign composers (often leading violinists), the plight of their native counterparts, and the perhaps surprising reception accorded to the respective quartets of Haydn and Pleyel. The importance of London's concert milieu in stimulating such highly public chamber-music activity becomes most obvious in a comparison with string quartet performance in two other European capitals. While no evidence exists for the public performance of a string quartet by professionals in either Paris or Vienna before the turn of the century,[1] London concert audiences became familiar with this new chamber idiom from the 1770s onwards through professional performances by leading exponents.

In this context, Joseph Haydn's contribution is beyond doubt the best known. But it should be stressed that the path to Haydn's celebrity as a quartet composer was, in England, far from smooth.[2] His quartets were initially slow to infiltrate the English market and were only sporadically performed in comparison with those of other composers whose contribution has been largely overlooked. Haydn's two visits to England in the early 1790s and the music he composed for London audiences have been the subject of much scholarly attention.[3] But

---

1 Philippe Oboussier, 'The French String Quartet, 1770–1800', in Malcolm Boyd, ed., *Music and the French Revolution* (Cambridge: Cambridge University Press, 1992), p. 74; and Mary Sue Morrow, *Concert Life in Haydn's Vienna: Aspects of a Developing Musical and Social Institution* (Stuyvesant, NY: Pendragon Press, 1989), p. 161.

2 See David Wyn Jones, 'Haydn's Music in London in the Period 1760–1790: Part One', *Haydn Yearbook*, 14 (1983), pp. 144–72.

3 For example, see H. C. Robbins Landon, *Haydn in England 1791–1795*, Haydn Chronicle and Works, vol. 3 (London: Thames & Hudson, 1976); H. C. Robbins Landon and David Wyn Jones,

162   MEREDITH McFARLANE AND SIMON McVEIGH

fresh insights are gained when the focus is shifted from a specific composer to the genre as a whole. This chapter presents a comprehensive survey of the string quartet in the London concert repertoire, highlighting three opuses – by Felice Giardini, Dieudonné-Pascal Pieltain and Ignaz Joseph Pleyel – as indicative of its compositional idioms. Given the extensive documentation elsewhere, the circumstances surrounding Haydn's 'London' quartets (opp. 71 and 74) are only briefly reiterated: instead we hope to illuminate the wider context for string quartet composition and performance in the capital.

The information for this study has largely been extracted from newspaper advertisements and reviews, which provide the most comprehensive picture of how the string quartet was represented in London concert programmes, and thus enable the first systematic analysis of trends in repertoire to be made. The perils associated with the interpretation of such material (ranging from the hidden agendas of concert promoters to the very basic problem of knowing whether a performance actually took place) should not be overlooked.[4] While we will briefly consider how the genre was represented in public during the 1770s, rigorous examination is possible only from the next decade onwards. Before 1783 detailed programme information was not regularly provided in newspaper announcements, and even then, while composer and genre are usually listed, it is extremely rare for the precise work to be identified (see Fig. 9.1 for a typical advertisement).

The public face of the string quartet in London

The date of the first known performance of a string quartet on the London concert stage was 27 April 1769. During the next 30 years, the string quartet established a firm foothold in London concert programmes, as is clearly demonstrated by Table 9.1. While figures for the 1770s cannot be regarded as wholly comprehensive or reliable,[5] Table 9.1 does suggest that the new genre was only cautiously received in the early years of the decade. A gentle rise in activity around 1780 reflected more entrepreneurial attempts by concert organizers to expose London audiences to the very latest chamber-music idiom. But in 1787 there was

---

Haydn: His Life and Music (London: Thames & Hudson, 1988); David P. Schroeder, *Haydn and the Enlightenment: The Late Symphonies and their Audience* (Oxford: Clarendon Press, 1990); Simon McVeigh, *Concert Life in London from Mozart to Haydn* (Cambridge: Cambridge University Press, 1993); Simon McVeigh, 'London', 'Quartet: 10' and 'Symphony: 9' in David Wyn Jones, ed., *Haydn*, Oxford Composer Companions (Oxford: Oxford University Press, 2002).

4   Information has been compiled from Simon McVeigh, *Calendar of London Concerts 1750–1800*, database, Department of Music, Goldsmiths College, University of London, whence further references can be obtained. See also Simon McVeigh, 'London Newspapers 1750 to 1800: a Checklist and Guide for Musicologists', in Michael Burden and Irena Cholij, eds, *A Handbook for Studies in 18th-Century English Music VI* (Oxford: Burden & Cholij, 1996). Aside from those in newspaper sources, few printed concert programmes have survived from this period.

5   The Bach–Abel concerts are just one example of a series for which the programmes were not specified.

Fig. 9.1 Newspaper advertisement for the first concert of the 1790 Professional Concert series (*The Public Advertiser*, 15 February 1790)

Table 9.1 Number of advertised concerts including string quartet performances, 1769–1799

Year	Total number of advertised concerts	Number of advertised concerts including string quartet performances
1769	67	1
1770	74	0
1771	73	0
1772	64	0
1773	82	1
1774	79	3
1775	86	1
1776	96	0
1777	97	2
1778	91	3
1779	89	5
1780	58	4
1781	72	3
1782	59	2
1783	63	3
1784	71	4
1785	76	4
1786	106	6
1787	88	20
1788	88	28
1789	68	22
1790	83	23
1791	72	17
1792	85	19
1793	87	8
1794	71	8
1795	65	3
1796	53	11
1797	36	5
1798	36	1
1799	35	3

This table includes concert series and benefits, oratorio series and 'readings and music', but excludes concerts at musical societies and the summer pleasure gardens. Two programmes included two string quartets.

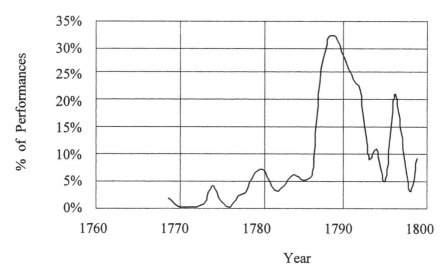

Fig. 9.2 String quartet performances as a percentage of total number of known concerts

a sizeable leap in the number of string quartet performances, coinciding with the keen appetite for new works displayed by London audiences during the 'rage for music', that exceptionally fertile period in London's concert life in the late 1780s. A peak was reached in 1788, with 28 concerts including string quartets: even more significantly this represented a peak as a proportion of the number of concerts overall (see Fig. 9.2).

For a total of seven years (1787–92 and 1796) over 20 per cent of all advertised concerts included string quartet performances. Interest in the genre was undoubtedly bolstered by the visits of Haydn (1791–92 and 1794–95) and Pleyel (1792), but already a gradual tailing-off had begun, arrested only by the brief revival of Johann Peter Salomon's concerts in 1796 (see further, Tables 9.7–9.8). This decline mirrors a downward trend in the number of concerts generally: 'with the exception of 1796, each season from 1794 to 1800 supported only one major orchestral series ... The number of benefit concerts held each year also diminished dramatically. Other aspects of London's concert life tell a similar story.'[6] It was a trend not to be decisively reversed until the foundation of the Philharmonic Society in 1813.

Rarely would more than two items of chamber music be featured in any given concert, despite the fact that programmes usually lasted three hours or more. Quartets vied for inclusion with duos, trios and quintets, all of which were also popular concert genres; usually they featured in the first half of the programme, perhaps as second or third item. This fact gains in significance when one realizes

---

6   McVeigh, *Concert Life in London*, p. 68.

Table 9.2 Types of concert featuring string quartet performances, 1769–1799

Type of concert	Number of concerts including string quartet performances
Concert series	
Pantheon (1774–82, 1784–85, 1790)	19
Hanover Square (1783–84)	2
Professional (1785–93)	46
Mara (1787–88)	9
Salomon (1786, 1791–94, 1796)	18
Opera (1795–98)	4
Total	98
Concert benefits	110
Readings and music	2

that it was the done thing to arrive late at a concert: Haydn's request for his new symphonies to be performed after the interval is not an isolated example of saving highlights until the second half. That quartets were often relegated to an early position may reflect a certain antipathy towards the genre, or at least a covert recognition that it was the especial preserve of connoisseurs.

Benefit concerts and subscription series, both of which were widely promoted in the press, were the two main types of professional concert to feature modern music, and indeed it was through exposure at these events that the string quartet gained its popularity. Table 9.2 shows that quartets were only rarely performed in any other public context, such as the occasional mixed concert of 'readings and music': certainly they were not regularly included at the summer concerts at the pleasure gardens, given their entirely different nature.[7]

String-players often introduced quartets at their benefits to display their technical and musical skills in the very latest chamber context, the quartet thus supplanting the genre more traditionally devoted to this purpose, the violin solo.[8] But it was at the main West End subscription series that it achieved the highest profile, as well as the serious attention of London's critics and taste-leaders such as the Prince of Wales, himself a keen quartet cellist. These prestigious weekly

---

7   This was not just a matter of the acoustics outdoors or in the Ranelagh rotunda, but rather reflects the *al fresco* character and distinctly populist tone of concerts at the gardens. Only two pleasure garden concerts including string quartets have been identified: one at the Apollo Gardens on 26 June 1789 with quartets by Haydn and Pleyel (billed only as a students' practice), and a more significant benefit at Ranelagh on 1 June 1798 where the Ashley family played a Pleyel quartet.

8   Simon McVeigh, *The Violinist in London's Concert Life 1750–1784: Felice Giardini and his Contemporaries* (New York: Garland, 1989), p. 244.

concerts encapsulated the glamour and sensation associated with London's public concert life, its 'exclusive principle' cultivated in terms of both audience and musical product. This international, high-profile image was gained through star soloists and the never-ending presentation of new repertoire: it is, therefore, no accident that string quartets were programmed at all the principal series in the 1780s. The string quartet was the latest new genre – indeed it was still being developed – and recent compositions by notable continental composers flooded into London in both manuscript and published form, thus fulfilling many of the prerequisites for a successful concert item.

That the Professional Concert so significantly featured string quartets in comparison with the other series partly reflects the fact that it was the only one to run 12 concerts a season for many years.[9] But more significantly, its unconventional organization – a cooperative of professional instrumentalists led by London's foremost violinist, Wilhelm Cramer – must also have encouraged the prominence of chamber music, with Pleyel quartets a particular speciality. The Pantheon concerts and those promoted by Gertrud Elisabeth Mara were more dependent on singers. But Haydn's appearance at Salomon's concerts in 1791 posed a serious threat through his chamber music as much as his symphonies, resulting in open rivalry when the Professionals engaged Haydn's pupil Pleyel the following year. It is striking that despite Pleyel's obvious popularity as a quartet composer, Salomon did not include a single quartet by him throughout his subscription series,[10] instead focusing on the latest quartets of Haydn (including op. 64) and those of other Viennese composers. His efforts in promoting Haydn quartets are largely responsible for his series ranking so highly in Table 9.2.

After the Professional Concert foundered in 1793, Salomon went on to present his most successful season the following year, introducing Haydn's specially written quartets of opp. 71 and 74. But for all Salomon's pre-eminence in chamber music, the number of quartet performances was already on the wane. In the remaining half-decade, string quartets were performed far more often at benefit concerts – the restoration of Salomon's series in 1796 provides only a temporary exception – and even when Cramer attempted a revival of the Professional Concert in 1799 no quartets were programmed.

London's string quartet performers

Nearly all London's most prominent string-players took part in the performance of string quartets at some stage, and some fairly stable quartet groups can be traced over several seasons (see Table 9.3). The main quartet leaders throughout

---

9   Simon McVeigh, 'The Professional Concert and Rival Subscription Series in London, 1783–93', *RMARC*, 22 (1989), 1–135, with complete programmes. Further relevant programmes are reproduced in Landon, *Haydn in England*.

10   Salomon nonetheless shrewdly programmed popular Pleyel string quartets at his benefit concerts in 1788–90 and elsewhere.

this period were Cramer and his two principal rivals: Giardini in the 1770s and Salomon thereafter. Second violinists and viola-players seem to have been more or less interchangeable, reflecting the similar demands of these inner parts, although the fact that Blake moved from viola to second violin in 1789 (when Borghi was indisposed) suggests that this was regarded as a promotion. By far the most stable ensemble, regularly performing together from 1784 to 1792, was the Professional Concert quartet, comprising Cramer, Borghi, Blake and Cervetto or Smith. Their main competition in 1791–92 was from Salomon, Peter Dahmen, Hindmarsh and Menel: this was the ensemble that provided the inspiration for Haydn's notoriously difficult 'London' quartets, opp. 71 and 74, premiered in 1794 by the same violinists with Fiorillo and Johan Dahmen.

There is convincing evidence of Cramer's superior qualities as London's pre-eminent orchestral leader. His dominance was sustained and far-reaching as a result of his position as both leader of the Opera orchestra and impresario of the primary subscription series. Cramer was personally responsible for transmitting the rigour and precision of Mannheim symphonic practice to London, and his authority at the head of an orchestra was unchallenged: it was precisely this element of control that was reputedly missing from Salomon's playing.[11] While this certainly affected Salomon's chances in securing regular engagements as an orchestral leader, his quartet-playing was widely revered, as much by concert audiences as among London's private circles of musical cognoscenti.[12] He was considered to be unsurpassed in the interpretation of Haydn quartets and repeatedly received the approbation of newspaper critics in this regard:

> We mention Haydn last, because among unrivalled excellence itself, he is still supreme: and to Salomon's praise be it spoken, no man perhaps studies him more ardently, and we may say affectionately. The new Quartet abounded with beauties, and the imagination of Salomon while playing it, gave continued delight.[13]

Comparisons between Cramer and Salomon were almost a cliché during the 1780s. That discriminating amateur musician Thomas Twining provided Charles Burney with an illuminating appraisal of the competitors' respective qualities:

> [16 June 1785]
> I heard Salomon too, whom I had not heard before. I like him much better than Cramer. Cramer is very good [at] mechanism. Salomon played as many hard tricks as the lover of difficulty could wish; but with more appearance of taste, I think, – more tone, more glow, more symptoms of feeling, than Cramer. With my eyes shut, I could tell that the fiddle was played on by a human creature.

---

11   See Ian Woodfield, *Salomon and the Burneys: Private Patronage and a Public Career*, Royal Musical Association Monographs, 12 (Aldershot: Ashgate, 2003), p. 22.

12   For examples of Salomon's activities in the private sphere see Meredith McFarlane, 'The String Quartet in Late Eighteenth-Century England: A Contextual Examination', D.Mus. diss. (Royal College of Music, 2002), pp. 87, 90, 93–5, 110.

13   *Morning Chronicle*, 26 Mar. 1794.

THE STRING QUARTET IN LONDON, 1769–1799
169

[16 September 1785]
We had Cramer, & Cervetto. Surely, Cramer is much improved since I had heard him! – in tone, in fancy, in taste &c.? I still believe, that were I to hear Salomon & Cramer play Quartetts of Haydn, tour à tour, in a room, I sh^d prefer Salomon. But I beg to swallow part of the unjust contempt that I expressed for Cramer, in my last letter. I did not do him justice. He is [a mas]terly player, & has more soul & energy than he used to have: is it not so?[14]

Similar comparisons, again focused on chamber repertoire and favouring Salomon, were made by newpaper critics:

In the 2d Act was performed, the famous Quartetto of Pleyel, by which Salomon has acquired such deserved celebrity. Indeed Salomon enters so happily into the spirit of the author, and throws in such a multitude of notes, (all of them of meaning and effect,) that he becomes in some sort *author*, as well as *performer* and shares the praise of composition with Pleyel, Cramer plays the passages of the Quartetto exactly as they are printed. – I shall enter no further into the comparison. I believe every candid critic will allow that Salomon's execution of this piece cannot be excelled, and that Cramer's fame would have suffered no diminution, had he left Pleyel in the undisturbed possession of his rival.[15]

Such chamber music was not simple domestic repertoire, but concert music designed for professional soloists. These soloists were the orchestral section leaders, very familiar with each other's style and experienced in playing together. The importance of the genre to professional string-players is demonstrated by the inclusion of so many names in a subscription list appearing in the first London edition of Pieltain's *Six Quartettos for Two Violins, a Tenor and Violoncello ...*, op. 2 (1785) – a rare extant exemplar in a quartet publication (see Fig. 9.3). Those names marked with an asterisk are also found in Table 9.3, while others include the Paris virtuoso Joseph Bologne (Chevalier de Saint-Georges) and the orchestral violinist Giuseppe Soderini. Also listed are the prominent London musicians Carl Friedrich Abel, Charles and Charles Rousseau Burney, Louis Decamp, Tebaldo Monzani, Venanzio Rauzzini and John Relfe.

A new wave of violinists – Giornovichi, Janiewicz and especially Viotti – eventually eclipsed both Cramer and Salomon in the 1790s, but there is no evidence that these prestigious soloists regularly performed the quartet repertoire outside a private or domestic setting.[16] This may simply have reflected the waning role of chamber music in London's concert life generally; yet it also points to the increasingly competitive nature of a solo career, driving the international stars to concentrate on the more overtly virtuosic concerto for public appearances.

---

14 British Library, Add. MS 39929, fos 359, 361 (referring to performances in Cambridge; also cited in Woodfield, *Salomon and the Burneys*, p. 15). Susan Burney similarly observed a mechanistic quality in Cramer's quartet-playing at a benefit concert in May 1789: 'Cramer led, & played a Quartetto of Pleyell's very finely, but a little too much like a Machine ...' (ibid., p. 41).

15 *The Times*, 27 Sept. 1788.

16 Only one public quartet performance before 1800 involving any of these three violinists is recorded (by Giornovichi in 1793).

Table 9.3 Advertised string quartet performers

Violin I	Violin II	Viola	Cello	Dates of performances	Total
Vachon	Cramer, W	Giardini	Crosdill	21/5/77	1
Giardini	Wilton	Napier	Crosdill	1/12/77	1
Cramer, W	Giardini	Wilton	Crosdill	22/4/79	1
Giardini	Wilton	Hackwood	Crosdill	26/4/79	1
Giardini	Bulkley	Wilton	Crosdill	22/3/80; 5/5/80	2
Salomon	Dance	Napier	Crosdill	29/3/84	1
Cramer, W	Borghi	Blake	Cervetto, J	5/5/84; 27/2/86; 1/5/86; 12/2/87; 5/3/87; 19/3/87; 26/3/87; 16/4/87; 11/2/88; 18/2/88; 25/2/88; 10/3/88; 24/3/88; 31/3/88; 7/4/88; 14/4/88; 15/2/90; 15/3/90	18
Ashley, G	Ashley, J	Ashley, R	Ashley, C	11/3/85; 24/2/86; 1/5/87	3
Cramer, W	Salomon	Blake	Cervetto, J	24/4/86	1
Pieltain, DP	Cramer, W	Blake	Smith	12/4/87	1
Cramer, W	Borghi	Blake	Crosdill	23/4/87; 7/5/87	2
Cramer, W	Borghi	Blake	Mara	10/5/87	1
Salomon	Borghi	Hindmarsh	Smith	23/5/87	1
Salomon	Borghi	Blake	Mara	25/5/87	1
Raimondi	Hindmarsh	Ashley	Mara	21/2/88; 3/4/88; 10/4/88; 17/4/88	4
Salomon	Cramer, W	Raimondi	Eley	27/3/88	1
Raimondi	Hindmarsh	Flack, J	Phillips, F	14/4/88	1
Cramer, W	Borghi	Blake	Smith	5/5/88; 7/2/91; 21/2/91; 28/2/91; 21/3/91; 4/4/91; 25/4/91; 5/3/92; 12/3/92; 19/3/92; 26/3/92; 16/4/92; 23/4/92; 30/4/92	14
Salomon	Borghi	Blake	Smith	12/5/88	1
Cramer, W	Blake	Shield	Cervetto, J	2/2/89; 16/2/89; 2/3/89; 9/3/89; 23/3/89; 20/4/89	6
Hindmarsh	Flack, J	Lavenu	Menel	30/3/89	1
Cramer, W	Blake	Shield	Smith	1/5/89	1
Cramer, W	Stabilini	Raimondi	Smith	17/6/89	1
Weichsell	Lavenu	Hindmarsh	Sperati	28/1/90; 4/2/90	2
Hindmarsh	Flack, J	Lavenu	Sperati	15/3/90	1
Clement	Bridgetower	Ware	Attwood, F	2/6/90	1
Salomon	Mountain	Hindmarsh	Menel	24/2/91	1
Salomon	Dahmen, P	Hindmarsh	Menel	18/3/91; 1/4/91; 15/4/91; 6/5/91; 13/5/91; 27/5/91; 24/2/92; 16/3/92; 23/3/92; 13/4/92; 1/6/92	11
Hindmarsh	Flack, J	Mountain	Menel	27/4/91	1
Mountain	Lavenu	Close	Kotzwara	12/5/91	1
Salomon	Dahmen, P	Abrams	Menel	20/3/92	1
Cramer, C	Cramer, W	Cramer, F	Lindley	27/4/92	1
Salomon	Barthélemon	Hindmarsh	Schram	28/5/92	1
Cramer, W	Mountain	Blake	Smith	4/3/93; 11/3/93; 15/4/93	3

THE STRING QUARTET IN LONDON, 1769–1799

Table 9.3 *continued*

Violin I	Violin II	Viola	Cello	Dates of performances	Total
Salomon	Dahmen, P	Hindmarsh	Mara	19/3/93	1
Cramer, W	Cramer, F	Blake	Smith	3/5/93	1
Giornovichi	Pieltain, DP	Fiorillo	Sperati	24/5/93	1
Cramer, W	Cramer, F	Lavenu	Smith	19/6/93	1
Salomon	Dahmen, P	Fiorillo	Dahmen, J	17/2/94; 10/3/94; 24/3/94; 31/3/94	4
Cramer, W	Cramer, F	Hindmarsh	Smith	6/3/94	1
Cramer, W	Cramer, F	Mountain	Reinagle, J	19/5/94	1
Cramer, W	Cramer, F	Hindmarsh	Lindley	23/5/94	1
Cramer, W	Cramer, F	Smart, H	Lindley	10/4/95; 11/2/96; 31/5/97	3
Cramer, W	Cramer, F	Abrams	Lindley	24/4/95	1
Salomon	Cardon	Smith	Schram	25/2/96; 14/4/96; 21/4/96; 18/5/96	4
Cramer, W	Cramer, F	Pieltain, DP	Lindley	14/3/96; 4/4/96; 25/4/96; 9/5/96; 16/5/96; 20/5/96	6
Salomon	Cramer, W	Pieltain, DP	Lindley	27/2/97	1
Cramer, W	Cramer, F	Shield	Lindley	30/5/98	1
Salomon	Cramer, F	Shield	Lindley	26/4/99	1

Spelling of names has been standardized; initials are editorial, with the exception of those of the Cramer family.

From Table 9.3 it appears that female string-players, in any case a very rare breed in English musical life, were excluded from public quartet performance. While Alyson McLamore indicates that participation of a woman 'in a chamber ensemble of some sort, such as a duet or trio, and even quartets and quintets' was not unheard of,[17] no public performances of string quartets have thus far been uncovered. One possible example is provided by Madame Hartog, who was, quite exceptionally, the leader at her own benefit on 26 March 1792, when she programmed a Pleyel quartet. But while the successful violinist Louisa Gautherot played in a trio at her benefit on 1 May 1789, it is surely significant that the string quartet on this occasion was performed by an all-male group. Leading a string quartet was evidently as much of a male preserve as leading a full orchestra.

---

17 'Symphonic Conventions in London's Concert Rooms, *circa* 1755–1790', Ph.D. diss. (University of California, Los Angeles, 1991), p. 25.

SUBSCRIBERS

His Royal Highnefs the Prince of Wales.

His Royal Highnefs the Duke of Cumberland.

A
- Earl of Abingdon
- Lord Afhburnham
- Capt.ⁿ Armftrong
- S.ʳ W.ᵐ Afton Bar.ᵗ
- M.ʳ Abel
- M.ʳ Arnofte
- J.L. Archdracon Efq.ʳ

B
- Lord Brudenel
- Lord Balgonie
- Count Brawn
- H. Bluncoe Efq.ʳ
- D.ʳ Burney   2 fets
- _ Brotherton Efq.ʳ 2 D.º
- M.ʳ De Boulogne
- M.ʳ Bartolozzi
- M.ʳ Berckenhoff
- M.ʳ Bifhop
- M.ʳ Baron
- M.ʳ R.ᵈ Blake 2 fets
- M.ʳ Bernard
- M.ʳ Blake✳
- M.ʳ J. Baptift, Chefter
- M.ʳ Barbeaux
- W. Bradyll Efq.ʳ
- B. Barrette Efq.ʳ
- M.ʳ Borghi✳
- M.ʳ Burchell, Manchefter
- M.ʳ Burney
- M.ʳ Bland   7 fets

C
- _ Chelwood Efq.ʳ 2 fets
- M.ʳ Collett   6 D.º
- M.ʳ Cramer ✳
- _ Caflon Efq.ʳ
- M.ʳ Croffdill✳
- J. Churchill Efq.ʳ
- M.ʳ J. Corfe
- M.ʳ Caracoli

D
- S.ʳ H.ʸ Dafhwood Bart.
- M.ʳ Le Chevalier Dupuis
- M.ʳ Dufour
- M.ʳ Defries
- M.ʳ Dagueville Tunⁿ.ʳ
- M.ʳ Deves
- M.ʳ De Camp
- M.ʳ Denys   2 fets

E
- W.B. Earle Efq.ʳ
- M.ʳ Eckard
- S. Ellis Efq.ʳ
- M.ʳ Evans, Bath

F
- Rev.ᵈ M.ʳ Fermer
- M.ʳ Fifin   2 fet

G
- Prince Galiazin 2 fets
- The R.ᵗ Honble Lord Gray de Wilton
- W.ᵐ Grant Efq.ʳ
- Major Goodenough
- G. Grand Efq.ʳ
- M.ʳ B. Gompert
- M.ʳ Nicolas Grimfhaw
- M.ʳ Gibfon

H
- Tho.ˢ Hammerfley Efq.ʳ
- D.ʳ Huet 2 fets
- A.H. Hole Efq.ʳ
- John Harrifson Efq.ʳ
- J.C. Hankey Efq.ʳ
- R. Hankey Efq.ʳ
- M.ʳ Hamoir   2 fets
- M.ʳ Hair, Briftol
- M.ʳ Hill, Briftol
- M.ʳ Henry
- M.ʳ Harker
- M.ʳ Hobbs

H
- M.ʳ Hanway

T
- M.ʳ Johnfon
- W.ᵐ Jacob Efq.ʳ

K
- George Kerr Efq.ʳ

L
- _ Laurence Efq.ʳ
- M.ʳ Lanzoni 6 fets
- L. Loches Efq.ʳ
- Mefs.ʳˢ Longman & Broderip 6 fets
- M.ʳ J. Levy
- M.ʳ Lefouef

M
- W.ᵐ Morreton Efq.ʳ
- For the Mufical Society at Manchefter
- M.ʳ Monzani
- M.ʳ Moller

O
- M.ʳ Olivier
- M.ʳ Okell
- M.ʳ Otely

P
- Capt.ⁿ Phillips
- _ Prado Efq.ʳ
- W.ᵐ Pradyll Efq.ʳ
- M.ʳ Prager
- M.ʳ Parke Sen.ʳ

R
- S.ʳ J.ˢ Reachy Bart.
- _ Ryland Efq.ʳ Ireland
- John Ruffel Efq.ʳ
- D.ʳ Richmond, Bath ✳
- M.ʳ John Rainagle 2 fets
- M.ʳ Ruffell
- M.ʳ Rauzzini
- M.ʳ Relfe

S
- Walter Scott Efq.ʳ 2 fets
- Hugh Scott Efq.ʳ
- _ Smith Efq.ʳ Ireland 2 D.º
- D.ʳ Shepherd 2 D.º
- Ralph Sheldon Efq.ʳ
- Edw.ᵈ Stevens Efq.ʳ
- J.B. Simpfon Efq.ʳ
- For the Mufical Society at Salifbury
- M.ʳ Salomon 3 fets✳
- John Sabatier Efq.ʳ 6 D.º
- M.ʳ Soderini
- M.ʳ Smart 2 fets
- M.ʳ Secoud, Bath

T
- Rev.ᵈ M.ʳ Twening at Colchefter
- M.ʳ Timerman
- M.ʳ Troyer
- M.ʳ Tibbs, Richmond, 2
- M.ʳ Toper

V
- M.ʳ Vanfanten 2 fets
- M.ʳ Valouis
- M.ʳ Villeneuve

W
- The Right Honble Lord Vifcount Wentworth
- Rich.ᵈ Winn Efq.ʳ
- W.ᵐ Webbe Efq.ʳ 2 fets
- Edw.ᵈ Wilfon Efq.ʳ
- M.ʳ Woodward
- M.ʳ Wafborough, at Briftol.

Fig. 9.3 Subscription list from Dieudonné-Pascal Pieltain, *Six Quartettos for Two Violins, a Tenor and Violoncello …*, op. 2 (London: Printed for the Author [1785])

Concert societies

A further important context for string quartet performance in London was the concert society, especially the Anacreontic Society and the Thatched House morning concert. Although separate from mainstream concert life, these societies had a considerable bearing on public concerts, particularly in the case of the Anacreontic Society. While its bourgeois origins and its committee of merchants and bankers belonged firmly to the musical life of the City (the commercial heart of London), the Anacreontic Society was one of the key organizations at the height of London's concert life. The evening's entertainment at the Crown and Anchor Tavern in the Strand ended in the traditional way with supper and convivial renderings of songs and glees.[18] But it opened with a concert that, exceptionally for such a gentlemen's club, was given by top professional performers; and chamber music including string quartets was often featured alongside symphonic works. By the late 1780s the regular programming of chamber music mirrored that of London's West End concerts, and newspaper reviews show that string quartets by Haydn and Pleyel were performed at most meetings between 1787 and 1789 and again in 1791. Cramer (first violin) and Smith (cello) were the two regular performers, with the inner parts usually filled by Dance, Napier, Blake or Hindmarsh; Pieltain also appeared as a quartet leader on occasion. Most of the performers were thus identical with those at West End subscription concerts, as is borne out by William Parke's description of the society's 'grand concert, in which all the flower of the music profession assisted as honorary members'.[19]

It was also, however, an arena for trial and experimentation. According to R. J. S. Stevens, 'all the eminent Musicians that arrived from the Continent, used to make their debut at the Anacreontic Society, in order to give a specimen of their abilities'.[20] It augured well for those new musicians and works that received 'the stamp of approbation' from the assembly before exposure to 'more fashionable *amateurs*' at London's West End concerts.[21] Composers, performers and publishers alike were thus significantly affected by the activities of the society. Some unfamiliar names turn up among the string players who performed quartets, for example, the violinists Condell, Almash and Scheener. The amateur violinist and composer John Marsh recalled hearing one of Pleyel's quartets 'played by the Chevalier St. George', the French virtuoso who never appeared in a more public

---

18 Contemporary descriptions of a typical evening at the Anacreontic Society are to be found in *Recollections of R. J. S. Stevens: An Organist in Georgian London*, ed. Mark Argent (London: Macmillan, 1992), pp. 24–8; William Parke, *Musical Memoirs* (London, 1830), vol. 1, pp. 80–84; and Michael Kelly, *Reminiscences* [1826], ed. Roger Fiske (London: Oxford University Press, 1975), p. 225.

19 *Musical Memoirs*, vol. 1, p. 81.

20 *Recollections*, p. 27.

21 *Morning Herald*, 4 Feb. 1785. This subject will be explored more fully in a forthcoming study of the Anacreontic Society by the present authors.

174 MEREDITH McFARLANE AND SIMON McVEIGH

light in London.[22] It was through the Anacreontic programmes that Mozart's chamber music was introduced to London audiences, but it presumably failed to impress sufficiently to infiltrate into mainstream concert life.[23]

Quite different was the Thatched House morning concert, established by the musician and publisher William Napier, in an attempt 'to harness West End amateur music-making into something resembling a City society'.[24] Despite these aspirations, there is little doubt that only top professionals took part in the performance of a Vanhal quartet in March 1785:

> As we intend in future occasionally to notice some musical entertainments, which have not hitherto attracted public attention, we shall begin with the Thatched House morning concert, which is this year conducted by Messrs. Salomon and Napier, and which deserves commemoration not only on account of the admirable performance of Mr. Salomon and other great masters, but as being now the fashionable lounge of the Thursday's levee. This little concert, we believe, was first projected by Napier as an academy for *amateurs*, in which he has been occasionally assisted by the most eminent performers. Barthelemon, Vachon, Cramer, Schroeter, Stamitz, and many others, have contributed to render it the favourable resort of the musical cognoscenti. The last concert was particularly distinguished by a new quartetto of Vanhall, which was heard with the most rapturous attention ... [25]

As a leading London publisher, William Napier was closely attuned to the amateur market and the musical requirements of wealthy dilettantes. While remaining ostensibly focused on such a clientele, the aims of the professional directors in 1792 (Cramer, Smith and Napier) 'for improving or displaying the taste and science of the amateur, and for introducing modest professional merit to the highest patronage' reveal a less altruistic agenda.[26] John Marsh sheds some light on the involvement of gentlemen amateurs, suggesting that they were restricted to playing in orchestral works for larger forces. The performance of a quartet of his own (a chamber work by an English composer, and an amateur at that) was surely quite exceptional:

> I called at Napiers & was introduc'd by him to a weekly morning concert at the Thatch'd House Tavern, led by Cramer, where I took a fiddle in the full pieces ... Having taken my new Quartetto in E. with me, Mr Napier was so good as to get it played there Cramer & Shields taking the fiddle parts, myself the tenor & Cervetto the bass. With 3. out of 4. such capital performers, the piece went off as might be expected to my utmost satisfaction.[27]

---

22 Presumably on 4 April 1787: *The John Marsh Journals: The Life and Times of a Gentleman Composer (1752–1828)*, ed. Brian Robins (Stuyvesant, NY: Pendragon Press, 1998), pp. 400, 410. This was the French violinist Joseph Bologne whose name has already been seen in Pieltain's subscription list.

23 There is no specific evidence that Mozart string quartets were performed here, although the Viennese edition of his 'Haydn' quartets was imported into London as early as 1787 (David Wyn Jones, 'From Artaria to Longman & Broderip: Mozart's music on sale in London', in Otto Biba and David Wyn Jones, eds, *Studies in Music History presented to H. C. Robbins Landon on his Seventieth Birthday* (London: Thames & Hudson, 1996), p. 113).

24 McVeigh, *Concert Life in London*, p. 49.

25 *Gazetteer*, 19 Mar. 1785.

26 *Morning Chronicle*, 28 Jan. 1792.

27 14 May 1779: *The John Marsh Journals*, ed. Robins, pp. 197–8. Marsh reported another such

THE STRING QUARTET IN LONDON, 1769–1799 175

Table 9.4   Advertised string quartet performances, 1769–1779

	1769	1770	1771	1772	1773	1774	1775	1776	1777	1778	1779	Total
Davaux							1				3	4
Haydn										1		1
Kammel	1											1
Kelly						2						2
Pugnani				1								1
Rauzzini										1		1
Sacchini										1		1
Unknown						1			2		2	5
Total	1			1	3	1			2	3	5	**16**

The London concert repertoire

The composers of string quartets performed in late eighteenth-century London may be divided into four categories: native English composers; continental composers who settled in England and resided there for a lengthy period of time (at least 10 years); continental composers who made visits to England at some stage of their careers; and finally, continental composers who never visited England. The vast majority fit into the second and third categories: that is, European composers in direct contact with the environment where their works were performed. Clearly some of these composers had already established their name well before their arrival in London, Haydn and Pleyel being the outstanding examples. Of the 212 advertised performances of string quartets before 1800, all except 71 were by these two composers. Yet, surprisingly, Pleyel's string quartets were performed over twice as often as those by Haydn during this period (99 as against 42).

Many less significant composers, from Kammel in 1769 onwards, contributed to the establishment of the genre in London. Tables 9.4–9.8 show how these composers were represented from 1769 to 1799, demonstrating London's receptivity to music from Paris, Mannheim and Vienna alongside that of European settlers such as Kammel, Abel, Giardini and Barthélemon. The cosmopolitan outlook of the capital welcomed and encouraged the influx of continental music, and it is hardly surprising that most major quartet composers were represented in concerts there.

Tables 9.4–9.5, giving data for the first 16 years, are not wholly representative, for those reasons already mentioned. In these early developmental years no single composer (or group of composers) can be seen to be leading the way, but this could

---

occasion on 3 September 1781: 'I went to Napier's to hear a famous fiddle player lately arriv'd of the name of Pieltain, where I also met Mr Schroeter the famous piano forte player & composer (who play'd the 2d. fiddle in some quartettos, Napier playing the tenor)' (ibid., p. 248).

176   MEREDITH McFARLANE AND SIMON McVEIGH

Table 9.5   Advertised string quartet performances, 1780–1784

	1780	1781	1782	1783	1784	Total
Abel				1	1	2
Barthélemon		1				1
Giardini	1					1
Haydn					2	2
Stamitz				1		1
Vanhal	1			1	1	3
Unknown	2	2	2	1		7
Total	4	3	2	4	4	**17**

simply reflect the availability of data rather than performance trends, as so many composers remain unidentified in advertisements. It is likely, for example, that London audiences would have been much more familiar with Abel's quartets than is suggested here, as his works were presumably performed regularly in the long-running Bach–Abel concert series starting in 1765, for which no programmes were advertised.

While Haydn is the only composer to figure throughout the entire period, at this early stage he was only one of many foreign quartet composers represented, some of whom never visited London. Among these was another prominent Viennese composer, Johann Baptist Vanhal, whose quartets, however, never matched the popularity of his symphonies in London. More successful perhaps were the works of Jean-Baptiste Davaux. The light style of the Parisian *quatuor concertant*, with its agreeable exchanges between four solo instruments, was an important influence on many quartet composers across Europe, and it may well be significant that the violinist responsible for three Davaux performances at the Pantheon in 1779 was Felice Giardini.[28]

Curiously, only one public performance of a quartet by Giardini himself is known in this period (at his 1780 benefit), though his position as a leading quartet composer would suggest that this tally falls well short of the true picture. Indeed he was a pioneer in London of the *concertante* quartet, which matched his typically easy-going melodic style and flashy (but not especially demanding) virtuosity. As early as 1751, the year of his arrival in London, he had explored *concertante* idioms in his op. 3 sonatas for harpsichord and violin, and he continued to develop soloistic textures in his string trios during the 1770s, especially after he took to playing the viola in trios with Cramer in 1776. This idiom was then transferred

---

28   Possibly from Davaux's op. 9, published in Paris that year and shortly afterwards in London by William Napier. Roger Hickman has highlighted the influence of the Parisian style on every Viennese composer of the time, including Haydn himself ('The Flowering of the Viennese String Quartet in the Late Eighteenth Century', *Music Review*, 51 (1989), 159–60).

Ex. 9.1 Felice Giardini, *Six Quartetto's*, op. 22 (London: J. Blundell, *c.*1779), no. 1 in F major, first movement

continued overleaf

Ex. 9.1 *continued*

Ex. 9.1 *continued*

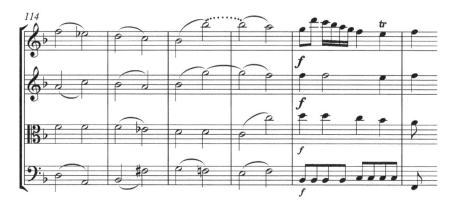

to the quartet published by Napier in the same year, a work markedly different in character from those of Bach and Abel in the same collection.

Giardini's quartets op. 22 (published by James Blundell around 1779) explore open sonorities and constantly shifting textures, with contrasts sharply delineated by changes in register, dynamics and rhythmic pace (Ex. 9.1). Each instrument plays a strongly individual part, and indeed all four instruments receive lengthy extrovert solos – with astonishingly high cello writing and prominent viola passages, no doubt with his own performance in mind (Ex. 9.2). These kaleidoscopic shifts of texture and vivid interplay were clearly allied to the Parisian *quatuor concertant*, but they were developed with an attention-seeking and soloistic flair that chimed with the very public environment of London's concert life. The need to display the virtuosity of four concert soloists acted against the intimate conversational idiom of Haydn and the Viennese school, replacing a gradually unfolding and tightly integrated motivic argument with one that puts texture and colour at its centre.

Other renowned London violinists whose quartets were sporadically performed include Antonín Kammel and François-Hippolyte Barthélemon. The latter was originally brought to London by the important musical amateur and patron Thomas Alexander Erskine, sixth Earl of Kelly. Well known as an ambassador for the Mannheim style in Britain, following his studies with Johann Stamitz, he was the first British quartet composer to be represented in London's public concerts (in 1774). Although none of his quartets was published, a quartet in A major in the recently discovered Kilravock Manuscript provides a compelling exemplar of the *Sturm und Drang* style.[29] The only genuine Mannheimer to be represented in London concerts was the travelling viola virtuoso Carl Stamitz, who performed extensively in London in the late 1770s: one of his quartets was performed under Cramer's direction in 1783.

---

29 David Johnson, 'Kelly, the 6th Earl of', *New Grove2*, vol. 13, pp. 464–5.

Ex. 9.2 Felice Giardini, *Six Quartetto's*, op. 22 (London: J. Blundell, *c.*1779), no. 5 in E major, first movement

Ex. 9.2 *continued*

Italian composers are the best represented of any national group in Tables 9.4–9.5. Giardini's contribution has already been noted; another representative of the Turin violin school was the outstanding violin virtuoso Gaetano Pugnani, who visited London twice between 1767 and 1773. His second set of string quartets was published there in 1770, and in 1773 he led one of his own quartets at a benefit, only the second recorded performance of a quartet in London. The string quartets of his compatriots Venanzio Rauzzini and Antonio Sacchini were heard at two singers' benefits in April 1778. It is notable that these rival opera composers should have turned to the string quartet at the very time it was beginning to achieve public recognition. Sacchini published his op. 2 quartets in 1778, while Rauzzini's opp. 2 and 7 appeared around 1777 and 1778 respectively.

The first known London performance of a Haydn string quartet took place on 20 February 1778 at the Freemasons Hall, presumably under the leadership of Cramer, who performed a concerto at this 'Anniversary Concert'.[30] Haydn was still little known through concert performances, his English reputation allied mainly to his quartet publications: at this point 'Haydn's opp. 1, 2, 9, 17 and, possibly, 20 were available plus a set of unauthentic works'.[31] The next documented performance of a Haydn string quartet was not until six years later on 18 February 1784 – again led by Cramer, but this time at a concert of the established Hanover Square series; by this date Haydn's op. 33 quartets can be added to the list of publications above. The composer's popularity in England had sharply escalated in the intervening years. His symphonies – the focus of a new and sustained public craze – were increasingly being made available by London publishers, coinciding with greater opportunity for their performance; and

---

30 Simon McVeigh, 'Freemasonry and Music in London', in David Wyn Jones, ed., *Music in Eighteenth-Century Britain* (Aldershot: Ashgate, 2000), p. 97.
31 Jones, 'Haydn's Music in London', p. 165.

182 MEREDITH McFARLANE AND SIMON McVEIGH

Table 9.6   Advertised string quartet performances, 1785–1789

	1785	1786	1787	1788	1789	Total
Giardini				1	1	2
Haydn	2	1	2	4	5	14
Pieltain		1	3			4
Pleyel		4	12	17	15	48
Raimondi				3		3
Salomon				1		1
Stamitz	1					1
Unknown	1	1	3	2	1	8
Total	4	7	20	28	22	**81**

already there had been attempts by concert promoters to entice Haydn to England. Recognition of his achievements as a quartet composer was to follow not far behind.

The total number of known quartet performances in the 16-year period up to 1784 represents less than a third of those in the following five years (1785–89, Table 9.6). This intense period of string quartet activity includes 1788, the peak year for the genre in London during the eighteenth century. Haydn, Stamitz and Giardini were the only three composers from the preceding 16 years whose quartets continued to be performed. Though Giardini had not yet returned from a period of absence in Italy, his quartets were performed at least twice, once by his rival Cramer in the 1788 Professional season, and once at the 1789 benefit of his former quartet partner Borghi in the form of a 'MS quartet', possibly from Giardini's op. 29, to be published in London the following year.

Works by the latest immigrant violinists were featured in this five-year span, including quartets by Salomon, Raimondi and Pieltain. But where previously such violinist-composers might have performed a solo (sonata with continuo) as a display piece, now the string quartet provided a more modern alternative, usually performed in manuscript under the leadership of the composer. Ignazio Raimondi led performances of his string quartets on three occasions in 1788, twice as director of Mara's subscription series and once at Hindmarsh's benefit; none of Raimondi's string quartets was published, and only one has survived in manuscript.[32] Salomon's quartets remained similarly unpublished,[33] with only one performance known from this period: this took place at the 1788 concert for the New Musical Fund, an annual high-profile event with massed performers, with Cramer as second violinist and Raimondi on viola.

---

32   In the library of the Conservatorio di musica Giuseppe Verdi, Milan.
33   An obituary mentions 'some violin quartetts' found 'among his unpublished compositions' (*The Harmonicon*, 8 (1830), 47), but these are not extant.

Ex. 9.3 Dieudonné-Pascal Pieltain, *Six Quartettos*, op. 2 (London: Printed for the Author [1785]), no. 1 in A major, third movement

The Flemish violinist Pieltain, less important than Salomon but a more brilliant virtuoso, similarly led one of his own string quartets at the 1787 New Musical Fund concert. His quartets were particularly popular that season with three known performances, probably from op. 2, 'printed for the author' in 1785 and subsequently published by William Napier. Pieltain's quartets were primarily designed to show off his own outstanding technique, with an array of violinistic effects. Catchy melodies are contrasted with lively figurative passage-work that exploits a wide variety of bowing patterns and forays into high positions. Ex. 9.3 illustrates a characteristically piquant episode in which the first violin is set in high relief by the strongly hierarchical texture, while in Ex. 9.4 a striking enharmonic modulation is enacted by a brilliant solo that intricately combines separate and slurred bow strokes. While there are occasional solos and interplay for the other instruments, the attention here is firmly focused on the first violin. But quartets

Ex. 9.4 Dieudonné-Pascal Pieltain, *Six Quartettos*, op. 2 (London: Printed for the Author [1785]), no. 2 in D major, first movement

Ex. 9.4 *continued*

characterized by this violin-dominated texture were not nearly so successful with London audiences as those exploiting a more equal-voiced *concertante* style, where the quartet itself appears as a virtuosic concert instrument.

Haydn's quartets were gradually gaining favour, with five known performances in 1789. Four of these took place at the Professional Concert, performed by Cramer's quartet, with the fifth at Cramer's own benefit. While it is not possible to pinpoint exactly which quartets were performed, opp. 42, 50, 54 and 55 are all possible candidates, with op. 54 the most likely, since one English edition describes it on the title-page as 'performed at the Professional Concert Hanover Square, 1789'.[34]

---

34 RISM H3511. Although opp. 54 and 55 were composed together, 'Op. 55 was probably not sent at this time; the publication was not entered at Stationers' Hall until March 1790, and copies have a manuscript note indicating 1790 performance at the Professional Concert, although no performances of Haydn quartets at that series are recorded' (McVeigh, 'The Professional Concert', 11).

186 MEREDITH McFARLANE AND SIMON McVEIGH

Yet in truth Haydn was completely overshadowed during this period. Pleyel's quartets were first introduced by Cramer at the Professional Concert on 27 February 1786, and they quickly became an established feature of concert programmes. In 1787 they were regularly programmed at the two leading subscription series and at benefits for London's finest musicians. As with the genre overall, 1788 marked a peak for the performance of Pleyel's string quartets in London, with no fewer than 17 concert performances documented. At the time of the genre's greatest popularity in London Pleyel's ascendancy was beyond question. His chamber music is now little known, but in the late eighteenth century his quartets were extensively published across Europe with numerous reprintings.[35] In London, his popularity was patent not only in this domestic market but also on the concert stage, where his flamboyant quartet writing perfectly matched the fashionable milieu.

Pleyel was adept at slipping into all the current quartet idioms, including a rather facile version of the Haydnesque conversational quartet and its simple, tuneful cousin designed for the amateur market (with which style Pleyel is, quite mistakenly, principally associated today). Naturally, however, it was the works in the attention-grabbing *concertante* idiom that were the key to his success on the London concert platform. His brilliant manner is epitomized in the set of quartets dedicated to the King of Prussia (B.331–42, 1787), where he projects a collective quartet virtuosity even more strongly than Giardini, with showy exchanges and elaborate solos for all four players.[36] His more sophisticated tonal palette, derived from his studies with Haydn, allows for more forceful contrasts, as harmonic dislocations combine with precipitous pauses in dramatically disrupting the musical flow. But Pleyel goes still further in developing the public impact of the quartet by adopting orchestral sonorities and a truly symphonic manner. This is most obvious in sudden *fortissimo* outbursts, powerful unison or chordal passages, and agitated rhythmic accompaniments; but it can also be identified in theatrical *pianissimo* and *morendo* effects that serve to heighten the dramatic argument. All of these characteristics can be seen in the fine C minor quartet (Ex. 9.5), where the force of a tutti section is ingeniously suggested by some elaborate arpeggiation in the first violin part at bars 220–22.

This set was Pleyel's most popular in terms of the number of editions issued,[37] and their likely London exposure is confirmed by the inclusion of B.334–6 in the Anacreontic Society repertoire. Although Pleyel's set, composed in Strasbourg in 1786, can hardly have been intended for public concert use, the combination of brilliant soloistic writing and driving orchestral sonorities perfectly matched

---

35   See Jiesoon Kim, 'Ignaz Pleyel and his Early String Quartets in Vienna', Ph.D. diss. (University of North Carolina, Chapel Hill, 1996), pp. 13 ff. and 28 ff. for data relating to Pleyel's string quartet publications; and Rita Benton, *Ignace Pleyel: A Thematic Catalogue of his Compositions* (New York: Pendragon Press, 1977).

36   See the example from B.334 quoted in Landon and Jones, *Haydn: His Life and Music*, pp. 290–91.

37   Kim, 'Pleyel and his Early String Quartets', p. 27.

Ex. 9.5 Ignaz Joseph Pleyel, *Three Quartettos ... Dedicated to the King of Prussia*, op. 9, book 4 (London: W. Forster, 1787), no. 2 in C minor [B.341], first movement

continued overleaf

Ex. 9.5 *continued*

Ex. 9.5 *continued*

continued overleaf

Ex. 9.5 *continued*

THE STRING QUARTET IN LONDON, 1769–1799

Table 9.7   Advertised string quartet performances, 1790–1794

	1790	1791	1792	1793	1794	**Total**
Callcott		1				1
Cambini			1			1
Gyrowetz	3		2			5
Haydn	1	7	5	1	5	19
Kozeluch		1				1
Pieltain	1					1
Pleyel	17	7	9	5	2	40
Rawlings		1				1
Unknown	1	1	1	2	1	6
Total	23	17	19	8	8	**75**

the public orientation of the capital's musical life. The immediate popularity of Pleyel's chamber music surely inspired other composers in London, most obviously Haydn in the opp. 71 and 74 quartets.

Three composers stand out in the period 1790–94: Haydn, Pleyel and Adalbert Gyrowetz (Table 9.7). The prominence of Haydn's quartets naturally coincided with his two visits to London, during which time he quite simply dominated English musical life. While Pleyel's continued popularity in terms of numbers of performances alone is indisputable, the shifting audience focus between these two popular quartet composers is illuminating. In 1791, the year of Haydn's arrival, the number of Pleyel quartet performances plummeted from 17 in the previous year to just seven. For the first time Haydn quartet performances matched Pleyel in number: mainly they took place at Salomon's concerts in the composer's presence. The latest set of quartets, op. 64, was also the source of a profitable alliance, with Salomon securing the rights to performance in London and John Bland those to publication there. Haydn's personal involvement was emblazoned on the title-page: 'PERFORMD under his DIRECTION, at Mr. Salomon's Concert, the Festino Rooms Hanover Square'.[38]

Pleyel's arrival in London in 1792, with a new stock of instrumental music for the rival Professional Concert, swayed the balance again in the newcomer's favour.[39] But Pleyel stayed for only one season, and by 1794 his popularity had diminished. Haydn's opp. 71 and 74 quartets, specially composed for his second London visit in 1794, were from the outset enthusiastically received in newspaper reviews. Nonetheless, it has to be accepted that they did not attract the high profile

---

38   Ian Woodfield, 'John Bland: London Retailer of the Music of Haydn and Mozart', *Music & Letters*, 81 (2000), 211, 230, 235–7. The edition naturally did not appear until June, after the concert season had ended.

39   This repertoire probably included the string quartets B.359–64.

of the late symphonies and hardly the public recognition that might be expected of brilliant new chamber works specifically created for this concert environment. Only five Haydn quartet performances are recorded in 1794. Was the vogue for quartets already abating, or was Haydn pushing back the boundaries faster than London concert audiences were ready to accept?

Although it is generally held that Haydn's op. 64 quartets were a 'relative failure in England',[40] a comparison between the known performances of the two sets – op. 64 in 1791 and opp. 71 and 74 in 1794 – in fact reveals a slightly more favourable reception for the former. Salomon's 1791 series included five performances of three quartets from op. 64, but in 1794 only four performances of two quartets from opp. 71 and 74. Bearing in mind the intense competition with the Professional Concert in 1791, the op. 64 quartets could scarcely have borne multiple performances in the face of a cool audience response.[41] Perhaps it was intended that the opp. 71 and 74 quartets would be performed in the 1795 season, but the amalgamation of Salomon's interests with the Opera Concert intervened: in the event some quartets in the set can never have been performed at London concerts during Haydn's visit.

So much has been written about the opp. 71 and 74 quartets and Haydn's marked divergence from his normally intimate chamber style and 'conversational' idiom that it would be redundant to reiterate their London background in any detail here.[42] Mary Hunter has aptly summarized those aspects of their performance context that scholars have found reflected in the music itself:

> László Somfai, for example, remarks on the utilitarian 'noise killer' beginnings to some of the public quartets, while H. C. Robbins Landon and others have pointed to the 'symphonic' presence of slow introductions, rare in Haydn's previous quartets. Most students of these works have also noted that the formal processes and sonic qualities of the Op. 71/74 quartets ... are well-adapted to the listening circumstances of large audiences. Singled out in this respect are the quartets' blocks of clearly contrasted material, their 'conspicuous' tonal shifts, and their use of 'orchestral' sound effects like tutti tremolos ... In addition, both Landon and Charles Rosen refer to the 'popular' character of some of the quartet tunes, again associating this with their function as public works.[43]

---

40 Cliff Eisen, 'String Quartet', *New Grove2*, vol. 24, p. 586.

41 It should be added that chamber works enjoyed a relatively short shelf-life: there was only one performance of a Haydn quartet (probably again from op. 64) at Salomon's 1792 series, although he was responsible for their inclusion at a number of benefit concerts.

42 See Landon, *Haydn in England*, pp. 455–82; László Somfai, 'The London Revision of Haydn's Instrumental Style', *PRMA*, 100 (1973–74), 159–74; László Somfai, 'Haydn's London String Quartets', in Jens Peter Larsen, Howard Serwer and James Webster, eds, *Haydn Studies: Proceedings of the International Haydn Conference, Washington, D.C., 1975* (New York: Norton, 1981), pp. 389–92; Landon and Jones, *Haydn: His Life and Music*, pp. 253, 289–96; Roger Hickman, 'Haydn and the "Symphony in Miniature"', *Music Review*, 43 (1982), 15–23; and McVeigh, *Concert Life in London*, pp. 105 and 159.

43 'Haydn's London Piano Trios and his Salomon String Quartets: Private vs. Public?', in Elaine Sisman, ed., *Haydn and his World* (Princeton: Princeton University Press, 1997), pp. 103–4.

There can be little doubt that London's public concert milieu and its conventions acted as a catalyst; and that such diverse factors as concert-hall acoustics, audiences of 500 or more, and professional soloists, combined with advances in the design of stringed instruments and bows, all contributed to Haydn's transformed quartet style.[44]

Hickman has observed a similar break in style in the quartets of the Bohemian composer Adalbert Gyrowetz, who visited London between 1790 and 1793: the striking orchestral character of his quartets from this period was evidently likewise inspired by the overtly public aspect of London's concert life.[45] Gyrowetz's quartets, already popular on the continent, were performed by Salomon at his 1792 series, and the esteem in which he was held by the English is reflected in multiple quartet performances during his stay.

By contrast, the quartets of other celebrated continental composers who did not visit London were only rarely performed there. Giuseppe Maria Cambini, so prominent an exponent of the *quatuor concertant* in Paris, was apparently little regarded; only one performance (by Salomon in 1792) is known in London throughout this entire period. The prevalent anti-French sentiment may have contributed to the lack of interest in his substantial chamber-music output. The Viennese composer Leopold Kozeluch was similarly represented by just a single quartet performance by Salomon the previous year: this despite the fact that he had been involved in lengthy negotiations with John Bland concerning both publication and performance.[46] Completely absent are performances of quartets by Boccherini and – most noticeable of all – Mozart, whose instrumental music was still regarded as obscure and difficult, despite several London publications as well as performances at the Anacreontic Society during the 1780s.[47]

Less surprisingly, perhaps, quartets by British composers were rarely heard in London concerts, with only three documented performances in the 1790s. The renowned glee composer John Wall Callcott opportunistically included in his 1791 benefit a quartet 'Composed under Direction of Haydn', following lessons with Haydn in instrumental composition – an ineffective attempt to broaden his musical

---

44   Roger Hickman also draws attention to the implications of this stylistic change in a wider European context: 'The new style quickly spread to all of the important centres for chamber music, even those where quartets were still primarily performed in chamber rooms. In Vienna, quartets were not performed regularly in public concerts until after 1800, but still almost every leading Viennese quartet composer incorporated orchestral features into his quartets during the 1790s' ('Haydn and the "Symphony in Miniature" ', 21).

45   'Haydn and the "Symphony in Miniature" ', 17–21, with an extended and powerful example from op. 13 (or 25) no. 1.

46   It is true that Kozeluch was better known for his piano music and symphonies, his quartet output being limited to two sets of three quartets each. His protracted negotiations with Bland are discussed in detail in Woodfield, 'John Bland: London Retailer'. Although acting from Vienna, Kozeluch demonstrated considerable acumen in achieving the best possible deal for the English publication of his op. 33 quartets, by playing off the rival publishers Longman & Broderip and Bland. He was also much concerned about the leader of the London premiere, initially proposing Cramer, to whom the set was dedicated.

47   See n. 23.

Table 9.8 Advertised string quartet performances, 1795–1799

	1795	1796	1797	1798	1799	Total
Davy		1				1
Gyrowetz		1	1			2
Haydn	1	3	1		1	6
Pleyel	2	5	3		1	11
Unknown		1		1	1	3
Total	3	11	5	1	3	**23**

horizons, as it turned out. More exceptional was the case of the young Thomas Rawlings, still a fledgling orchestral musician when the Professionals promoted one of his string quartets in 1792: it was an extraordinary show of support at a time of cut-throat competition, and was favourably received by the critics.

Turning now to the final five-year period (Table 9.8), 1795 was a sparse season for string quartet performance with the main subscription series subsumed into the Opera Concert; the three known performances of Pleyel and Haydn all took place at benefit concerts. Following Haydn's departure, the revival of Salomon's concerts in 1796 not only stimulated a brief renaissance but also spurred competition. The Opera Concert (directed by Giornovichi and led by Cramer) now felt compelled to programme more instrumental items, including quartets on three occasions, probably older showpieces by Pleyel and Haydn. Salomon also performed a Haydn quartet but, true to form, introduced two 'new MS' quartets: one by Gyrowetz (possibly in an attempt to fill Haydn's niche) and another by the little-known English composer John Davy. The former misfired: public favour for the departed Gyrowetz had apparently turned against him and one review was damning ('a collection of passages without meaning, without relation, and consequently without unity').[48] Davy was the only new quartet composer to be introduced in this final five-year period. None of his string quartets was ever published, and little instrumental music has survived in comparison to his prolific output of songs and theatrical scores.

It is clear from the Tables that quartets by continental composers, mostly resident in London at some stage, were overwhelmingly predominant. The lack of encouragement of native composers in London's concert life is starkly revealed: of the 212 advertised performances of string quartets before 1800 a mere five were written by British composers. This may partly have reflected the paucity of available British repertoire, to which many different factors contributed; but it was more directly indicative of a general antipathy towards the works of local composers. Even the highly skilled composer and string-player William Shield,

---

48 *Morning Chronicle*, 27 Feb. 1796.

THE STRING QUARTET IN LONDON, 1769–1799   195

who performed for many years in the ranks of the Professional Concert and had quartets published by Napier, never received a single public quartet performance.

This lack of engagement by British musicians might seem to imply a relatively passive culture: major string quartets were apparently written by leading European composers to be played by the top concert artists. Certainly the question arises as to whether there was the same relationship between public concert performance and amateur music making as there clearly was in the case of piano music or songs. One crucial difference is that whereas any young lady of social pretension could be expected to be reasonably accomplished on the piano, nothing similar could be said of her male counterparts, who only rarely found the time or motivation to become proficient string quartet players. Quartets were generally advertised in publishers' catalogues alongside symphonies under the heading 'For Concerts', putting them in a different class from simple flute duets and the like. Indeed most of the published repertoire was well beyond the normal amateur technique, as is clear from William Napier's advertisement for his edition of some easy quartets:

> It has been a general Complaint among the Lovers of Music, that the Quartettos which have been lately published, although many of them are excellent and well composed, yet are so very difficult that none but the best Masters are capable of performing them.[49]

If this was the case in 1776, one can only guess what most amateurs must have made of Haydn's opp. 71 and 74.

Yet there were certainly others who discovered in domestic string quartet playing a vital musical outlet, enthusiasts who sought out new and demanding repertoire to try out wherever they could. John Marsh's passion for quartet-playing has already been remarked, and his persistence was rewarded in a performance of one of his own quartets with some of the best players in the country. The Duke of Cumberland (George III's brother) engaged Giardini as his music-master, and regularly played the violin in chamber-music parties at Windsor Lodge and Cumberland House. But the most enthusiastic devotee was the Prince of Wales, who was taught the cello by John Crosdill and regularly engaged Giardini, Cramer, Salomon and others to join him in chamber music at Carlton House: 'The Prince's morning parties are chiefly devoted to the quartettos of Haydn, Pleyel, Stamitz, and the charming trios of Schroeter.'[50] That this was more than a superficial hobby is evident from another newspaper comment: 'The Prince's musical parties are now generally in the morning, but without company – He is too great an amateur to suffer the buzz of conversation to interrupt the harmony of his concerts.'[51]

This is of more than passing significance. The Prince of Wales was in direct contact with Pleyel during the late 1780s: he was the dedicatee of the seventh

---

49   *Public Advertiser*, 18 Jan. 1776.

50   *Public Advertiser*, 11 Jan. 1787. Further on the quartet in private circles, see McFarlane, 'The String Quartet in Late Eighteenth-Century England', pp. 86–143.

51   *Morning Herald*, 5 May 1786.

set of quartets (B.346–51), published in 1788, and the same year he presented some new *concertante* music by Pleyel to the Professional Concert, of which he was principal patron and a regular supporter.[52] Whether this included recent chamber music is not specified, but there can be little doubt that the Prince's personal enthusiasm for Pleyel's quartets directly influenced the programming of the Professional Concerts. The future George IV, now mainly reviled for his profligacy and debauchery, thus played no small part in the chain of events that led to Haydn's opp. 71 and 74, those outstanding examples of the London quartet inspired by the public concert environment.

---

52   McVeigh, 'The Professional Concert', p. 64.

PART THREE

Contexts for Concerts

CHAPTER TEN

Music and Drama at the Oxford Act of 1713

H. Diack Johnstone

The Treaty of Utrecht, by which the War of the Spanish Succession was, between Britain and France at any rate, brought finally to an end, was signed on 11 April 1713 (31 March OS). But the prospect of peace had been on the horizon for many months past.[1] Thus George Frideric Handel, now firmly resolved to settle in London, had already composed a setting of the Te Deum in anticipation of the day on which the nation might be expected to celebrate the event, as it had the various outstanding Marlborough victories of the war, with a great service of thanksgiving in St Paul's Cathedral. The autograph is dated 14 January 1713. By 5 May, the day on which the peace itself was formally declared, the work had been publicly rehearsed no fewer than three times.[2] Though a day of national rejoicing had originally been planned for 16 June, the preparations took rather longer than expected, and in the event it was postponed until 7 July when, up and down the country, civic authorities went in procession to local services of thanksgiving and celebrated an end to hostilities with much public merriment (including bonfires and fireworks at nightfall).[3] In London, both Houses of Parliament ('richly dressed upon the Occasion') set out from Westminster 'about noon' and slowly made their way up Whitehall, and thence into the Strand where some 4000 charity children standing on specially erected 'scaffolds' were waiting to greet them with hymns

---

1   For a good short survey, see A. D. MacLachlan, 'The Road to Peace, 1710–13', in Geoffrey Holmes, ed., *Britain after the Glorious Revolution 1689–1714* (London: Macmillan, 1969), pp. 197–215; also chs 12–14 of David Green's eminently readable book, *Queen Anne* (London: Collins, 1970).

2   For dates together with a very useful account of the relevant political background, see Donald Burrows, 'Handel and the English Chapel Royal during the Reigns of Queen Anne and King George I', Ph.D. diss. (Open University, 1981), vol. 1, pp. 98–106.

3   Many of these are noted in the London papers in the wake of the event. Musically one of the most impressive celebrations outside the capital must have been that at York where, according to *The Evening Post* of 9–11 July, the Lord Mayor and Corporation went in procession 'with Drums, Trumpers [*sic*] and the City Waits' to the Minster: there, in the presence of the Archbishop of York, they 'heard Divine Service, and had the *Te Deum* set by Mr. Purcell, and the whole Service, perform'd in an extraordinary Manner, With Violins and Trumpets in Concert with the Organ'. The Purcell Te Deum 'with the Symphonies and instrumental parts, on Violins and Hautboys' was also performed at Worcester; see Michael Tilmouth, 'A Calendar of References to Music in Newspapers published in London and the Provinces (1660–1719)', *RMARC*, 1 (1961), 86.

199

in honour of the Queen and the peace. The last lap took them up Ludgate Hill to St Paul's Cathedral where they would have been joined (we presume) by the Lord Mayor and Aldermen of the City – though there is, rather oddly, no mention of them in the papers – and together taken part in the great service of national thanksgiving at which Handel's 'Utrecht' Te Deum and Jubilate had its first official performance. Though Queen Anne was also supposed to have been there, she was at the last minute prevented by illness from attending, and was thus forced to give thanks privately in the Chapel Royal at St James's Palace where there can have been very little, if any, music.

The service probably began somewhere round about 2 p.m., and in those days of one-hour-plus sermons, it evidently went on for a good three and a half hours at least.[4] In addition to the 'Utrecht' Te Deum and Jubilate, it also included the first performance of an anthem, 'This is the day which the Lord hath made', specially composed for the occasion by William Croft (1678–1727), Organist and Master of the Choristers at Westminster Abbey, and Organist and Composer (since 1708) of Her Majesty's Chapel Royal. Unlike the Handel, Croft's setting of verses from Psalm 118 was for voices and organ only.[5] According to *Dawks's News-Letter* of 9 July, referring not simply to the Croft but also the Handel, the music 'was as Excellently performed as it was exquisitely Composed'. Chorally, both the choirs of St Paul's and the Chapel Royal would have been involved (and almost certainly that of Westminster Abbey as well). Among the soloists who performed the Croft anthem (and the Handel Te Deum and Jubilate also) were several of the leading English male singers of the period: Francis Hughes and Richard Elford (altos), John Freeman and John Church (tenors), together with Bernard Gates, Daniel Williams and Samuel Weely (basses). Three days later most of them, and so too, we may suppose, many of the instrumentalists who had also taken part, were in Oxford; there, on Friday the 10th, they gave the first performance of two Croft odes, one English and one Latin, and both also in celebration of the peace.

The occasion was the so-called 'Oxford Act', a grand academic gathering convened for the purpose of conferring degrees, chiefly Masters of Arts, but also Doctors of Theology, Law, Medicine and occasionally Music. The date was always the first Monday after 7 July, and by statute it ought to have taken place annually. But by the eighteenth century a public celebration of the Act was only very rarely held: the last had been in 1703, and the next, in 1733 (when Handel made his celebrated appearance in Oxford), was, as it turned out, to be the very

---

4   According to the papers, Henry Compton, the Bishop of London (who was also too ill to attend) died about 6 p.m., 'the Time when the Service in Thanksgiving for the Peace was just finish'd in his Lordship's Cathedral'.

5   It may be that Richard Brind, as organist of St Paul's, played for the service, but he himself was no composer. Croft's anthem was later published in *Musica sacra* (1724), vol. 2, pp. 95–116. The principal MS source (Royal College of Music MS 839) is a copy in the hand of his pupil James Kent, with autograph annotations; there is another somewhat later Kent copy in Oxford, Bodleian Library, MS Mus. d.173.

MUSIC AND DRAMA AT THE OXFORD ACT OF 1713   201

last observance of the Act in its traditional form.[6] (The annual Encaenia which shortly afterwards replaced it, and was originally but one of its component parts, is now a one-day event designed to commemorate the university's benefactors and is confined to the awarding of honorary degrees.) The 1713 Act, however, must have been conceived as Oxford's official celebration of the Peace of Utrecht, since nothing much appears to have happened on 7 July other than the preaching of a sermon in St Mary's, the university church. It seems rather extraordinary therefore that as late as 25 June Thomas Hearne, the prickly Oxford diarist and antiquary whose remarks on Mr Handel and 'his lowsy Crew' 20 years later were subsequently to earn him a place in musical history, should be writing to a friend that 'we are uncertain as yet whether we shall have an Act. The Vice-Chancellor seems against it, and so does his Lady. And the Proctors are also as unwilling to have one. Yet Preparations are making as tho' there would be one ...'.[7] Clearly Hearne was wildly out of touch with what was actually going on, since the 1713 Act must obviously have been planned some months in advance, and the Vice-Chancellor (Bernard Gardiner, Warden of All Souls) must also have been very closely involved. Though Gardiner, a staunch Hanoverian Tory, may well have been (as he is described in *DNB*) a 'conscientious, indomitable, stern, [and] uncompromising man', he must also have been a man well disposed to music, for he himself had been a member of the Oxford Music Club in the 1690s when all its members had also to be performers.[8]

The actual degree ceremony on Monday was preceded by a number of other academic events starting on Friday afternoon with a 'Comitia Philologica' at which some 20-odd young men delivered themselves of a series of Latin orations in both prose and verse; most were solo performances, but some – the 'Carmine Amoebaeo' – were in dialogue form involving two or three speakers. As the 1713 Comitia itself was 'in Honorem Annae Pacificae', the subjects on which they spoke were mostly a foregone conclusion. The Saturday was given over to 'lectures' in the various 'Schools' and to disputations (in Latin) on a small number of 'Quaestiones' put to candidates in advance. Except for the lectures, everything took place in the Sheldonian Theatre, which had been opened in 1669 and designed by Sir Christopher Wren specifically to house such academic ceremonies as these. On Sunday there would have been two services (Matins and Evensong) in St Mary's, each with a sermon and also, most probably, though we do not actually know this to have been the case in 1713, special music – which may or may not have involved Croft and his team of London performers. With Colley Cibber and the Drury Lane theatre company also in residence the city would have been crammed with visitors, not only persons 'of quality and distinction', but also no

---

6   For details of the latter see H. Diack Johnstone, 'Handel at Oxford in 1733', *Early Music*, 31 (2003), 248–60.

7   Letter from Hearne to H[ilkiah] Bedford. See *Remarks and Collections of Thomas Hearne*, vol. 4, ed. D. W. Rannie (Oxford: Clarendon Press for the Oxford Historical Society, 1898), p. 205.

8   See Margaret Crum, 'An Oxford Music Club, 1690–1719', *Bodleian Library Record*, 9/2 (Mar. 1974), 83–99 at 89.

202 H. DIACK JOHNSTONE

doubt a good many Cambridge men come over to witness the proceedings. As one
Oxford academic writing to another who had been absent on the occasion put it,

> The Town has been so exceeding full this Act beyond what was ever known before, I
> think, that [t]here was too great a Hurry & Confusion for us to be able to doe as we
> ought, either for the Satisfaction of our friends or the Reputation of the University.
> Friday's performance was to the Satisfaction of Every One; but y[e] Great Crowd on
> Monday was a little too Mobbish –[9]

Whilst it is by no means impossible that one or other if not both Croft odes were
specially commissioned for the 1713 Act – their words, in celebration of the peace,
were in both cases, after all, the work of Joseph Trapp (1697–1747), a Fellow of
Wadham College and the university's first Professor of Poetry – they were also
to serve as his D.Mus. exercise. Also taking a doctorate in music on the same
occasion and no doubt sharing many of the same performers (since candidates for
degrees in music were expected to bear the cost of a public performance of their
exercises) was the expatriate German composer J. C. Pepusch (1667–1752).[10]
Both men, travelling together perhaps – the journey up from London then took the
best part of two days – had arrived in Oxford by Thursday the 9th when they were
formally matriculated, one as a member of Christ Church, the other as a member
of Magdalen College;[11] as the sons of gentlemen ('Gen.fil.') they each paid five
shillings. Their respective merits as musicians had in fact already been put to a
meeting of Convocation (then the official governing body of the university) by the
Chancellor, the Duke of Ormonde, in two letters dated St James's, 28 May 1713.[12]
In supporting Croft, the Duke invited the university to consider not only his
composition of, but also 'his great charge in performing the entertainment of
Musick for the Encaenia for this p[res]ent Act, which he had long since undertaken
when intended for the peace'.[13] Pepusch he describes as 'a Forreigner and
Protestant who hath long resided in England who is a Person of good Learning
and singular Skill as well in Theory as [in] the Practice of Musick', adding – rather
interestingly since nothing ever came of it – that it was Pepusch's intention 'shortly
to Publish a Treaty [sic] of Musick from Severall Tracts now in the Bodleian
Library & other Collections of his own already made'.

---

9   Letter of 15 July 1713 from Dr Arthur Charlett, Master of University College, to William
Dobson, the President of Trinity. Oxford, Bodleian Library, MS Ballard 21, fo. 192.

10   Though we nowadays might think the B.Mus. to have been an essential prerequisite, it was not
uncommon during this period for an already established composer to proceed straight to the doctorate.

11   Oxford University Archives, MS SP 6 (Matriculation Register, 1699–1714); not paginated or
foliated.

12   Oxford University Archives, MS NEP/Subtus/Bd (Register of Convocation, 1704–1730),
fos 97[v] and 98. Ormonde had succeeded his father, the first duke, as Chancellor of the university in
1688; and, though hamstrung by Parliament, he had also served as commander in chief of the allied
forces since the Duke of Marlborough's dismissal in December 1711. In this latter capacity he had of
course been intimately involved in the final stages of the War of the Spanish Succession.

13   This, combined with the fact that Trapp's words were elsewhere said to have been 'made ...
by the Direction of the University', sounds to me very much like a commission. For further evidence
pointing in this direction, see my discussion of the partial setting of 'Laurus cruentas' by Richard
Goodson on pp. 214–15.

MUSIC AND DRAMA AT THE OXFORD ACT OF 1713

Somewhat surprisingly, however, and no doubt embarrassingly for him, Pepusch arrived to find himself in breach of the university regulations which required a candidate for D.Mus. to produce a 'Canticum' in 6 or 8 parts (with instruments) as part of his exercise[14] – and his 'Song' in praise of Queen Anne would appear to have had only a four-part concluding chorus. He had thus that same day (9 July) to appeal to Convocation for permission to proceed, his failure to meet the statutory requirements of the degree notwithstanding.[15] Luckily the oversight was condoned. Although the exercise itself does not survive, we can tell from the libretto – published as a single double-sided wordsheet for the audience – that it contained, recitatives apart, no fewer than 11 movements: 7 arias, 2 duets, a trio and concluding chorus all in da capo form.[16] Three allegorical characters, 'Peace', 'Apollo' and 'Britain', are involved (and a solo trumpeter also in the penultimate aria); if we allow for an introductory overture or sinfonia as well, the piece must have taken the best part of an hour (or more) in performance. Who was responsible for the words we do not know – it could even have been Pepusch himself – but they are pretty dire on the whole, as the opening four lines (sung by Peace) suffice to show:

> Hail Queen of Islands! Hail illustrious fair!
> No more give way to sorrow and despair,
> Raise up thy drooping head, recal[l] thy Charms
> And welcome me to Earth with open Armes!

Joseph Trapp on the other hand was a real poet, if not a particularly distinguished one, and his libretti for Croft are both thoroughly competent and well stocked with the sort of imagery designed to evoke a positive response from the composer. And Croft does not disappoint; though tied by their texts to a particular occasion, both odes are well worth performing and, dare one say it, far more interesting than some earlier Oxonian Act music which has recently found its way onto disc. With one in Latin, the other English, they also make a nicely contrasted pair, one a somewhat subdued and basically minor-key piece, the other a much more brilliant and essentially ebullient work in the major, framed by movements in which a solo trumpet is added to an orchestra consisting otherwise of oboes and strings. Their overtures too are very happily contrasted, one a two-movement French overture, the other a four-movement Italian symphony (though not actually so called). The style of both is firmly assured and on the whole rather more Italianate than English. The following analytical chart (see Table 10.1) shows not only the number of movements involved, but also their scoring and the carefully devised tonal balance of the whole. Oboes, though specified only twice,

---

14 See *Oxford University Statutes*, tr. G. R. M. Ward, vol. 1 (London: William Pickering, 1845), p. 50; and for the original Latin text, John Griffiths, ed., *Statutes of the University of Oxford codified in the year 1636* (Oxford: Clarendon Press, 1888), p. 60.

15 Oxford University Archives, MS NEP/Subtus/Bd, fo. 101.

16 Two copies only are known, one in the Bodleian Library, Oxford, press-mark G.A. Oxon. b.111, the other in the library of Lambeth Palace.

H. DIACK JOHNSTONE

Table 10.1 Structural breakdown of Croft's two Oxford odes showing number of movements, metre, scoring and key

Laurus cruentas

1 Overture[a]	(a)	C	strings a4	G minor
	(b)	3/4	strings a4	G minor
2 Laurus cruentas		3/2	Duet: two altos + bc	G minor
3 Nunc quotquot urget		¢	Solo: alto + 2 vns and bc	B♭ major
4 O quis arduos		3/4	Solo: bass + 2 obs and bc	F major
5 Surge fama		¢	Trio: 2 altos, bass + bc	C major
6 Justam dum regit		C	Solo: alto + 2 vns and bc	E minor
7 Gentes amicae plaudite		¢	Chorus a8 + strings	G major

With noise of cannon

1 Overture	(a)	C	strings and trumpet	D major
Allegro	(b)	¢	strings and trumpet	D major
Adagio	(c)	C	strings only	D minor
Allegro	(d)	3/8	strings and trumpet	D major
2 With noise of cannon[b]		C	Solo: bass + 2 vns and bc	D major
3 A milder, a happier strain		¢	Solo: alto + 2 vns and bc	D minor
4 Tuning to peace		¢	Chorus a4 + strings	D minor
5 Peace is the song		3/4	Duet: alto and bass + ob and strings	G minor
6 The soul of music		C	Chorus a4 + strings	B♭ major
7 Nor will we ev'n the martial trumpet spare		C	Solo: alto + tpt and strings	D major
8 Where mighty Anna		C	Verse: AATTBB + strings	B minor
9 O mighty Anna		C	Chorus a8 + tpt and strings	D major

a Modern edition of the overture, ed. Maurice Bevan, *Musica da Camera* 44 (London: Oxford University Press, 1977). It should perhaps be noted that Croft's setting rides rough-shod over the verse structure of the Latin text.

b For a short extract (in score), see Ex. 2.3 in Susan Wollenberg, *Music at Oxford in the Eighteenth and Nineteenth Centuries* (Oxford: Oxford University Press, 2001), pp. 24–5. The movement has also been recorded by David Thomas and the Parley of Instruments on a 1979 Meridian disc of music by Croft, since reissued as Meridian CDE 84234. An eighteenth-century keyboard arrangement of the overture is included in *William Croft: Complete Harpsichord Works*, ed. Howard Ferguson and Christopher Hogwood, 2 vols (London, 1974; rev. 1981), vol. 2, pp. 23–30.

MUSIC AND DRAMA AT THE OXFORD ACT OF 1713   205

once in each ode, would almost certainly have doubled the violins in some at least of the other movements.

Though one or two movements were later abstracted and circulated in manuscript copies, no fewer than three manuscript copies of both odes survive.[17] Much the most important of these is a beautiful presentation copy made by Croft's pupil James Kent (then aged 13), and given by the composer, almost certainly in advance of the Oxford Act, to his good friend and colleague John Dolben (later Sir John), an Oxford (Christ Church) man who was then Sub-Dean of the Chapel Royal.[18] Still in its original binding, it is now in the music library of the University of Washington in Seattle (M 782.8 C874t), and, like several other Dolben MSS, it was once owned by John Lucius Dampier.[19] The others are all in the Bodleian Library (and in a single unidentified hand) as Tenbury MSS 1221 ('With noise of cannon'), 1308 ('Laurus cruentas', but lacking the final chorus) and 1231 (which contains both odes). None of these Oxford copies has any real textual authority, but the first (Tenbury 1221) is particularly interesting in that the opening words of the last two movements have been changed to 'O Great Victoria', thus suggesting the possibility of a late nineteenth-century revival; a large number of pencilled alterations in the score also point in the same direction. Quite who was responsible we do not know, but one might perhaps hazard a guess that it was Sir Walter Parratt, who was appointed Master of the Queen's Musick in 1893.

Some time after the 1713 Oxford Act, Croft himself published both works in a handsome folio volume entitled *Musicus Apparatus Academicus*. Though originally performed the other way round, 'With noise of cannon' comes first here (as it also does in Tenbury 1231 and the Seattle MS) and both are very much more fully figured in print than in manuscript.[20] On opening the volume, one is faced with a splendidly baroque title-page designed by John Devoto and engraved by Thomas Atkins (see Fig. 10.1), a second copy of which is also placed before

---

17   Single movements survive as follows: 'Justam dum regit', 'With noise of cannon' and 'A milder, a happier strain' (all in Oxford, Christ Church MSS 68, 70, 71 and 73, and all copied by Richard Goodson jun. in the late 1730s); also a somewhat shortened version of 'Peace is the song' in BL Add. MS 31455 together with the concluding chorus 'O mighty Anna' (here in C major). Very curiously, bits of the last chorus of both odes were later adapted by the Swedish composer Johan Helmich Roman (1694–1758), and incorporated in an anthem (with Swedish text): see Ingmar Bengtsson, *Mr. Roman's Spuriosity Shop: A Thematic Catalogue* (Stockholm: Swedish Music History Archive, 1976), p. 59, and Supplement No. 1 (Stockholm, 1980), pp. 5–6. As a pupil of Pepusch, Roman was in England from about 1715 to 1721. A mid-nineteenth-century copy of the trio 'Surge fama' used as an illustration in one of Edward Taylor's Gresham College lectures on English opera is in Royal College of Music, MS 2103 (at fo. 70ᵛ).

18   On Dolben (1684–1756) and his patronage of Croft, see Donald Burrows, 'Sir John Dolben, Musical Patron', *Musical Times*, 120 (1979), 65–7.

19   See Donald Burrows, 'Sir John Dolben's Music Collection', *Musical Times*, 120 (1979), 149–51. For information which prompted me to investigate this source rather more fully than I might otherwise have done, I am indebted to Professor Graydon Beeks.

20   The published version incorporates a number of minor changes not evident in the MS sources which, as a set, are unusually closely related; internal evidence suggests that they were all copied, most probably from an autograph no longer extant, some time in advance of the premiere (and in the order: Seattle, Tenbury 1308/1221, and Tenbury 1231).

Fig. 10.1 William Croft, *Musicus Apparatus Academicus* [1720], title-page designed by John Devoto

'Laurus cruentas', and here, as in the Seattle source (and Tenbury MS 1231 also), both odes are separately paginated. A second title-page, much less striking but more informative, follows, and there is also a further introductory page – an 'Address to the Reader' in effect – explaining for what purpose the works were written, and how 'having done their Work and answered the end for which they were Compos'd', they have 'lain by neglected' until, that is, 'the Importunity of some Friends ... prevailed with me to make them publick'.[21] Quite when the volume appeared has hitherto been a matter of conjecture, some authorities (like *New Grove2*) assigning it to 1715 while others opt for 1720 or, more cautiously, a date of publication somewhere between the two. Of three copies in the Bodleian Library, one (press-mark: fol. BS 49) is clearly a presentation copy from the composer to the library, and this much is evident from the inscription 'Bibl. Bodl. d.d. Auctor' on the front fly-leaf. The volume is still in its original eighteenth-century binding, while the damage to the outer edge of the front cover (together with its original press-mark: C.1.17 Jur) shows that it was once chained to the shelves in Selden End.[22] Having got that far, one has only to look up the acquisitions records (in Library Records MS e.10) to discover that it was donated to the Bodleian some time between November 1719 and November 1720 as number 25 in a list of 44 items given to the library during that year. To get beyond that point, however, a careful trawl of contemporary newspaper advertisements is required. Given the composer's natural modesty, evident even in the explanatory note partially quoted above, one is hardly surprised to learn that the forthcoming publication of *Musicus Apparatus Academicus* was not widely advertised; indeed, I could find only one reference to it, and that in *The Post-Boy* of 5–8 March 1719/20 where Croft tells us that not only the two Oxford odes, but also a book of anthems – obviously the first book of *Musica sacra* – which had 'for some time past ... been Engraving in Score upon Copper Plates' were 'now finished and printing off; and will be ready to be deliver'd to such Persons as have desired, or may be desirous of having the same, before Easter next'. Though a further announcement in 'the Gazette and other publick Papers' was promised, it seems that no such press release was ever issued, and that the publication of *Musica sacra* was in fact held back until 1724 when this first volume eventually appeared, together with a second batch of Croft anthems.[23]

Unlike 1733 when the university was obviously at some pains to repair a few political fences and to dispel any lingering image of Oxford as a den of covert Jacobite sympathizers, the 1713 Act was a blatantly Tory affair designed not only to celebrate the peace, but also to sing the praises of those who were publicly

---

21 The second much plainer title-page and following authorial explanation are reproduced as pl. 4 in Wollenberg, *Music at Oxford*. John Dolben must surely have been one of the 'Friends' who nudged the composer into print.

22 I am grateful to Peter Ward Jones, head of the Bodleian Library music staff, for an explanation of what the damaged outer edge together with the obviously earlier press-mark must imply.

23 A seemingly unique copy of Croft's proposals for the publication of *Musica sacra* survives in the New York Public Library, and is dated London, 25 March 1724.

208   H. DIACK JOHNSTONE

perceived to have been responsible for bringing it about, chiefly of course the Queen. This is clearly evident in the several orations delivered as part of the Comitia Philologica on the Friday afternoon (10 July), the third of which is entitled 'Ormondus Imperator'. It must also account for a specific reference to the Earl of Oxford – an *éminence grise* if ever there was one – in the final stanza of 'Laurus cruentas' as printed in the official wordbook published by the University Press for the occasion.[24] Thus it is with a ringing endorsement of 'Illi cui dederunt Oxonii titulos Camenae' that Croft's setting ends. And since this formed no part of the text as originally set – it appears only as a last-minute addition to Tenbury MS 1231 (and is preserved also in the 1720 print) – we must suppose that Robert Harley himself was also in attendance.[25] Academic members of the audience were almost certainly provided with copies of the Comitia Philologica (which, in addition to the words of both odes, also contained the texts of almost all the Latin orations delivered during the course of the ceremony). For members of the general public, a separate wordsheet with 'Laurus cruentas' on one side and 'With noise of cannon' on the other was also printed, presumably at Croft's expense, and here, curiously, there is yet another version of the Latin text in which the last four lines as set are replaced by eight others which run as follows:

> Tu, Fama, reple Buccinam, & aeream
> Intende vocem; non regionibus
>   Audita solum, quas jacentes
>   Sub gelido videx Axe Phoebus;
>   Sed nota Terris Imperio additis
>   Ingentis ANNAE, quas nova Pax dedit
>   Recens *Britannas*, & remoto
>   Oceanus lavat *Indus* Orbe.

Whether this was Trapp's ending as originally conceived is not entirely clear, but he himself was already known as an outspoken Tory. During the course of what must have been a very long afternoon, both Croft odes were performed, 'Laurus cruentas' between the opening 'Proloquium' and a first block of 11 orations (the so-called 'Concentus Primus'), and 'With noise of cannon' between the 'Concentus Secundus' (containing a further 10 orations) and the concluding 'Concentus Tertius' or 'Peroratio' by which the proceedings were brought finally to an end. That music was traditionally performed at these points is evident from a number of late seventeenth-century sources, some of which are specifically designated as being for 'Act Saturday'.

---

24   Copies in the Bodleian Library, press-mark Pamph. 311 (47), and BL, press-mark G. 2502 (4); other copies elsewhere. On the Earl of Oxford's relations with the university, see G. V. Bennett's essay in *The History of the University of Oxford*, vol. 5: *The Eighteenth Century*, ed. L. S. Sutherland and L. G. Mitchell (Oxford: Clarendon Press, 1986), p. 66.

25   By creating 12 new Tory peers expressly for the purpose of rigging the vote in the House of Lords, it was Harley – Prime Minister in effect – who can be regarded as the chief architect of the peace. Though he himself was subsequently impeached and sent to the Tower (in 1715), he was acquitted two years later; shortly before his death (in May 1724) he signed on as one of 155 subscribers for Croft's *Musica sacra* (see n. 23 above).

From a long account of the event in one of the London papers (*The British-Mercury* of 15 July), it would appear that Croft's contribution made a very considerable impression:

Oxford, *July* 10. This Day the publick Act began ... with the utmost Pomp and Magnificence. The Celebration of Peace brought an innumerable Concourse of Persons of Distinction, and inspir'd all that were publickly concern'd, with uncommon Zeal and Emulation in their several Performances. ... and what adds much to the Solemnity, is, that Mr. Croft, Organist and Composer to her Majesty, &c. and Mr. Nepusch [*sic*] commence Doctors. The Act was open'd with a most surprizing [*sic*] Piece of Harmony compos'd by Dr. Croft, which lasted about an Hour. The Words were made by the Reverend Mr. Trap[p] upon the Peace, by the Direction of the University. The Performance in all its Parts was done with great Exactness and Applause: The Vocal by Mr. Elford, Mr. Hughs, Mr. Freeman, Mr. Gates, Mr. Weely, and several other [of] the best Voices. The instrumental Parts by Mr. Goodson, Musick Professor here, Mr. Isham, and the best Hands of her Majesty's Musick, and in the Opera-House. The Harmony, Solemnity, and Variety of which Piece, has given all that are Judges an unspeakable Esteem for that exquisite and inimitable Master. We expect on Monday next to be very well entertain'd by Dr. Nepusch's Exercise.

The misspelling of Pepusch was corrected in the next issue (of 22 July), and so too the error in referring to Croft's exercise as a single piece; the two odes, it now points out, 'took up near two Hours in the Performance; and ... was so extraordinary, that at the Request of the University, the *English* Part was perform'd again on Monday following'.

Sadly, perhaps, there is no further comment in any of the London papers, so we have no idea what sort of impact, if any, the Pepusch 'Song' made on the assembled company; it may well have been – indeed probably was – outshone by the far greater formal variety of 'With noise of cannon'. With two such substantial works set amid the academic ritual of the occasion – and music was only one of the subjects involved – this too must have been another very long afternoon. In presenting them for their doctorates, the Heather Professor of Music played no part, for that duty was then assigned (by statute) to one or other of the two Savilian Professors (of astronomy and geometry). But the Heather Professor, Richard Goodson senior (*c*.1655–1718), was undoubtedly there, seemingly as a member of the orchestra; though primarily a keyboard-player, it is not inconceivable that, as a violinist, he also led the band. How many other local musicians also took part it is impossible to say, but it could be that one or two of the more accomplished players in the Oxford Music Club were conscripted for the occasion. The chorus trebles too would almost certainly have been provided by one or more of the Oxford choral foundations, most probably Christ Church, of which Goodson was organist – and to which Croft now belonged by virtue of the matriculation ceremony which had taken place on 9 July. Whether or not the two men were known to each other in advance of the Act we cannot say, but it seems not unlikely. Similarly perhaps with Pepusch, who may well have chosen Magdalen simply because in London he was friendly with Daniel Purcell who had

210   H. DIACK JOHNSTONE

been organist at Magdalen from 1688 to 1695. But all this is conjecture. What is certain is that some time after the event – less than 10 years in Croft's case – both men had their portraits painted in all their academic finery, the Oxford D.Mus. gown and hood being then (as it still is) quite the most resplendent thing of its kind.[26]

In 1713 as in 1733, and with the expectation no doubt of attracting thereby a greater number of auditors than usual, the Saturday morning 'Musick Lecture' was moved from its customary home in the Schola Musicae to the Sheldonian Theatre, and it says something for the fortitude and enthusiasm of our eighteenth-century forebears that they might reasonably be expected to turn out for such an event at the (to us) unearthly hour of 6 or 7 a.m. By this date, what had originally been a lecture as such had evidently become a concert for which Richard Goodson, as Heather Professor of Music, was entirely responsible. Who played and sang, and what the normal format of the programmes was, we do not know, but it is by no means impossible that on this particular occasion some music by Croft or Pepusch was performed, though we may well doubt whether either of them was personally involved. Whilst it could be that the chance survival among a volume of stray instrumental parts associated with Oxford of a suite for two violins and cello ascribed to Croft and hitherto unnoticed is a legacy of the 1713 Musick Lecture,[27] it would appear more likely from the titles of the individual movements ('1st musick', 'Round O', '2d musick', 'Slow Ayre', 'Hornpipe', untitled movement in duple time, 'Roundo minuet', untitled movement in *alla breve* time, and 'Overture') that this is actually a theatre set for some as yet unrecognized play, conceivably one of those brought down by the Drury Lane company for its 1713 Oxford season. Unfortunately the first violin part is lacking all but the first four movements.

As organist not only of Christ Church but also of the university church (St Mary's), Goodson would also have been expected to organize the music for the two services on Act Sunday (12 July). In 1733, the out-of-town performers took part in a performance not only of two orchestrally accompanied anthems, both by Handel, but also of his 'Utrecht' setting of the morning canticles. Whether anything similar happened in 1713 is not recorded, but if it did, then only Croft is likely to have been involved since nearly all of Pepusch's church music is rather

---

26   The Thomas Murray portrait of Croft was later given to the university by the widow of his great friend and admirer, Humphrey Wyrley Birch (for whom see Hawkins, *History*, vol. 2, p. 796), and now hangs in the Oxford Faculty of Music; an engraving (in reverse) by George Vertue serves as frontispiece to *Musica sacra* (1724) and there is another (by J. Caldwall) in Hawkins, *History* (loc. cit.). Thomas Hudson's fine portrait of Pepusch must obviously have been painted rather later and is now in the National Portrait Gallery, London (but currently hangs in Beningbrough Hall, a National Trust property near York).

27   Oxford, Bodleian Library, MS Mus. Sch. c.44, fos 130–34. On the use of the so-called 'Monke Sonata' (by Lambert Pietkin) in this same MS, see Peter Holman, 'Original Sets of Parts for Restoration Concerted Music at Oxford', in Michael Burden, ed., *Performing the Music of Henry Purcell* (Oxford: Clarendon Press, 1996), p. 15.

MUSIC AND DRAMA AT THE OXFORD ACT OF 1713   211

later in date.[28] Neither do we know whether or not a London performance of either composer's D.Mus. exercise was ever given. But in Oxford, at any rate, the event was not quickly forgotten. On 15 February 1714 the members of the Oxford Music Club met to perform 'Dr. Croft's Musick' which, with only this one work mentioned and three shillings paid for choristers on the occasion, strongly suggests that at least one if not both odes were done again within a year of their first performance.[29] In the meantime, an Oxford clergyman, the Rev. William Dingley of Corpus Christi College (and senior non-performing member of the Music Club), had also paid homage to the composer by dedicating to him the published version of his sermon in praise of church music delivered to the university on St Cecilia's Day, 1713.

By Tuesday 14 July, the dust of the Oxford Act was starting to settle, and most of the London performers were probably headed back to town. But two at least appear to have stayed on until the end of the week when, inspired no doubt by the splendour of the occasion, they decided to supplicate for the degree of B.Mus. They were John Isham (d. 1726) and William Morley (d. 1721), two men, obviously friends, who had recently published a joint *Collection of New Songs*, one of which was later to find its way into the last volume of Hawkins's *History* (1776).[30] Morley, a lay vicar of Westminster Abbey, had been appointed a supernumerary Gentleman of the Chapel Royal earlier that year, while Isham, mentioned in the newspaper notice quoted above, was a former pupil of Croft who had succeeded him as organist of St Anne's Soho when Croft finally relinquished the post in 1711.[31] On Thursday (the 16th), Convocation held its last meeting of the academic year, and was presented with two letters from the Duke of Ormonde dated St James's, 13 July, supporting their application.[32] The following day they were both matriculated as members of Merton College, and since they were

---

28   The obvious candidate in the case of the morning canticles is Croft's orchestrally accompanied setting of the Te Deum and Jubilate of 1709. It seems not unlikely, however, that the anthem on the occasion was Goodson's symphony anthem 'Rejoice in the Lord O ye righteous', on the front page of which (Christ Church MS 1219) Philip Hayes many years later wrote: 'The Author's original manuscript. Probably compos'd for the Public Act in 1713 and Perform'd at S' Mary's or still earlier, upon the Accession of King William [in 1689]'. If 1713 seems more likely in terms of style than 1689, the date is no more than a guess on Hayes's part and replaces what, following a note in Richard Goodson jun.'s hand at the end of the anthem, appears originally to have read 1734; beneath the erasure, the third digit at any rate was clearly '3'.

29   See Crum, 'Music Club', 93, and Oxford, Merton College MS 4.33 (unpaginated). The only other recorded performance (of 'Dr Croft's Song for his Degree, and a great Deal of other Musick') was given by the musical society in Wells on 23 November 1719 as part of their annual celebration of St Cecilia's Day; see *The Diary of a West Country Physician, A.D. 1684–1726* [Claver Morris], ed. Edmund Hobhouse (London: Simpkin, Marshall, 1934), p. 74.

30   See modern reprint of 1853 edition, pp. 799–800.

31   For the most up-to-date biographical information on Morley see *A Biographical Dictionary of English Court Musicians 1485–1714*, compiled by Andrew Ashbee and David Lasocki assisted by Peter Holman and Fiona Kisby, 2 vols (Aldershot: Ashgate, 1998), vol. 2, pp. 809–10; on Isham (who held no court appointment) see ibid., s.v. 'Croft', and Donovan Dawe, *Organists of the City of London 1666–1850* (Padstow: Donovan Dawe, 1983), p. 114.

32   Oxford University Archives, NEP/Subtus/Bd (Register of Convocation, 1704–1730).

212 H. DIACK JOHNSTONE

designated 'Pleb. fil.' in the register, it cost them each only two shillings and six pence.[33] But as neither had an exercise at the ready, and the opportunity for performing such had in any case now passed them by, each was required to lay down 'such a pecuniary Caution as shall be required of him for ye performance of his Exercise within one year'; that done, they would be allowed to take the degree on payment of the statutory fees.

Quite when their exercises were formally presented we do not know, but it must certainly have been some time within the next 12 months as specified in the Register of Convocation. And since a public performance was required, we may safely assume that they were given in succession, no doubt in the Schola Musicae, which was then the normal venue for all such performances as were not part of an official Public Act. Both are short orchestrally accompanied odes in honour of the Queen and in celebration of the peace, and, as it happens, the scores and parts of both have survived in the Bodleian's Music School collection. Morley's 'Let the shrill trumpet's loud alarms' (MSS Mus. c.6, fos 23–40^v and Mus. Sch. 131) opens with a three-movement overture in which the fugal allegro is followed by an *alla breve* adagio in the tonic (C) minor. Then comes a brief secco recitative for bass and continuo, a duet for alto and tenor, a treble solo whose last clause is reworked as a short four-part chorus, a bass solo, another duet, this time for alto and bass, and finally the Canticum a5 specified in the statutes. The overture and concluding chorus are both in C major (except, that is, for the aforementioned adagio) with the central movements in a rather surprising succession of minor keys: A, E, G and C. The scoring, as is the case with the Isham ode also, is for strings (and continuo) only. The Isham ode (MSS Mus. Sch. d.341 and Mus. Sch. c.140) is also in C, and with four movements, the third of which is slow (and in the tonic minor), the last a jovial allegro in 6/8 time; the overture to 'O tuneful god and all ye sacred nine' is clearly modelled on that to Croft's 'With noise of cannon'. Between that and the final five-part chorus are an alto and bass duet (in C minor), a bass solo (in C major) and an alto solo (in A minor). Musically, however, neither has anything much to offer.

In the case of the Morley, both score and parts are in the hand of the composer, but Isham had his score (and most of the two solo vocal parts) copied by James Kent, the 13-year-old pupil of Croft who produced the handsome presentation copy of the two Croft odes now in Seattle. So similar is the word 'Overture' at the head of both scores that one might almost imagine one to be a photocopy of the other. How any child could have developed such a distinctive and beautifully formed hand by the age of 13 is amazing (see Fig. 10.2). From the number of parts in MS Mus. Sch. c.140 ('O tuneful god'), two each of first and second trebles, alto,

---

33 Oxford University Archives, MS SP 42 (Register of Subscriptions at Matriculation, 1694–1714). In MS SP 6 (Matriculation Register, 1699–1714) the date is wrongly given as 16 July: it was in SP 42 that they actually signed. It is interesting that the university obviously operated a sliding scale of fees by which matriculands were charged according to the social status of their fathers, and 'Paup. fil.' had nothing whatever to pay. On the different social categories of students in eighteenth-century Oxford, see vol. 5 of *The History of the University of Oxford*, pp. 311–14.

Fig. 10.2   William Croft, 'Laurus cruentas', first page of the first vocal movement as copied by James Kent in 1713

214 H. DIACK JOHNSTONE

tenor and bass (with soloists also singing in the choruses) and two each of first and second violins and bass with a single 'tenor' or viola part, it would appear that there were at least ten singers and seven string-players involved – possibly more if the trebles sang two to a part, and the instrumentalists also shared. The Morley on the other hand has only one of each – but with a second 'First Trebble' (i.e. first violin) part and a separate figured 'Through Bass' part which may be the residue of a second duplicate set copied locally. Who the performers were is anyone's guess, but it could well be that, trebles apart, both singers and string-players came down from London to support their colleagues.[34]

There is, however, one further musical by-product of the 1713 Oxford Act which also needs to be discussed, and that is a second setting, evidently by Richard Goodson, of the opening four lines of 'Laurus cruentas'.[35] The autograph survives in Oxford, Christ Church MS 1142 A (fos 21–2) and is really no more than a rough compositional sketch which breaks off after an opening bass solo and four-part choral setting of the words 'Heu, heu, satis et super / victorias inter quere lasque / ambigui cecinere [Vates]'. In Croft's setting (as sung on 10 July), the same passage runs: 'Heu, heu, satis et super / Non caede gaudentes Poetae / Ambiguis cecinere plectris'. Nevertheless it was with a Latin text almost identical with that set by Goodson that Croft was originally presented, the only difference being that 'inter quere lasque' now read: 'inter atque querelas'; and it is this latter version which is to be found not only in the Seattle MS but also in Tenbury 1308. By the time Tenbury MS 1231 came to be copied, Trapp's words had been revised yet again (presumably by the poet himself) to match the version actually performed, and the ending altered to incorporate that judicious tribute to the Earl of Oxford previously mentioned.[36] Perhaps the most likely explanation is that some time quite early on in the year, the university decided to celebrate the peace with an official public Act and asked Trapp (as Professor of Poetry) to produce an ode specially for the occasion. Goodson, getting wind of this, might naturally have assumed that as Heather Professor he would be called on to produce the music, as he had done on several similar occasions in the past: most recently, it seems, in 1705, to celebrate

---

34   On the implications for performance of these and other surviving sets of Oxford parts, see Holman, 'Original Sets of Parts', pp. 9–19.

35   I am grateful to Professor John Caldwell for drawing this further setting to my attention; also to my colleague Dr Margaret Howatson, formerly Tutorial Fellow in Classics at St Anne's College, Oxford, for her invaluable assistance not only with the text of 'Laurus cruentas', but also with a good deal of sloppy Latin in some of the documents in the University Archives to which reference has earlier been made. The translation of 'Laurus cruentas' included here as an appendix is hers.

36   Croft's original ending is preserved in both the Seattle MS and in Tenbury MS 1231; in the latter, however, it is clearly indicated that the original ending is to be replaced by the music written beneath – and completed some 30 pages earlier on a single blank sheet which is in fact the verso of the last page of 'With noise of cannon'. That the final chorus in Tenbury 1308 breaks off after only five bars may well reflect some indecision on the part of the copyist as to what exactly was about to happen with the rest of that movement. Unless Croft began work on his two Oxford odes even earlier than Handel had his 'Utrecht' Te Deum and Jubilate, all three MS sources together with Tenbury 1221 must have been copied within a six-month period prior to the Act.

the victory at Blenheim in the summer of the previous year.[37] He thus embarked on a setting of 'Laurus cruentas' which was abandoned once he discovered that Croft was already at work on his setting of the same text, a setting which, we may suppose, had quite possibly been commissioned by the university. But this too is purely conjectural: there is no evidence in the university archives of any arrangements made in advance of the actual Act.

When William Croft and J. C. Pepusch arrived in Oxford on Thursday 9 July, the Drury Lane theatre company under the management of Colley Cibber had already been in residence for a couple of weeks, thus adding a variety of dramatic entertainment to the forthcoming academic spectacle and musical attractions of the Act itself. According to an unspecified newspaper advertisement for their performance of *The Tempest* on 23 June, this was to be 'positively the last time of Acting till Winter, the Company being obliged to go immediately to Oxford'.[38] During the latter part of the seventeenth century such visits by various London theatrical companies had, by permission of the Vice-Chancellor, been a more or less regular feature of the Act. But plays and theatre-going in general were regarded by a great many Oxford academics like Hearne as a morally corrupting influence on the young, and in 1710 the players were actually banned.[39] Though they were allowed back in 1713, this was in fact to prove their last visit. In 1733 they were forced to perform in Abingdon, a small country town about 6½ miles south of the city; and four years later, with university backing, Parliament would be invited to consider a bill prohibiting the performance of stage plays in either Oxford or Cambridge,[40] presumably as part of the so-called Licensing Act by means of which the London theatres too were to be more rigorously controlled. With no proper playhouse in which to operate, the actors had either to set up their own theatrical booth or make do with whatever indoor spaces were available, generally it seems a tennis court. Latterly (and very probably in 1713 too) this appears to have been the one belonging to Merton College which, incidentally, still stands, and is now, appropriately, the headquarters of the Oxford University Tennis Club.

For what little we know of the 1713 Oxford theatrical season we are chiefly dependent on Cibber's own account of the visit in his *An Apology for the Life*

---

37 For a list of Goodson's Oxonian odes, mostly undated, see T. A. Trowles, 'The Musical Ode in Britain c.1670–1800', D.Phil. diss. (University of Oxford, 1992), vol. 2, pp. 75–8; and for a valuable discussion of the late seventeenth-century background together with a fuller account of the purely musical features of Croft's two odes than is attempted here, see ibid., vol. 1, pp. 32–54. Two of Goodson's odes ('Ormond's glory, Marlborough's arms' and 'Janus did ever to thy wond'ring eyes', the latter his contribution to the university's Blenheim celebration) have been recorded on a recent disc ('Music from Ceremonial Oxford', CD GAU 222) to which passing reference has earlier been made.

38 See *The London Stage*, Part 2: 1700–1729, ed. E. L. Avery (Carbondale, Ill.: Southern Illinois University Press, 1960), vol. 1, p. 305.

39 See Graham Midgley, *University Life in Eighteenth-Century Oxford* (New Haven and London: Yale University Press, 1996), p. 131.

40 See *A Register of English Theatrical Documents 1660–1737*, comp. and ed. Judith Milhous and Robert D. Hume, 2 vols (Carbondale and Edwardsville, Ill.: Southern Illinois University Press, 1991), vol. 2, items 4088 and 4104.

of Colley Cibber, first published in 1740.[41] Thus we learn that 'It had been a Custom for the Comedians, while at *Oxford*, to act twice a Day; the first Play ending every Morning, before the College Hours of dining, and the other never to break into the Time of shutting their Gates in the Evening'. From other sources, it would appear that the normal period for which the players were allowed to remain in Oxford was 12 days. In 1713, however, they were there for a full three weeks, but performed only once a day. This meant, as Cibber says, that not only might the actors 'be fresher for every single Performance', but also that they 'might be able to fill up the Term of their Residence, without the Repetition of their best, and strongest Plays'. What those 'best, and strongest Plays' were we can only guess, the only one actually mentioned by Cibber being Addison's *Cato*, first performed at Drury Lane on 14 April 1713 and given a run of 20 performances there before the company set out for Oxford at the end of June; and since Addison himself was a distinguished Oxford man, it evidently attracted a good deal of local interest as well, the author's Whiggish political affiliation notwithstanding. According to Cibber, 'the Death of *Cato* triumph'd over the Injuries of *Caesar* every where' – from which latter remark we may safely perhaps infer that *Julius Caesar* was also done. And so too, it would appear from 'The Players Epilogue. Spoken by Miss Willis at their leaving the University this Summer', were *Othello*, *Sir Courtly Nice* (by John Crowne), and Cibber's own *Hob, or The Country Wake*.[42] Assuming all the players took the same parts in Oxford as they had done in London earlier in the 1712–13 season, then the company must have comprised at least fifteen men and seven (possibly eight) women.[43] And if one were to add the three other plays in which Miss Willis herself had been involved, then it could be that Oxford audiences also had a chance to see Vanbrugh's *The Pilgrim*, Betterton's *The Amorous Widow*, and *Bartholomew Fair* (by Ben Jonson). All in all, the 1713 theatrical invasion appears to have been a considerable success: 'our Reception at *Oxford*', said Cibber, 'exceeded our Expectation', and on taking their leave 'we had the Thanks of the Vice-Chancellor, for the Decency, and Order, observ'd by our whole Society; an Honour which had not always been paid, upon the same Occasions'. Though the overall number of performances was slightly down on previous years, the box-office takings were obviously greater, so much so it appears that the company could afford to make a donation of £50 towards the repair of St Mary's, the university church. As Miss Willis put it in the final lines of 'The Players Epilogue':

---

41   Modern edn, ed. with an Introduction by B. R. S. Fone (Ann Arbor: University of Michigan Press, 1968), pp. 254–6. Writing at least 15 years after the event, Cibber (1671–1757) wrongly remembered the date as 1712. For further details see Sybil Rosenfeld, 'Some notes on the players in Oxford 1661–1713', *Review of English Studies*, 19 (1943), 366–75, esp. 372–4.

42   See Rosenfeld, 'Some notes on the players'; Miss Willis's epilogue is there reproduced in full.

43   For a complete roster of the Drury Lane company during the 1712–13 season, see *The London Stage*, Part 2: 1700–1729, vol. 1, p. 284; and for cast lists, the individual plays mentioned here. Biographical details of Miss Willis and all the other actors and actresses involved are to be found in Highfill et al., *Biographical Dictionary*.

MUSIC AND DRAMA AT THE OXFORD ACT OF 1713   217

Beyond our Hopes we've found a Welcome here,
And wish (with some of you) it might be ev'ry Year.

If in the history of the university the 1713 Act is remembered at all, it is chiefly
for the fact that it was in that year that the Vice-Chancellor finally succeeded –
much to Hearne's disgust – in suppressing the activities of the 'Terrae filii', a pair
of licensed undergraduate buffoons whose speeches in the Sheldonian were a
considerable embarrassment, and had, by their vulgarity and unchecked slanging
of academic authority, not only brought the university into disrepute, but also run
the risk, some thought, of courting governmental intervention in the university's
affairs. But both musically and dramatically, as I hope to have shown here, the
Oxford Act of 1713 was a good deal more interesting than that, and has left us with
two works, 'Laurus cruentas' and 'With noise of cannon', both of which are well
worth hearing again.

APPENDIX

The following is the text of 'Laurus cruentas' as set and first performed on 10 July
1713. As printed in the Comitia Philologica (and also the separately published
wordsheet presumably issued by the composer) the stanzas are unnumbered. A
unique copy of the latter source survives in Oxford, Bodleian Library MS Ballard
47 (at fo. 103), and here, stanza 5 is replaced by two others which may well
represent the original ending of Trapp's poem. The English translation is by
Margaret Howatson.

st.1   Laurus cruentas, & faciles nimis
     Mori *Britannos* heu! satis & super
     Non caede gaudentes Poetae
     Ambiguis cecinere plectris.

Of laurels stained with blood, and British
     men too prepared, alas! to die, the Poets,
     though not rejoicing in slaughter, have
     sung enough and more than enough
     in music of ambiguous strain.

st.2   Nunc quotquot urget *Pierius* labor,
     Feliciori ascendere spiritu
     Jubent Camenae, gratuletur
     Ut melior Lyra mitiores

Now our Muses bid all those whose labour
     is for poetry to ascend with happier
     inspiration, so that a better Music may
     celebrate the gentler

st.3   Pacis Triumphos. O! quis ad arduos
     Sublimis ausus materiam valet
     Aequare versu? Surge Fama
     Irrequieta potentis ANNAE

Triumphs of Peace. O who is bold enough
     and able, raised aloft, to match his
     theme in verse to those hard-won
     triumphs? Arise, Glory, of mighty
     ANNE the unresting

st.4   Ministra, Justam dum regit Arbitra
     Mundi Bilancem, Regnaque ponderat,
     Felix Olivae, dissitasque
     Sola sciens sociare gentes;

Attendant, while She wields the Scales of
     Justice as Arbiter of the whole World,
     and weighs Kingdoms in the Balance,
     rejoicing in the Olive Branch, alone
     knowing how to unite peoples at
     variance.

st.5 Gentes amicae plaudite, plaudite
Paci faventes Castalidum Chori,
Reginae et Illi cui dederunt
Oxonii titulos Camenae.

Friendly peoples applaud, applaud you
Choirs of Castalian nymphs whose
devotion is to Peace, to the Queen and to
Him to whom our Muses have given
the title of Oxford.

Replacement stanzas (from MS Ballard 47):

st.5 Tu, Fama, reple Buccinam, & aeream
Intende vocem; non regionibus
Audita solum, quas jacentes
Sub gelido videt Axe Phoebus;

st.6 Sed nota Terris Imperio additis
Ingentis ANNAE, quas nova Pax dedit
Recens *Britannas*, & remoto
Oceanus lavat *Indus* Orbe.

You, Glory, give the Trumpet its theme,
and direct its brazen voice; not only
heard in those regions which Phoebus
sees lying beneath the icy Pole;

but also known in those Lands which have
been added to the Realm of mighty
ANNE, which the new Peace has lately
rendered British, and which are bathed
by the Indian Ocean in the farthest part
of the Globe.

CHAPTER ELEVEN

The Pleasures and Penalties of Networking: John Frederick Lampe in the Summer of 1750

Roy Johnston

After his contract of employment with Thomas Sheridan of the Smock Alley theatre in Dublin expired in 1750, John Frederick Lampe went to live and work in Edinburgh, where he died in the following year. There is a substantial period of more than five months between the close of Sheridan's season at the end of May and Lampe's arrival in Edinburgh in November. A re-examination of the evidence in the light of fresh research leads to the conclusion that Lampe was occupied for part of that summer in the unusual venture, for that period, of a preliminary visit to Edinburgh. In investigating this, the opportunity is taken to observe the career interrelationships among Lampe, Henry Carey, Thomas Arne, Mrs Lampe and Mrs Arne, the actors Macklin and Garrick and the actor and theatre manager Thomas Sheridan; and to throw further light on the advantages and difficulties of using networking to enhance careers in the middle of the eighteenth century.

Lampe in London

Johann Friedrich Lampe, born in Brunswick and graduate in law at Helmstedt, moved to Hamburg and then arrived in London in 1725 or 1726 in his early twenties, where he started to play the bassoon for Handel, a fellow-Saxon. In 1732, in a project to promote opera in English at the Little Theatre in the Haymarket, Lampe wrote three full-length serious operas 'after the Italian maner [*sic*]' within a year. The project failed and all the operas, by Lampe and others including the young Thomas Arne, lost money; his *Amelia*, however, to a libretto by Henry Carey, had 13 performances, a good many more than any of the others. In a different genre, his *The Opera of Operas or Tom Thumb the Great* came out in November 1733 at Drury Lane; as a successful burlesque opera it made opera and opera singers the objects of ridicule rather than plays and actors, and established Lampe in the theatre. Handel had turned from *opera seria* in Italian to oratorio in English with *Esther* in 1732, particularly to satisfy a perceived demand for dramatic music in English. Carey was quick to realize the burlesque potential, and

219

220 ROY JOHNSTON

he and Lampe collaborated in 1734 on a 'grand oratorio' burlesque, *The Dragon of Wantley*, in which Carey ridiculed Italian opera by transferring its artificial conventions and high-flown sentiments to a down-to-earth English folk-tale set in Yorkshire. Lampe set Carey's ribald lines to elaborate and seemingly serious music, accurately parodying Handel. John Rich put on a three-act version at Covent Garden in 1737:

> The Musical Connoisseurs are desired to take Notice, that the Company keeps up strictly to the Italian Taste, the Notes being full of Grandeur and Harmony, and the Words full of low Nonsense ... [Moore, the hero] shall come as near the Figure of the Divine Farinello [*sic*] as possible.[1]

It was phenomenally successful: it ran for 69 performances, seven more than the first run of *The Beggar's Opera*, and played for 57 successive nights, interrupted only by the death of the Queen. The libretto was reprinted more than 14 times in its first season and the music was published in 1738. Taken up by other companies, it held the stage till 1782. It was followed by *Margery, or a worse Plague than the Dragon*, performed at Covent Garden in December 1738. Though less effective and less successful, it confirmed Lampe as London's most prominent theatre musician, a position he consolidated by marrying his leading lady, Isabella Young. He and Thomas Arne thus became relatives; Arne had married Isabella's sister Cecilia. Later in the same season as the premiere of *The Dragon of Wantley*, Arne had success with his masque *Comus*, at Drury Lane.

In the 1740s several notable actors were beginning to feel their way towards a new conception of 'natural' acting. In 1741 Charles Macklin won sudden fame at Drury Lane for his portrayal of Shylock. A few months later the young David Garrick, at an outlying playhouse, Goodman's Fields, made an immediate success as Richard III in the new style which ensured both his entrée to the London theatres and a dominance there which he never lost. It was a theatrical phenomenon which was bound to increase the popularity of Shakespeare in particular and the spoken drama in general, to the detriment of the musical theatre in which Lampe and Carey were now established. Lampe's *The Sham Conjurer*, 'a court masque of Speaking, Singing, Dancing', failed after three performances at Covent Garden in April 1741. His company tried its luck in the provinces (Charles Burney as a student saw a shortened version of *The Dragon* in Chester in 1741)[2] and he wrote nothing more for the London theatres except two works given at the Little Theatre in the spring of 1744, one described as an 'operetta'. Henry Carey, his inspired writer of 'low nonsense', failing to make any headway in the new theatrical climate and in deep depression, took his own life in 1743.

What blew in the face of the others turned out to be a following wind for Arne who, in contrast, put himself in a good position. Masque seemed to be a more durable genre than burlesque opera, and he followed up *Comus* with *The Judgment*

---

1   Rich's advertisement in *The Daily Advertiser*, 16 May 1737.
2   J. Norman Gillespie, 'The Life and Work of Henry Carey', Ph.D. diss. (University of London, 1982), p. 146.

of Paris at Drury Lane in March 1742. Handel had gone to Dublin in the previous year, and Arne and his wife decided to go there too, arriving in 1742 in the close season; for a short time, Dublin had the three of them in residence. Arne formed the impression that a prolonged stay might be to his advantage, went back to London that summer to sort things out and returned to Dublin in the autumn. He and his wife stayed for two years. Cecilia's singing was much praised and in great demand. *Comus* and *The Judgment of Paris* were both performed, and acting on their success Arne revised a masque which he had composed for private performance in 1740, and had it performed at the Smock Alley theatre in March 1744. This was *The Distresses and Conquest of King Alfred*, being given its first public performance – and the first time 'Rule Britannia' had been heard in public. On his return to England Arne found himself with a trio of successful masques which put him in as good a position in the changed theatrical climate as could have been expected. Lampe on the other hand had what was to be his last opera, *Pyramus and Thisbe*, produced at Covent Garden in January 1745. Based on the mechanics' play in *A Midsummer Night's Dream*, it was taken up by provincial companies but did not lead to further opportunities in London.

Thomas Sheridan

At the Smock Alley theatre in Dublin in January 1743, the player who made his debut on the stage (named simply as 'a Gentleman') playing Shakespeare's Richard III was Thomas Sheridan, father of Richard Brinsley Sheridan.[3] He was 23 years of age and came of good family; the problem of his social position as a gentleman and an actor plagued him for much of his life and was regarded by many of his contemporaries as a contradiction in terms. In 1732 his father, who put on plays in the boys' boarding school which he ran in the family home in Dublin, sent him for two years to board at Westminster;[4] Thomas Sheridan was soon spending several nights a week at the major London theatres. After graduation at Trinity College, Dublin he was preparing to enter his father's profession, but his interest in the stage had continued. A farce he wrote, *The Brave Irishman, or Captain O'Blunder*, was to have a fair success in Dublin theatres over many years as a vehicle for a good comic actor. He wanted only a gentleman's reason for stepping on the boards, but, as he said,

> the miserable State in which I found the Stage, and the Meanness of the Performers at that Time, had brought the Profession itself into such a Degree of Contempt, as was sufficient to deter a Young Man of my Spirit, who had gone through an entire Course of a liberal Education, from entering into it.[5]

---

3   *Dublin Gazette*, 25–9 Jan. 1743.

4   Esther K. Sheldon, *Thomas Sheridan of Smock-Alley* (Princeton: Princeton University Press, 1967), pp. 10–13.

5   Thomas Sheridan, *An Oration, Pronounced before a Numerous Body of the Nobility and*

In the summer of 1742, the group of actors who came to Dublin to play a summer season after the London season ended included David Garrick. Sheridan's interest in the theatre brought the two young men together (Garrick was the elder by two years) and a friendship developed. Garrick's style of acting had given him a solid popularity with the public; also, his respectable background had not kept him from the stage. Sheridan's last scruple was removed. Within five months of Garrick's final performance in Dublin he was making his own Smock Alley debut. He became a leading actor overnight in tragedy and Shakespeare. On his return to Dublin in 1745 from a successful spell at Covent Garden and Drury Lane, he found himself manager of the united theatres of Smock Alley and Aungier Street; Aungier Street was abandoned as a playhouse except for special occasions and the acting company moved permanently to Smock Alley. His goals became clear to him: he would raise the social status of the stage, make the actor's profession respectable, and restore the theatre to its classical role as a cultural institution.[6] He took steps, ultimately successful, to get rid of the great inconvenience of allowing people to be admitted onstage during the performance. He also addressed, with less success, the nuisance of the upper gallery. The servants who had spent hours before the play saving unreserved seats elsewhere for their masters and mistresses sat there and became the most notoriously rowdy section of the audience, throwing apples and even stones at the band during the music before the play.

Sheridan was not a musician, but he saw music as a powerful ally in the realization of his hopes for an orderly and well-run theatre. At the beginning of the 1747–48 season the great stumbling block continued to be the upper gallery. Convinced that part at least of the trouble stemmed from boredom with inferior preliminary music, he hired the best band he could find in town, hoping, he said, to please the town in general, but especially the gallery audience – who, having come early for seats, ought to welcome some first-rate music to make the time pass less heavily. But the problem persisted. When several musicians had been injured and their instruments damaged, Sheridan had to warn his audience that 'they could expect "worse Hands" or no music at all, if such behaviour continued'.[7]

He had nonetheless made strides. With the main part of the Dublin theatre audience he was now on congenial terms. There was work to be done to consolidate the good opinion, acceptance and patronage of Dublin Castle and the aristocracy. One way to this, he was quite sure, was to increase the Shakespeare content of the Smock Alley repertoire. Another, he remained convinced, was by music. Mid-eighteenth-century ballad opera and dancing, performed by the acting company, were not the fare to attract the Castle. Musicians and singers of real quality would ensure that the music in which the Shakespeare plays and others abounded would be properly performed, and in some cases recomposed. Ballet and full-length opera might not be too far out of reach.

Gentry, Assembled at the Musick-Hall in Fishamble-Street, on Tuesday the 6th of this instant December, and now first Published at their unanimous Desire, 2nd edn (Dublin, 1757), p. 21.

6   Sheldon, *Thomas Sheridan*, pp. 27–31.

7   Ibid., pp. 116–17; *Faulkner's Dublin Journal [FDJ]*, 21–4 Nov. 1747.

The 'Musical Tribe'

When Sheridan went to London in 1748, then, he was looking as usual for actors and actresses, but primarily on this occasion for the best singers, instrumental musicians and composers in the metropolis. Handel was not to be enticed back: in any case his music had been performed in the concert room, not the theatre. Arne on the evidence of his visit to Dublin earlier in the decade would have suited well, and his wife had every quality Sheridan wanted in his star singer. But Arne was well placed now with Covent Garden, Drury Lane and the pleasure gardens. Sheridan turned to Lampe. *The Dragon of Wantley* had a vitality of its own which enabled it to keep the stage, but burlesque, being – like parody – a parasite, had lost its contemporary relevance as its host, the Italian opera, receded from view. Lampe, however, still enjoyed the prestige which *The Dragon* had brought him, and his operas, including *Pyramus and Thisbe*, had been performed in Dublin.[8] His wife, who as mentioned was a sister of Mrs Arne, was a superlative singer.

Among the singers recruited by Sheridan, besides Mrs Lampe, there was Elizabeth (Betty) Storer. She had sung with Mrs Arne and was well known and well liked in Dublin over several seasons, with a valuable capacity to appeal to every area in the theatre as well as performing oratorio in the concert room. Mrs Mozeen had sung for Handel when she was Miss Edwards, including roles in the premieres of *Imeneo*, *Deidamia* and *Samson*, and in the first London performance of *Messiah*. Daniel Sullivan, a counter-tenor, had begun his career as a boy singer in Dublin, and encountering the Lampes in Chester in 1741 sang Moore in *The Dragon*, then sang the role again at Drury Lane in 1743. Handel recruited him in 1744; he took the part of Athamas in *Semele*, Joseph in *Joseph and his Brethren*, Mical in *Samson* and David in *Saul*. He had also been in Dublin for Sheridan in the 1745–46 season.

Lampe was not to be in a position of sole charge. At about the time that Sheridan made his acting debut at Smock Alley there had arrived in London a young Italian of the same age, Niccolo Pasquali. He had become well known as a violinist in the London theatres. Sheridan, having Lampe as composer anchored to the harpsichord and needing an imported first violin, contracted him to come to Smock Alley and conduct the band. With Lampe, Pasquali, and his star singers and instrumentalists from London on two-year contracts, Sheridan began his 1748–49 season. During the summer of 1748 he had carried out an elaborate remodelling of Smock Alley's interior, which included an enlargement of the orchestra to accommodate 'the extraordinary Number of Hands' engaged for the season.[9] The band, larger than that of Covent Garden at this time, consisted of 10 violins, a

---

8   *Pyramus and Thisbe*, on its first appearance in December 1746, had assisted Sheridan in his anti-stagesitters campaign; no person whatsoever was to be admitted behind the scenes, 'as the Machinery would be much obstructed by it': *FDJ*, 13–16 Dec. 1746.

9   Sheldon, *Thomas Sheridan*, p. 130.

224   ROY JOHNSTON

harpsichord, two double basses, a viola, a cello, two oboes, two bassoons, two French horns and a trumpet.[10]

Through late arrival the Lampes did not make their entry on the musical scene until late October. By that time the others had appeared at Smock Alley, acting and singing in plays. Pasquali had also made his debut as a composer in *As You Like It* 'with new Pieces of Musick, particularly a grand Concerto for the Violin, Solo', 'several Entertainments' in *The Beggar's Opera*, and his concerto again in *The Merchant of Venice*.[11] The *Merchant of Venice* programme was repeated the following evening 'by Command of the Lords Justices',[12] no doubt to Sheridan's satisfaction. With the singers and the band, Pasquali had also conducted a Charitable Society concert in the Philharmonic Room in Fishamble Street.[13] For the King's birthday on 30 October Lampe composed an ode in which Mrs Lampe sang, 'being the first time of her Appearance here in Publick'.[14] Earlier in the day, in an occasion of pomp and ceremony at Dublin Castle,[15] another ode had been performed. Matthew Dubourg, born in the same year as Lampe, had at the age of 25 succeeded to the post of Master and Composer of State Musick in Ireland, being preferred, for religious reasons, to his teacher Geminiani. He held the post for 24 years, until he was appointed to lead the King's Band in London in 1752. Dubourg was an active influence in the Dublin musical community and led the band in the first performance of *Messiah*. The high standard of string playing in Dublin, remarked on by Handel, was owed to Dubourg and Geminiani. In every year from 1741 Dubourg composed a royal birthday ode, and he continued to do so after he left Dublin, until 1759.

Both Lampe's and Dubourg's odes received second performances, Lampe's in Smock Alley,[16] Dubourg's the following evening in the Philharmonic Room, with Dubourg conducting and Miss Oldmixon singing 'songs out of the latest operas'.[17] The English soprano Eleanor Oldmixon had established herself since 1746, singing in the oratorio concerts with Dubourg; for her benefit performance in the previous February, Dubourg had conducted the first Dublin performance of *Samson*. The week which commenced with the King's birthday celebrations ended with another new composition. *The Triumphs of Hibernia*, described as a 'new Masque', by Pasquali, was performed at Smock Alley as afterpiece to *Tamerlane*;[18] Sheridan saw fit to repeat it six times in the remaining months of

---

    10   *FDJ*, 24–7 Sept. 1748.
    11   Sheldon, *Thomas Sheridan*, p. 330; *Dublin Courante* [*DC*], 1–4, 4–8 Oct. 1748.
    12   Sheldon, *Thomas Sheridan*, p. 331.
    13   *FDJ*, 22–5 Oct. 1748.
    14   *FDJ*, 29 Oct.–1 Nov. 1748.
    15   *FDJ*, 29 Oct.–1 Nov. 1748.
    16   Sheldon, *Thomas Sheridan*, p. 331; *FDJ*, 29 Oct.–1 Nov. 1748.
    17   *FDJ*, 25–9 Oct., 29 Oct.–1 Nov. 1748, *DC*, 21–5 Oct. 1748. The Philharmonic room in Fishamble Street opposite St John's church (Brian Boydell, *A Dublin Musical Calendar 1700–1760* (Dublin: Irish Academic Press, 1988), p. 268) is to be distinguished from Neale's Music Hall, also in Fishamble Street, where *Messiah* was first performed.
    18   *FDJ*, 29 Oct.–1 Nov. 1748.

JOHN FREDERICK LAMPE IN THE SUMMER OF 1750

1748.[19] In this single week, some lasting features in the two years of the Sheridan contracts had made themselves evident: the primacy of Dubourg as conductor and composer in the ceremonial music centred on the castle and in the Charitable Society concerts in the Philharmonic Room; the entrenchment of Miss Oldmixon as Dubourg's preferred soloist in the latter; and young Pasquali's flying start as player, conductor and composer.

The Dragon of Wantley, conducted by Lampe on 30 November, had three performances during December and one in January 1749.[20] At the end of January *The Dragoness* was given, with the libretto published by a printer in Dame Street at threepence;[21] three performances followed in February, two in March and one in April. Lampe had consolidated his reputation as a composer of proven successes. In writing new songs for plays he seems to have been less than prolific; over the two seasons he would produce new songs for *Oroonoko* in February 1749,[22] *Theodosius* in April 1749,[23] for an afterpiece, *The What D'ye Call It*, in December 1749[24] and 'a new song at the end of each act' in *King John* in April 1750.[25] *Diana*, a solo cantata for his wife 'in hunting style', was performed in Cecilia Arne's benefit in Fishamble Street on 7 February 1749.[26] If it seems not to have had further performances, it may well be because Pasquali upstaged both Lampe and Dubourg with a new piece which had its first performance at Smock Alley two nights later. The War of the Austrian Succession had ended in the Treaty of Aix-la-Chapelle in October 1748. It merited observance in the many countries of Europe which had been on the winning side. The advice from England was that a major festivity was planned in London for the early spring. Dubourg may well have been waiting to hear the form it would take, to ensure a worthy response by him from Dublin Castle (the London event, when it took place, was the occasion of Handel's Fireworks Music). It was Pasquali who leapt in, without waiting for firm news from London (or perhaps with a swifter informant) with a masque, *The Temple of Peace*, described as being 'on occasion of the present happy Peace established over Europe'. A compilation, it included 'several favourite songs of Mr Handel, Boyce, Purcell and other eminent Masters; the rest of the Musick composed by Signor Pasquali'. No doubt its being ready for Sheridan so promptly owed something to its having 'Machinery and Scenes ... contrived and executed by Pasquali Junior, brother to Signor Pasquali'.[27] By 21 April, when the London celebration took place, it had had four performances. The official Dublin counterpart to the London celebration, complete with fireworks on St Stephen's

---

19 Boydell, *Calendar*, pp. 129–30; *FDJ*, 1–5, 8–12 Nov., 3–6, 5–10 Dec. 1748; Sheldon, *Thomas Sheridan*, pp. 331–2.
20 Ibid., p. 332.
21 *DC*, 4–7 Feb. 1749.
22 *FDJ*, 7–11 Feb. 1749.
23 Sheldon, *Thomas Sheridan*, p. 336.
24 Ibid., p. 339.
25 Ibid., p. 344.
26 *FDJ*, 14–17, 24–8 Jan., 31 Jan.–4 Feb. 1749.
27 *FDJ*, 4–7, 7–11 Feb. 1749.

226   ROY JOHNSTON

Green, took place on Tuesday 25 April.[28] Two evenings later, Pasquali's masque was given its fifth performance at Smock Alley 'by particular desire'.[29] Lampe had had no part as a composer in the treaty celebrations. A fortnight earlier, Pasquali had had a further first performance of that season, a 'musical entertainment' entitled *Apollo and Daphne*,[30] with four further performances. Lampe on his part had *Tom Thumb the Great* performed in May.[31] If Lampe had been hired as the composer and Pasquali the leader of the band, Pasquali had certainly ventured into composition with more success. Mrs Lampe had had a successful season as a singer, but neither she nor her husband had made significant entry, as the Arnes had done, into the oratorio world dominated by Dubourg and Miss Oldmixon.[32] During the 1748–49 season, Mrs Lampe, Sullivan and Mrs Mozeen had benefits at Smock Alley; Mrs Storer, popular as ever, had two. Pasquali had a benefit, as did the box-keeper, treasurer and prompter. Lampe had none.[33]

In his first uninterrupted season since he became manager of Smock Alley Sheridan had justified the improvements he had made to the fabric of his theatre. He had attracted the notice and favour of the nobility and gentry and consolidated his good standing with the Dublin public. He had indulged his predilection for Shakespeare with impressive success, with himself and Macklin as leading actors; of the 102 performances of mainpieces in the season, 29 were of 13 Shakespeare plays, of which *The Merchant of Venice* had four performances and *The Tempest* five. Although there were only two musical mainpieces, *The Beggar's Opera* and *Comus*, and neither Lampe nor Pasquali would compose one during the two-year contract, it was in the afterpieces, the incidental music in the plays, and in the music before the plays and between the acts, that the London musicians pulled their quantitative and qualitative weight. But there was no ground for complacency. Benjamin Victor, Sheridan's treasurer, had disapproved of Sheridan's extravagance in hiring too many performers at too high salaries from the start. He particularly resented the 'Musical Tribe', as he called them, with their two-year contracts, and referred to them as 'woeful bargains'.[34] A few months into the first season he seemed to have modified his view, declaring in a letter to Colley Cibber that 'the Profits of this Winter promise already, to be much greater than were ever yet known in this Kingdom [Ireland]'.[35] But his considered view of the whole season was a gloomy one; the musicians' salaries had totalled nearly £1400 and were 'a dead loss to the Manager'.[36]

---

28   *DC*, 22–5 Apr. 1749; and see the illustration in Boydell, *Calendar*, p. 126.
29   Sheldon, *Thomas Sheridan*, p. 335.
30   *FDJ*, 8–11 Apr. 1749.
31   *FDJ*, 23–7 May 1749.
32   For the 1743–44 season five years earlier, Dubourg and Arne had advertised six Handel oratorios to be performed by subscription, the singers to include Mrs Arne and Mrs Storer: *FDJ*, 23–5 Oct. 1743; Boydell, *Calendar*, p. 94n.
33   Sheldon, *Thomas Sheridan*, p. 330.
34   Benjamin Victor, *The History of the Theatres of London and Dublin, from the year 1730 to the present Time*, 2 vols (London, 1761), vol. 1, p. 143.
35   Ibid., vol. 2, p. 212.
36   Ibid., vol. 1, p. 137.

The Musical Tribe were bound by their contract not to perform anywhere in public before 1 June, other than at the theatre, without written permission. Sheridan, aware of the favourable publicity to be gained by making his musicians known outside the theatre, had allowed them occasionally to perform at concerts so long as Smock Alley was not inconvenienced and, no doubt, for a financial consideration. Away from the Smock Alley ambience, and out of season, the musicians were free to act on their own initiative. The London pleasure gardens were enjoying their heyday, and the reputations gained by Vauxhall, Marylebone and Ranelagh as fashionable places of summer resort had attracted imitators. Dr Bartholomew Mosse, founder of the Lying-in Hospital (later known as the Rotunda), had leased a plot of land bordering Great Britain Street on the undeveloped outskirts of the city. There he laid out his New Gardens for the support of the hospital in the style of Vauxhall. The first concert was advertised to take place on Tuesday 27 June 1749; an ode on the hospital, 'written by Mr Jones the Brick-Layer and set to Musick by Mr Pasquali' would be performed.[37] Sullivan and Mrs Storer were advertised to sing during the season.[38] Summer concerts had also been given in Dublin at the Marlborough Bowling Green since 1728;[39] in the summer season of 1749, well advertised in advance, Lampe was to conduct and his wife to sing every Monday, Wednesday and Friday.[40] The entertainments were 'for the support of the unemployed, native Musicians of this Kingdom';[41] whoever the supporting instrumentalists were, they were certainly not Sheridan's. Both gardens put on performances of Handel's new Fireworks Music.[42]

For the 1749–50 season the Charitable Society had made an arrangement with Sheridan to have the services of the Smock Alley band for every Tuesday (which was not a theatre night). The amity between Sheridan and the society was shown by the theatre closing on Friday 15 December to allow the musicians to sing and play in the society's *Messiah*. Otherwise, the second season proceeded on the same pattern as the first. Lampe's *Tom Thumb* had three performances in November. The new year was to bring performances of *The Dragon*, *The Dragoness* and *Pyramus and Thisbe*. In January he had on sale 'Mr Lampe's *The Lady's Amusement: A collection of Songs, Ballads with Symphonies and Thorough Bass*, sold by Manwaring, College Green, Dublin, engraved and printed for the Author'.[43] Pasquali had his *Triumphs of Hibernia* repeated and wrote a new masque for Congreve's *All for Love*. Sheridan's other theatre, in Aungier Street, had a larger stage than Smock Alley but it was draughty and had an unsatisfactory acoustic. Sheridan had found a profitable use for it by adapting it for 'festinos' of music, refreshments and dancing, which became popular monthly events

---

37 *FDJ*, 24–6 June 1749.
38 *DC*, 25–9 July, 5–8, 8–12 Aug. 1749.
39 Boydell, *Calendar*, p. 266.
40 *FDJ*, 4–8 Apr., 27–30 May 1749; Boydell, *Calendar*, p. 127n.
41 *The Censor, or Citizens' Journal*, 3 June 1749.
42 *FDJ*, 2–5 Sept. 1749 (Marlborough), 9–12 Sept. 1749 (Great Britain Street).
43 *FDJ*, 27–30 Jan. 1750.

and provided another way of making the Smock Alley band more financially productive.[44] Having made his way into the esteem of the nobility and gentry, Sheridan decided to entertain them further by carrying out a remodelling of Aungier Street 'in order to have Dramatick Operas exhibited there'.[45] The band was well up to the new challenge, but nothing that his two resident composers had written fitted the concept. *Comus* did, and it was with Arne's masque that Aungier Street opened in its new guise on Saturday 10 February.[46] The enterprise was immediately successful, and *Comus* was repeated on the two following Saturdays. It was to be succeeded by the biggest musical success of the two seasons. Purcell's *King Arthur, or The British Worthy*, a five-act semi-opera to a libretto by Dryden, first performed in London in 1691, was given at Aungier Street on Saturday 17 March.[47] It proved hugely popular. Of the innovations at Smock Alley the most notable was Boyce's *The Chaplet*, played as an afterpiece, which made its first appearance – with its libretto on sale at the theatre – on 20 February.[48] Sheridan brought his season to an end in the last full week of May with a flamboyant and concentrated display of his dramatic and musical talent. Tuesday 22nd had the season's fifth performance of *King Lear*, with for afterpiece the ever-popular *The Mock Doctor*, Wednesday had the fourth performance of *Macbeth* followed by *The Chaplet*, Thursday *The Earl of Essex* by Henry Brooke with an entr'acte violin solo by Pasquali and *The Dragoness* for afterpiece. The grand finale was reserved to Aungier Street with the fourth performance of the season of *Comus* on Friday and the eighth of *King Arthur* on Saturday 26th, the Musical Tribe at full, triumphant stretch.[49] It was a season in which Sheridan had accomplished the unbelievable in eighteenth-century Dublin: a Shakespearean revival without any loss – indeed with a gain – in his audience and treasury. Victor hailed it as 'the most profitable Season to the Manager; the Sum total was increased two thousand Pounds beyond any of the preceding Years'.[50]

But it had not been the happiest of seasons. Encouraged by the success of his new venture at Great Britain Street, Dr Mosse had determined not to wait for summer but to open his pleasure garden in March, at 12 noon on Wednesday 7th. Early in January Stephen Storace, as Mosse's emissary, had approached some Smock Alley musicians and had word back from Pasquali that Sheridan would agree to let them perform at the garden, but only at such times as he 'had no Occasion for them'. Pasquali apparently also reassured the musicians that they might engage with Mosse, that it was not necessary to put Sheridan's leave in writing, and that Smock Alley rehearsals could be arranged so as not to interfere with the noon-to-three performances at the garden. But when Sheridan saw to his

---

44 Sheldon, *Thomas Sheridan*, pp. 132–3.
45 *FDJ*, 31 Oct.–4 Nov. 1749.
46 *FDJ*, 3–6 Feb. 1750; the use of Saturday did not conflict with the Smock Alley schedule.
47 Sheldon, *Thomas Sheridan*, p. 343.
48 Ibid., p. 342.
49 Ibid., p. 346.
50 Victor, *History of the Theatres*, vol. 1, p. 148.

JOHN FREDERICK LAMPE IN THE SUMMER OF 1750

alarm from Mosse's advertisement that the music at the garden would continue until the end of April and from then on every evening – a serious overlap with the Smock Alley season – he put his foot down and, spurning intermediaries, demanded to meet Mosse himself. Mosse had not complied by the opening day. When the 'numerous and polite' audience gathered at the garden for the opening concert they were to be disappointed, for Sheridan had kept his musicians rehearsing *King Arthur* in preparation for the first night at Aungier Street 10 days later. Accusations and counter-accusations appeared in the press, followed by argumentative pamphlets.[51]

Nor was the row with Mosse the only source of worry. The Musical Tribe had helped Sheridan in attaining his objectives, but the charms of music had not soothed the savage breast of the upper gallery. Early in the second season Victor had had to place an advertisement offering a reward of 10 guineas 'for the Discovery of any Person who shall throw anything at the said Band of Musick'.[52] Two months later Sheridan had to step in with a threat to close the section,[53] and he found further measures necessary, including the doubling of the price of seats in that part of the house. In the remodelling of the Aungier Street theatre for the highly successful 'dramatick Operas', the upper gallery, significantly, was closed off.[54]

Sheridan, disillusioned and with his treasurer constantly on his back, abandoned music as an aid and a solution. Notwithstanding the fact that the excellence of the large band and the talented singers had provided a musical dimension of great quality and variety for the two remarkable seasons, the hard truth was that they were an expensive icing on the cake. To his treasurer's relief, when the second season ended Sheridan did not renew the contracts. In the Smock Alley company of the next season, only Pasquali remained, on sufferance.[55]

The summer of 1750

To some of the Musical Tribe, perhaps a good many, conditioned to the vagaries of a nomadic existence and accustomed as of second nature to keeping an ear to the ground, the non-renewal did not come as a surprise. Lampe had not done well in Dublin; Sheridan, by hiring young Pasquali and preferring him, had sidelined him. Upstaged by Arne in the past and Pasquali in the present, he must have known well before the end of the second season that the sooner he left Sheridan the better, and so he began casting around for an advantageous exit. To move to another Dublin theatre was not feasible. Sheridan commanded the Dublin theatre scene; there was no counterpart to the presence in London of both a Covent Garden and a Drury

---

51 Sheldon, *Thomas Sheridan*, pp. 145–6; Brian Boydell, *Rotunda Music in Eighteenth-Century Dublin* (Dublin: Irish Academic Press, 1992), p. 31.
52 *FDJ*, 3–7 Oct. 1749.
53 *FDJ*, 9–13 Jan. 1750.
54 *FDJ*, 3–6 Feb. 1750; Boydell, *Calendar*, p. 135n.
55 Pasquali went to Edinburgh in 1752 after Lampe's death; he died there in 1757.

230 ROY JOHNSTON

Lane. To make a career in the concert and oratorio world of Dublin, Lampe had the musicianship and the antecedents, and his wife the voice, but that area was still dominated by Dubourg and his preferred soprano Miss Oldmixon. Arne and his wife, Mrs Lampe's sister, had been accepted into that charmed environment; the Lampes had not. A return to London, then? Handel had returned from Dublin to a revitalized career. Arne, with his knack for making the right choices and being in the right place at the right time, had achieved a special position in the theatres and pleasure gardens. The prospect for Lampe of gaining a worthwhile foothold on return to London was thus problematic. The provinces?

It is the contention of this chapter that at some stage in these anxieties there came an approach from Edinburgh. It is some time before the approach can be retrospectively confirmed; until then the narrative has the character of supposition. Edinburgh was the third largest city in the British Isles. Although it had ceased to be a capital city when James VI of Scotland ascended the English throne as James I, it remained the centre of Scotland's church and legal systems, and the home base of a considerable and ancient Scottish nobility and gentry. That there was a musical society and a musical life in Edinburgh was known. So, disconcertingly, was an inimical attitude to the theatre, but that was said to be changing. 'Everyone knows', says Fraser Harris,

> how Allan Ramsay in 1736 had ruined himself financially (and the Town Council and clergy thought morally as well) by refitting at his own expense a building in Carrubber's Close, known as The Theatre. The feeling on the part of the Town Council against 'stage-plays' was at that time so strong that the manager of the company either in the Taylors' Hall or later in the Canongate Theatre would advertise 'a concert of music' on such-and-such a night. Everyone knew that a play was going to be acted; occasionally some purely musical performance was given before the play began, oftener not. In this way the edict of the Town Council forbidding plays was technically evaded, but that acting went on was an open secret.[56]

Perhaps the approach was made to Lampe in particular, or, on the grapeshot principle, to the Musical Tribe at large. It was Lampe and his wife, with Mrs Storer, who were attracted by what Edinburgh had to offer. A provisional deal was probably in place by the time Henry Thomson, describing himself as 'Hen. Thomson, Actor of great Merit', placed an advertisement in the Edinburgh press to the effect that he and Thomas Davies had bought 'right, title and interest of the new Concert Hall' and that they would open it 'in the first week of November next with several new and approved good Actors, clothes, scenes &c.' In the same advertisement Thomson had also in mind 'to open his Great House and Gardens at Lauriston ... the first Monday in June, with publick breakfasting as at Ranelaugh, &c'.[57]

---

56 David Fraser Harris, *Saint Cecilia's Hall in the Niddry Wynd* (Edinburgh and London: Oliphant, Anderson & Ferrier, 1899), pp. 277–8.

57 *Caledonian Mercury* [*CM*], 7 May 1750. Once the enterprise had begun he backed away from the 'breakfasting', but kept up an advertising campaign for a 'four-hour entertainment beginning at 5 p.m.': *CM*, 21 June 1750; *Edinburgh Evening Courant* [*EEC*], 5 July 1750.

JOHN FREDERICK LAMPE IN THE SUMMER OF 1750   231

During this time, a series of advertisements was placed not in Dublin but in the *Belfast News-Letter*.[58] Belfast in 1750 was a dilapidated little town. By 1786, when John Nixon painted his watercolour of High Street (see Fig. 11.1), it was much improved, but two buildings encountered by the Lampe party remained. On the right is the old market house (the Assembly Rooms) with its distinctive diamond-shaped clock. The horseman is entering the Donegall Arms, which was probably in 1750 the Royal Boot.

The first advertisement announced that on Wednesday 13 June there would be a concert in which Mrs Lampe and Mrs Storer would sing, Mr Manwaring would play a Violin concertino and there would be a German flute piece by Mr Rocke.[59] In the next issue of the newspaper a further concert was advertised.

> *By Particular Desire,*
> *At the Assembly Room in Belfast, On Wednesday*
> *next, being the 20th of June, will be Perform'd,*
> A CONCERT of Vocal and Instrumental
> Musick. Act the First, Overture; Songs, Shepherd,
> what art thou pursuing? by Mrs. STORER. Wou'd you
> gain the tender Creature? by Mrs. LAMPE. Act the
> second, A Concerto. Songs, Hush ye pretty Warbling
> Quire, by Mrs. LAMPE. To Wisdom's cold Delight; by
> Mrs. STORER. Act the third, A Concerto; by Mr.
> ROCKE. Songs, 'Tis Liberty; by Mrs. STORER. You
> tell me I'm Handsome; by Mrs. LAMPE. A Solo, by Mr.
> MANWARING. Jocky and Jenny; a Dialogue by Mrs.
> LAMPE and Mrs. STORER. After the Concert will be a
> BALL. Tickets to be had at the Royal Boot opposite the
> Assembly Room, at half a Crown each.
> N. B. This will be the last Time of Performance.[60]

There was a further advertisement in the same newspaper a fortnight later, but for a different venue:

> *At the Market House in Downpatrick.*
> Every Evening during the Races there, will be a Concert of Vocal and Instrumental
> Musick. The Vocal parts by Mrs LAMPE and Mrs STORER; and a Solo on the Violin
> by Mr MANWARING. Price a British Half Crown.
> N.B. Two Bows of Violins were lately lost at Bannbridge: Whoever brings them to
> Mr Lee in Belfast, shall receive 5s. 5d. reward, if they be not broke.[61]

Downpatrick, the county town of Down, was some 20-odd miles from Belfast. In 1750 the Races took place on Tuesday 3, Wednesday 4, Thursday 5 and Friday 6 July.[62] In these advertisements, Mrs Lampe and Mrs Storer are familiar names. Bartholomew (Barty) Manwaring was prominent in Dublin musical life, had

---

58   This newspaper first appeared in 1737 and has remained in continuous publication until the present day.
59   *Belfast News-Letter [BN-L]*, 12 June 1750.
60   *BN-L*, 15 June 1750.
61   *BN-L*, 29 June 1750.
62   *BN-L*, 12 June 1750.

Fig. 11.1 Nixon's watercolour of High Street, Belfast

conducted a number of Handel oratorios and played violin solos and concertos in concerts; his brother William owned the music shop which had published Lampe's songs. Of Rocke, the player on the 'German flute', no information has come to light. As will be seen, Charles Storer would have been with the company; by profession an actor, he was well used in his career to following in the footsteps of his popular wife. The omission of Lampe's name is not significant; he was rarely mentioned in specific concerts in Dublin. Of the music, three songs are from *Acis and Galatea*. 'To wisdom's cold delight' is a solo cantata by John Stanley, possibly the one which Mrs Storer sang between the acts of a play on 24 April 1749.[63] 'Jocky and Jenny' is by Henry Purcell. A further concert was advertised for Belfast, but for 7 September: the vocal parts would be by Mrs Lampe and Mrs Storer, and there would be a solo on the violin by Mr Manwaring.[64]

Meanwhile, there had been concert activity in Edinburgh, and a proven connection between Thomson and Lampe, if not yet made, comes closer. No musicians had been named in Thomson's advertisements of his concert hall and gardens. But there was an advertisement in mid-July for a concert of vocal and instrumental music in St Mary's Chapel. The programme included songs by Mrs Lampe ('Come, ever smiling Liberty', 'Myself I shall adore') and Mrs Storer ('See from the silent grove', 'Eileen Aroon'), a solo by Mr Manwaring, and two duets, one of them 'Jonny [*sic*] and Jenny'.[65] On Monday 30 July in the new concert hall in the Canongate, 'by desire of several persons of distinction', there would be a concert of music, 'after which will be given, gratis, The BEGGARS OPERA: Polly, Mrs Storer; Macheath, Mrs Hamilton; Lucy, Mrs Lampe, with entertainments of dancing'.[66]

Hopes of a connection appear to be dashed by the statement of a Scottish authority, James C. Dibdin, who claims that it is impossible that these performances ever took place.[67] From that Scottish summer, however, there survives in the library of Edinburgh University an original document bearing the date 22 August 1750 (Fig. 11.2).[68] There is no indication on the face of the document that any of the four signatories signed by proxy, or that they did not all sign on the same day, in the same place. A proven connection, *pace* Dibdin, is made. Thomson and Davies had secured their star attractions for the first season of their new concert hall. A few weeks later they placed a substantial advertisement for its opening at the end of October:

Whereas Hen. Thomson and Thomas Davies have purchased of the proprietors of the NEW CONCERT HALL all their Rights, Title and interest in the same, together with cloaths, scenes and everything else thereunto belonging, they humbly beg leave

---

63 Sheldon, *Thomas Sheridan*, p. 335.
64 *BN-L*, 4 Sept. 1750.
65 *EEC*, 16 July 1750.
66 *CM*, *EEC*, 26 July 1750.
67 James C. Dibdin, *Annals of the Edinburgh Stage* (Edinburgh: Richard Cameron, 1884), p. 66.
68 La.II.451/1/56.

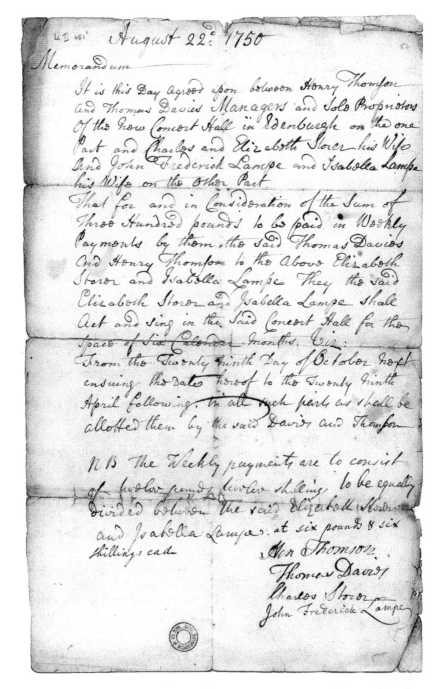

Fig. 11.2 Agreement of Thomson and Davies with Lampe and Storer, 22 August 1750

JOHN FREDERICK LAMPE IN THE SUMMER OF 1750

to inform the Nobility and Gentry that having engaged several new Actors, Singers, Dancers &c. they shall open the said Hall under their direction on Mon 29 October with a concert of music, after which will be given gratis
The BEGGARS OPERA: Polly, Mrs Storer; Lucy, Mrs Lampe; with several new entertainments of dancing.
NB: the Orchestra will be enlarged, and the Voice accompanied with a Harpsichord, on which Mr Lampe is to perform. ...
The Managers engage that there shall be at least 30 concerts exclusive of benefits.[69]

The advertisement was given a number of repeats; that of 1 October added the information that several plays of Shakespeare would be revived, including *Romeo and Juliet* with Davies as Romeo and Mrs Storer as Juliet.[70]

The Lampes, Storers and Manwaring were back in Dublin in the early half of October.[71] On Wednesday 10th, Manwaring was advertised to play at the Philharmonic Society.[72] On Friday 12th, Mrs Lampe and Mrs Storer were to sing at the Marlborough Bowling Green.[73] On the following Thursday (18th) there was to be a benefit at the Fishamble Street Music Hall for Mrs Lampe and Mrs Storer, the performance to be conducted by Manwaring.[74] It had to be postponed, and was readvertised for a week later, the 25th.[75]

But with the opening of Thomson's concert hall to take place only four days later in Edinburgh, there was plainly something wrong. There had indeed been a disconcerting development, and Thomson's hall did not open on the stated day. On 30 October – the day after it was to open – there was published an extract from a letter received by Henry Thomson; it was dated a fortnight earlier, 15 October, and presumably had just arrived. It had been written by Charles Storer in Dublin:

Sir,
I had the favour of both your obliging letters, but the pleasure I received from the contents of them was very soon soured by the unlucky and most mortifying accident that possibly could have happened. Mrs Lampe has kept her bed these 16 days in a high fever, one day given over, the next the greatest hopes of recovery, and so alternately for above a fortnight past. As to setting out before her, the very thoughts of being left alone would absolutely kill her; nor could the entertainments be the least forwarded without Mr Lampe. We are doing all we can in this troublesome situation ... I have secured all the Musick of *Romeo and Juliet, Merchant of Venice, Tempest* &c., &c., and shall leave nothing undone that I have power to be of service in. I have only this to say, as that we are out of all manner of business, our inclination and interest both join to make us set out with utmost expedition.
    I am, Sir, your most obedient servant, Charles Storer.

---

69   *CM*, 24 Sept. 1750.
70   *EEC*, 1 Oct. 1750.
71   Rocke is not mentioned in the Scottish advertisements, but he seems to have been with the party in Belfast on their return. He placed an advertisement in *BN-L* (25 Sept. 1750) referring to himself as 'of the late Concert', offering tuition in a variety of instruments and a willingness to stay in the area 'if encourag'd'.
72   *FDJ*, 2–6 Oct. 1750.
73   *FDJ*, 6–9 Oct. 1750.
74   *FDJ*, 2–6 Oct. 1750.
75   *FDJ*, 16–20 Oct. 1750.

The advertisement added, 'NB. The opening of the concert hall, which was design'd on Wednesday next, the Managers are obliged to put off until the Arrival of Mrs Storer and Mr Lampe, &c.'[76] Mrs Lampe was ill, then, when she came back to Dublin at the end of the summer, and this explains the postponement of the benefit concert on 18 October for her and Mrs Storer. The benefit eventually took place and Lampe, with a party which included his wife and the Storers, arrived the following month in Edinburgh. Barty Manwaring stayed behind in his native Dublin, where his career was firmly established.

Report, review or comment being rare in the newspapers, the evidence for the summer concerts in Edinburgh is in the advertisements, and a concert advertised is not proof that it took place or that it took place as advertised. These reservations make it not unreasonable for James C. Dibdin to declare, on other evidence, that they never happened. The apparent improbability of a party of musicians making a brief visit to Edinburgh, going back to Dublin and returning a few months later in the same year would seem to have supported his judgement. The summer visit, however, is to be seen in a context of networking. The grapevine was an essential element. At the one extreme, Sheridan by making frequent visits to London reduced its importance (while by no means nullifying it). At the other stood the Edinburgh Musical Society. Formed in 1728 and composed almost entirely of nobility, gentry and lawyers,[77] it had good local professionals ('Masters') of the calibre of McGibbon, but was at pains to recruit for its leaders the best in Europe. Difficulties occurred where long distances were involved, direct audition was impossible and there was a need for linguistic intermediaries. As their minutes attest, a great deal of time, energy and initiative went into finding likely musicians, confirming their quality through foreign-based contacts and getting them appointed and transported to Edinburgh.[78] Henry Thomson, at pains to secure big names for his opening concert season, thus making enquiries and following up rumours at long if not longest range, would have heard about the situation in Dublin; the Musical Tribe contained the sort of people he wanted. For Lampe, once an arrangement had been made, the summer months offered the opportunity of an exploratory visit to Edinburgh. After his experience of the Dublin scene he needed to make a proper reconnaissance, to form an impression at first hand of the musical life of the city and the present attitude to the theatre, together with the likelihood of his finding an honourable place in it, and to see Thomson and make sure he was not encountering another Sheridan. His brother-in-law Thomas Arne had sampled Dublin in the summer of 1742 before committing himself and his wife to a longer sojourn. Thomson, with his new enterprises needing his attention,

---

76   *CM*, 30 Oct. 1750.

77   See the list of members in Fraser Harris, *Saint Cecilia's Hall*, pp. 290–99.

78   For example see the references, *passim*, in the minutes of the Edinburgh Musical Society to Passerini, from his being attracted from St Petersburg in April 1749 to his arrival in Edinburgh in January 1751. See also, in a different but related context, Curtis Price, Judith Milhous and Robert D. Hume, *The Impresario's Ten Commandments: Continental Recruitment for Italian Opera in London 1763–64* (London: Royal Musical Association, 1992).

JOHN FREDERICK LAMPE IN THE SUMMER OF 1750

was not in a position to come to Dublin, but no doubt he encouraged Lampe. It would enable Thomson to make up his own mind; summer engagements could be arranged for Mrs Lampe and Mrs Storer, to see their calibre and also to trail the new concert hall.

For the Arnes, the route travelled between London and Dublin had been long established and well used. It was less easy to determine a way between Dublin and Edinburgh. To go by sea to Holyhead, then by Chester and across England to pick up the regular road northward, meant a long sea journey and a longer road journey. There was an alternative route, shorter in distance and with a shorter sea crossing. For 20 years at least, Dublin theatre companies had been travelling to Belfast and other northern towns, playing summer seasons.[79] The direct route, some 90 miles to Belfast travelling due north, had its difficulties in the northern part, particularly the passage through hilly country known as the Gap of the North.[80] But from the town of Donaghadee in County Down, some 20 miles further, there was a sea crossing of the North Channel to Portpatrick in Scotland which was only some 25 miles long. And from there, as Thomson and others could have told Lampe, there was a well-used land route to the Scottish towns and universities (Edinburgh some 140 miles) travelled by generations of Ulster-Scots merchants, professional men and students. Lampe persuaded Barty Manwaring and Rocke, who had no career interest but added a valuable instrumental dimension, to accompany himself, his wife Isabella, Betty and Charles Storer on the unfrequented (at least by musicians), but not unknown, northern route. On the way they put on concerts in Belfast and Downpatrick and possibly elsewhere.[81] By late August, having completed the passage to Edinburgh and performed there, the Lampes and Storers had seen enough of the city and of Thomson and Davies, and they of them, to agree on the arrangement set out in the legal document. The party could then return to Ireland by the same route, put their affairs in order, and and leave Dublin for good as soon as they were free of some residual musical obligations which had nothing to do with Sheridan, and in time for the opening of Thomson's new hall.

There is nothing in the chronology (see Table 11.1) which precludes such a visit. As can be seen, on 26 May 1750 the final performance of the season at Smock Alley took place, effectively the end of Thomas Sheridan's employment of the Lampes and Storers. The party had ample time to make the journey north for their first advertised concert in Belfast on 13 June. The dates of the Downpatrick

---

79   At the close of the Dublin season of 1735–36 Lewis Duval's Smock Alley company made its way to Belfast; in 1741 Duval went 'as usual' to Belfast and Newry: Robert Hitchcock, *An Historical View of the Irish Stage*, 2 vols (Dublin, 1788–94), vol. 1, pp. 97, 114.

80   The first mail coach service, established in 1752, took three days each way for the journey: *BN-L*, 19 June 1752.

81   The Downpatrick advertisement suggests that they may have given a concert in the County Down town of Banbridge. In this regard, if his violin bows were not recovered unbroken, Manwaring could have had professional services in Belfast. Adair Ainsworth, 'in the upper end of North Street', advertising in 1763 to the effect that he was 'recommended and approved by the best Judges both for making and mending Fiddles for these several years past', included the information that he also made 'screw and plain Bows or fluted for Gentlemen': *BN-L*, 4 Nov. 1763.

Table 11.1 Chronology of 1750

	Dublin	Belfast and Downpatrick	Edinburgh
May			7: Thomson's advt for concert hall and open-air concerts
	26: final performance of the season at Smock Alley		
June		13: first Belfast concert	
		20: second Belfast concert	
July		3–6: Downpatrick concerts	
			18: concert with Mrs Lampe, Mrs Storer, Manwaring
August			6: *Beggar's Opera*, Mrs Lampe and Mrs Storer
			22: Lampe and Storer sign contract with Thomson and Davies
September		7: Belfast concert with Mrs Lampe, Mrs Storer, Manwaring	
			24: advt: new concert hall to open 29 Oct. with Lampes and Mrs Storer
	25: appointment of new organist to St Werburgh's announced (Lampe 'a judge')	25: Rocke advertises tuition as 'one of the late Concert'	
	30: onset of Mrs Lampe's fever		
October			1: repeat advt 24 Sept.

Table 11.1 *continued*

	Dublin	Belfast and Downpatrick	Edinburgh
	6: concerts advertised involving Mrs Lampe, Mrs Storer, Manwaring		
	10: concert, Manwaring to play a solo		
	12: concert, Mrs Lampe and Mrs Storer		
	15: Storer writes to Thomson, Mrs Lampe ill 'these 16 days'		
	18: benefit concert Mrs Lampe and Mrs Storer, postponed		
	25: *Acis and Galatea*, conducted Manwaring, benefit Mrs Lampe and Mrs Storer		
			29: new hall to open
			30: Storer's letter published, new hall opening postponed
November			19: arrival of Lampes and Storers in Edinburgh

concerts are in the first week of July; they had until 18 July to get to their first advertised concert in Edinburgh. After they signed their agreement with Thomson on 22 August, their concert in Belfast was not until 7 September. Lampe's responsibility for the St Werburgh appointment was discharged by the end of September. The final Dublin engagements, the expected departure for Scotland in October, and the early part of the Lampes' and Storers' commitments in Edinburgh were thrown into disarray by Mrs Lampe's illness.

Dibdin, who declared that it was impossible that the July concerts in Edinburgh took place, gave as his reason that 'Mrs Storer certainly did not arrive in Edinburgh until November 5th, Mr Lampe accompanied her'.[82] This on its own is not conclusive proof that a summer visit was not made.[83] It is certainly not strong enough to stem the tide of evidence in the other direction. Of that evidence one important particular is the existence of the legal agreement of 22 August which shows that Lampe and Storer, at least, were in Edinburgh at that time. The presence of their wives is confirmed by the advertisement of the concert at the Marlborough Bowling Green for Friday 12 October at which they were both to sing, 'being the first time of their performance since they arrived from Scotland'.[84]

The event in the new concert hall on Friday 25 November contained an afterpiece in which Mrs Storer would sing.[85] The Allan Ramsay convention still obtained: the 'concert' of 26 November was followed, 'gratis', by *Hamlet*, in which Storer played Laertes, and *The Devil to Pay*, in which his wife played the lead.[86] Mrs Lampe took some time to recover from her illness. It was not until Christmas that she appeared in an advertisement, singing Lucy to Mrs Storer's Polly in *The Beggar's Opera*; in the same bill Storer was to appear in the pantomime, and the advertisement ended: 'N.B. The orchestra is to be enlarged, and the Voices will be accompanied with an Harpsichord, to be performed by Mr Lampe'.[87] Lampe was to have a successful start to his new career, with performances promised of *The Dragon of Wantley*, *The Dragoness* and *Tom Thumb*. In the following summer he was holding open-air concerts in Heriot's Gardens.[88] Then came his death on 25 July 1751, of 'fever'. Fraser Harris prints the laconic entry in the register of burials, gives a photograph of the tomb in the Canongate churchyard and transcribes its substantial tribute.[89]

The Irish towns in which the Lampes and Storers, Manwaring and Rocke gave concerts on their way to and from Edinburgh from Dublin had not yet had concerts, certainly not by musicians of this calibre. Concert life generated by the town itself does not appear in Belfast until the appearance of the Belfast Musical

---

82 Dibdin, *Annals*, p. 66.
83 And, incidentally, whatever Dibdin's source may have been, both the Edinburgh newspapers announced Mrs Storer as not arriving until the 19th: *CM*, *EEC*, 20 Nov. 1750.
84 *FDJ*, 6–9 Oct. 1750.
85 *CM*, 24 Nov. 1750.
86 *CM*, 27 Nov. 1750.
87 *CM*, 20 Dec. 1750.
88 *EEC*, 3 June 1751.
89 Fraser Harris, *Saint Cecilia's Hall*, pp. 267–8.

Society in 1768 (although it may have come into being without the benefit of newspaper before that). Not many musicians, we can be reasonably certain, had travelled by this route from Dublin to Edinburgh; the days when musicians used networking as a necessary component of a career were, considering the rigours of travel, some time in the future. What can be said is that, long before Belfast by means of its expansion to a major industrial city placed itself by sheer weight of population on the premier British touring circuits, the route taken by the Lampes and Storers had become regularly used by musicians travelling between Dublin and Scotland.

CHAPTER TWELVE

'So much rational and elegant amusement, at an expence comparatively inconsiderable': The Holywell Concerts in the Eighteenth Century

Susan Wollenberg

Glance at the current programme and you'll be astonished at the starry window-dressing it details ... One wonders what makes such artists glad to take the road to Oxford now and then ... It's the venue partly, that's for sure: it exerts unrivalled charm, and has, besides, acoustic properties to die for.[1]

These remarks were made apropos of a modern-day series of weekly chamber concerts held at the Holywell Music Room, Oxford.[2] But they could equally well have served to describe the original subscription concerts housed at the Holywell Music Room in its first phase of existence. The audience's sense of constituting a regular gathering of friends and acquaintances; the mixture of local musicians and visiting performers; the intimate surroundings with seating for only a few hundred; these and a host of other factors – including even the involvement of the coffee houses[3] – all make the present-day 'Coffee Concerts' seem in many ways descended from the Holywell concerts in the eighteenth century.

The original concerts were an eighteenth-century version of the same sort of phenomenon: a popular and successful venture offering a carefully chosen variety of aural experience. It is to be hoped that their modern counterpart will long continue to flourish. The Coffee Concerts' eighteenth-century predecessors extended for a period of over 40 years before the troubled times (from 1789 onwards) brought with them a destabilizing of musical life, as of so many aspects

---

1   Derek Jole, 'Informality pulls in chamber music fans', *Oxford Times*, Arts 7, 31 Jan. 2003. I am grateful to the editor, Derek Holmes, for his help in tracing this article and for permission to quote from it.

2   The 'Oxford Coffee Concerts', January to April 2003.

3   In the eighteenth century the coffee houses acted as outlets for the sale of concert tickets. By 1740 there were approximately 13 such establishments in Oxford; by 1800 their numbers had increased to about 20 (see *Encyclopædia of Oxford*, ed. C. Hibbert and E. Hibbert (London: Macmillan, 1988), p. 97, which also points out that 'the first coffee house in England was opened in Oxford ... in 1651'). Actually the 'Coffee' element in the present-day concerts is tied in with what are really descendants of the taverns, which also in the eighteenth century acted as sales outlets for concert tickets.

244 SUSAN WOLLENBERG

of English society. Even after 1789, though, the Holywell concerts were subject to constant efforts to revive their fortunes, and it was not until 1840 that the room virtually 'ceased to retain any definite connection with the art of music, except its name'.[4]

The 250th anniversary of the Holywell Music Room (which opened in 1748) provided a welcome opportunity to reassess aspects of its history. In doing so, I have paid some attention also to the 'history of its history'; to the ways, in other words, that its story has been told, and what the cumulative achievement and effect of those tellings might be. In any such endeavour, pride of place must clearly be given to the work of John Henry Mee. Mee's book, *The Oldest Music Room in Europe* (1911), was in many respects a remarkable pioneering effort. But it was not the first history of the Holywell Music Room. That was achieved by William Hayes (1708–77), Heather Professor of Music at Oxford from 1741.[5] The history of the room in its telling is thus almost as old as the room itself.

When in 1800 the stewards of the Musical Society at Oxford (who were responsible for the management of the Holywell concerts) were provoked by the difficulties of the times to appeal to the public for support, they summoned up a sense of the history attached to these concerts, balanced by an appeal to reason:

> The Stewards ... take the liberty of submitting to the consideration of the public – whether after a commodious Room has been built and furnished at a great expence, and the Orchestra has been provided with a complete set of Musical Instruments and Books; and after a Band of Instrumental Performers, of acknowledged abilities in their profession, has been collected; they will suffer the Room and its Furniture to be rendered useless, and the Performers to be dispersed, by withdrawing their support from an Institution, which has been established upwards of fifty years, and which provides so much rational and elegant amusement, at an expence comparatively inconsiderable.[6]

---

4 John Henry Mee, *The Oldest Music Room in Europe: A Record of Eighteenth-Century Enterprise at Oxford* (London and New York: John Lane, 1911), p. 199. In fact the Holywell Room continued to be used for occasional concerts, these featuring among a miscellany of events and uses including auctions and exhibitions. Andrew Clark, in his edition of Wood's *Survey of the Antiquities of the City of Oxford* (Oxford Historical Society, 1889: full reference n. 5 below), p. 392, noted that 'till within the last few years the building was occasionally employed for its old purposes, concerts, etc. being given here. For some short time it was rented for its meeting room by the Oxford Architectural and Historical Society', but that 'it is now used by Mr. John Galpin for a fencing school and for assaults at arms'.

5 William Hayes, 'History of the Music Room', Oxford, Bodleian Library, MS Top. Oxon d. 337; cf. Sir John Peshall, ed., *Wood's Antient and Present State of the City of Oxford* (London, 1773), pp. 247–8, and Andrew Clark, ed., Anthony Wood's *Survey of the Antiquities of the City of Oxford*, Oxford Historical Society, 3: vol. 1 (Oxford: Clarendon Press, 1889), pp. 390–92 ('an account of the Music Room [in Holywell Street] from the pen of William Hayes, Mus. D.'). For further details of Hayes's 'History' see also Susan Wollenberg, *Music at Oxford in the Eighteenth and Nineteenth Centuries* (Oxford: Oxford University Press, 2001), ch. 4, pp. 48–9. It was on the basis of the eighteenth-century descriptions of the room's interior that the University Surveyor's office planned and carried out the restoration of the Holywell Music Room in 1959–60. (See Wollenberg, *Music at Oxford*, pl. 7 for a contemporary photograph of the interior restored.)

6 *Jackson's Oxford Journal* [*JOJ*], 8 Feb. 1800; text of the Stewards' appeal also in Oxford, Bodleian Library, Mus. 1 d.64/1 (reproduced in facsimile in Wollenberg, *Music at Oxford*, p. 145).

THE HOLYWELL CONCERTS IN THE 18TH CENTURY 245

A number of features of this text are especially significant in relation to the development of the concerts over those 'fifty years [and upwards]', among them the initial call to the public:

MUSIC ROOM, OXFORD.
February 4th, 1800.
The Stewards of the Music Room are sorry to be under the necessity of representing to the Subscribers, and the University and City at large, that the present state of their fund is wholly inadequate to the necessary expences of the Concert.[7]

The reference, as here, to 'town and gown' recurs as a constant refrain throughout the concert notices over the 50-year period and beyond. Formulae such as 'the Ladies and Gentlemen of the University and City, and of its vicinity' convey an important facet of the Holywell enterprise: performers and audience were drawn from both spheres, and they may have harmonized more easily in the context of music than in some other areas. Moreover, as Graham Midgley has pointed out, the Holywell Music Room provided 'a setting where ladies could be introduced with safety and decorum'.[8]

Like its modern descendant, the original concert series was significantly supported by the local press. From the founding of *Jackson's Oxford Journal* in 1753, the Musical Society had a regular outlet for its publicity. Concert-goers would have become accustomed to finding under the standard heading 'MUSIC ROOM, OXFORD' the notices of forthcoming events, as well as the occasional special announcements. It was largely from these, as well as from advertisements, notices and obituaries (all also carried by the *Journal*) relating to individual musicians, that Mee constructed his history of the Holywell Music Room: thus he acknowledged his particular indebtedness 'to the proprietors of Jackson's *Oxford Journal* for placing at my disposal the early files of their newspaper'.[9]

In addition, Mee used the programme collection housed in the Bodleian Library, which he identified as 'bound in two volumes called "Oxford Concert Bills"'.[10] Drawing on these, together with 'a very scarce document' that included an early Catalogue of Music belonging to the Society,[11] Mee developed a

---

7   Ibid.
8   Cf. *JOJ*, 28 Oct. 1820; and Graham Midgley, *University Life in Eighteenth-Century Oxford* (New Haven and London: Yale University Press, 1996), p. 141. On decorum in general, Mr Salmon in his *Present State of the Universities and of the five adjacent counties…* (London, 1744), p. 40, noted apropos of Oxford that 'the People of the Place are more Civilized than the Inhabitants of any other Town in *Great-Britain*'; and on students' leisure pursuits he also suggested 'that *Time* is not always thrown away, which is not directly employ'd in the *Particular* Study they are engaged in. *Relaxations* from Business prepare them to be equal to the *Difficulties* of it. They will return to it with greater *Vigour* …' (ibid., p. 400).
9   Mee, *Music Room*, Preface, p. v.
10   Mee, *Music Room*, p. 115. From Mee's description these volumes constitute the collection now under the shelf-mark Mus. 1 d.64. He also mentions a collection 'in the possession of the writer', containing programmes from 1797 to 1819; this appears to constitute the further collection of programmes recently acquired by the Bodleian Library.
11   This Mee comments on (*Music Room*, p. 44) as follows: 'In all likelihood the only copy extant belongs to the present writer.' The document is now in the Library of the Faculty of Music, University of Oxford (Rare Books).

246 SUSAN WOLLENBERG

wide-ranging account of the repertoire of the concerts, and the circumstances of its performance. Moreover he looked beyond these immediate sources, gathering information from a variety of other printed and manuscript items relating to the Holywell musicians and their concerts. The result is a richly woven account whose basic outlines have remained at the heart of subsequent histories. While William Hayes, in recording the origins and genesis of the Music Room project in the mid-eighteenth century, clearly recognized its special status, it is surely above all to Mee's work that the establishing of the legendary reputation of the Holywell Music Room (as, indeed, 'the oldest Music Room in Europe') is to be credited.

The Rev. John Henry Mee was himself something of an Oxford legend. He took the musical degrees at Oxford (B.Mus. 1882; D.Mus. 1888) and was phenomenally active in the musical life of the university and its colleges; his name appears almost ubiquitously in the documentation from the late nineteenth and early twentieth centuries, on occasions and in contexts that range from conducting the statutory performance of his D.Mus. exercise (for which 'there was an overflowing audience in the Sheldonian Theatre' in 1888)[12] to his singing among the tenors (with Mrs Mee among the altos) in a Merton College concert in December 1887.[13]

Mee's unstinting generosity, both in material terms and in the giving of his time, is well documented by his contemporaries. Among a number of tributes published in his lifetime, perhaps the acknowledgement in the 50th anniversary programme of the Eglesfield Musical Society at Queen's College in 1910 conveys most vividly the wholehearted commitment that he gave to a range of musical projects in Oxford:

> There has been no one who has spent himself more freely in the interests of this Society than the Rev. J. H. Mee, D. Mus., formerly Scholar of the College. Not only has he composed works for the performances, [and] financed the Society through days of difficulty, but [also he] has ... been a member of the chorus in every concert since 1872.[14]

He was warmly praised by his colleagues in the University Musical Union (OUMU: of which he was a founder member) when together they published the two volumes of proceedings, 1884–94 and 1894–1904; it was noted that during the year 1890–91 he had given to this society an organ with two manuals and pedals, 'found to be of great practical use to members'.[15]

---

12 *Musical Times*, 29 (1888), 732: 'The public performance which the rules of the University impose upon every candidate for the degree of Mus.Doc. is usually ... entirely without general interest. But an important exception to the rule occurred on Friday ... when the Rev. John H. Mee directed his "Exercise" ...'. The *Musical Times* went on to praise the composer and his work in judicious critical terms: 'The composer is an enthusiastic amateur, and his new work proves him to be a highly accomplished musician ... as a whole the work is not only scholarly but effective.'

13 Merton College archives, Q. 2.36 (programme of 2 Dec. 1887).

14 Queen's College archives, News cuttings album, p. 23.

15 *Ten Years of University Music in Oxford, 1884–1894*, ed. P. C. Buck, J. H. Mee and F. C. Woods (Oxford: W. Bowden, 1894), p. 6.

THE HOLYWELL CONCERTS IN THE 18TH CENTURY   247

By 1904 Mee and his co-editor for the second volume, E. Kemp, were able to report the OUMU's move to new premises – the Holywell Music Room. The restoration of the Music Room to fully musical use in 1900–1901 signalled the start of a new and immensely significant chapter in its history, and the importance of this event was well recognized in the local press:

> An interesting transfer is being this Term accomplished in the Oxford musical world. The old Holywell Music Hall, after being during the last century the centre of Oxford music and the scene even of the Commemoration concerts, had fallen on dark days, and had been largely eclipsed by younger rivals. It is now passing into the tenancy of the Oxford Musical Union, and so will once more take a prominent place among the agencies by which good musical traditions are advanced and maintained here.[16]

In recording in 1904 that the move to the Holywell had been accomplished, Mee and Kemp also mentioned that Mee's history of the Music Room was in progress.[17] Thus Mee was working on his Music Room book precisely in the period when the room was once more reclaimed for the use of Oxford's music-lovers generally, and in particular as the headquarters of a university musical society (although contemporary photographs show that the layout of the interior, with the club's tables and chairs, was very different from its eighteenth-century disposition).

In spite of this vantage-point, Mee constructed his Holywell history distinctly in terms of past glories and their coming to an end. Around the central discussion of the music and musicians (ch. 3: 'The Music belonging to the Society') he ranged, first, two introductory chapters on 'The Oxford Music Room' and 'The Management of the Music Room', and then two concluding chapters entitled 'Suspension of the Concerts' and 'The End of the Music Room'. This last chapter begins: 'The third period in the history of the Music Room is a gloomy one ...' and depicts the process that it sets out to examine, in correspondingly melodramatic terms: 'at last the enterprise, so vigorously started in 1748, and so sturdily maintained even during the greatest political and military struggle that ever engaged the energies of the English nation, comes to an inglorious end in 1840'; then resumes the narrative in the same spirit – 'Our immediate task is to trace the progress of decay'.[18]

To some extent this portrayal invites a retrospective imposition of 'the progress of decay' on the earlier period of the Music Room's history. There is a sense – not entirely wrong – that for such a decline to have happened there must have been the seeds of failure embedded in the project in its previous phases (if not indeed from the start).[19] The present chapter, taking its cue from all this, examines the Holywell

---

16   *Oxford Magazine*, 19 (1901), 233.

17   *Ten More Years, 1894 to 1904, of University Music in Oxford* (Oxford: J. Vincent, 1904), p. x.

18   Mee, *Music Room*, p. 175. Only in the final sentence of the book (p. 202) does Mee comment briefly (though enthusiastically) on the changed situation vis-à-vis the room's use from 1901 onwards.

19   Thus Jenny Burchell, *Polite or Commercial Concerts? Concert Management and Orchestral Repertoire in Edinburgh, Bath, Oxford, Manchester, and Newcastle, 1730–1799* (New York: Garland, 1996) focuses on management-related problems.

248 SUSAN WOLLENBERG

scene in the eighteenth century with the intention of redressing the balance at least somewhat. My concern here is not primarily to chart the changing fortunes of the Musical Society's concerts at Holywell during the second half of the eighteenth century and beginning of the nineteenth. Their outline has been amply reconstructed by Mee from the range of documentary sources at his disposal. Supplementary items that have come to light since, whether further examples of programmes and notices in the press, or diaries of the time such as those of Richard Paget, and John Marsh, have added nuance and detail without radically altering the picture he drew.[20] But the material presented by Mee is certainly open to further interpretation and analysis, as well as the amplification made possible by these additional sources.

The focus here, then, is on identifying and investigating some of the factors that lent stability to the Holywell enterprise in the eighteenth century;[21] or indeed, to put it more strongly, the 'secrets of its success' – for it undoubtedly enjoyed a considerable success. As soon as one begins to look at these, it becomes evident that the concerts functioned within a perhaps unusually close-knit social and musical context, with the status of Oxford as a university city clearly affecting the nature of the environment for music. The university and its colleges created a city centre of a particular kind – an area relatively densely populated (by 1801 the university comprised a tenth of the total population of the city) and with a preponderance of young men who expected to spend their time at Oxford in the pursuit of leisure as well as occasional study. As the Oxford historian Vivian Green has put it:

> [The undergraduate's] day would start with breakfast either in his rooms or in the Common Room, or at a coffee house; and then he would probably do some work (not all of them would do any work): dinner ... either three or four o'clock in the afternoon, was a very formal occasion for which undergraduates had to dress formally. And after that, then there was either time for reading or for a great many of them playing cards, casting a wager, and drinking (and often drinking to excess) ... The day was a pretty leisurely one ... by and large the pressure of work was not all that enormous, either for undergraduates or for dons. What they did for recreation varied intensely: the rich I suppose went foxhunting, some went boating ... there was a lot of walking, there was a certain amount of cockfighting, there were players, there were things that went on in the coffee houses and the taverns, and all that in addition of course to the musical performances.[22]

In a period when the value of music to society was the subject of considerable debate,[23] one strand of thought regarded music as a potentially civilizing influence

---

20 For extracts from Paget's diary, see Wollenberg, *Music at Oxford, passim*; for Marsh see *The John Marsh Journals: The Life and Times of a Gentleman Composer (1752–1828)*, ed. Brian Robins (Stuyvesant, NY: Pendragon Press, 1998).

21 For discussion of some of the destabilizing elements see Mee, *Music Room, passim*, esp. pp. 115 ff.

22 Dr Vivian Green, in conversation with Susan Wollenberg: 'Oxford', British Cities ('Fairest Isle'), BBC Radio Three (23 May 1995).

23 For selected excerpts from the literature, see Ch. 14 below.

THE HOLYWELL CONCERTS IN THE 18TH CENTURY   249

that would 'tempt gentlemen from "midnight Drinkings" '.[24] On the other hand, attendance *en masse* at musical performances occasionally provoked 'a tumult of young men' to riotous behaviour, as in 1792 with the case of the broken violin, reported by William Crotch.[25]

That colourful incident may partly have been encouraged by the intimacy of the Holywell Room, and the relative proximity of audience and performers that it afforded. The Room itself with its famed acoustic (it was observed that there was 'not one pillar to deaden the sound') was clearly a strong element in the attractions offered by the eighteenth-century subscription concerts at Holywell. As Peter Borsay points out,[26] it represented a category that was exceedingly rare for the period: a building purpose-made for music, as distinct from the vastly more prevalent usage of pre-existent buildings. The Holywell Music Room was envisaged from the start as a 'space for music'; its existence was owed to a perceived need, as William Hayes's 'History' made clear (for an architectural sketch see Fig. 12.1).[27] These two factors alone – that it was custom-built, and that it was put up in response to an existing cultural and social need – while not guarantees of the concerts' success, made it a more likely prospect.

Within the university there had been distinguished precedents over the previous century and a half for the designing and creation of new purpose-built edifices in response to a 'perceived need', together with a vision of how best to fulfil that need. Sir Thomas Bodley's Library (1602) and Wren's Sheldonian Theatre (1669) – the university's grand assembly room – are examples remaining, like the Holywell Music Room, in lasting use through to the present day for the purpose for which they were originally intended. (The Sheldonian was connected with musical performances from the time of its opening onwards.)[28] In the case of the Music Room, the building project set up during the 1740s, and so graphically described

---

24   Sir Charles Mallet, *A History of the University of Oxford* (London: Methuen, 1924–27), vol. 3, p. 145.

25   Oxford, Bodleian Library, MS Mus. d.32, facing p. 1. It was on this occasion that Malchair's 'fine Cremona' violin 'on which he used to lead' the Holywell Band was 'broken by an Orange thrown at the Orchestra'. For an earlier reference to 'a riot in the true spirit of the times' at the Holywell see Donald Burrows and Rosemary Dunhill, *Music and Theatre in Handel's World: The Family Papers of James Harris 1732–1780* (Oxford: Oxford University Press, 2002), p. 589 (Edward Poore to James Harris, 15 May 1770).

26   See Ch. 2 above.

27   Hayes, 'History of the Music Room', fo. 2ᵛ. Hayes's account conveys an acute awareness of the difficulties inherent in the earlier phase of the Musical Society, with the use of tavern accommodation for its meetings. His detailed description of the Music Room and its furnishings and fittings (in Peshall, reference as n. 5 above) provokes the thought that he was surely consulted on the design. (Its architect, Thomas Camplin, was Vice-Principal of St Edmund Hall.)

28   On the Bodleian, see Ian Philip, *The Bodleian Library in the Seventeenth and Eighteenth Centuries* (Oxford: Clarendon Press, 1983); on Wren, and Sheldon's Theatre, see Lisa Jardine, *On a Grander Scale: The Outstanding Career of Sir Christopher Wren* (London: HarperCollins, 2002), esp. pp. 215 ff. Oxford was in the forefront of the creation of public buildings: the Bodleian Library is one of the oldest public libraries in Europe, while the Ashmolean (1683) is the oldest museum open to the public in Britain.

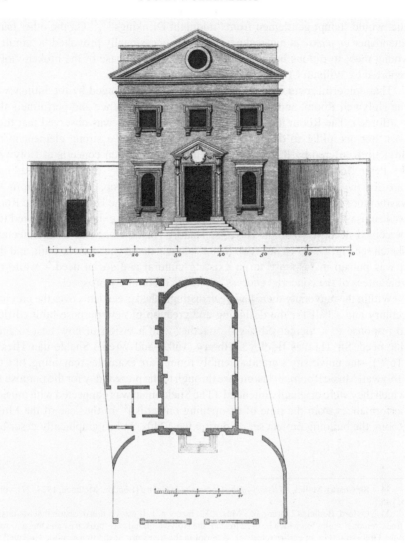

Fig. 12.1 Holywell Music Room, architectural sketch

by Hayes,[29] marked a crucial and inspired shift from the club atmosphere of the Musical Society's meetings at the King's Head Tavern to the public subscription concerts put on by the Musical Society at the Holywell from the mid-century forward.

Hayes's involvement linked the earlier and later phases of Oxford's eighteenth-century musical life – pre- and post-Holywell. One vital element in the establishment of the Holywell subscription series was a sense of continuity. As Heather Professor, William Hayes was responsible for the direction of the concerts.[30] A distinctive feature of William Hayes's tenure of the Heather chair (and indeed already a feature of the earlier part of his career) was his devotion to the music of Handel, and especially the choral works.[31] Two landmark occasions when Hayes's Handelian sympathies were in evidence were the 1733 Act, when Hayes travelled to Oxford to hear Handel's performances; and the opening of the Radcliffe Library (later known as the Radcliffe Camera) in April 1749, for which Hayes himself directed a series of performances of works by Handel, including *Messiah* (in its first hearing in the English provinces). The taste for choral music in general, and Handel's English oratorios and other vocal works in particular, was built in to the Holywell repertoire.

In fact this taste was established, together with a potential audience with a vested interest in the project, in the process of fund-raising for the Music Room during the 1740s – when the resonances of Handel's 1733 visit were still echoing strongly in Oxford. The renowned Oxford counter-tenor Walter Powell (who as a chorister had earned a shilling or two on occasion taking a singing part for the musical club at the King's Head) also formed a link between the pre-Holywell phase, and in particular Handel's visit to Oxford, and the Music Room project. Powell, by this time a senior figure in the academic and musical establishment, had taken a leading role (that of Joad, the High Priest) in the premiere of Handel's *Athalia* at the Sheldonian Theatre in July 1733. He also took a central role in promoting the subscription scheme for the new Music Room in the 1740s. As the number of subscribers increased, so the plans for the new room took shape.[32] The purchase of 'the Ground whereon the present Music Room stands' (as Hayes described it; the description itself still stands today) for £100 from Wadham College, after a false start with a different site – the Racket Court – seemed to mark the decisive launch of the project.[33]

---

29 William Hayes, 'History of the Music Room', fo. 3.

30 There could be advantages and disadvantages to this arrangement; under Philip Hayes's direction (when he succeeded his father, William, as Heather Professor), elements of dissension surfaced repeatedly, no doubt owing partly at least to his irascible temper.

31 William Hayes's championship of Handel's music is widely documented. On this, and on Handel's Oxford connections, see particularly: Donald Burrows, 'Sources for Oxford Handel performances in the first half of the eighteenth century', *Music & Letters*, 61 (1980), 177–85; also Ch. 7 above; H. Diack Johnstone, 'Handel at Oxford in 1733', *Early Music*, 31 (2003); and Susan Wollenberg, 'Handel in Oxford: The tradition c.1750–1850', *Göttinger Händel-Beiträge*, 9 (2002), 161–76.

32 Hayes, 'History of the Music Room'.

33 Apropos of the Racket Court, on the use of such spaces for theatrical performances see Ch. 10 above.

252   SUSAN WOLLENBERG

At that stage, with a total of some £500 raised in subscription money, the prospects for the building were evidently regarded optimistically. When ('by the Time the Walls were raised') the money was 'swallowed up' and the project came to a halt, after further discussion at the Club it was decided to put on monthly performances of choral music to obtain the money needed for finishing the building: Hayes records that £176. 13*s*. 3*d*. was raised thereby. This display of initiative produced successful results; 'the Workmen were employed, the Floor laid …' and the room fitted out ready to accommodate the total of '400 persons commodiously' for whom Hayes describes it as calculated.[34] In the course of this process, then, an audience for choral music had been established. The penchant for this repertoire became enshrined in the structure of the Holywell subscription concerts.[35]

Oxford audiences were particularly prone to adopt favourite composers and repertoire over a long period of time. A kind of 'long memory' operated in Oxford's musical life; whether or not all the hundreds of 'Persons' seated 'commodiously' (or perhaps crowded less comfortably) at the Music Room enjoying the 'Quarterly Choral Performances' from the 1740s onwards had been present at Handel's performances in Oxford in 1733, certainly they were collectively primed to regard this composer as in some way their own. The Handel choral repertoire – using the term broadly to encompass the oratorios, anthems and miscellaneous vocal genres – was able to be quarried in different ways to fulfil the variety of needs consonant with the current taste in programme planning. The oratorios especially lent themselves to this versatile usage. Their overtures formed effective opening items to the 'Acts' into which the concert programmes were divided; they were also found to serve well as concluding pieces, as with the 'OVERTURE to Judas Macchabaeus, (with the Side Drum.)' included at the end of 'Act II' of the weekly concert at the Music Room, 24 October 1785.[36] They also yielded incidental instrumental pieces; various combinations of these were favoured, such as the opening cluster of 'Act II' in the programme of 6 December 1773, featuring 'OVERTURE – "Saul," with the Dead March'.[37]

Vocal extracts ranged from solo airs (often billed as 'SONG') to full choruses, with a variety of ensemble settings in between: in 1785, for instance, Master Webb sang Handel's 'SONG. "Happy Iphis"', immediately preceding the overture to *Judas Maccabaeus* (and following Corelli's 'CONCERTO the 8th'), while in 1773 Mr Norris sang 'Love in her eyes sits playing', between two instrumental items,

---

34   Hayes, 'History of the Music Room', fo. 3. In general the evidence for the numbers that could be accommodated in various venues needs to be interpreted (these were no doubt sometimes given impressionistically, or intended metaphorically) but the casting of Hayes's account in documentary style tends to suggest accuracy of detail.

35   For further discussion of this see Wollenberg, *Music at Oxford, passim*, esp. chs 2 and 4, and 'Handel in Oxford: The tradition c.1750–1850'.

36   Programme in New College Archives. I am grateful to Caroline Dalton, Archivist, for alerting me to her discovery of this document.

37   Oxford, Bodleian Library, Gough Oxf. 90.

a Trio by 'Scwindl' [Schwindl] and a symphony by Ricciotti, in 'Act 1'.[38] The frequent programming of such excerpts was in addition to the performance of complete oratorios (a field in which Oxford, among provincial centres, took the lead).[39] When the 'ARTICLES of SUBSCRIPTION for the Support of the MUSICAL SOCIETY' published for 1775–76 set out the new scheme whereby in Easter and Michaelmas Terms 'instead of the Oratorios as usual' would be substituted 'two grand Miscellaneous Concerts', the organizers were concerned to reassure the subscribers that 'the Oratorio of the Messiah' would be 'performed as usual in Lent Term, and some other Oratorio, or Piece of Choral Music, in Act Term'.[40]

The programme for the Music Room, 24 October 1785, with its inclusion of Corelli's concerto, acknowledged a composer whose works, like those of Handel, were strongly embedded in the Musical Society's history. Corelli's chamber music was enthusiastically cultivated in Oxford during the earlier part of the eighteenth century.[41] Again as in the case of Handel, the intrinsic musical and practical reasons that ensured a lasting place for Corelli's works in the Holywell repertoire were joined by the new ideology of 'ancient music' and the growth of the canon in the later eighteenth century, which endowed such composers as these with a special status. Philippe Jung, the Oxford violinist of Viennese provenance, remarked of Malchair that he had 'a particular penchant for the music of the celebrated Handel, Geminiani, Corelli, and the other old masters'.[42]

At the same time, the 'miscellaneous' programming characteristic of the subscription concerts incorporated plentiful opportunities to hear modern music. Oxford's Holywell concerts, with their inclusion of Stamitz symphonies and Haydn quartets alongside Handel's choruses and Corelli's concertos, thus presented their audiences both with some of the most exciting of contemporary styles, and with the fine music of the 'old masters'. They served also as an important showcase for local composers, among them the successive Heather Professors of Music.[43]

The organizers and performers in these Oxford concerts can be seen to have espoused, in fact, virtually every contemporary trend in music making: they participated, for example, in the transfer of the glee from club-room to concert hall, and in the development of the new genre of keyboard concerto (in which

---

38   Sources of programmes as n. 36 and 37. 'Master Webb' would have been one of the choirboys from the college chapel establishments: in the eighteenth century (as nowadays) these treble soloists were a popular feature of the concert scene. Thomas Norris was among the distinguished ranks of the adult chapel singers in Oxford.

39   See especially Hans Joachim Marx, *Händels Oratorien, Oden und Serenaten. Ein Kompendium* (Göttingen: Vandenhoeck & Ruprecht, 1998).

40   *JOJ*, 1775–76 (*passim*). The university year was divided into four terms with breaks in mid-December, then around Easter, Whitsun and midsummer.

41   See Margaret Crum, 'An Oxford Music Club, 1690–1719', *Bodleian Library Record*, 9/2 (Mar. 1974), 83–99.

42   Quoted (in French) from Jung's *Guide d'Oxford* (1789) in Mee, *Music Room*, p. 79.

43   For a more detailed analysis of the Holywell repertoire see Wollenberg, *Music at Oxford*, chs 4 and 9.

Philip Hayes was among the pioneers: for a university whose Professors of Music at this time were invariably organists of distinction, this was a clearly appropriate 'growth area').[44] They were prompt to pick up on the latest fashionable pieces, for instance in the genres of vocal chamber music: thus William Jackson of Exeter's attractive chamber duets were drawn on for the Holywell programmes in the 1790s.[45] And as the stewards constantly secured appearances by visiting 'star' performers, these visitors no doubt brought new repertoire with them to Oxford.

Room was also found in the Holywell programmes to 'replay' evident audience (and performers') favourites repeatedly during a season or several seasons. Paxton's 'Indian Death Song' fell in this category, and made an appearance (sung by Mr Woodcock) in the programme of 9 December 1791 referred to above, as well as on 1 April 1791 (also sung by Mr Woodcock); earlier it had featured in programmes such as those of 27 November 1788 and 12 May 1790, sung by Mr Norris. Similarly demonstrating the taste for 'local colour', in this case in the popular Scottish vein, Philip Hayes's 'Farewell to the Rocks of Lannow' (to verses by 'Miss Seward') found a place in numerous programmes at Holywell during the late 1780s and early 1790s (it was also sung at the Concert of Ancient Music on 17 February 1791). The practice of providing full texts of all vocal items in the Holywell programmes, whether in English or a foreign language, enabled those listeners who so wished to savour every nuance of the poetry and its musical setting.[46]

The 'long service' characteristic of many of the resident performers at Holywell, and the tendency of the visiting performers to return (again, often repeatedly), gave a very particular kind of stability to the experience of attending the concerts. (An extreme example of the 'long memory' that might result comes in the comment by an Oxford critic in 1848 apropos of the cellist Robert Lindley: 'He is well remembered by several lovers of music in this City, as occupying, nearly 50 years ago, the same position as he did on the present occasion.')[47] The list of performers at Holywell over the period of 'fifty years and upwards' referred to by the stewards in their appeal of 1800 is a remarkably distinguished one.[48] Among the patterns that can be seen is a distinct tendency for child prodigies and young performers in the early stages of their concert careers to include an appearance at the Holywell in Oxford among their first engagements (the extreme example here being the 3-year-old William Crotch, future Heather Professor of Music, in 1779).[49] Outlining the early career of Mrs Billington (Elizabeth Weichsel), Sainsbury thought that at 'fourteen she came before the public as a singer at Oxford': in fact she was 17, but was still Miss Weichsel and had not yet

---

44 On the glee, see Ch. 8 above.

45 As in the programme of 9 Dec. 1791 (Oxford, Bodleian Library, Mus. 1 d.64/1).

46 Programmes in Oxford, Bodleian Library, Mus. 1 d.64/1.

47 *JOJ*, 8 July 1848.

48 For further details of performers see Wollenberg, *Music at Oxford*, esp. chs 4 and 9.

49 *JOJ*, 3 July 1779. Crotch returned as a more mature performer in 1783 (cf. Mee, *Music Room*, p. 66).

THE HOLYWELL CONCERTS IN THE 18TH CENTURY   255

made her first stage appearance in London (although she had performed in benefit concerts with her parents and brother).[50] Mee, surely rightly, attributes the strength of the list and the specific pattern of engagements (as discussed above) to the stewards' flair for spotting talent and snapping up promising newcomers soon after their debuts. A newcomer of a rather different kind, Joseph Haydn, was enticed to Oxford (where his works were already well established in the Holywell repertoire) just a few months after his arrival in England in 1791.

Aspects of the performers' professional networking and the geographical outlines of their concert circuit would in general have governed their Oxford appearances; but sometimes undoubtedly the performers governed the arrangements, as in 1786 when the subscription concert at the Holywell Music Room was 'postponed ... from November 20 to the next day' to suit Mrs Billington, 'inasmuch as she was engaged in London'.[51] Presumably many of the performers were also, like Mrs Billington, 'generously available for benefit concerts, without fee':[52] certainly many such occasions for members of the Holywell Band were enhanced by the contributions of the visiting stars. The right to hold benefit concerts was guaranteed to the principal performers in the band by the Musical Society's Articles. While the inclusion of this formal allowance may have been motivated by the wish to control the number of benefits, nevertheless it granted legitimacy to a concert genre which was to prove both enduring and flexible in its applications.[53]

In maintaining a core of resident performers attached to the Holywell (among the musicians regularly taking part in the concerts, besides the instrumentalists in the band, were numerous choristers and adult choir members from the collegiate foundations) the Musical Society ensured for its subscription series a stability which clearly could never have been achieved by reliance on outsiders alone. In regard to its musicians, too, Oxford was quite densely populated, and the ranks were notably swelled by the contribution of distinguished musical dynasties such as the Marshall, Mahon and Reinagle families. Many among the musical community lived (and often owned shops) centrally in the city, within a narrow radius of the Music Room (if not indeed in Holywell Street itself: see Fig. 12.2).[54] They worked together closely as colleagues, and formed close friendships.[55]

---

50   [John Sainsbury], *A Dictionary of Musicians*, 2 vols (London, 1824), vol. 1, p. 88.
51   Highfill et al., *Biographical Dictionary*, vol. 2, p. 125.
52   Ibid., p. 128.
53   For examples of benefits in Oxford in different contexts and at different periods, see Wollenberg, *Music at Oxford*, esp. chs 4 and 9.
54   For instance, a number of members of the band and of the choirs kept music shops (or more general emporia) in the streets near Holywell such as High Street (Mathews, Hardy, Jung), Catte Street (Mathews) and Turl Street. Musicians' dwellings in the area included those of Francis Attwood (High Street) and Philippe Jung (Holywell). Information on musicians' addresses is found in Mee, *Music Room*, and *Jackson's Oxford Journal, passim*, as well as in advertising bills and in notices at the foot of the concert programmes.
55   Among particularly close working partnerships was that of Thomas Norris (tenor) and William Mathews (bass): for their careers see, *inter alia*, Highfill et al., *Biographical Dictionary* and (on their Oxford performances) Wollenberg, *Music at Oxford*. An account of the remarkable friendship

256   SUSAN WOLLENBERG

Recent research in various areas has brought to light new information about many of the Holywell performers. Where Mee was obliged to record regretfully in his book that 'some [individual musicians] ... such as Lates, Lambourne, and Miss Reynolds, remain mere names', quite full accounts of these individuals can now be constructed.[56] And Mee's expression of frustration in dealing with the prolific Mahon family ('It is greatly to be wished that more information were forthcoming with regard to a family named Mahon, which was evidently closely connected with the Music Room for a great number of years') can now be tempered as a result of the researches of Betty Matthews and others.[57] This new information, as well as illuminating the circumstances of the individuals concerned, helps us to build up a fuller picture of the ways in which the musicians' careers were developed, and to see in more detail how it was possible to sustain a living as a musician in such a community.

The benefit concerts allowed to the performers have already been mentioned: these were advertised using a variety of 'marketing ploys' and in terms designed to elicit the maximum response, as in the case of Mr [R.] Wall's 'Benefit Concert of Vocal and Instrumental Music' in August 1791, permitted by 'the Vice-Chancellor, from a Motive of Humanity'. Presenting his 'humble Respects to the Publick', Mr Wall sought to engage their sympathy by confiding the unfortunate personal circumstances that gave rise to this occasion: as 'the Performers [had] been so kind to promise him their Assistance', he 'thankfully' embraced this opportunity, 'having been confined by a long illness', and expressed his hopes for their generous support.[58] Presumably if members of the band were unable to play, they received no pay. In 1800 the 'Stewards of the Music Room' pointed out that 'by the plan of the Institution no fixed Salary is ensured to the Performers; but each depends intirely for what he is to receive upon the contingent produce of the [subscription] fund'. With 'only 141' subscribers the 'prospect of subsistence' was not considered a realistic hope.[59] (Matters improved thereafter, thanks to the stewards' efforts.)

---

between Crotch and Malchair is extant in Oxford, Bodleian Library (Crotch's memoir of Malchair: MS Mus. d.32). There are also possible connections among the Oxford musicians through Free-masonry. An advertising bill for Mathews's shop in the High Street, Oxford (Bodleian Library, John Johnson collection) has its text surrounded by masonic symbols. It was in addition an international community, with, besides those musicians of continental origins already mentioned, others such as Paul Alday and his wife (of the Paris Concert spirituel) and Andreas Lidl (a member of Haydn's band at Eszterháza) joining the Holywell ranks.

56   Mee, *Music Room*, pp. 68–9. On Lates see David M. Lewis, *The Jews of Oxford* (Oxford: Oxford Jewish Congregation, 1992), p. 5; and Stanley Sadie (rev. S. Wollenberg), 'Lates, James', *New Grove2*. (Further on Lates see the present chapter, below.) For Lambourn, see Ch. 7, p. 138 above. On Miss Reynolds (assuming the same person) see, *inter alia*, Ch. 14 below, and *New Grove2*.

57   See Betty Matthews, 'The Musical Mahons', *Musical Times*, 120 (1979), 482–4; also the discussion in H. Diack Johnstone and Roger Fiske, eds, *The Eighteenth Century*, Blackwell History of Music in Britain, 4 (Oxford: Blackwell, 1990), *passim*; and the entries in Highfill et al., *Biographical Dictionary*.

58   *JOJ*, 6 Aug. 1791.

59   Stewards' appeal, reference as n. 6 above.

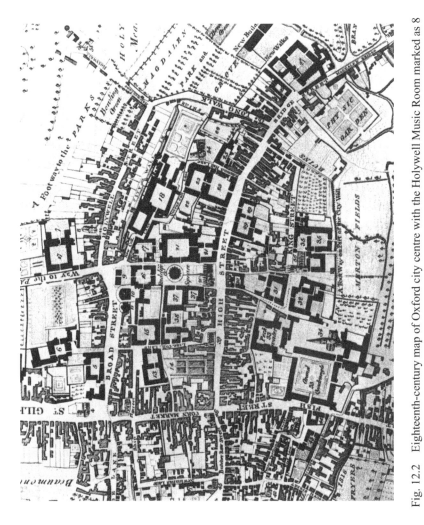

Fig. 12.2 Eighteenth-century map of Oxford city centre with the Holywell Music Room marked as 8

258   SUSAN WOLLENBERG

The career of James Lates (d. 1777) illustrates the range of musical activity and connections that the performers might cultivate. Lates (from his billing alongside Malchair) seems to have been principal second violin in the Holywell Band; he was also household violinist to the Duke of Marlborough at Blenheim.[60] The string chamber sonatas of his op. 5 were dedicated to the Duke, 'for whose private amusement they were principally composed'. His duets for violins or flutes of op. 1 and op. 2 were dedicated to 'Richard Kaye Esq. of Brazen-Nose College in the UNIVERSITY OF OXFORD' as a 'little Tribute of Gratitude and Esteem … humbly offered'. Evidently the dedicatee was a patron, and possibly a pupil. Sir Richard Kaye, Bart., matriculated at Brasenose in 1754, aged 17; he took the BCL in 1761, DCL in 1770, became an FRS, held various distinguished church offices and was appointed 'chaplain to the king' in 1766.[61] In addition to the previously known publications, a manuscript copy of violin minuets by James Lates has recently come to light.[62] Each of the 16 minuets bears a lady's name: 'Miss Day's Minuet', 'Miss Nichol's Minuet' and so forth. Presumably these ladies, also, were Lates's pupils – and he married one of them (assuming that 'Miss Day' is Joanna Day, the lady 'of exceeding good Accomplishments, with a very handsome Fortune' to whom Lates was reported in *Jackson's Oxford Journal*, 5 November 1768, as having been married on 29 October of that year). Lates's achievements were summed up in the description of him, in the *Journal*'s obituary, as an 'Eminent Musician' of the locality.[63]

The Holywell concerts, the 'Eminent Musicians' who performed in them, and the Music Room itself, chimed in with not only local needs and tastes, but also aspects of eighteenth-century English cultural life more broadly: the provision of attractive 'public spaces' for entertainment; the sociability that characterized life in general, and the life of a university city in particular; the cherishing of traditions, together with the keen desire to follow the newest trends and to hear the latest talents; and the creation of an engine of publicity fuelled by the exploitation of

---

60 On his early career, see *New Grove2*. For more detail on his performances with Malchair see esp. 'Malchair the Musician' in Colin Harrison, ed., *John Malchair of Oxford: Artist and Musician* (Oxford: Ashmolean Museum, 1998); and on his publications (and the subscribers to these), see Wollenberg, *Music at Oxford*, pp. 52–3.

61 Joseph Foster, *Alumni Oxonienses* (Oxford: Parker & Co., 1888; repr. 2000), vol. 2, p. 780. Lates's family's connection with the university may have helped him: his father David Francis (Francisco) Lates is described in early records as 'teacher in Oxford by leave of the Vice-Chancellor of Italian, French, Spanish, Portuguese, and Hebrew, and "In Musica Magister"' (William Dunn Macray, *Register of the Members of St. Mary Magdalen College, Oxford*, vol. 5, 'Extracts from the Registers and Accounts', 1758: p. 18).

62 BL, MS Mus. 137; inscribed 'S: S: Banks 1764'. The first part consists of a copy of 'A Collection of new Minuets For the year 1764 Perform'd at Court on His Majesty's Birthday', scored 'for the Harpsichord, Violin and German Flute'. The second part is entitled 'Sixteen Minuets for the Violin Composed by Mr. James Lates'. (Lady Sarah Sophia Banks was the sister of Sir Joseph Banks, friend of Burney.) Nicolas Bell of the British Library, Music Collections kindly informed me of the recent acquisition of this manuscript.

63 *JOJ*, 22 Nov. 1777. Posterity has acknowledged Lates's role in the development of English string style (cf. Robin Stowell, ed., *The Cambridge Companion to the Violin* (Cambridge: Cambridge University Press, 1992), p. 179).

such 'marketing devices' as consumer loyalty, and novelty. With the Music Room advertisements nestling in the pages of *Jackson's Oxford Journal* among alarming reports of footpads, or the case of the silver spoons stolen (surely unwisely) from the Judge's Lodgings,[64] the price of grain, and 'wanted' notices for sober servants – among all this paraphernalia of daily existence, music was presented as an integral part of Oxford life. The qualities that sustained the Holywell concerts for so long were subsequently channelled into an ever-widening range of concert enterprise in nineteenth-century Oxford.

---

64 *JOJ*, 15 Mar. 1775.

CHAPTER THIRTEEN

Gigs, Roadies and Promoters:
Marketing Eighteenth-Century Concerts

Rosamond McGuinness

As the title of this chapter suggests, there are parallels to be drawn between promotional opportunities and procedures in London of the late seventeenth and early eighteenth centuries, and the present day. In both periods, technological advances gave rise to new possibilities for communication. In the early period these took the form of printing, with its by-products of newspapers and advertising; in the latter period, the computer and the internet. There are other parallels as well: the rise of the City and of market forces; of upwardly mobile people and shifting social barriers; investment opportunities and disappointments; deceived investors grouping together to recoup their losses; insider traders being imprisoned; the diversification of business interests; media censorship; and, further, the growth of a consumer society preoccupied with the acquisition of possessions and the status these could bring, together with the perception of music as a commodity with considerable financial potential.

Today's context for music includes the pop world and 'crossovers'. The notions of highbrow, middlebrow and lowbrow have been blurred with, for instance, such CDs as 'Tearjerkers – Classical Music to Move the Mind, Body and Soul' (Warner Classics). In the eighteenth century the musical scene was newly focused on the public concert, also a shifting social and cultural phenomenon, functioning in a milieu in which court patronage was virtually non-existent and private patronage rare. Public concerts, particularly benefits, were ideal as a supplementary source of income for the many musicians drawn to London. By the early years of the eighteenth century they were one of the mainstays of musical life in the metropolis. The freelance tradition so essential in England today was born.

What role did intuitive marketing play, if any? Intuitive, because the versatile composer-performer who organized, managed and promoted the concerts did not have today's specialized training or literature, and thus operated instinctively without, for example, Maslow's hierarchy of universal needs which underpins today's advertising (see Appendix, p. 268 below, Example A); nor Freud's studies of the unconscious and its application to subliminal persuasion and motivational analysis; and without astronomical amounts of money, or a system of rhetoric with formulated conventions and codes.

261

To be sure, there was the precedent of medical advertising in the newspapers and great bills (posters) which were particularly apt for a walking city, as London then was; and restrained formal notices about books, lost property or missing servants in the early official government newspaper, the *London Gazette*, from the 1660s onwards (see Appendix, Examples C, D and E for examples regarding music).

But those who advertised in the many London newspapers that emerged subsequently, after the lapsing of the Licensing Law in 1695, had to use their ingenuity. These newspapers are invaluable as a source for our reconstruction of the history of the public concert only if used with caution, bearing in mind that they were not calendars, nor conceived to be, nor were they a mirror of society. Their musical references need to be seen within the context of the variables of each newspaper title: its structure, ownership, management policies, political stance, readership, costs and profits; production practices, distribution methods, circulation figures, and relationship with such institutions as postal services, theatres and coffee houses where newspapers were read for two pence. 'The fondness of the English for these papers is incredible', wrote the French Benedictine Abbé Prévost, visiting London around 1720. 'They spread from the Capital into the farthest corners of the provinces, and there is no one, down to the lowest seaman, who does not spend twopence a day to satisfy his curiosity.'[1] Coincidentally, both coffee houses and newspapers came into their own just when concerts were on the move from private, informal gatherings to public, more formal occasions, with entry charges. Newspapers, then as now, served as the focal point of a complex, subtle system involving a cultural and commercial transaction between a variety of coinciding interests. Their view of reality was and is limited, coloured by the particular outlook and practices of those in control.

Caution is also needed when thinking of concerts. 'A concert is a concert is a concert'? – with apologies to Gertrude Stein. The eighteenth-century concerts – variably called 'consorts' or 'entertainments' – were differentiated by their venue, audience, cost, organizer's intentions, contents, accompanying non-musical activities or commodities. There was no established impresario; no custom-built, large concert hall; no audience reverentially listening. They were more akin to contemporary jazz concerts in London's restaurants – Pizza Express and so forth: they provided opportunities to socialize and conduct business – 'to see and be seen' while eating and listening; to purchase a musical machine or win a hand-painted miniature picture, have entertainment at the horse races, take part in a lottery or even participate in the performance. Thus we need to imagine going to the Royal Festival Hall or Carnegie Hall with the advice that if we attended dressed up in the costumes of one of the *commedia dell'arte* characters, we could join the orchestra playing thus clothed. Concerts were held in any place considered to be economically viable. Venues used ranged from tennis courts, chocolate rooms and

---

1 Abbé Prévost, *Adventures of a Man of Quality*, Broadway Library of Eighteenth Century French Literature (London: Routledge & Sons, 1930), pp. 119–20.

taverns to the theatres, guildhalls and public gardens. By the late 1720s and 1730s there were at least 100 different venues used for public concerts in a small area within the City of London and Westminster, usually with more than one concert on an evening.

Concerts were but one element in a commercial complex which, to mention only a few of its ramifications, embraced music publishers who had shares in newspapers and periodicals, manufacturers of musical playing cards and musical fans, and makers of the musical machines already noted above. Accounts of what was printed and available for home consumption, especially for women and children, show just how much the domestic replication of the concert experience was exploited as a money-spinner. Music in its various guises was big business, the public concert in particular, and increasingly so as it became popular. Indeed this was so much the case that by 1754 one commentator in the *London Magazine* was complaining that 'Music [was] never intended ... in itself to become the labour, principal attention, great business of a people. Yet, how far, how scandalously it has of late prevailed, as such, in our country, let the shameful number of concerts now declare.'[2]

What brought this about? What made music apparently so popular? One answer is astute marketers, through blanket bombarding, projecting music as being one of the most desirable status symbols. It is one thing to be a modern consumer and the target of the persuasive messages being sent. Even then it is sometimes difficult to decipher the message. The difficulties may actually reside in the power of the message, constructed – as is frequently found today – ambiguously, as for example in the English advertisements with no words. Their ambiguity is an effective way of counteracting the phenomenon which the American economist John Kenneth Galbraith discussed in his book *The Affluent Society* (1958): 'Advertising will beat helplessly on ears that have been conditioned by previous assault to utter immunity.'[3] The eighteenth-century 'spoof' concert advertisements may be a parallel here, presupposing as they do more than the information that appears on the page.[4] Sometimes today a holding company may be advertising across products. The same applied with people such as John Walsh who, I believe, had shares in a number of newspapers and was also somehow involved with concert rooms.[5]

It is quite another thing to have to enter vicariously into the mentality of those living about 300 years ago. It is particularly difficult when the sort of evidence we would like to have does not seem to be extant at present. Nevertheless, I find it is possible to draw together here some of my initial impressions about the advertisements from about 1670 to 1750. By concentrating upon advertisements I do not mean to imply that advertising existed in a separate sphere from marketing.

---

2   *London Magazine*, Nov. 1754.
3   John Kenneth Galbraith, *The Affluent Society* (London: Hamish Hamilton, 1958).
4   On these, see p. 265 below.
5   This is something I am currently exploring.

I am well aware that today advertising is considered to be an element of promotion along with sales drives and publicity, and that promotion's function is to capture the attention of potential customers to what is being sold and induce them to buy. And further, I recognize that this is but one aspect of the so-called 'Marketing Mix': Promotion, Price, Produce and Place, People, Process and Physical Evidence; and also that market positioning is important and that differences exist between advertising and market/product positioning. The decision of the English Co-op Bank to try to reach ethical investors is one example of market positioning. Another is Mick Jagger's systematic study of where a niche might exist to make his group portray an image different from that of the Beatles. Although a first-class student in his first year at the London School of Economics (so one of his classmates informs me), Jagger went onto the television show 'Juke Box Jury' and purposely spoke in a way which masked his intellectual capacity. Nigel Kennedy (as 'Kennedy', *tout court*) in his contrived speech and dress has done the same.

Marketing, which is both a concept and practice permeating all the activities and personnel of any company today, is subject to fashion. There is transactional or traditional marketing where the focus tends to be on one single transaction and the emphasis upon acquiring new customers and not keeping old ones. Today, with relationship marketing and customer franchises, the concern is with the long-term value of the customer, thus the customer's loyalty. Heinz (as in 'Beanz meanz Heinz'), for instance, with its contents, its packaging and its marketing over the years, has been promoted to provide comfort in conformity. The question of what were the marketing concepts and practices prevalent during the first half of the eighteenth century in London represents at this stage very much work in progress.

Before the public concerts began there was a potential audience both converted and unconverted. There was, for instance, a long tradition of amateur music making for the privileged. There were many popularized publications in circulation from the seventeenth-century music publisher John Playford, and there was a mercantile class with both the wherewithal and the will to acquire the attributes of the people of quality.

Although too few of the early predecessors of newspapers have survived to enable us to count or study their advertisements, the existence of diatribes, for example, in the middle of the seventeenth century, particularly concerning the medical advertisements, attests to the prevalence of advertising. The *London Gazette* refused to insert advertisements at first, maintaining repeatedly that they were 'not properly the business of a Paper of Intelligence'. When advertisements for musical performances were inserted in the early newspapers they initially appeared mainly as short informative notices, existing side by side with advertisements ornamented to varying degrees with persuasive words; however, none of them ever reached the hyperbolic heights of those used for medicine and for commodities such as coffee promoted as medicine (Appendix, Example B). In the advertisements with 'hype' the words used are ones used today generally for commodities and not for musical performances. However, for every persuasive word or every incentive offered, there are parallels today (new, best, varied …).

Not only that: the universal needs articulated by Maslow are all addressed, not necessarily in every single advertisement but over the whole range of advertisements. There sometimes seem to be variations in the nature of advertisements and in the language used by different newspapers and the different venues. What this reflects I am currently trying to ascertain.

In whatever newspapers the advertisements for concerts were printed, novelty, then as today, seems to have been of prime importance. Today, however, in the UK at least, advertisers are entitled to use 'new' on a product only for one year if that product has not been changed. In the eighteenth century there were no such restrictions; no codes of advertising existed. The idea of novelty finds its expression in a whole host of words which are peppered throughout the majority of advertisements (Appendix, Example H). 'NEW', as the twentieth-century advertising guru David Ogilvy stated in a lecture, 'is one of the most powerful words in the advertising dictionary.'

Music advertisers, like those advertising other products and activities, made all sorts of claims, were obsequious, used hyperbole liberally and even, at times, flirted with the truth (Appendix, Examples F, G). Advertising in general provoked both Joseph Addison in the *Tatler* on 10 September 1710, and Samuel Johnson in the *Idler* on 20 January 1759, to complain about its practices. By the time Johnson was writing, advertisements were highly stylized, bringing with them the danger of the resistance to advertising that Galbraith later identified. Johnson addressed this when he wrote critically and cynically about advertisements generally, though not mentioning concert advertisements specifically: 'Whatever is common is despised. Advertisements are now so numerous that they are very negligently perused, and it is therefore become necessary to gain attention by magnificence of promises, and by eloquence sometimes sublime and sometimes pathetic. Promise, large promise, is the soul of an advertisement.'

Of all the colourful advertisements and techniques used in the eighteenth century for music, including some of the highly amusing spoof ads already mentioned, my favourite example is that of the man who was publicized as performing in a quart bottle. The Earl of Sandwich was convinced that through advertising one could make people believe anything. Lord Chesterfield, his friend, entered into a bet with him that people would go to the theatre if he announced that a man would play the 'music of every instrument now in use' on a walking cane and would go into a 'common Wine Bottle' and sing. The advertisement was placed in several newspapers in 1749. The theatre was jammed, but when the artist did not appear, the house was wrecked as a response.[6]

When evaluating advertisements, whether in eighteenth-century or in modern sources, I have come to see that what advertising does and how it does it is more

---

6   A modern parallel (showing a similar perception and exploitation by management of the 'low taste' of its audience/customers) is the Gerald Ratner fiasco in England when Ratner, the head of a large jewellery chain which catered to a middle- to lower-class market, alienated his 'customer base' by referring to his product as 'crap' at a board meeting. After extensive media publicity, socially aspiring customers took that judgement as an evaluation of themselves, bringing Ratner and the company down.

complex, unpredictable and subtle than at first I thought to be the case. For, as in all communication – musical performances included – its effects do not depend only on what the advertiser does: consumers select the stimuli to which they respond and whether they will respond at all. And this latter component is perhaps the most difficult to decipher with certainty 300 years after the event. That being so, I have come to think of advertisements as a kind of sounding-board. Advertisers have to be sensitive to emerging trends and amplify them. It seems clear to me that, with their advertisements, those promoting concerts in the eighteenth century were reinforcing the idea that what had been the preserve of the privileged was now well within the reach of the socially mobile, and that concerts were among the appurtenances of life, even indeed to be reckoned among the social necessities. Those promoters certainly muscled in to the market. But what, if anything, did they contribute to music's popularity?

Earlier in this chapter I observed that in the eighteenth century music in general was popular, and the public concert in particular. 'How and why', I asked, wondering whether marketing played a role. The interpretation of 'popularity' is, like the advertising related to it, both subtle and complex. It has long been fashionable to attribute the rage for music in eighteenth-century England mainly to the aspirational ideals of a rising mercantile class, with their wealth and time for leisure, as well as to the growth of London. Such an explanation is not adequate in itself. One of the things that is needed to supplement or even replace this view is an understanding of the cultural roots of demand, gleaned through a systematic study of the devices used to stimulate it; and of the determination on the part of the entrepreneurs who employed these devices. Here my computer database is useful as a tool in helping to address the following questions: How far can one attribute this popularity to the marketing procedures that were being used at the time? Was the consumer response advertisement-led? How far did a reciprocity exist between the advertiser's response to an audience already existent, and the creation of an audience? Did the language of advertising used by the early composer-performer entrepreneurs imbue music in its various guises with certain images which were designed to stimulate interest in what was to be gained from what was being promoted? I say 'what was to be gained' because, in studying advertising over these past 25 years, I have constantly been made aware that it operates on two levels, whether today or 300 years ago: the obvious and the subliminal. It seems to be manipulating us into thinking that we need what it is trying to promote, when in fact it is projecting the idea that what it is trying to promote can help us obtain something else which we feel we need (Maslow's Motivation and Personality). The goal is to get the consumer to think and feel 'I want, I need, I cannot live without that something that the promoted product or activity can give me'. The creation of such appetites was an essential for eighteenth-century London musicians. Intuitively many knew what to do and did it, prompting me to want to write an article in a contemporary marketing magazine under the title 'So you think what you are doing is new, eh?'

I have touched only the surface of an intricate tapestry with all sorts of interwoven strands. The questions I have raised are only a few of those strands. There are many issues that still have to be unravelled. I should like to find out, by examining the language used in advertisements both for musical events and for other items in a particular newspaper, to whom the individual newspapers appealed. How far did the marketing mix apply? What did advertising procedures signify? What factors impinged upon the methods and content of musical advertisements? Were they predominantly concerned with monetary, political or cultural factors? Did these factors determine what sort of music a paper advertised? Further, by examining the content of musical advertisements is it possible to disentangle the various overlapping interests of those with vested interest? What was the relationship of the format of the advertisement and the popularity of particular concerts? Was there such a thing as a Whig or Tory concert? And if so, what was the difference between the kind of musical offerings a Whig audience preferred as compared to those attended by Tories? What is the significance of the pattern that appears to exist between particular venues and specific coffee houses? What was the character of the named coffee houses? What was the level of competition in the newspaper market at the time? And what was the readership profile (types of reader and levels of readership)? How many opportunities to perform existed (numbers, capacities and fullness of concert venues?) What was the nature of the audiences? Were any differentiation strategies in evidence in the advertisements (pricing and positioning) and is there any evidence of the composers seeking out 'opinion formers' to channel messages (to reach like-minded customers)? And the one question that recurs subliminally throughout this chapter like an *idée fixe*: how is one to discern whether the advertisements were designed to create an audience or to draw in an existent audience? Is it possible to know with certainty whether the newspapers were dictating to the reader what they thought the taste should be or what it actually was?

Clearly I have my work cut out here: work that can continue to benefit from cutting across the boundaries of disciplines and extending into the real world of business today.

Appendix

Note: where emphasis has been added to the original, this is indicated by bold type.

Example A

Abraham Maslow's 'Hierarchy of Needs', taken from J. Blythe, *Essentials of Marketing* (London: Financial Times Management, 1998), p. 176.

Self-
actualizing
Needs

Aesthetic needs

Cognitive needs

Esteem needs

Belonging needs

Security needs

Survival needs

Example B

Publick Advertiser, 19–26 May 1752

In Bartholomew Lane, on the back side of Old Exchange, the drink called *Coffee*, which is a very wholsom and Physical drink, having many excellent virtues, closes the Orifice of the Stomach, fortifies the heat within, helpeth Digestion, quickeneth the Spirits, maketh the heart lightsom, is good against Eyesores, Coughs or Colds, Rhumes, Consumptions, Headach, Dropsie, Gout, Scurvy, King's Evil, and many others, is to be sold both in the morning, and at three of the clock in the afternoon.

Example C

London Gazette, 30 December 1672

These are to give notice, that at Mr. John Banisters House, now called the Musick-School over against the George Tavern in White Fryers, this present Monday, will be Musick performed by **excellent** Masters, beginning precisely at 4 of the clock in the afternoon and every afternoon for the future precisely at the same hour.

Example D

London Gazette, 11 December 1676

On Thursday next the 14th instant, At the Academy in Little Lincolns-Inn Fields will begin the first part of the Parley of Instruments. Composed by Mr. John Banister, and perform'd by **Eminent** Masters at Six a Clock, and to continue Nightly, **as shall by bill or otherwise by Notified.** The Tickets are to be deliver'd out from One of the Clock till Five every day and not after.

Example E

London Gazette, 26 November 1694

The Consort of Musick in Charles-street, Covent-Garden, will begin again next Thursday with the Addition of **two new Voices,** one being a **young Gentlewoman of 12 years of Age, the Room being put in good condition;** and there to continue this Season.

Example F

Post Boy, 20 November 1697

These are to give Notice **to all Lovers of Musick,** and the Art of Singing that Mr. James Kremberg is **lately come out of Italy, and shall keep a New Consort of Musick by very great Masters, of all sorts of Instruments: with fine Singing, in Italian, French, English, Spanish, German, Dutch and Latin, after the newest Italian and French manner.** At Mr. Hickford's Dancing-School in Panton-street, near the Hay-Market, or in James-Street over-against the Tennis-Court, just by the Blew-Posts, there being a Door out of each Street to the Room. This Consort will begin on Wednesday, the 24th of this Instant, at Eight a Clock at Night, and will continue Weekly the same Day; **always with New Compositions.** Price Half a Crown.

Example G

Post Boy, 6 September 1701

Mr. Abell **having had the Honour lately to Sing to the Nobility and Gentry of Richmond and the Neighbouring Towns,** thinks himself bound in Gratitude to give an Invitation to the said **Noble** Assembly to return his most humble thanks with a Performance of **New Musick,** in **English, Latin, Italian, French, &c.** On Monday next, being the 8th of September, 1701, at Three of the Clock exactly, in that **most Excellent Musick-Room of Richmond Wells; being Honour'd and Accompany'd by the Greatest Masters of Europe,** it being the last time of his Singing this Summer. Each Ticket Five Shillings, to be had at the Wells. **The Dancing will begin as soon as the Consort ends. Note, That the Tide of Flood serves to go and return the same day. Moonlight.**

270 ROSAMOND McGUINNESS

Example H

From a variety of characteristic newspaper advertisements:

Novelty

never performed before; first time of singing; never before heard in England; newly come from Rome; newest, the whole thing being entirely new; fresh Set of Musick; a New Voice, exceedingly admir'd; Famous Seniora Anna, lately come from Rome, who never Sung on the Stage; a Manner never yet perform'd in England; first time perform'd; first time of his Singing since his Arrival; not yet perform'd; every Consort will have new Varieties; Compos'd new for the day; several new Voices; some new Voices; etc.

Value

favourite; excellent; the greatest Italian masters; several eminent masters; by the greatest performers extant; best; unique; best Hands from the Opera; several new Foreign Pieces, chose out from the greatest Authors; who hath so often perform'd with the greatest Applause; finest Voices and Hands in Town; a celebrated song; extraordinary; chiefest Masters; best Masters in Town; greatest masters in Europe; the famous Italian; fine Consort; late famous Purcell; choicest songs; several new Foreign Pieces, chose out from the greatest Authors never sung before; the like Number is not at any other Place in Epsom, nor at any other publick Wells in England; All compos'd by that Great and much esteem'd Master; several of the best English Voices; Magnificent Entertainment; etc.

Convenience and comfort

There will be country Dances after the Consort, in two large Rooms that will contain 40 Couples, with good Fires in them; Coaches and Chairs may come into James-street, or into Panton-street, there being a Passage into the Room both ways. There are made a commodious Pair of Stairs for the Convenience of the Company that come by Water; The Walks in the Gardens are made very pleasant, and will be always open for the Company to walk and divert themselves; Note, that the Moon will shine, the Tide serve, and a Guard placed from the College to St. James's Park, for the safe Return of the Ladies; to begin exactly at 7 a Clock, for the better Accommodation of the Company; Tickets are given out at the Place [York Buildings] the same day by Mr. Pinkeman, who has taken care to provide places for Persons of Quality at Five Shillings each, and the lower at half a Crown; beginning at 5 and to be ended at 8 for the conveniency of the Qualities resorting to the Park after; room put in good condition; etc.

Prestige and status

at the request of several Persons of Quality; at the request of several Gentlemen; at the request of the Nobility and Gentry; There is now a new Consort goes down this Year, which have been approved of by several Nobleman and Gentlemen; at the approval of Mr. Handel; by their Majesty's authority; to all Lovers of Musick; etc.

MARKETING 18TH-CENTURY CONCERTS

Value added

A Book, containing the Order and Words of the whole Entertainment will be given gratis to ech Person at Entrance; There will be Country Dances after the Consort; Italian lights; variety of new Artifical Water-Works; and Mr. Morphy (for the better Entertainment of his Friends) has made an Addition to the said Consort; concluding with a Ball; raffling of a harpsichord; after [the Consort] a Masquerade, and a fresh Set of Musick; Beginning exactly at 7 of the Clock.

CHAPTER FOURTEEN

Women Pianists in
Late Eighteenth-Century London

Nicholas Salwey

As Charles Rosen comments, 'that Haydn late in life found an English widow equal to the technical demands of his imagination at the keyboard should not blind us to the fact that these are the exceptions'.[1] They may indeed be the exceptions but one should not deduce from this that many women pianists did not attain a high standard at the piano. Indeed, one must remember the technical challenges posed by Haydn's late keyboard music, for while several foreign virtuosi residing in London would have met these challenges, it is unclear whether any English male pianists were of a similar standard. It has become common practice to perpetuate the view that women pianists in the late eighteenth century were almost exclusively amateurs, but as I hope to show, this was not necessarily the case. The reputation of all women pianists was regularly tarnished by the inherent amateurism implied in remarks by men such as Charles Burney, who wrote in 1776 that 'in general his [J. C. Bach's] compositions for the piano forte are such as ladies can execute with little trouble', or the description on publications such as Steibelt's sonatas op. 35, entitled 'Amusement for the ladies, being a sett of easy sonatas for the piano forte'.[2] While piano playing was indeed a necessary accoutrement and accomplishment for any young lady who wished to advance in life and to marry at or above her station, and thereby created a large market for less challenging compositions, numerous young women did excel at the piano and did so on the public platform alongside the leading male pianists of their generation. While they may not have provided serious competition for the foreign virtuosi who dominated London concert life, English female pianists appear to have been well able to hold their own with their native male counterparts, and both in their choice of repertoire and their own compositions, there is no apparent recourse to less virtuosic writing.[3] However, a career as a pianist was virtually impossible

---

1 Charles Rosen, *The Classical Style* (London: Faber, 1971), p. 46.

2 Charles Burney, *A General History of Music*, 4 vols (London, 1776–89), vol. 4, p. 482. Steibelt's sonatas op. 35 (*c*.1797) were issued both by Longman, Clementi & Co. as 'Three Sonatas for the piano forte …', and as above by Longman & Broderip.

3 Concert information is drawn from Simon McVeigh, *Calendar of London Concerts 1750–1800, Advertised in the London Daily Press*, database, Goldsmiths College, University of London. For a complete listing of harpsichord and piano performances, see Nicholas Salwey and

for women, because of the clear restrictions placed upon them by the rigid conventions of late eighteenth-century society.

Women pianists had to struggle against the male-enforced norms of feminine interests and conduct. The 'careers' of those who performed in public all fit a similar pattern – the child pianist, relinquishing the piano in her late teens, perhaps in favour of the greater prestige of the vocal art but more often for marriage. Marriage appears to have been an impediment to performing on the piano in public. Only two instances occurred during the second half of the eighteenth century of performances by married women,[4] and it has been argued that these very years coincided with a suppression of the liberties which had been gradually gained over the previous decades. As Amanda Vickery points out, the years from 1780 to 1850 'saw the rise of "separate spheres"'.[5] For women, this period represented a setback after previous gains:

> With the eighteenth-century glorification of 'Man' came a radical narrowing of women's participation in and contribution to productive and social life, and a drastic diminution of women's stature. It was not merely a relative decline. Pre-capitalist woman was not simply relatively eclipsed by the great leap forward of the male achiever; she suffered rather an absolute setback.[6]

The stirrings of a revolt were at least in place, led by the eloquent and forthright writings of Mary Wollstonecraft, whose most famous work, *Vindication of the Rights of Woman*, published in 1792, was received with a mixture of outrage and enthusiasm. As Wollstonecraft asks,

> Do the women who, by the attainment of a few superficial accomplishments, have strengthened the prevailing prejudice, merely contribute to the happiness of their husbands? Do they display their charms merely to amuse them? And have women who have early imbibed notions of passive obedience, sufficient character to manage a family or educate children?[7]

Marriage is presented as the primary goal of such an education: 'To rise in the world, and have the liberty of running from pleasure to pleasure, they must marry advantageously, and to this object their time is sacrificed, and their persons often legally prostituted.'[8]

Simon McVeigh, 'The Piano and Harpsichord in London's Concert Life, 1750–1800: A Calendar of Advertised Performances', in Michael Burden and Irena Cholij, eds, *A Handbook for Studies in 18th-Century English Music VIII* (Oxford: Burden & Cholij, 1997), pp. 27–72. For further details, see Nicholas Salwey, 'The Piano in London Concert Life, 1750–1800', D.Phil. diss. (University of Oxford, 2001).

4   Out of some 622 advertised performances on the piano and harpsichord between 1750 and 1800, 210 were by women, this representing over a third of the total.

5   Amanda Vickery, *The Gentleman's Daughter: Women's Lives in Georgian England* (New Haven and London: Yale University Press, 1998), p. 3.

6   M. George, 'From Goodwife to Mistress: The Transformation of the Female in Bourgeois Culture', *Science and Society*, 37 (1973), 6, as quoted by Vickery, *The Gentleman's Daughter*, p. 2.

7   Mary Wollstonecraft, *A Vindication of the Rights of Woman* (London, 1792; Harmondsworth: Penguin Books, 1985), p. 119.

8   Ibid., p. 152.

WOMEN PIANISTS IN LATE 18TH-CENTURY LONDON 275

To gain a clearer understanding of the difficulties that might have been faced by those women who managed to perform on London's stages, one needs to look closely at the historical background in order to comprehend the limited opportunities available to them and the need to impress with their abilities. This picture of young women acquiring accomplishments is to be found in much of the art and literature of the time. Portrait artists appear to have been exclusively male, and they excelled in depicting the subtle nuances of the relationship between the sexes. As Richard Leppert has discussed, by the end of the eighteenth century a portrait of a young lady will typically include a pianoforte, and if a male is also present he is almost invariably depicted standing beside, or leaning against the piano with the woman seated beneath him. Leppert paints a picture of the male commissioning a portrait according to some form of agenda, the woman appearing to be tied to the piano as if to the sink, and he reaches a very clear conclusion:

A woman who became an accomplished performer signaled a variety of changes in her relationship to her husband and to her place in society. She became *visually* prominent, especially if she performed outside the drawing room, particularly if she gave a public recital, thus upstaging her husband and, implicitly, suggesting to her husband's friends that she was out of control, leading a life of her own not defined by domestic regulations and responsibilities. A well-bred woman who took music so seriously constituted a threat to social boundaries.[9]

Virtually without exception, women did indeed cease to perform in public after their marriage. Perhaps they had achieved the main goal of learning the piano in the first place and saw no need to play, perhaps their hands were indeed tied with children, social duties and the like, but it does seem highly probable that public performance would have been seen as some form of threat in a highly male-dominated society. In the literature of Jane Austen and the Brontë sisters the same agenda is apparent, with numerous depictions of women exhibiting their abilities at the piano. They are without exception unmarried, often performing before unmarried men, and it is in such circumstances that the piano invariably makes its appearance in novels of the first half of the nineteenth century.

Such sources have been studied exhaustively, and one example will suffice to portray the importance that pianistic ability held, as portrayed in fiction.[10] Even in Austen's first novel, *Pride and Prejudice* (1797), the word 'instrument' has come to denote the piano, which features prominently throughout. At a party at the home of Sir William Lucas, the 'middle-class' Bennet daughters demonstrate proficiency at this vital accoutrement of respectable breeding. Austen makes it apparent that any pianistic ability cannot begin to outweigh lack of beauty, and that in any case, performances of 'Scotch and Irish airs' are more likely to impress than a rendition of a concerto:

---

9   Richard Leppert, *Music and Image: Domesticity, Ideology and Socio-Cultural Formation in Eighteenth-Century England* (Cambridge: Cambridge University Press, 1988), pp. 39–40.

10   For further sources see Arthur Loesser, *Men, Women and Pianos* (New York and London: Victor Gollancz, 1955), and Patrick Piggott, *The Innocent Diversion: A Study of Music in the life and writings of Jane Austen* (London: Douglas Cleverdon, 1979).

276   NICHOLAS SALWEY

Her [Elizabeth's] performance was pleasing, though by no means capital. After a song or two, and before she could reply to the entreaties that she would sing again, she was eagerly succeeded at the instrument by her sister Mary, who having, in consequence of being the only plain one in the family, worked hard for knowledge and accomplishments, was always impatient for display.

Mary had neither genius or taste; and though vanity had given her application, it had given her likewise a pedantic air and conceited manner, which would have injured a higher degree of excellence than she had reached. Elizabeth, easy and unaffected, had been listened to with much more pleasure, though not playing half so well; and Mary, at the end of a long concerto, was glad to purchase praise and gratitude by Scotch and Irish airs, at the request of her younger sisters.[11]

Literature of the late eighteenth and early nineteenth centuries rarely fails to evoke such a picture of female life. Much rarer are accounts which provide any information regarding the apparently ambivalent relationship between men and music. Two such accounts, written almost a century apart, illustrate the lack of any advance in female liberty whilst also shedding light on the contrasting attitudes to music between the two sexes. John Locke, writing in 1693, speaks of music as being 'so light and airy an amusement', and comments that

a good hand upon some instruments is, by many people, mightily valued. But it wastes so much of a young man's time to gain but a moderate skill in it; and engages often in such odd company, that many think it much better spared: and I have, amongst men of parts and business, so seldom heard anyone commended or esteemed for having an excellency in music, that amongst all those things, that ever came into the list of accomplishments, I think I may give it the last place.[12]

A similarly damning indictment can be found a century later, in 1788, in a 'Letter to a young Man on his too Strong Attachment to Singing and Music':

In the first place, my dear cousin, these pleasures of sound may take you off from the more desirable ones of sense, and make your delight stop at the ear, which should go deeper, and be placed in the understanding; for, whenever a good singer is in company, adieu to all conversation of an improving or intellectual nature. In the second place, it may expose you to company, and that perhaps not the best or most eligible. Hence your business and your other more useful studies may be greatly, if not wholly neglected, and very possibly your health itself be impaired. In the third place, it may tend, which it naturally does, to enervate the mind and make you haunt musical societies, operas, and concerts; and what glory is it to a gentleman, if he were a fine performer, that he can strike a string, touch a key, or sing a song, with the grace and command of an *hired* musician?[13]

'Hired musicians' were often foreign, for music was not an acceptable profession for gentlemen, and this must surely be one of the principal reasons why women pianists were as prominent as they were on the London platforms. The only leading male performers were almost exclusively foreign and from musical

---

11   Jane Austen, *Pride and Prejudice* (London, 1813; Harmondsworth: Penguin Books, 1996), p. 24. Originally entitled 'First Impressions', it was rejected by Cadell, a London publisher, in 1797, and only eventually published in 1813.

12   John Locke, *Some Thoughts on Education*, 1693 (London, 1836), p. 310.

13   [E. Newbery], *Newbery's Familiar Letter Writer* (London, 1788), pp. 78–9.

families. This situation was to remain unchanged throughout the first half of the nineteenth century. One example of a hired musician was Johann Samuel Schroeter, the oft-praised German virtuoso fortepianist, who first appeared in London in 1773 and whose name was still being used as a byword for perfection some 20 years later. His years in England provide a remarkable example of upper-class attitudes to the musical profession. When Schroeter eloped with one of his students, a young lady of 'good family', her father settled a yearly allowance upon him of £500 on condition that he abandon his career as a public performer, thus saving the family from the disgrace of having a professional musician as a family member.[14]

There appears to have been no such disdain meted out to young ladies who were of a standard to perform, and numerous accounts state that this level of attainment was the ultimate goal. Soon after the first public performance on the piano in London in 1767, piano playing had become the most important of the accomplishments, and certainly the most public one. The notion of families spending their evenings being entertained by their daughters performing at the piano is confirmed in the autobiography of Adalbert Gyrowetz, composer-pianist resident in London from *c*.1790 to *c*.1793. He comments that 'the daughters ... are for the most part musical, and are either very proficient in piano playing or singing, and know how to spend the evenings very pleasantly in this way'.[15] By 1814 Allatson Burgh had stretched the social parameters of women pianists to include 'Daughters of Mechanics' and he remarked on music as having 'insinuated itself into the social enjoyments of every rank in Society'.[16] A farmer, in an undated letter, complained that 'Our Daughters, instead of being taught their Duty, and the Business of a Dairy at home, receive their Education at a Boarding School, are taught to dance, to speak French, and to play upon the Harpsicord'.[17]

Studying the piano inevitably featured prominently in women's etiquette manuals and in books about teaching. Erasmus Darwin listed the subjects that should be taught in order of priority, with 'Musick and Dancing' coming second, after 'The Female Character', and before 'Reading, Writing, and Grammar'.[18] Burton described music as 'a polite accomplishment' which 'may be considered as one of the most agreeable arts of pleasing practiced by the fair sex',[19] while for the Rev. John Bennett,

---

14   Charles Neate was to find himself in a similar situation in 1816: indeed the stereotype of the lascivious male music teacher eloping with the younger female pupil may date from this very period. Amongst the London pianists, Schroeter, Clementi, Dussek, Steibelt and Hüllmandel all married their pupils.

15   As quoted and translated by Howard Craw, *A Biography and Thematic Catalogue of the Works of J. L. Dussek (1760–1812)* (Ann Arbor: UMI, 1980), pp. 453–4.

16   Allatson Burgh, *Anecdotes of Music, Historical and Biographical; in a Series of Letters from a Gentleman to his Daughter*, 3 vols (London, 1814), vol. 1, p. v.

17   British Museum, Add. MSS 27, 827, fo. 101, as quoted by Miriam Kramnick in the introduction to Wollstonecraft, *Vindication* (Harmondsworth: Penguin Books, 1985), p. 31.

18   Erasmus Darwin, *A Plan for the Conduct of Female Education in Boarding Schools* (Derby, 1797), p. vii.

19   J. Burton, *Lectures on Female Education and Manners* (London, 1793), p. 97.

278 NICHOLAS SALWEY

> Musick ... is a very desirable acquisition in any woman, who has time and money enough to devote to the purpose, for it requires no inconsiderable portion of *both*. It will enable you to entertain your friends; to confer pleasure upon *others*, must increase your *own* happiness, and it will inspire tranquillity, and harmonize your mind and spirits, in many of these *ruffled* or *lonely* hours, which, in almost every situation, will be your lot.[20]

It would be easy to underestimate the time that budding female pianists might have spent in practising, but many young pianists appear to have devoted a large part of their youth to mastering this instrument. Hannah More quotes 'a person of great eminence' as having remarked to her that

> Suppose your pupil to begin at six years of age and to continue at the average of four hours a-day *only*, Sunday excepted, and thirteen days allowed for travelling annually, till she is eighteen, the state stands thus; 300 days multiplied by four, the number of hours amount to 1200; that number multiplied by twelve, which is the number of years, amounts to 14,400 hours![21]

To judge by the account of one girl's youth, such a calculation does not seem far-fetched. For the 15-year-old Maria Holroyd, genuine enthusiasm is evident, and music making played a prominent part in her life:

> I get up at 8, I walk from 9 to 10; we then breakfast; about 11, I play on the Harpsichord or I draw. 1, I translate, and, 2, walk out again, 3, I generally read, and, 4, we go to dine, after Dinner we play at Backgammon; we drink Tea at 7, and I work or play on the Piano till 10, when we have our little bit of Supper and, 11, we go to Bed.[22]

Later she describes her pleasure at the arrival of a certain Sir G. Webster, who 'has brought a Fidler (who attends upon his lady), which is very agreeable, as he accompanies one on the Pianoforte every evening'.[23]

The evidence is clear that so many hours spent practising were deemed to be worthwhile if they were 'to increase a young lady's chance of a prize in the matrimonial lottery'.[24] Mary Bennet (in *Pride and Prejudice*) clearly felt obliged to try to excel at the piano on account of her plain looks; as the Edgeworths observed, 'Next to beauty, they [accomplishments] are the best tickets of admission into society'.[25] In Austen's *Emma*, Miss Fairfax's apparent success with Mr Churchill even induces the heroine to do some practice: 'She did unfeignedly and unequivocally regret the inferiority of her own playing and singing. She did

---

20 Rev. John Bennett, *Letters to a Young Lady, on a variety of useful and interesting subjects*, 2 vols (Warrington, 1789), vol. 1, p. 234.

21 Hannah More, *Strictures on the Modern System of Female Education*, 2 vols (London, 1799), vol. 1, p. 81.

22 *The Girlhood of Maria Josepha Holroyd [Lady Stanley of Alderley]. Recorded in Letters of a Hundred Years Ago: From 1776 to 1796*, ed. J. H. Adeane (London: Longmans, Green, 1896), p. 14.

23 Ibid., p. 23.

24 Maria and Richard Lovell Edgeworth, *Practical Education*, 2 vols (London, 1798), vol. 2, p. 522.

25 Ibid., vol. 2, p. 525.

most heartily grieve over the idleness of her childhood and sat down and practiced vigorously an hour and a half.'[26] That the skills acquired were almost certain to be neglected after marriage is never an issue:

> Out of the prodigious number of young women who learn music and drawing, for instance, how many are there, who ... after they have the choice of their own amusements, continue to practise these accomplishments for the pure pleasure of the occupation? As soon as a young lady is married, does not she frequently discover, that 'she really has not *leisure* to cultivate talents which take up so much time.' Does not she complain of the labour of practising four or five hours a day to keep up her musical character? What motive has she for perseverance; she is, perhaps, already tired of playing to all her acquaintance. She may really take pleasure in hearing good music; but her own performance will not then please her ear so much as that of many others. She will prefer the more indolent pleasure of hearing the best music that can be heard for money at public concerts. She will then of course leave off playing, but continue very fond of music. How often is the labour of years thus lost for ever![27]

Even 50 years later, in *Vanity Fair* (1847–48), Thackeray expressed cynicism both at the expense of learning and at the reasons for learning in the first place: 'What causes them to labour at pianoforte sonatas, and to learn four songs from a fashionable master at a guinea a lesson, and to play the harp if they have handsome arms and neat elbows ... but that they may bring down some "desirable" young man with those killing bows and arrows of theirs?'[28] One (seemingly hypothetical) mother summoned up by the Edgeworths to prove their points described how

> I would give anything to have my daughter play better than anyone in England. What a distinction! She would be immediately taken notice of in all companies! She might get into the first circles in London! She would want neither beauty nor fortune to recommend her! She would be a match for any man, who has any taste for music! And music is universally admired, even by those who have the misfortune to have no taste for it.[29]

It is impossible to assess the standard of the teachers, but there is little reason to assume that women were well taught. Charles Dibdin relates with horror how 'The regular progression of rules ... are totally neglected, and Miss, the very first day, sits down to play abstruse passages out of HAYDN and PLEYEL. ... Passages, and not music then, are what young ladies are now taught.'[30] Later he refers to 'a lady of fashion' who 'in short ... could play arpegeos [*sic*] and consecutive octaves, with the right hand by wholesale, but not one single favourite air:– she could not even count the time of it'.[31] Joel Collier claimed to be able 'to give any young lady of tolerable parts, a *shake* in two lessons, and a *swell* in three'.[32]

---

26   Jane Austen, *Emma* (London, 1816; Harmondsworth: Penguin Books, 1994), p. 174.
27   Edgeworth, *Practical Education*, vol. 2, pp. 523–4.
28   William Thackeray, *Vanity Fair* (London, 1847–48; Harmondsworth: Penguin Books, 1985), pp. 57–8.
29   As quoted by Edgeworth, *Practical Education*, vol. 2, pp. 521–2.
30   Charles Dibdin, *A Letter on Musical Education* (London, 1791), pp. 9–10.
31   Ibid., p. 18.
32   Joel Collier, *Musical Travels through England* (London, 1775) , p. 83.

280 NICHOLAS SALWEY

Peripatetic teachers may well have had to teach several subjects and several instruments: the accounts of a Hertfordshire music-master, Thomas Green, 'record that in addition to his private pupils he taught music and drawing to pupils at four boys' schools and five girls' schools during his career from 1740 to 1790'.[33]

Two accounts by leading musicians from the first half of the nineteenth century shed some light on the selecting of teachers and the standard of the pupils they might encounter. The 22-year-old George Smart described his audition to teach music at a school in London in 1798:

> The first question put to me was: 'Can you play at sight?' I boldly answered 'Yes.' He then placed before me a very difficult sonata, and put his ear close to the pianoforte. I saw at once that the sonata was too much for me, but I dashed at it and rattled over the right and wrong notes. Mr. Twiss expressed his perfect satisfaction and reported to Mrs. Cameron that I must be a very capable teacher.[34]

The young Samuel Wesley started teaching at a London school in 1784, and appears to have had nothing positive to say about the experience, commenting that 'the profits are inadequate to the slavery' and referring to the 'drudgery of more dunces assaulting my ear … this contemptible, frivolous work of hammering sounds into blockheads'.[35]

Despite their own accomplishments, there is little evidence of talented female pianists making a living solely from teaching the piano. The one notable exception is Therese Jansen, who married the famous engraver Gaetano Bartolozzi in 1795. As a teacher she 'was eminently successful; so much so, indeed, that she and her brother … realized rather more than two thousand pounds per annum'.[36] A pupil of Clementi, she was the dedicatee of Dussek's three sonatas for piano and violin, op. 13 (1793), the Grand Sonata for pianoforte, op. 43 (1800), Clementi's three piano sonatas, op. 33 (1794), and Haydn's last three piano sonatas, Hob. XVI: 50–52 (1794), and piano trios, Hob. XV: 27–9. She is one of only three women pianists in Haydn's list of pianists in London from the First London Notebook (1791–92), but her only recorded performance during this period, of a Haydn sonata at the Anacreontic Society, occurred before Haydn's arrival in London.[37]

The first woman pianist to make her mark in London was Elizabeth Weichsel, whose success at the piano has tended to be all but eclipsed by her renown as a singer following her marriage in 1783 to her singing teacher, James Billington. Sainsbury's *Dictionary* is rare in giving credit for her pianistic abilities:

---

33 Gillian Sheldrick, ed., 'The accounts of Thomas Green, music teacher and tuner of musical instruments, 1742–90', *Hertfordshire Record Society*, 8 (1992), Appendix 3.

34 H. Bertram Cox and C. L. E. Cox, *Leaves from the Journals of Sir George Smart* (London: Longmans, Green, 1907), p. 6.

35 James T. Lightwood, *Samuel Wesley, Musician: The Story of his Life* (London, 1937; New York: Benjamin Blow, 1972), pp. 115 and 117.

36 *Memoirs of the Life, Public and Private Adventures of Madame Vestris* (London, 1839), pp. 3–4.

37 She also performed twice in 1806. See Salwey, 'The Piano in London Concert Life', p. 86, for further details.

WOMEN PIANISTS IN LATE 18TH-CENTURY LONDON

This celebrated singer, musician, and piano-forte player was ... trained to music at the earliest possible age, and even performed on the piano-forte and violin ... at the Haymarket Theatre, at six years old ... Her first master was Schroeter, an excellent teacher of the piano-forte, and her father superintended her musical education with a degree of severity that could be scarcely justified even by the proficiency of the pupil. Few persons have attained the perfection that Miss Weichsell reached upon this instrument.[38]

Burney says of her that 'after distinguishing herself in early childhood as a neat and expressive performer on the piano-forte, [she] appeared all at once, in 1786, as a sweet and captivating singer'.[39] One of the only other contemporary accounts of her piano playing occurs in the scurrilous *Memoirs of Mrs Billington* by James Ridgway, which caused a considerable stir when published in 1792 – by which time she had forsaken the piano for a career as a singer:

It may be depended upon as a fact, that at twelve years of age, when her fingers were so short that she could hardly extend her hand, to four notes of the piano forte, she was then desirous to grasp large things, by attempting Octaves, or EIGHTHS; the utmost extent of performance, with the right or left hand and she had always a remarkable fine shake when her father was performing with her, as she is certainly indebted to him, for every *perfection*, she now has, in her performance upon the *Piano Forte*.[40]

Her own opinion of her talents is memorably cited in a letter to her mother in 1784: 'it would give you great pleasure, I make no doubt, for you to hear me applauded very near <u>three</u> minutes after I am off the stage, though it may seem as if I wanted to praise myself; but I assure [you] I am counted a very pretty actress, and every body that has heard me play on the pianoforte, say I am the greatest player in the world.'[41] Her successes as a pianist on the London stage are without parallel for the time; she performed only twice on the harpsichord, but gave the first recorded public performance on a grand piano in 1781, performed a concerto on the piano at the age of seven, and appeared in 13 concerto performances in 1778 at the age of 11, including 10 in which she was performing exclusively for the Oratorio Series at Covent Garden. She played a concerto of her own composition at the age of 15, and had published two sets of sonatas before she was 12; and in 1792 Goulding published her *Three Sonatas for Violin and Pianoforte*, one of which was performed in a Professional Concert of that year by William Dance and

---

38 [John Sainsbury], *A Dictionary of Musicians*, 2 vols (London, 1824), vol. 1, pp. 87–8.

39 Burney, *History*, vol. 4, p. 681.

40 [James Ridgway], *Memoirs of Mrs Billington, from her birth* ... (London, 1792), pp. 33–4. The private lives of musicians had now become fair game for the gossip-mongers: 'It is now generally agreed that public performers, whose morals are flagitious, are the proper objects of censure' (p. xv). The author (also the publisher) goes so far as to make claim of rape: 'Some of my readers may object to the last expression, yet the truth is, her father was detected in attempting an intercourse with his musical offspring, before she could *possibly*, from her tender years, have had any tendency to vice' (pp. 3–4). Haydn remarked that 'It is said that her character is the worst sort, but that she is a great genius, and all the women hate her because she is so beautiful. N.B. She is said, however, to have written the most scandalous letters, containing accounts of her amours, to her mother'; H. C. Robbins Landon, *Haydn in England 1791–1795*, Haydn Chronicle and Works, vol. 3 (London: Thames & Hudson, 1976), p. 123.

41 Ridgway, *Memoirs*, p. 61.

282   NICHOLAS SALWEY

William Cramer. As was the norm, her appearances as a pianist ceased in the year of her marriage, at the age of 16.[42] Nevertheless she had been, if briefly, the most prominent pianist performing publicly in London. A measure of her success may be deduced by the names of the only other two pianists to have performed exclusively for the Oratorio Series at Covent Garden; Clementi in 1790, and Dussek in 1796–99. Her compositions, which must presumably reflect her own pianistic abilities, reveal a considerable proficiency.

During the 1780s, and indeed through to the end of the century, women pianists played an increasingly significant role on London's concert platforms. While none attained the prominence gained by Elizabeth Weichsel, names such as Maria F. Parke, Jane Mary Guest, Maria Hester Reynolds and Cecilia Maria Barthélemon must have become familiar to the concert-going public. Moreover, a large number of the performances by males are one-off appearances, while the above names clearly enjoyed considerable popularity and acclaim. Reynolds and Guest performed for the Hanover Square Concert Series, while Parke played for the Oratorio Series at Drury Lane and for the Salomon Concerts and the Professional Concerts at Hanover Square.[43] Miss Guest's abilities are confirmed by Burney who placed her alongside Clementi and Cramer.[44] Born in 1762, the daughter of a tailor, and brought up in Bath, she studied with Rauzzini, Sacchini and Thomas Linley before moving to London to study with J. C. Bach.[45] It is from these early years that Fanny Burney's description (1780) of her playing dates, which she compares with that of her own sister Esther, who was listed as a pianist by Haydn, and was the wife of another leading pianist, Charles Rousseau Burney:

> Miss Guest is very young, but far from handsome; she is, however, obliging, humble, unassuming, and pleasing ... She began with playing the third of Eichner, and I wished she had begun with something else, for I have so often heard our dear Etty in this, that I was quite spoiled for Miss Guest, or, I firmly believe, for anybody; because in Eichner, as in Bach of Berlin, Echard and Boccherini, Etty plays as if inspired, and in taste, expression, delicacy and feeling, leaves nothing to wish. Miss Guest has a very strong hand, and is indeed a very fine player – so fine a one as to make me think of Etty while she plays, though always, and in all particulars, to this poor girl's disadvantage. She next played the second of Clementi, which seemed to want nothing but a strong hand [op. 2 no. 2?], and therefore I was full as well content with the player as with the music, but not enchanted with either.[46]

---

42   See Salwey, 'The Piano in London Concert Life', p. 86, for details of a piano performance of hers in 1806.

43   Miss Reynolds and Elisabetta de Gambarini are exceptional throughout the entire 50-year period in appearing both before and after marriage. As Mrs Park (née Reynolds), the former played a sonata and concerto at her own benefit concert in 1791, some seven years after her previous appearance.

44   Burney, *History*, vol. 4, p. 682: 'Keyed-instruments are perhaps nowhere on the globe better played in every different style, than at present in this country, by Burney, Clementi, Cramer jun., Miss Guest, Hulmandel, the two Wesleys, and many others, not only professors but dilettanti, who though not public performers, one hears with great pleasure in private.'

45   [Sainsbury], *A Dictionary of Musicians*, vol. 2, p. 161.

46   Fanny Burney, *Diary & Letters of Madame d'Arblay (1778–1840) as edited by her niece*

WOMEN PIANISTS IN LATE 18TH-CENTURY LONDON   283

Fanny Burney displays a clear bias in favour of her sister; but the young Miss Guest's abilities must have been pronounced, for she was to teach one of the Thrale daughters, whose other music teachers included Burney himself.[47] Miss Guest's first London performance occurred in April 1779 at a benefit concert for the oboist Johann Fischer. Two years later, at her own benefit concert at the Hanover Square Rooms in July 1781, she performed a sonata and a concerto in a concert that saw her appearing alongside the singer Tenducci as well as a concerto performance by Salomon. In 1783 she was the most prominent pianist at the Hanover Square concert series, where she was featured five times, and twice more in benefit concerts at the same venue, performing Schroeter's concerto, op. 5 no. 6 at her own benefit and also accompanying the leading violinist Pieltain in a sonata by Boccherini. The following year she attempted to start her own concert series at the Tottenham Street Rooms, performing a concerto at the first concert, and a Handel concerto and a sonata of her own at the third (and last) concert later that year. This was presumably the last and the only unaccompanied sonata of her six sonatas, op. 1 published in London that year, and in Paris and Berlin in 1784 and 1785. These are dedicated to Queen Charlotte (with whom the young Miss Guest had clearly already found favour), and the subscription list includes some 500 names, among them prominent members of the aristocracy and many of London's leading musicians.

This performance appears to have been her last in London, and she married in 1789. As Mrs Miles, she taught the piano and appeared in Rauzzini's concerts in Bath during the 1790s,[48] and in 1804 and 1806 she was appointed teacher to the young Princesses Amalie and Charlotte. In Sainsbury's *Dictionary* she is praised for the concertos she wrote for her performance in Bath, and indeed to find her mentioned therein is surprising in view of her absence from London's platforms.[49] A very brief space of time, a mere three years, was enough to gain a sufficient reputation for her to be described by Papendiek as 'the renowned pianist' or by William Parke as 'the admirable piano-forte player, Miss Guest, afterwards Mrs Miles', who 'played in a similar way [to Schroeter]'. She is praised in the *European Magazine* in 1784 for her 'fleetness and facility of finger, expression of touch, diversity of grace, and general mastery upon the instrument [which]

Charlotte Barrett, with preface and notes by Austin Dobson, 6 vols (London: Macmillan & Co., 1904), vol. 1, pp. 358–9.

47   Mrs Thrale wrote on 17 September 1780 that 'Mr Johnson praises Hester's diligence at her Classical Studies ... She has made vast Improvements too under Miss Guest & Piozzi; & Dr Burney is jealous of that I see', *Thraliana*, ed. Katherine Balderston, 2 vols (Oxford: Clarendon Press, 1942; 2nd corrected edition, 1951), vol. 1, p. 455.

48   See Jenny Burchell, *Polite or Commercial Concerts? Concert Management and Orchestral Repertoire in Edinburgh, Bath, Oxford, Manchester, and Newcastle, 1730–1799* (New York: Garland, 1996), p. 160.

49   'Her manuscript concertos, which she reserved for her own performance exclusively at the Bath concerts, under the direction of Rauzzini, have given such proof of genius in composition, that we lament they should remain unknown to the lovers of music', [Sainsbury], *A Dictionary of Musicians*, vol. 2, p. 161.

is without rivalship, and thrills through the hearts of all who hear her'.[50] Most remarkable is the fact that a tailor's daughter from Bath, with no apparent musical connections (a feature that distinguishes her from the majority of women pianists), achieved such acclaim and the public recognition of teaching the young princesses. This is remarked upon in a review of her sonatas which describes it as the 'production of a wonderful female performer on the harpsichord, whose connections, from her extraordinary practical merit, are not only high, but uncommonly extensive', referring to the 'lustre and magnitude' of the subscription list.[51]

One of Mary Guest's last public performances in London was at the benefit concert for Maria Hester Reynolds on 29 April 1783, at which the two pianists played a duet. Notably, neither of these two artists had made early appearances as child prodigies; both were to succeed in establishing a considerable reputation through performance and composition. Reynolds, born in 1760, had made her first public appearance in 1782 in the Hanover Square concert series with a concerto on the harpsichord alongside concertos by Wilhelm Cramer (violin) and Johann Fischer (oboe). Her brief performing career was cut short by her marriage in April 1787 to the engraver and writer Thomas Park.[52] She appeared on only three other occasions, playing a Clementi duet in April 1783 with the young Maria F. Parke, a concerto performance at her own benefit concert at Willis's Rooms in March 1784, and her solo performance as Mrs Park ('late Reynolds') in May 1791. Maria Hester Reynolds was to gain much greater renown as a teacher (the Duchess of Devonshire was among her pupils) and as a composer.

The similarity of the two names, Miss Maria F. Parke and Mrs Maria Hester Park (née Reynolds), has led to considerable confusion.[53] Maria Parke was the daughter of the oboist John Parke, and therefore also the niece of the oboist and composer, William Parke. Born in 1772 or 1773, she was over 40 years of age at the time of her marriage in 1815, and in the previous years she had managed to forge a considerable career first as a pianist and later as a singer. As was almost certainly the case with Elizabeth Weichsel, her entrance onto London's concert

---

50 *European Magazine*, July 1784, pp. 6–7.

51 Ibid., p. 6.

52 Thomas Park's numerous publications include *Nugae Modernae: Morning Thoughts and Midnight Musings* (London, 1818) in which his devotion to his wife is the subject of three poems, pp. 78 and 95–7. Among the subscribers for the book were Mrs Miles, Thomas Haigh and William Crotch.

53 The two identities are confused in *New Grove*, 1st edn (London, 1980), and, based on that source, in Salwey and McVeigh, 'The Piano and Harpsichord in London's Concert Life', where, in the index on p. 71, Mrs Park (née Reynolds) should read Mrs Maria Hester Park (née Reynolds), and Miss Maria Hester Parke should read Miss Maria F. Parke. The correct distinction was made in the relevant articles by Olive Baldwin and Thelma Wilson in *The New Grove Dictionary of Women Composers*, ed. Julie Anne Sadie and Rhian Samuel (London: Macmillan, 1994), pp. 361–2. More recently, Thomas Tolley has clarified the situation with his article 'Haydn, the engraver Thomas Park, and Maria Hester Park's "little Sonat"', *Music & Letters*, 82 (2001), 421–31. As Tolley points out (p. 427 n. 38), 'Unfortunately these authors [Baldwin and Wilson] mar the latter entry by following earlier authorities (such as Landon, Bartha, Fiske in *The New Grove*) in assuming that the "Mistris Parck" to whom Haydn presented a sonata in October 1794 was John Parke's daughter (Miss Maria [F.] Parke) rather than Mrs (Maria Hester) Park.'

platforms was greatly facilitated by her musical relatives; she made her first appearance at the age of eight at her father's benefit concert in April 1781 performing a 'favourite' concerto of Schroeter's, very likely the same concerto (op. 5 no. 6) that she played at her father's benefit at the same venue and in the same month of the following year. Four years later, in 1785, she performed this work at the Oratorio Series at Drury Lane (as the only pianist to perform there that year), while her performance of a 'favourite' sonata of Clementi's in 1784 and a new unpublished sonata of his in April 1785 might well indicate that she took lessons from him. Certainly, the latter occasion was likely to have been the first public performance of one of Clementi's Sonatas op. 13, which were registered at Stationers' Hall on 26 May 1785.

Miss Parke was now in her early teens and this event may neatly mark her coming of age as a performer. She appeared three times during the following year, as the only pianist to perform at Salomon's Concert Series at the Hanover Square Rooms, and most notably performing a Mozart concerto in April 1786, while during the years from 1788 to 1791 she appeared at the Professional Concerts alongside such prestigious names as Clementi, Cramer and Dance. The 1790s saw the number of her appearances at the piano slowly declining as her career as a singer increased, and after 1794 she appeared at the piano only at her own benefit concerts, at which her public profile was foremost as a singer. At her benefit concert in 1796 Miss Parke performed a 'new' sonata of her own, advertised as still being in manuscript, presumably one of the *Three Grand Sonatas*, op. 1 that were published in 1799, one of which was also presumably the unspecified sonata she played at her benefit that year.

It is particularly notable that she ceased to play concertos after 1790: during the years from 1781 to 1790 she performed a total of nine concertos and six sonatas, while during the 1790s she performed just six sonatas, and there is no evidence of her playing concertos in the years thereafter. Her late marriage may have enabled her to be visible in public as both a singer and a pianist, but it would seem that her vocal career was responsible for causing her to eschew the more public and virtuosic nature of the concerto genre at a time when concerto performances were significantly more common than sonata performances.[54] Maria Parke seems to have appeared in public on the piano for the last time in 1798; she may have performed sonatas after 1800, but she is not listed at all in Ellsworth's survey of piano concerto performances in the first half of the nineteenth century.[55] Curiously, programme information shows her to have performed a wider range of repertoire than any other pianist of the time, with concertos by Schroeter, Mozart and Krumpholtz, and sonatas by Clementi, Pleyel and herself. Despite her greater renown as a singer, she was, with nine performances, the most prominent

---

54 During the 1790s there were a total of 170 concerto performances, as compared with 66 sonata performances.

55 Therese Marie Ellsworth, *The Piano Concerto in London Concert Life between 1801 and 1850* (Ann Arbor: UMI, 1992).

286 NICHOLAS SALWEY

pianist on the London stage during the 1790s excepting only the likes of Clementi, Dussek, Cramer and Field.

Cecilia Maria Barthélemon was another pianist whose musical pedigree assured her an easy passage onto London's concert platforms. Her father, François-Hippolyte, was a composer as well as being one of London's foremost violinists for over four decades, leading the orchestra variously during this time at Covent Garden, Drury Lane, the King's Theatre, Marybone and Vauxhall Gardens, and elsewhere. Her mother, Mary Young, was a leading soprano of the time, who performed before Marie-Antoinette in Paris and was accompanied at the piano by Haydn in 1792. A pupil of Schroeter's, Miss Barthélemon made her debut performing a concerto (accompanied by her father on the viola d'amore) at her parents' benefit concert in 1782 when only 12 years old, and participated in similar events in 1783, 1785, 1786 and 1787. She made only one other public appearance as a pianist, at a benefit for a 'gentleman of rank' in 1788. It is perhaps tempting but would be unwise to dismiss her merely as a musically able scion of her parents, dependent upon them for performing engagements. Her career was most likely to have been cut short as her prowess as a singer increased, as well as by two marriages, but her few performances demonstrate a considerable variety of repertoire – including concertos by Schroeter, Kozeluch and Mederitsch, and sonatas by Clementi – and her own compositions demonstrate very considerable ability. One account claims that she received some instruction from Haydn himself,[56] to whom she dedicated her most accomplished composition, the Sonata in G major, op. 3 (1794). Haydn includes her twice in his list of musicians in London (1792), both as a singer and as a pianist, and she appears in Doane's *Directory* (1794) as a soprano, harp-player, and pianist.[57]

Of the pianists who performed in public in the 1790s particularly, a very significant number are female. While none of them comes close to the prominence of Weichsel, whose 18 appearances in 1777–78 account for over half of the piano performances during these years (and can only be matched by Dussek in the entire 50-year period), nevertheless over a quarter of the pianists appearing in the 1790s were female, and the works of Dussek and Cramer feature prominently amongst the music they performed. Indeed the final concert of this period is of a Dussek concerto played by a young blind lady. Numerous 'lesser' figures also appeared throughout the decade, such as Miss Diot, Miss Macarthur, Eliza Abrams, Dussek's wife Sophia and his sister Veronika Cianchettini, yet they performed as

---

56 'In the course of the years 1791 and 1792, the great Haydn, who had been engaged by Salomon to compose and direct his concerts at the Hanover Square Rooms, spent much of his time with the Barthelemons at their retreat in Vauxhall, and, among other occupations, gave music lessons to the daughter of the house'; Charles Higham, *Francis Barthelemon* (London, 1896), p. 11. See also Landon, *Haydn in England*, p. 169, for Cecilia's own accounts of Haydn's visits to the house.

57 The copy of Schroeter's concerto op. 5 no. 6 in the Bodleian Library, Oxford includes a handwritten annotation at the top of the score by C. M. Barthélemon: 'I had the honour of playing *this* Concerto to H.R.H. the Prince of Wales, at the Pavilion at *Brighton*, when my beloved Parents attended His R.H's *Concerts 1796*' (Mus. 131 c.58). Joseph Doane, *A Musical Directory for the year 1794* (London: R. H. Westley, 1794; repr. London: Royal College of Music, 1993).

WOMEN PIANISTS IN LATE 18TH-CENTURY LONDON   287

often as any excepting those from the exclusively male preserve of the so-called London Pianoforte School. Miss Diot is not generally mentioned in contemporary accounts, but to judge from her six performances in 1796–97 she must have displayed considerable talent. This is evident in a review of her performance of one of Cramer's concertos on 14 March 1796: 'It is with true satisfaction we do justice to the great talents of a Pupil of the eminent Composer Mr. CRAMER, Mademoiselle DIOT, who performed last Monday, with an infinite exactness, a Concerto upon the Piano Forte, at the Concert of the Opera.'[58] Her London debut occurred for the opening of the new Pantheon in Oxford Street, and her other appearances were for the Opera concert series at the King's Theatre Room, at which Bertini was the only other pianist to appear that year, and at which Steibelt alone performed in 1797. On four occasions she performed a concerto by Dussek, as well as one by Cramer, and she joined John Braham at his benefit in a Clementi duet on one piano. She appears advertised as both Madame and Mademoiselle, and no further details are evident, though it seems likely that she may have been a relative of Francis Diot, listed in Doane's *Directory* as being a resident of Exeter, a Master of Music and Dance, and a member of the New Musical Fund.

Miss Macarthur is another whose fleeting presence on the concert platforms does not appear to indicate any lack of talent. A slightly ambivalent review comments that 'A Miss McARTHUR, who came from the East Indes, played a Concerto on the Piano Forte, in a manner highly creditable to her talents'.[59] Her eight appearances during 1795–97 included works by Dussek and Cramer, but more pertinently, she and Dussek were the only pianists to perform for the Oratorio Series at Covent Garden. Miss Eliza Abrams is referred to in Sainsbury's *Dictionary* as a 'celebrated singer and composer of songs', and there are no accounts that detail her abilities as a pianist, but in the annual benefit concert for the Abrams sisters her performances (from 1787 to 1796) played a prominent role. These encompassed a wide repertoire, including concertos by Klöffler, Vanhal, Attwood and Janiewicz, and a sonata by Dussek, providing further proof of the much greater variety of repertoire performed by women of the time than by men.

Dussek's wife, sister and nephew all played a part in London's concert life during the 1790s. Sophia Corri had made her debut as a pianist in Edinburgh at the age of four, and performed publicly twice in London before her marriage to Dussek on 31 August 1792. When she was 16 years old, Dussek had joined her in a duet at her benefit concert in June 1791 and had himself played a concerto, and in the following March she played a concerto of his at her benefit concert. In both concerts she also appeared as a singer, and she was to follow the established path by relinquishing the piano after her marriage, although she resumed public appearances as a pianist following her husband's abrupt departure for the continent in 1799. She played a leading role as a singer throughout the 1790s, but did not appear again in public as a pianist until 1800. She performed at the Oratorio Series

---

58   *True Briton*, 15 Mar. 1796.
59   *True Briton*, 5 Mar. 1796.

in March 1800 on the harp accompanied by her singing teacher at the piano; this was the vocal performer, violin virtuoso and composer Giovanni Battista Cimador. Her three solo performances as a pianist took place later in 1800 at her own benefit concert, and at the only two concert series that were held that year, the Oratorio Series and those at Willis's Room. That she appeared again as a pianist so rapidly would imply that she may have been fulfilling contractual obligations for her absent husband. For the Oratorio series she played her husband's hugely successful 'Military' concerto, on an instrument advertised as a 'new patent Grand pianoforte by Corri and Dussek, with tambourine and triangle'. She performed a concerto on only one other occasion, playing a work of Cramer's at her benefit concert in 1814.

Dussek's sister Veronika Cianchettini doubtless hoped to make a career in London in the wake of her brother's success. She had arrived in London by 1799, in which year she gave birth there to her son Pio. She made her debut at her own benefit concert in June 1800, performing Dussek's 'Military' concerto as well as a sonata of her own composition, likely to be her Sonata in F major (with variations on 'Adeste Fideles') published in London in the same year. While she performed concertos at her own benefit concerts (in 1801, 1804 and 1807), her son achieved some fame as a prodigy, making his debut at the age of five, and performing a concerto of his own at the age of eight.[60]

The French Revolution saw a considerable exodus of musicians fleeing across the Channel. Doane's *Directory* of 1794 includes a number of French musicians, amongst whom Mesdames Ducrest, de Sisley and Delaval all appear listed as sopranos. Similar customs to those in England may have prevailed in France, as all three appeared as pianists if only briefly, preferring instead to establish their reputations as singers, or in the case of Delaval as a harpist. Madame La Marquise Ducrest was 'an unfortunate emigrant, the wife of a man of rank', who had met his death at the guillotine: according to *The Sun* she deserved 'public attention, as well for her talents as her misfortunes'.[61] She appeared only once as a pianist, performing a Dussek sonata at her benefit concert in May 1793, but she sang frequently at the Concert of Ancient Music and at the Salomon concerts. She and Dussek were presumably acquainted, Dussek having dedicated his Concerto in E flat, op. 3, C33 (1787), during his Paris years, to her husband the Marquis Ducrest. Madame de Sisley, whose husband had perished on the first day of the French Revolution, 14 July 1789, made her debut singing at the final Salomon concert of 1791: 'Salomon and Haydn were both warm-hearted and generous men, and it is typical that they launched her at their final concert.'[62] The following year, at her own benefit concert for which Salomon led the orchestra, she performed a piano sonata of her own composition, in addition to singing several arias.

---

60 His Two Fantasias, composed at the age of seven, were dedicated to the Prince of Wales; on the frontispiece (London, 1807) he is even described as 'Mozart Britannicus', but neither his career as a performer nor his compositions begin to justify such comparisons.
61 *The Sun*, 18 Feb. 1794, as quoted by Landon, *Haydn in England*, p. 236.
62 Ibid., p. 85.

Madame Delaval appears in Doane's *Directory* as a pianist and harpist, and in the former capacity made her debut at a Professional Concert in 1791, playing a duet for piano and violin with Agathe-Elisabeth-Henriette L'Arrivée.[63] The two artists performed again at Delaval's benefit concert in 1794, in a Concertante for piano and harp, the latter played by L'Arrivée. Delaval's two solo appearances as a pianist occurred at her own benefit concerts in 1792 and 1796, and she was to achieve true success as a harpist, replacing an indisposed Madame Krumpholtz (her teacher) for the Second Salomon Concert of 1792, having earned considerable praise for her performance at the First Concert the previous week.

Difficult as it is to assess the standard of women pianists, it is no less difficult to gauge the quality of their compositions. With the majority of keyboard works being conceived for the composer's own performance, the incentive to compose after marriage would have been slight. Milligan has calculated that of the concertos for all instruments performed during the 1790s, only some 10 per cent were ever played by anyone other than their composer, and the same situation is clearly visible with regard to sonata performances.[64] The incentive for women to publish concertos therefore was very slight indeed, and if publication and the likelihood of reasonable sales was the aim then the domestic market was incomparably more favourable than that of the public market. The youthful and occasional sonata publications by the women pianists may not rank alongside those of the leading members of the London Pianoforte School but they certainly compare alongside those of their native male counterparts. The works of Jane Guest or Maria Parke show no lack of technical prowess and are as accomplished as those of such contemporaries as Haigh, Mazzinghi or Attwood.

To judge both from performance data and from references in contemporary literature, it is unfair to perpetuate the myth of the female amateur. Even if piano playing was widely perceived merely as a necessary 'accomplishment' and an integral part of the education of 'ladies', there were clearly many who excelled and who were held in high esteem by the leading virtuosi of the time, as witness the array of virtuosic keyboard works dedicated to Therese Jansen by Clementi, Dussek and Haydn. An analysis of the number of performances during this period reveals that women pianists were rarely outshone by their male counterparts, and when this did occur it can be largely explained by the exclusive use of one of the leading foreign male pianists for a particular concert series. If the leading members of the London Pianoforte School are excluded – such as Clementi, Dussek, Cramer and Steibelt – one finds that women pianists are as prominent as the English male pianists, and this is all the more marked for the brevity of their careers, these being cut short by marriage. Amongst them are many who may well

---

63 See *Morning Chronicle*, 15 Mar. 1791 for a review of L'Arrivée's performance. The sonata is likely to have been one of Madame Delaval's 'Three Sonatas for the Harp or Piano Forte, with an Accompaniment for the Violin, op. 1', dedicated to the Countess of Shaftesbury, published by Birchall in 1790.

64 See Thomas Milligan, *The Concerto and London's Musical Culture in the Late Eighteenth Century* (Ann Arbor: UMI, 1983).

have deserved greater praise than it was customary to give to women; and who, in a less restrictive society, might have continued to play to considerable acclaim for many years.

Index

Abel, Carl Friedrich 8, 12, 100–1, 103, 108, 169, 175, 176
Abrams, Eliza 286, 287
Academy of Ancient Music 7
Addison, Joseph 85, 216, 265
Alday, Paul 107, 250, 256
Aldrich, Henry 40
amateur musicians 4
Anacreontic Society 4, 148, 173–4, 193, 280
Anne, Queen 200, 208
applause 3
Applewaite, Mr 156
aqua-concerts 28
Arden, Richard Pepper 156
aristocracy and music 78
Arne, Cecilia (née Young) 219, 220, 221, 225, 230
Arne, Thomas 12, 159, 219, 220, 221, 223, 229, 230, 236
Arnold, John 145
Arnold, Samuel 96, 104–5
Artaria 111
artists, portrait 275
Ashley, John 9, 13
assembly rooms 26–7, 29, 30, 31, 32
Astrop 22
Atkins, Thomas 205
Atterbury, Luffman 151
Austen, Jane 275–6, 278–9
Avison, Charles 13, 69, 70
    Durham concerts and 59, 61–3, 64, 66, 70
    music publication 97, 98, 107
    Newcastle concerts and 10, 56, 58, 59, 61, 66, 67, 70
Awbery, John 122–5, 127, 129
Aylward, Theodore 149

Bach, Carl Philipp Emanuel 110, 111
Bach, Johann Christian 8, 12, 101, 103, 107–8, 110, 112, 273
Banister, John 1, 36

Barber, Joseph 97
Barbican (London) 9
Barnard, Lord 60, 69
Barrett, Mr 149
Barthélemon, Cecilia Maria 282, 286
Barthélemon, François-Hippolyte 103, 108, 175, 179, 286
Bartleman, James 160
Bartolozzi, Gaetano 280
Bath 13, 14, 22, 32–3, 38
    assembly rooms 26–7, 30, 31, 32
    catch/glee clubs 146, 148, 149, 150, 151, 153, 154, 155, 156
    churches and chapels 29–30
    concerts in 8, 10
    pleasure gardens 27, 30, 32
    promenades 28
    spa 28, 30
beau monde
    London 8, 71–2, 74–5, 77–81
        politics of cultural quarrels 81–5
        towards modernity 85–9
    Paris 72, 74–5, 78
Beckwith, John 133
Belfast 231, 233, 237, 240–1
benefit concerts 8, 166, 255, 256
Bennett, G. V. 37
Bennett, John 277–8
Bever, Thomas 121, 137
Beverley, Music Room 21
Biddlecomb, William 120
Billington, Elizabeth (née Weichsel) 254–5, 280–2, 284, 286; *see also* Weichsel, Elizabeth
Birmingham 25, 32
    festival 32
    music societies 25
    pleasure gardens 27
Bisse, Thomas 31, 40
Blake, Benjamin 11, 168, 173
Bland, John 11, 193
Blenkinsop, Peter 69
Blundell, James 179

291

INDEX

boats, music on 28
Boccherini, Luigi 193
Boden, Anthony 40
Bodleian Library (Oxford) 249
Bologne, Joseph (Chevalier de Saint-
    Georges) 169
Bond, Mr 46, 49
Borghi, Luigi 108, 168
Borsay, Peter 249
Boyce, William 96
    The Chaplet 48, 49, 228
    Solomon 36, 48, 69
Bremner, Robert 6, 98, 101, 110, 111–12
Bridgnorth 22
Bristol 22
    catch/glee clubs 146, 148, 149, 150,
        151, 153, 156
    pleasure gardens 27
    river parties 28
British-Mercury, The 209
Britton, Thomas 1, 36
Broderip, Robert 148, 150, 156
Brontë sisters 275
Brooke, Henry 228
Brooke, Lady Frances Evelyn 88
Brooks, James 96, 151
Brydges, James, Duke of Chandos 8, 37
Bucholz, R. O. 74
Burgh, Allatson 277
Burney, Charles 9, 12, 14, 46, 49, 50, 168,
    220, 273, 281, 282
Burney, Charles Rousseau 169, 282
Burney, Fanny 2, 282–3
Burton, John 277

Callcott, John Wall 142, 151, 193
Cambini, Giuseppe Maria 193
Cambridge
    concerts in 22, 23
    music societies 37
Camidge, Matthew 96
Cantelo, Ann (later Mrs Harrison) 12
Canterbury 4
    catch/glee clubs 146, 147, 148, 149,
        150, 152, 154, 155, 156
    concerts at 159
    music societies 7
Carey, Henry 219, 220
Carmarthen, Lady 78
Castle Society 3
catch clubs 6, 141–60; *see also* Noblemen
    and Gentlemen's Catch Club
Cervetto, James 168, 169

Chalklin, Christopher 24
Chandos, Duke of *see* Brydges, James,
    Duke of Chandos
Charle, Christophe 87
Charles, Mr 10, 49, 68
Chesterfield, Lord 142
Chevill, Elizabeth 143, 147
Chichester 4
    catch/glee clubs 146, 148, 149, 150,
        152, 153–4, 155, 157, 158, 160
    music societies 7
Chilcot, Thomas 29
Church, John 200
Church, Richard 135
churches
    cathedral musicians 55–6
    concerts in 23–4, 29–30, 31
    see also clergy and music
Cianchettini, Veronika 286, 288
Cibber, Colley 201, 215–16
Cimador, Giovanni Battista 288
Claget, Charles 67–8
Clark, J. C. D. 88
Clark, Peter 25, 147, 156
Clarke, Charles 46
Clarke, William 46
Clementi, Muzio 10, 11, 12, 103, 108
clergy and music 37–8, 53
Cluer, John 94
Coke, Lady Mary 78, 81
Colebatch, Henry 45
Collier, Jeremy 76
Collier, Joel 279
Concert of Ancient Music 3, 87, 89, 254
concerts 5, 20–1
    amateur and professional musicians 4,
        7, 11
    applause 3
    benefit concerts 8, 166, 255, 256
    conversation at 2–3, 80–1
    new music 4
    organization 5–6, 7–8, 9–10
    programmes 2, 61–3, 93, 252–4
        string quartets 175–96
    promotion 261–71
    seventeenth century 1–2
    subscription 8, 166
    tours 10
    see also St Cecilia's Day celebrations
conversation at concerts 2–3, 80–1
Cooke, Benjamin 151
Cooke, William 39, 40, 41, 42, 43, 46, 48
Corelli, Arcangelo 63

INDEX

293

Corfe, Joseph 149, 156
Cork, Countess of 88
Corri, Sophia (later Mrs Dussek) 286, 287–8
Coventry 13, 22
Cowper, Earl 57, 58
Cowper, Spencer 57, 58, 60, 61, 62, 63, 65, 66, 68, 69
Cramer, Johann Baptist 108
Cramer, Wilhelm 108, 167, 168, 169, 173, 174, 181, 186, 194
Croft, William 96, 200, 201, 215
    odes for Oxford Act (1713) 200, 202–11, 212, 217–18
Crosdill, John 195
Crotch, William 249, 254, 256
Cumberland, Henry Frederick, Duke of 11, 14, 195

Dahmen, Peter 168
Dampier, John Lucius 205
Danby, John 96, 151
Dance, William 173
dances 29
Darwin, Erasmus 277
Davaux, Jean-Baptiste 176
Davies, Thomas 230, 233
Davy, John 194
Dawks's News-Letter 200
Day, Joanna 258
Dean, Winton 38
Delaval, Madame 288, 289
Dennis, John 84
Devoto, John 205
Dew, Thomas 41, 47
Dibdin, Charles 151, 279
Dibdin, James C. 233, 236, 240
Dingley, William 211
Diot, Francis 287
Diot, Miss 286, 287
Dolben, John 58, 120, 205
Downpatrick 231, 237
Dublin 13, 14
    theatre in 221, 222, 224–9
Dubourg, Matthew 13, 224, 225, 230
Ducrest, Madam La Marquise 288
Dupuis, Thomas Sanders 96
Durham
    cathedral musicians 55–6
    concerts in 56–8
        collaboration 58–9, 69–70
        decline 65–8
        personal and professional relations 68–9

repertoire 61–3
rivalry with cathedral 60–1, 63–5
Dussek, Jan Ladislav 286, 287–8
Dussek, Sophia (née Corri) 286, 287–8
Dyer, Mr 45

Eagleton, Terry 79
Ebdon, Thomas 70, 96
Edgeworth, Maria and Richard 278, 279
Edinburgh 14, 219, 230, 237
    music societies 6, 7, 14, 111, 236
    St Cecilia's Hall 3, 21
    theatre in 230, 233, 236, 240
Egan, Pierce 27
Elford, Richard 200
Erskine, Thomas Alexander, 6th Earl of Kelly 179
European Magazine 12, 283–4
Exeter, music societies 37

Fawcett, Richard 117–19, 121, 133
Fawconer, Edward 144
Felton, William 39, 40, 42, 43, 46, 47
festivals 5, 10, 32, 52
    Birmingham 32
    Norwich 32
    Salisbury 38, 159
    Three Choirs 10, 14, 22, 23, 31–2, 38, 40, 41, 42, 48, 49, 51, 159
Field, John 12
Fiennes, Celia 22
Fiorillo, Federigo 168
Fischer, Johann Christian 283
Forster, William 101, 112
Frederick of Orange, Prince 156
Freeman, John 200

Gainsborough, Thomas 13
Galbraith, John Kenneth 263, 265
Gardiner, Bernard 201
Gardiner, William 143, 158, 160
Garrick, David 219, 220, 222
Garth, John 13, 59, 60, 63, 65, 66, 68, 69, 70, 107, 108
Gates, Bernard 200
Gautherot, Louisa 171
Gelson, Cornforth 58, 64–5
Geminiani, Francesco 9, 224
George III, King 3, 14
George (Prince of Wales) 195–6
George, James 45–6, 50
Giardini, Felice 12, 13, 62, 64, 68, 162, 168, 175, 176, 179, 181, 182, 195

294 INDEX

Giornovichi, Giovanni Mane 169, 194
glee clubs 10, 141–60
Gloucester, music societies 10, 35
Gloucester Journal 41, 42, 49
Gluck, Christoph Willibald 82
Goodban, Mrs 147, 148, 149
Goodson, Richard junior 117, 118
Goodson, Richard senior 209, 210, 214
Gore, Israel 149
Goss, John 149
Green, Thomas 280
Green, Vivian 248
Greene, Maurice 48, 96
Greggs, William 55
Guest, Jane Mary (later Mrs Miles) 282–4, 289
guild halls, concerts in 22, 31
Gyrowetz, Adalbert 191, 193, 194, 277

Habermas, Jürgen 73, 79
Hall, Henry 40
Hall, Jennifer 87
Hall II, Henry 40
Handel, George Frideric 4, 14, 24, 62–3, 116, 219, 221, 230, 251, 252
 Acis and Galatea 62, 63, 69, 115–16
 Alexander's Feast 35, 57, 62, 69, 115, 119, 124
 Athalia 133, 135, 251
 Cecilia volgi un sguardo 124
 Commemoration at Westminster Abbey (1784) 5
 Concertos op. 3 48
 Deidamia 117, 223
 Imeneo, 223
 Israel in Egypt 123–4
 Judas Maccabaeus 23
 Messiah 5, 62, 129, 223, 224, 251
 Ode for St Cecilia's Day 133
 opera 219, 223
 oratorios 9, 219, 251–2
 publication 94, 96
 Samson 62, 115, 223
 Saul 63, 117, 223
 Te Deum ('Utrecht') 199, 200
 Twelve Concertos op. 6 35–6
 visit to Oxford 200, 251
 Water Music 28
Hanover Square concert room (London) 3
Harington, Henry 145, 151
Harley, Robert 208
Harris, David Fraser 230
Harris, George 58

Harris, James 14, 24, 116, 117–18, 120, 121, 149
Harrison, Mrs *see* Cantelo, Ann
Hartog, Madame 171
Hawarden, Lord 156
Hawkins, John 36, 41, 211
Haydn, Joseph 7, 14, 112, 165, 166, 280, 286, 288
 keyboard music 273
 'London' symphonies 8
 string quartets 11, 161, 167, 168, 173, 175, 176, 181–2, 185–6, 191–3, 194, 195, 196
 visits to London 4, 191
 visit to Oxford 255
Hayes, Philip 107, 124, 129, 131, 135, 144, 254
Hayes, Thomas 124, 131, 133
Hayes, William 96, 115, 116, 121, 122, 124, 125, 129, 131, 133, 135, 142–4, 149, 244, 249, 251
Hayes, William junior 131
Hearne, Thomas 116, 117, 201, 215, 217
Hellendaal, Pieter 96, 107
Hellier, Samuel 137, 138
Henley, Phocian 121
Hereford
 College Hall 24
 music societies 6, 10, 35, 36, 37, 39–52
Herschel, Alexander 148
Herschel, William 30
Hesletine, James 55, 58, 59, 61, 69
Hickman, Roger 193
Hindmarsh, John 168, 173
Hoeberechts, John Lewis 98
Holroyd, Maria 278
Holywell Music Room (Oxford) 1, 2, 3, 21, 243–59
Hook, James 105
Hooper, Graham 150–1
hostelries
 catch/glee clubs in 152–3
 concerts in 25, 26
Hughes, Francis 200
Hüllmandel, Nicolas 10
Hummel, Johann Nepomuk 10
Hunter, Mary 192
Husbands, William 37, 40

Idler 265
inns
 catch/glee clubs in 152–3
 concerts in 25, 26

INDEX

295

Isham, John 211, 212

Jackson, William 98, 150, 254
Jackson's Oxford Journal 115, 245, 258, 259
Jacob, Margaret 74
James, Walter 156
Janiewicz, Feliks 13, 169
Jansen, Therese 280, 289
Johnson, John 101
Johnson, R. 98
Johnson, Samuel 265
Jones, Colonel 150
Jones, David Wyn 111
Jones, Mr 46

Kammel, Antonín 175, 179
Kaye, Richard 258
Kelly, 6th Earl of *see* Erskine
Kemp, E. 247
Kent, James 205, 212
King's Lynn 22
King's Theatre (London) 76, 78, 81, 83, 84, 86
Kozeluch, Leopold 11, 193
Krumpholtz, Madame 289

Lambourn, John 138, 256
Lampe, Isabella (née Young) 219, 220, 223, 224, 233, 235, 237
Lampe, John Frederick 14, 219–21, 223–41
Lancashire witches 14
Lancaster, Music Room 21
Landon, H. C. Robbins 192
Lane, Mrs Fox 13
L'Arrivée, Agathe-Elisabeth-Henriette 289
late-coming 2
Lates, James 256, 258
Lee, Nathaniel 26
Leeds 13, 25
Leipzig, Gewandhaus 9, 77
Lennox, Lady Louisa 158
Leppert, Richard 275
Lichfield, music societies 36, 37
    catch/glee clubs 146, 147, 148, 153, 154, 155, 157–8
Lincoln, catch/glee clubs 146
Lindley, Robert 254
Linley, Elizabeth 159
Linley, Mary 159
Liverpool 13
    catch/glee clubs 146

Music Hall (Bold Street) 21
Llewellyn, George 37
Locke, John 276
London 19
    beau monde 8, 71–2, 74–5, 77–81
        politics of cultural quarrels 81–5
        towards modernity 85–9
    celebration of Treaty of Utrecht (1713) 199–200
    concerts in 1–3, 7–10, 11, 22, 76–7
        string quartets 161, 162–96
    music societies 7, 36
        Anacreontic Society 4, 148, 173, 193, 280
        Noblemen and Gentlemen's Catch Club 142, 143, 145, 146, 147, 150, 155, 156, 160
        string quartets and 173–4
    opera/musical theatre in 39, 75, 76, 219–21, 223
    pleasure gardens 159, 227
    theatre in 76
    see also King's Theatre
London Gazette 262, 264
London Magazine 263
Longman & Broderip 104–5, 109–10, 111, 112, 113
Love, Charles 55
Love, Nathaniel 55
Lysons, Daniel 39, 40–1, 42

Macarthur, Miss 286, 287
Macklin, Charles 219, 220, 226
McLamore, Alyson 171
McVeigh, Simon 86
Madrigal Society 142
Mahon, John 148
Mahon family 255–6
Malchair, John Baptist 121, 249, 253, 256, 258
Manchester, catch/glee clubs 146
Manwaring, Barty 231, 233, 235, 236
Mara, Gertrud Elisabeth 12, 167
marketing of concerts 261–71
Marlborough, Duke of 258
marriage 274
Marsh, John 4, 7, 81, 145–7, 149–53, 155–60, 173, 174, 195
Maslow, Abraham 265
Mathews, William 138, 255
Matthews, Betty 256
Mee, John Henry 244, 245–7, 255, 256
Menel, Mr 168

296   INDEX

Meredith, Edward 14
Middlesex, Lord 79
Middleton, Bartholemew 149
Midgley, Graham 245
Miles, Jane Mary *see* Guest, Jane Mary
Milligan, Thomas 289
modernity 73, 85–9
Montagu, John, 4th Earl of Sandwich 142,
    158, 265
Monthly Review 150
Moore, John 149
More, Hannah 278
Morley, William 211, 212
Morris, Claver 24, 25, 37
Mosse, Bartholomew 227, 228–9
Mountier, Thomas 56, 58
Mozart, Wolfgang Amadeus 193
Mozeen, Mrs 223
music
    copying 117–39
    networks 12, 14–15
    popularity of 4–5
    publication 11–12, 93, 94–109
        by author 98–100
        role of publisher 100, 109–13
        by subscription 94–8
    teaching 279–80
    see also concerts
music societies 5–7, 10, 35–53
    catch and glee clubs 6, 10, 141–60
    string quartets and 173–4

Napier, William 96, 112, 113, 173, 174,
    179, 183, 195
Nattes, John 30
networks 12, 14–15, 219–41, 255
Neville, Sylas 149
Newcastle 13, 14
    concerts in 10, 55, 56, 66, 68
        collaboration with Durham 58–9
        repertoire 61–3
    pleasure gardens 27, 66
Newcastle Courant 56, 57, 60
Newcastle Journal 67
Newmarket, Races 13
newspapers 262, 264–5
Nixon, John 231
nobility 78
Noblemen and Gentlemen's Catch Club
    (London) 142, 143, 145, 146, 147,
    150, 155, 156, 160
Noferi, Giovanni Battista 69, 70
Norris, Thomas 159, 252, 254

North, Roger 75, 141–2
Norwich 19
    assembly rooms 32
    catch/glee clubs 146
    festival 32
    music societies 25
    pleasure gardens 27, 32
    river parties 28
    St Andrew's Hall 21
    theatre 26, 32
Nottingham, catch/glee clubs 146

Oldmixon, Eleanor 224, 230
opera 39, 52–3, 75, 77, 80, 219–29
    politics of cultural quarrels and 82–3
Opera Concerts (London) 8, 13
oratorios 9, 23, 29, 53, 219, 251–2
Ormonde, Duke of 202, 211
Oxford 13, 14
    Bodleian Library 249
    catch/glee clubs 143, 144, 145
    concerts in 22–3, 115–16, 243–5, 252–4
    Holywell Music Room 1, 2, 3, 21,
        243–59
    music copying in 117–39
    music societies 3, 36–7, 40, 211, 245,
        246, 247
    Oxford Act (1713) 200–15, 217
    Sheldonian Theatre 201, 249
    theatre productions 215–16
Oxford, Earl of 208, 214

Paganini, Nicolò 10
Pall Mall Magazine 87
Pantheon (London) 2
Papendiek, Charlotte 3, 283
Paris
    beau monde 72, 74–5, 78
    Concert spirituel 9
    politics of cultural quarrels 82
Park, Maria Hester *see* Reynolds
Parke, Maria F. 282, 284–6, 289
Parke, William 14, 173, 283
Parratt, Walter 205
Parry, Robert 149
Pasquali, Niccolo 14, 223, 224, 225, 226,
    228, 229
Passerini, Giuseppe and Christina 14
Paxton, Stephen 64, 149
Paxton, William 69
Penrose, John 28
Pepusch, Johann Christoph 202, 203, 209,
    210, 215

INDEX

Phillips, Philip 121
pianists, women 273–90
Piccinni, Niccolò 82
Pieltain, Dieudonné-Pascal 162, 169, 173, 182, 183
pleasure gardens 27, 30, 32, 66, 159, 227
Pleyel, Ignaz Joseph 14, 162, 165, 167, 173, 175, 186, 191, 194, 195, 196
politics of cultural quarrels 81–5
Pomfret, Lady 22
Porter, Roy 143
Porter, Samuel 158, 159
Porter, Thomas 44, 45, 47
portrait artists 275
Portsmouth 13
Powell, Walter 121, 251
Preston, John 100
Preston, T. 100
Prévost, Abbé 262
private concerts 21
professional musicians 4, 11
programmes for concerts 2, 61–3, 93, 252–4
    string quartets 175–96
promenades 28
promotion of concerts 261–71
publication 11–12, 93, 94–109
    by author 98–100
    role of publisher 100, 109–13
    by subscription 94–8
Pugnani, Gaetano 181
Purcell, Daniel 209–10
Purcell, Henry 26, 228

Raguenet, Abbé 82
Raimondi, Ignazio 182
Rameau, Jean-Philippe 13, 62, 82
Ramsay, Allan 230
Randall, William 96
Rauzzini, Venanzio 8, 10, 14, 27, 108, 169, 181
Rawlings, Thomas 194
repertoire *see* programmes for concerts
Revel, Jacques 89
Reynolds, Maria Hester (Mrs Park) 256, 282, 284
Rich, John 220
Ridgway, James 281
Rogers, John 138
Romsey 22
Rosen, Charles 192, 273
Royal Academy of Music 39, 81
Royal Festival Hall (London) 75

Sacchini, Antonio 14, 181
St Cecilia's Day celebrations 24, 35, 47, 57, 121, 147
St Cecilia's Hall (Edinburgh) 3, 21
Saint-Georges, Chevalier de *see* Bologne, Joseph
Salisbury 4, 24
    catch/glee clubs 146, 148, 149, 152, 153, 154, 155, 156, 157
    Festival 4, 24, 38, 159
    music societies 38
Salmon, Eliza 13
Salomon, Johann Peter 3, 4, 8, 9, 11, 165, 167, 168, 169, 182, 191, 193, 194, 288
Sandwich, Lord *see* Montagu, John
Schroeter, Johann Samuel 277
Scroggs, William 137
Senhouse, Peter 39, 40
sexuality 80–1
Shaftesbury, Lord 79
Shaw, H. Watkins 116
Sheffield 13
Sheldonian Theatre (Oxford) 201, 249
Shenton, Richard 48
Shenton, Robert 45, 48
Sheridan, Thomas 219, 221–9, 236
Shield, William 194–5
Shrewsbury 14
Smart, George 280
Smith, John Christopher 9
Smith, Mr 168, 173, 174
Smith, Richard 156
Smith, Theodore 109
Snow, John 119, 121
social relationships
    concert-going and 31–2
    theatre-going and 79
Soderini, Giuseppe 169
Somfai, László 192
spas 28, 30
Spectator 79
Stamitz, Carl 100, 179, 182
Stamitz, Johann 179
Stanley, John 9
status
    catch/glee clubs and 154
    concert-going and 31
Steele, Richard 85
Steibelt, Daniel 273, 289
Stevens, Richard John Samuel 12, 152, 173
Storer, Charles 233–5, 237

298 INDEX

Storer, Elizabeth 223, 227, 230, 231, 233, 235, 237
string quartets 10, 161–96
  concert societies 173–4
  London repertoire 175–96
  performers 167–71
  public face 162–7
subscription
  concerts 8, 166
  publication by 94–8
Sullivan, Daniel 223, 227
Sun, The 288
Swarbrick, Henry 40, 41, 42

Tacet, Joseph 108, 110
Talbot, Charles 156
Tatler 79, 265
taverns
  catch/glee clubs in 152–3
  concerts in 25, 26
teaching music 279–80
Thackeray, William 279
theatres 26, 29, 32, 76
Thetford 22
Thompson, Edward 40
Thomson, Henry 230, 236, 237
Three Choirs Festival 10, 14, 22, 23, 31–2, 38, 40, 41, 42, 48, 49, 51, 159
Tilmouth, Michael 35
Toghill, Moses 149
tours 10
town halls, concerts in 22, 31
Trapp, Joseph 202, 203, 208, 214
Tunbridge Wells 13, 30
  promenades 28
Twining, Thomas 168

Uffenbach, Conrad von 37
urbanization 20, 38, 141
Utrecht, Treaty of 5, 199
  celebrations 199–200, 201

Valentine, Robert 108
Vanhal, Johann Baptist 176
Vauxhall Gardens 9, 27
Venice 75
Vestris, Signora 64
Vickery, Amanda 274
Victor, Benjamin 226, 228
Vienna 9, 78
Viotti, Giovanni Battista 13, 169

Wagner, Richard 87

Wall, R. 256
Walond, William junior 135, 137
Walpole, Horace 79, 89
Walsh, John 96, 110, 111
Warner, Richard 27
Warren, Edmund 150, 151
Wasborough, Rice 156
Webb, Master 252
Webbe, Samuel 96, 151, 152
Webber, Mr 149
Weber, William 23
Webster, G. 278
Weekly Journal 77–8
Weeks, Jack 153
Weely, Samuel 200
Weichsel, Elizabeth (later Mrs Billington) 254–5, 280–2, 284, 286
Welcker, John 100, 101, 113
Welcker, Peter 101, 113
Wellman, Francis 149
Wells 25
  Close Hall 24
  music societies 35
Wesley, Samuel 280
Whitefriars tavern (London) 1
Wilde, Mr 48
William V of Orange 156
Williams, Daniel 200
Willis, Miss 216
Winchester 7, 159
Wollstonecraft, Mary 274
women
  catch/glee clubs and 10, 147
  marriage 274
  performers 10
  pianists 273–90
  string quartet players 171
Wood, Bruce 40
Woodcock, Francis 41, 42, 45, 50
Woodcock, Francisco 45
Woodcock, John 44
Woodcock, Mr 254
Woodcock, Robert 41
Woodcock, Thomas 41, 42
Worcester
  Guildhall 22
  music societies 10, 35
Wren, Christopher 201
Wright, H. 96
Wynn, Watkin Williams 14

York 38
  assembly rooms 13, 26, 30

music societies 147
catch/glee clubs 146
York, Frederick, Duke of 156

York Buildings (London) 2, 75
Young *see* Arne, Cecilia
Young, Mary 286